Introduction by P E T E R J.

TREES
AND
THORNS

STUDIES *in the* FIRST FOUR
CHAPTERS *of* GENESIS

James B. Jordan

Theopolis
BOOKS

AN IMPRINT OF ATHANASIUS PRESS

TABLE OF CONTENTS

FOREWORD

ANYONE who attempts to write a commentary on a book of the Bible is bound to realize fairly soon how much he could talk about and how little space he has. John Owen wrote a six-volume commentary on Hebrews, but today a commentary that long would be a marketing disaster. And yet, the commentator realizes, there's so much he could say about virtually every verse.

James B. Jordan has not written a commentary on the whole of Genesis, though he has lectured on Genesis on several occasions, including the lengthy series of in-depth Sunday School classes available under the titles "Studies in Genesis," "Life of Abraham," and "Life of Jacob." His book *Primeval Saints* focuses on the stories of the major characters in Genesis, while *Creation in Six Days* focuses specifically on the question of the historicity and date of the events recorded in Genesis 1, but includes some exposition of Genesis 1.

Trees and Thorns is not a commentary on Genesis, nor is it even a fully-developed commentary on Genesis 2–4. It began life as a series of monthly "Thank You" newsletters for donors to Biblical Horizons. Jim had written a series of studies on Genesis 1 for *Geneva Review* and once intended to publish them under the title *Heptameron: The Seven Days of Creation*, and he started this series to complement those studies. He introduced them by saying, "Because these letters are 'relatively unpublished,' I am going to be more bold in sharing my thoughts, some of which are preliminary."

In this volume, those newsletter essays have been combined and organized into chapters. In some cases, we have made minor modifications to what Jim originally wrote in order to bring it into line with his later, more mature thought. For instance, in *Creation in Six Days* and in his essay "Merit Versus Maturity," Jim drew on these *Trees and Thorns* studies—and even quoted them at length—but made some adjustments and additions, and we have incorporated those here. In several cases, where Jim has changed his view significantly, we have kept his older view in the main text but pointed out the change in his view in the footnotes.

But in spite of our editorial work, the original newsletteriness is doubtless still evident and it remains true that Jim boldly shares his thoughts, even though some of them are preliminary. As he often says elsewhere, these studies are not intended to be the final word on the subject but it is his hope that they are a helpful word—in some cases, a helpful first word on some aspects of Genesis 2–4.

The reader will, on occasion, find that there is a certain amount of repetition as Jim revisits topics he has discussed earlier, sometimes revising them to some degree and several times amplifying them, showing how themes grow and develop and snowball through these opening chapters of Genesis and into the rest of Scripture. One might ask sometimes "Why didn't you say that earlier?" but an attempt on the part of the editor to "fix" things would have destroyed one of the pleasures of these studies, the pleasure of watching a careful and imaginative student let Scripture prompt him to think and rethink and of joining him in discovering more facets of Scripture's teaching.

And here we return to where we started. Genesis is one of the longest books of the Bible and a commentator who wants to discuss everything will find that he has used up his page limit before he has gotten far into the book. Who has time and space enough to talk at length about gardens and sweat and noses and so on?

There is a place for a commentary, even a relatively detailed commentary, that takes the reader through the whole book with what Calvin referred to as "lucid brevity." But there is also a place—and not only a place, but a great need—for someone to spend time on the small details that such a commentary might easily gloss over, to compare Scripture with Scripture, to tease out of the text of Scripture things we might otherwise miss as we hurry on to the next verse.

And that is what Jim does here, inviting us to slow down and to chew on and digest these three chapters of Scripture that lay the foundation for everything that follows in God's Word.

John Barach
Lake Charles, Louisiana

INTRODUCTION

TREES give shade, produce fruit and nuts, provide homes for sparrows and squirrels, monkeys, sloths, and koalas. Forests are the glory of the land, shelter for throngs of wild animals tended by our heavenly Shepherd. A tree is a world, linking soil and sky, with a canopy that stretches like a firmament adorned with fruited stars.

Cut and transformed, trees provide human habitats. Many of us live in tree houses, even if we don't live among tree branches. Leaves on deciduous trees glitter like emeralds in the summer sun, go crimson, rubiate, and golden in autumn on the way to becoming bare ruined choirs where late the sweet birds sang. Coniferous trees bravely keep alive the evergreen promise of spring, even as they shoulder mounds of snow. Trees show that our years run in a continuous cycle of wintry death and resurrection.

Thorns, by contrast, stick low to the ground. Some thorny plants produce fruit, but many are no more than pins and needles that grasp at the unwary. Animals that live among thorns are often dangerous; the serpent is a mobile thorn bush with scales. In Scripture, thorns are found in devastated landscapes bereft of any hope for renewal.

Some people are trees, fruitful and roomy, glorious ladders connecting heaven and earth. Some are unproductive thorn bushes, the kind of people who can find nothing better to do than to go into politics (Judg. 9).

Jim Jordan wrote the essays collected here as newsletter for donors to Biblical Horizons. On the surface, they are studies in Genesis 2–3, but, as always in Jim's work, there's much beneath the surface. He taught his friends and colleagues that everything in Scripture grows from the seeds planted in Genesis 1–3.

And, since Scripture touches on everything in the universe, Genesis 1–3 provides the frame and categories for understanding reality as a whole. Like everything Jim wrote, *Trees and Thorns* helps us see through new eyes—to see the whole world and its history refracted in the everyday contrast between fruitful trees and bramble bushes. These essays don't just teach us how to see. They teach us how to be. They're full of cautions: Watch out for the thorns. They're full of exhortations: Be a tree of life, planted by rivers of water, giving fruit and bearing leaves for the healing of nations.

I pray that *Trees and Thorns* will plant seeds in many readers, so every land will become fertile fields, and fertile fields a forest.

Peter J. Leithart
Beth-Elim
Gardendale, Alabama
Trinity Season 2020

1

THE GENERATIONS OF HEAVEN AND EARTH

GENESIS 2:4

GENESIS 2:4 reads like this: "These are the generations of the heavens and the earth when they were created, in the day that Yahweh God made earth and heaven." Or it reads like this: "These are the generations of the heavens and the earth when they were created. In the day that Yahweh God made earth and heaven...."

Do you see the difference? In the first translation, all of Genesis 2:4 is seen as introducing the stories of Adam and Eve and of Cain and Abel. In the second translation, the first sentence of Genesis 2:4 might go with Genesis 1:1–2:3 or it might also go with what follows.

This sentence, "These are the generations of...," occurs ten times in the Book of Genesis. Scholars have debated at length whether it should be seen as introducing a new section or as closing off the preceding one. Without going into the details here, we can agree with everyone by saying that this phrase is a boundary between one section of Genesis and the next—except for a couple of places where it introduces a short genealogy that is found within a larger story. I shall go with the majority and assume that this phrase introduces the section that follows it. In other words, "These are the generations of xyz" means "These are what came forth from xyz."

THE STRUCTURE OF GENESIS

The Book of Genesis can be seen as having an introduction and seven sections:

Introduction: The Creation (Gen. 1:1–2:3).

1. The Generations of the Heavens and the Earth (Gen. 2:4–4:26) – corresponding to Day 1, the creation of the heavens and earth out of formlessness (creation of man) and the separation of light and darkness (judgment on man; division of Cain and Abel).

2. The Generations of Adam (Gen. 5:1–6:8) – corresponding to Day 2, the establishment of a firmament to separate waters above from waters below. In my speculative opinion, the godly line of Seth was the human form of the firmament, and the corruption of that line is answered by the removal of the firmament and the re-coalescence of the waters in the Flood.

3. The Generations of Noah (Gen. 6:9–11:9) – corresponding to Day 3. There are two sections here:

   Day 3a: separation of land and sea – the Flood, and a new separation of land and sea (Gen. 6:9–9:29).

   Day 3b: multiplication of plants on land – the "Table of Nations" of Genesis 10, which is one of the sub-sections introduced by "These are the generations of … the sons of Noah," and the scattering at Babel (Gen. 10:1–11:9).

4. The Generations of Shem (Gen. 11:10–26) – corresponding to Day 4, the establishment of lightbearers of rule in the heavens. Not only are the godly called lights, but the patriarchs' lives were marked out in years that are the same as significant astronomical numbers.

5. The Generations of Terah (Gen. 11:27–25:11) – corresponding to Day 5, when the great swarming creatures were made and when God gave His first command to any creature. The themes of multiplication and law are highlighted in the story of Abraham, which Genesis 11:27–25:11 delineates.

6. The Generations of Ishmael and Isaac (Gen. 25:12–35:29) – corresponding to Day 6. It is the story of Jacob that is the major item here. Day 6 also has two sections:

Day 6a: creation of helpful animals – "the generations of Ishmael" subsection (25:12–18), for the Ishmaelites were not enemies of Israel.

Day 6b: creation of man – "the generations of Isaac" (25:19–35:29), a section mainly concerned with Jacob, the man who was able to wrestle with God and prevail!

7. The Generations of Esau and Jacob (Gen. 36:1–50:26) – corresponding to Day 7. The sabbath-rest theme is clear in the story of Joseph, "the generations of Jacob" (37:1–50:26). The "generations of Esau" (Gen. 36) point to the fall of man, which happened on the sabbath. Thus, a false sabbath rest is given to Esau, as he multiplies and takes control, while a true sabbath rest is given to the godly.

Is all of this speculative? Sure. What's wrong with tossing around some possibilities? Give it some thought, and see what you think.

THE OFFSPRING OF HEAVEN AND EARTH

We have seen that the phrase, "these are the generations of xyz" structures the book of Genesis. Now we need to press a bit further.

Ruth 4:18ff. reads, "Now these are the generations of Perez: Perez begat (fathered) Hezron; Hezron begat Ram; Ram begat Amminadab; etc." The meaning is clear: the "generations of xyz" are the things that emerged from— were fathered by—xyz. The same meaning is found throughout Genesis, as in Genesis 5, where the descendants of Adam are listed as "the generations of Adam."

Genesis 2:4, then, indicates that the section it introduces will discuss the offspring of the heavens and the earth. What follows is the creation of man. It is clear that man is regarded as in some sense the offspring of the earth, for man was formed from the dust of the ground (2:7).

This fact opens up much pregnant symbolism in the Bible. For instance, clay bricks and clay implements represent people. Plants, which grow out of the earth, represent people, especially the offspring of parents. Hence the title of this book: men are the trees and thorns. The "curse of the soil" is indirectly a curse against human life. (As we will see, the soil is not cursed, but mediates God's curse to human beings.)

3

Not only is man formed from the ground, but according to 2:19 so are all the animals and birds.

In what sense, though, is man the offspring of the heavens? Before we jump to a conclusion, we need to look carefully at what Genesis 1 has already taught us about the heavens. The highest heavens were created on Day One along with the primeval earth (1:1: "In the beginning, God created the heavens and the earth").

Then, on Day Two, God set up the firmament—the blue sky—above the ground and called it "heaven." Thus, the sky is an image of heaven within this world. Then, on Day Four, God set lights in the firmament to govern day and night, festival times, and so forth. So the sun, moon, and stars are also revealers of heavenly realities. Finally, on Day Five, God appointed the birds to fly above the earth in the open firmament of heaven. Birds, then, are also heavenly.

What Genesis 1 does not explicitly say, but what we must discern, is that the created highest heavens are the place where God's visible throne is to be found. Genesis 2–4 does not mention the birds, the stars, or the firmament. Thus, the only sense in which the "heavens" can have humanity as their offspring is in the sense that it was the Breath of God, proceeding from God's throne, that infused life into the earthly clay of the man's body and of the bodies of the animals (2:7, 19).

Heaven and earth cooperate in the creation of man. Heaven (God) is first and the earth second. God is the Divine Initiator, and the earth is the receiver. There is nothing sexual in this, but there is an obvious analogy to marriage. Awareness of this reality is crudely preserved in human mythology, when Father Sun marries Mother Earth and brings forth humanity.

This generating work of heaven and earth does not stop with the first creation. When Eve gave birth to Cain, she said that she had gotten a child with Yahweh's help (4:1). She confessed the same truth when Seth was born (4:25). Human life is always a result of God's Spirit breathing into human clay.

This theme—that heaven and earth generate human life—continues throughout this entire section of Genesis (2:4–4:26). When Adam sinned, God said, "cursed is the ground because of you" or "with reference to you." The ground is not itself cursed, and man is not directly cursed. The ground is cursed with reference to man. The idea is that God's judgments will be mediated to humanity through the ground. The ground will yield both trees and thorns. The first thorn was Cain, the first tree Abel.

As the generating power of God and the soil worked in human life, the curse worked its way progressively in the world. Thorns proliferated, choking out good plants. Abel was killed. Cain's descendants built a mighty civilization, culminating in Lamech. All of this was the offspring, the generation, of the heavens and the earth, as God worked with the ground to bring judgment and death to wayward humanity.

But there was a promise that someday heaven and earth would cooperate to bring forth a new humanity. From the clay of the woman would come forth the Son of God (3:15–16). The heavenly Spirit works with the earthly clay of His body to bring life, not a curse, to the new humanity, a point we confess whenever we eat His body and drink His blood in the Lord's Supper.

MAN THE LIGHT-BEARER

Genesis 2:4 has an interesting literary structure in Hebrew, a structure that we find very often in the Bible. The structure is called a chiasm or palistrophe and is characterized by parallelism arranged in a sandwich pattern, like ABCBA, or ABBA, or ABCDEFFEDCBA.

Here is Genesis 2:4 as we find it in Hebrew word-order:

A. These are the generations of the *heavens*

   B. And the *earth*

      C. In their *creation*

         D. In the *day*

      C'. Yahweh God *made*

   B'. *Earth*

A'. And *heavens*.

Notice that the idea of the heavens brackets the chiasm, while the idea of day is at the heart of it. Genesis 1 indicates that the heavens are the pattern for the earth. The heavens were made complete all at once, while the earth develops and grows from formlessness to form, darkness to light (evening to morning), and emptiness to fulfillment. The earth grows to become more heaven-like, a process we could call heavenization, or from the Greek, ouranification(!).

According to Genesis 1:3–5, God created light on the first day and called light by the name "day." Thus, "day" means "light-time." The alternation of night and day, evening and morning, began on the first day, and this shows us that these were ordinary weekdays. But because "day" means "light-time," it can be used to denote any time God in His glorious light draws near, which is thus called "Day of the Lord." Because "day" can refer to any "time of light," the Old Covenant can be seen as a time of night and the New Covenant as a time of day (cf. Mal. 4:2: the coming of Jesus is the dawn of the "sun of righteousness").

God created a firmament to separate waters from waters and called it "heaven" (Gen. 1:6–8). Thus, we now have within the "earth" a representation of the highest heaven. The sky above the ground points beyond itself to God's throne-heaven.[1]

On the fourth day God made lights in the firmament-heaven to regulate day and night (Gen. 1:14–19). These lightbearers are "day-makers," since they give off light and light is day. Thus, we see an association between heaven and day in Genesis 1. Daylight shines down from the firmament-heaven, and so day is something that shines forth from heaven. The Day of the Lord is thus a visitation from the God of heaven.

But on the fourth day we have an additional thought. The light-bearing day-makers are not only set up as signs to mark seasons (literally, festival times), days, and years and to give light on the earth (1:14–15); they are also specifically said to *govern* the day and the night (1:16, 18) and to *separate* light from darkness.

Immediately after this we find other governors set up on the earth. Those governors are men and women, who are to rule over all the creation (1:24–30). Men and women bear God's image, and thus like Him are light-bearing day-makers. They shine forth God's day-heaven over the earth. Thus, Moses' face shone when he was transfigured, and so did Jesus'. Similarly, "sun, moon, and stars" are frequent symbols of human powers in the Old and New Testaments.

It is interesting that the lightbearers were established both to govern day and night and to separate light from darkness. The theme of governing is applied to humanity in Genesis 1, while the theme of separating is applied to humanity in Genesis 2–4.

In Genesis 1, there is nothing bad or evil about darkness. Darkness is a time of lesser light (moon and stars) that gives way to a time of greater light (sun). Once sin becomes a factor, however, darkness becomes an image of depravity and evil. Man as light-bearing day-maker is to separate light from darkness and work against darkness.

---

1. James B. Jordan, *Through New Eyes: Developing a Biblical View of the World* (1988; reprint, Eugene, OR: Wipf and Stock, 1999), 42–47.

I am arguing that Genesis 1 culminates in the creation of humanity and that the features of Genesis 1 have application to humanity. I believe a careful and sensitive reading of Genesis 1 leads to this conclusion: The themes of heaven, day, and lightbearer find their culmination point in man, the image of God.

This helps account for what we read in Genesis 2:5–7. We are told that no plants or shrubs were yet on the earth and there was as yet no rain. There was, however, water coming up out of the ground and watering the whole surface of the earth. Then Yahweh God formed man from dust and breathed into him His own Breath, making man in His image. Compare this narrative with Genesis 1:2. There we find that the earth is empty, formless, and dark. There is water over everything, but also the Spirit of God is hovering over everything. Then God creates light.

The two pictures are too similar for us to fail to grasp the analogy. The Spirit of God made light; the Breath of God made man. The Spirit hovered over the waters and then made light-makers to govern the waters; God overshadowed clay and made man to govern the earth, which was covered by streams of water. When God made daylight in Genesis 1, there was as yet no vegetation on the earth. When God made man there was as yet no plant or shrub of the field.[2] Man in Genesis 2 corresponds to light in Genesis 1: Man is the earthly lightbearer.

SEVEN "DAYS"

Now that we have seen the close parallels between Genesis 2:4–7 and Genesis 1:1–3, I want to pursue that theme and argue that Genesis 2 recapitulates the days of Genesis 1 in a general way. Please note that I am not trying to argue that there are seven clear paragraphs in Genesis 2 that recap the days of Genesis 1 point by point. I do, however, see a general movement through the same themes, leading to the same point. The events of Genesis 2 happened on the sixth day but seem to recap the events of the first six days.

Genesis 2:4 is parallel to Genesis 1:1, as we have seen.

---

2. On Day 3, in Genesis 1, God had made fruit trees and grain plants, which are garden plants. Evidently, plants of the "field"—forests and the like—were not yet made when man was created.

In Genesis 2:5–7, we find that the earth is said to be empty of plants and shrubs "of the field." That is, the earth is formless, because the distinction between garden and field has not yet been established, and void because of the absence of these plants. As the land was covered by "the deep" in Genesis 1, here the earth is also covered with water, in the form of streams that water "the entire surface of the ground." Then, as God made light in Genesis 1:2, so God makes man to be lightbearer and governor in Genesis 2:7.

On Day 2 God set up the firmament to separate waters from waters, and on Day 3 He made the land appear and put food-plants on it. Genesis 2:8–14 speaks of the Garden and its food-plants, and of the land that arises in the center of the world. Since the rivers flowed out of Eden to water the whole earth, Eden was the highest point on earth. Thus Genesis 2:8–14 *seems* to be a recap of Day 3.

Actually, however, we should see the Garden of Eden as the place where man the lightbearer is placed, so that the Garden corresponds to the firmament-heavens that were set up on Day 2 and into which the sun, moon, and stars were placed on Day 4. Later on in the Bible, the Garden-sanctuary is associated with the firmament.[3] The Garden is between the Land of Eden and the rest of the world, since the river arises in Eden, and thus the Edenic Plateau was higher than the Garden. Similarly, the firmament is between the highest heaven and the cosmos.

So, Genesis 2:5–7 recaps Day 1, 2:8–9 recaps Day 2, and 2:10–14 recaps Day 3. Then in Genesis 2:15–17, God puts the man in the Garden of Eden to dress it and to guard it. Guarding involves separation and distinction, since the man has to know what to guard against. He must guard his own heart against disobedience and, as we shall see, he must guard the Garden against invasion. God tells him to distinguish between the ordinary trees and the two special trees and between the special tree that might be eaten (the Tree of Life) and the special tree that is temporarily forbidden (the Tree of the Knowledge of Good and Evil).

Thus we see in Genesis 2:15 the same themes as Day 4. Man is clearly *over* the Garden, in the same way as the lightbearers are over the earth. The lightbearers are to govern day and night, and the man is to dress the Garden. The lightbearers are to separate light and darkness, and the man is to distinguish between obedience and disobedience, between friend and enemy.

---

5. I have set out many of these associations in *Through New Eyes*.

On Day 5, God made the fish and birds to dwell in the seas and on the land, corresponding to Day 3. He also gave them the first command recorded in Genesis 1. In Genesis 2:16–17, we have God's command to Adam.

Day 6 is equivalent to Genesis 2:18–24. On Day 5 God created sea creatures and birds. On Day 6a He made the land animals, and on Day 6b He created man. Here in Genesis 2:18–24, God brought beasts and birds, representatives of the two days, before the man. When none proved suitable as a mate, God created woman. Thus we move from animals to humanity again.

This brings us to the seventh day. In Genesis 1, God rested on the seventh day. Genesis 2 brings out the notion that God rested not only because He was finished, but also because He had turned the administration of the world over to a steward. He turned the Garden over to Adam and Eve and departed.

It is clear that God departed, because after our first parents sinned, He returned. Genesis 2:24 also points to God's departure when it says "for this reason a man will leave his father and mother and stick to his wife." We are so used to seeing this sentence as an aphorism that we fail to take note of it in context. Adam's father is God. There is a sense in which Adam leaves God as earthly father and sets up his own household in Genesis 2:24. God continues, of course, to be Adam's heavenly father. This is a point of tension in the passage, because now the question comes: How will this young man fare now that he is on his own, captain of his own family and in charge of the Garden? It is the same question that parents ask themselves when they give their children away in marriage.

This sequence of events is a strong indication that the fall of man happened on the sabbath day. Another indication that this was the day of man's sin is that God came to visit Adam and Eve that very day, and God's visitation to man is always associated with the sabbath and the Day of the Lord.

Psychologically, we are almost forced to see the fall on the sabbath day, for this reason: If Adam and Eve had resisted the Tree of Knowledge once already, they would have begun to build strength of character, making it easier to resist the next time. Thus, they must have fallen the very first time they were confronted with the possibility of disobeying. It is very unlikely that Adam and Eve wandered around the Garden for several days before coming to the central grove where the two special trees were. Rather, we are compelled by common sense to believe that Adam pointed out the central grove to Eve right away and explained God's prohibition to her.

Additionally, since God invited Adam to eat of the Tree of Life and Adam had not yet done so when God appeared to judge him, Adam surely had not been in the Garden very long.

What emerges from this brief study is that Genesis 2 leads us to the same point of climax as Genesis 1: the sabbath. This is the day of man's test and of God's judgment: the Day of the Lord.

2

No Rain and No Man

Genesis 2:5

*And no shrub of the field had been made in the earth, and no plant of
the field had sprouted, for Yahweh God had not caused rain upon the
earth and there was no man to serve the soil (Gen. 2:5).*

GENESIS 2:5 tells us that "no shrub of the field had been made" and "no
plant of the field had sprouted" by the time of the sixth day. These events did
not occur until after man was created. If that is so, then what kinds of plants
were made on the third day of Genesis 1?

Genesis 1:11–12 tells us that two kinds of plants were made on the third
day. The first was "grains seeding seed" (literally) and the second was "trees
fruitbearing fruit." These two kinds of foods were given to Adam and Eve
as food in Genesis 1:29. These are the foundations respectively of bread and
wine. They are the kinds of plant food man encounters first, in the Garden-
sanctuary at the center of the world, on the sabbath day. They were made first
and already existed when man was made. They already existed for man to

eat with God on the first sabbath. As we shall see, however, the grain did not exist yet in mature (food) form; only the trees had produced food. Thus, man's first sanctuary food was fruit (wine), not grain (bread). We shall take up the reasons for this in the next chapter.

Genesis 2:5 tells us that certain of the other kinds of plants were not made on the third day. By itself, this shatters the "modified day-age interpretation" of Genesis 1. The "day-age interpretation" holds that each "day" was a stage in the evolutionary development of the world, but this is obviously wrong since it would mean plants existed before the sun, moon, and stars. Thus, the "modified day-age interpretation" says that each of the six "ages" of Genesis 1 means that for some reason the item mentioned is highlighted in that age. Plants were around for an age; the mists cleared to reveal the sun for an age; then came an age of dinosaurs, fishes, and birds; and then came mammals and man. This sounds okay (sort of), but Genesis 2:5 makes it impossible. We can hardly have only fruits and grains on the earth for millions of years before ferns, bushes, pine trees, and grass appeared![4]

Genesis 2:5 says that "no shrub of the field was yet in the earth." This means that such plants had not yet been created. But what are these "shrubs"? The word for "shrub" (*siach*) occurs only three other times in the Old Testament. Speaking of Hagar and Ishmael after they were driven out from Abraham, Genesis 21:15 says, "And the water in the skin was used up, and she left the boy under one of the shrubs." This associates shrubs with areas that are not "well watered throughout," as was the Garden of Eden (Gen. 13:10) and as is required for grain and fruit.

Speaking of trashy people, "whose fathers I disdained to put with the dogs of my flock," Job comments that they don't eat well: "Who gather mallow from the shrubs, and whose food is the root of the broom bush." Driven from the community for their crimes, "among shrubs they bray; under brush they huddle" (Job 30:1–7).

We can conclude that "shrubs" probably includes all plants that do not produce food in the form of grain or fruit. Some are indeed edible, but they are not the staple form of diet and are not included as sanctuary food (bread, wine, and oil). These plants did not exist until after the six days of creation

---

4. There are other problems with the "day-age interpretation"—primarily that it is exegetically impossible to take "day" in this sense in Genesis 1—but it is not our purpose to go into all that here.

week were over. Their creation was suspended until after man was made, for a reason implied in Genesis 3:18. God waited until He saw whether man would sin or not. If man did not sin, the shrubs would be one kind of plant; if man sinned, they would be "thorns and thistles."

Genesis 2:5 goes on to say "no plant of the field had yet sprouted." This implies that such plants did exist and indeed are the same as the grains created on the third day. Such plants had been brought forth, but no second generation had sprouted. Genesis 1:11, "let the earth sprout vegetation," uses *dasha'*, which implies growing up. Genesis 2:5, "had yet sprouted," uses *tsamach*, which implies budding. The grains grew on the third day, but had not sprouted buds until after the sixth. The grain plants had not yet sprouted their ears of grain.

Here again, I believe that the grains had not sprouted because it remained to be seen whether man would sin or not. Harvesting and winnowing grain is labor-intensive, and Genesis 3:18–19 says that sinful man will grow and harvest it by the sweat of his nose. God could have caused grain to sprout in a way that is not so labor-intensive. Thus, the sprouting of the grain awaited the decision of man to sin or not to sin.

According to Genesis 2:5, the shrubs did not exist and the grains had not sprouted because two factors were missing. First, the earth needed to be watered *by God*, and second, a man was needed to cultivate these plants. What this establishes for us is that man's work is done jointly with God's. God contributes water and man contributes labor, and this means that the field plants are kept under control and develop properly.

It also establishes that the world was never designed to grow apart from human cultivation. "Nature" has no balance in "herself." Man as God's under-shepherd (under-farmer) is part of the necessary mix. Against senseless exploitation of the world, however, we have to see that Genesis 2:5 implies that man works with God as cultivator of the creation.

FROM GARDEN TO FIELD

The distinction between garden (or vineyard) and field begins in Genesis 2. As we saw in the previous chapter, this relates to the ordering of the formless world. Plants of the field are contrasted with the garden planted by God in Genesis 2:5 and 8. Later on, under the Old Covenant the Israelites will be required to keep their field plants and vineyard plants separate (Lev. 19:19;

Deut. 22:9), just as we are to keep the eating of the bread and the drinking of the wine separate in the Lord's Supper.[5] God created fruit trees and grain plants on the third day and scattered them over the earth, but there is no indication that they were kept separate. The separation is set up here, when the Garden of Eden is separated from the Land of Eden.[6]

Genesis 2:5 states that man's labor of cultivating the field will involve him with the shrubs and with grain plants. It is clear from Genesis 2:15 that he will also be involved in cultivating the Garden, including fruit trees and grape vines. Why, then, are these field plants emphasized here in 2:5?

The reason, as we have seen in the previous section of this chapter, is eschatological. The passage looks forward to man's proceeding out the Garden of Eden and into the Land of Eden. The Sanctuary-Garden is the vineyard near the house, while the Land is the field. Man is not to live continually in the Garden but only to start there and return there each sabbath day. The goal implied by Genesis 2:5 is that man will act as God's image and move out of the Garden, cultivating the whole earth, the "field." Man proceeds from the center. The sanctuary does not exist for itself alone, but to train men to cultivate the world.

In fact, this is what happened. The judgment pronounced by God in Genesis 3:18 is phrased in terms of the two kinds of field plants. The shrubs will now include "thorns and thistles," and the grains will be eaten by the sweat of the brow. The orchard trees are not mentioned and, in a sense, are excluded. Throughout the Old Covenant, men were never allowed to drink wine in the presence of God, and the Nazirite had to swear off all grapes and raisins as well. The priests were, however, allowed to eat the showbread and the cereal offerings in holy places. Man could fellowship with God in the field under the Old Covenant, but he was not admitted back into the Garden until the New.

Sadly, throughout Church history men have rejected the opportunity to come back into the Garden and drink wine with God. For centuries the Church would not serve the cup to the laity, and most Protestants have never recovered the joy of weekly celebration of the Lord's Supper. Many Protestants

---

9. For a full discussion, see James B. Jordan, *From Bread to Wine: Creation, Worship, and Christian Maturity* (West Monroe, LA: Athanasius Press, 2019).

6. I have discussed this distinction at some length in my paper, "The Law of Forbidden Mixtures," *Biblical Horizons* Occasional Paper 6 (August 1989).

refuse wine and settle for grape juice. We have been given permission to return to the Garden, but we refuse it.

To return to Genesis 2 and 3, we can understand what is implied by Genesis 2:5. God drove Adam and Eve out of the Garden so that they could cultivate the thorny shrubs and tough grains. Had our parents not sinned, they would have followed the rivers out of the Garden into the field and cultivated nice shrubs and gentle grains instead. Thus, Genesis 2:5 points forward to man's eventual departure from the Garden, which was to happen after he had named the animals, gotten a helper, and resisted Satan.

Thus, we have an order of world development set out for us in Genesis 1–2. God first created the world, then set aside the fields of the "lands," and finally planted an orchard in a garden in the midst of a land. Man is the image of God. Man begins in God's orchard but is tasked with developing a land first. Man will start with field plants, which produce the grain that is necessary to sustain human life. He will in time also plant vineyards and orchards, which produce the fruits that are luxuries in human life.

God climaxes His work with the garden-orchard at the end of the first week. Then God passes on the world to His image, who labors for the second week. The climax of human labors will be a garden-orchard-city: the New Jerusalem. Because of Adam's sin, it remained for the Last Adam to do this manly work.

For man to do his work properly, he must start not with his orchard, and not even with his field. He must start by cultivating God's orchard (Gen. 2:15). If he does not cultivate and guard God's orchard, then when he starts his own field, it will be a perverse field, and when eventually he builds a city-orchard, it will be a perverse city. Man must bow the knee and start in God's house before he moves out to do his own works. Only then will his works be good works.

GRAIN AND FRUIT, BREAD AND WINE

Looking at Genesis 2:5 and 8, we have seen that man's first food was fruit, grown by God and given as a gift. Man's second food would be grain, grown by man and God together, offered to God and then received back as a gift. The same would be true of man's later fruit. Grace precedes works, here as always.

Fruit is grown in the vineyard, the orchard. Under the Old Covenant, the vineyard was kept separate from the field, where grain is grown. The vineyard, being analogous to the Garden of God, was holier under the Old Covenant than the field. Under the Old Covenant, the priests were allowed to eat grain in the sanctuary, but not wine. Wine was too holy, and man was not yet wholly sanctified.

Thus, the original order seems reversed. Originally, fruit came first and then grain. Now bread comes first and then wine. How are we to understand this?

We go back to Genesis 1, which mentions grain first and then fruit (Gen. 1:11–12, 29). God made the world first, then set aside the Land (field) of Eden and, last, separated the Garden (orchard) of Eden. Thus, the historical order is grain and then fruit, bread and then wine. Similarly, God worked six days and rested the seventh. This is the order of God's work and of the work of His image, man. Grain grows in a year; fruit takes longer. Under the Old Covenant, the Israelites had to wait until the fourth year to eat fruit (Lev. 19:23–24). Similarly, bread can be made quickly, while wine takes a longer time.

God worked, then rested. Man, however, was made late on the sixth day and his first full day was the day of rest. Man starts in rest and moves to work. Similarly, man started with God's fruit and then moved to his own grain and then to his own fruit. This is the order of grace, which always precedes works. Man started in the Garden and moved to the field and then to his own orchard. This establishes the theological fact that however much human work is involved in the production of bread and wine, they are ultimately gifts of God.

But how does wine (fruit) come first for us? Remember that wine is the blood of grapes and thus signifies blood, in which is life (Gen. 49:11; Deut. 32:14; Leviticus 17). In the order of creation, the blood of fruit comes first, then the bread. In the order of re-creation, the blood of Christ comes first, then the bread and wine of communion, which we make as a memorial before God. We must drink once and for all of the blood of Christ in the sense of John 6 (conversion) before we eat the bread and drink the wine of communion. I believe that this is why, on one occasion only, at the Last Supper, Jesus shared the wine before giving the bread and wine (Luke 22:17–20).

Let me go a bit further and suggest that baptism with water is to be associated with the fact that fruits came first. Wine is glorified water (John 2). Baptism—apart from our works—gives us the initial fruit of the Garden-sanctuary. We don't do anything to produce the water of baptism; in fact

Genesis 2:5 says that water comes wholly from God. The Lord's Supper—which involves our work of producing bread and wine, taken from field and garden—is the continuing food of the Kingdom.

With this in mind, we can return to Genesis 2 and see a further dimension of what is found there. Man was freely invited to the Tree of Life. God planted that tree, not man. Its fruit was a free gift. Thus, man gets life from God apart from works. This is signified by baptism, in the sanctuary-garden of the Church.

Man was also eventually to eat of the Tree of Knowledge,[7] apparently before going out into the field to cultivate grain. That fruit was also a free gift, but depended on man's faithfulness. It represented investiture with mature authority. It is also signified by baptism.

Only the man who has been given Life and Authority is free to bring his own grain and fruit, bread and wine, to God and eat with Him.

What is faithfulness then? Is it a work, in the sense of cultivating the ground? No, it is seen in Genesis 2–3 as the "work" of guarding the Garden, resisting Satan. This endeavor must precede all others. Only when men come to God for Life, resist Satan, and have been given Authority by God—only then—are they equipped to pursue the dominion mandate and cultivate the world. Only then are their works of producing bread and wine acceptable to God.

---

7. See James B. Jordan, "Merit Versus Maturity: What Did Jesus Do For Us?" in Steve Wilkins and Duane Garner, eds., *The Federal Vision*, 2nd ed. (Monroe, LA: Athanasius, 2014), 164ff.

3

A Spring to Water the Soil

Genesis 2:6

*And no shrub of the field had been made in the earth, and no plant of
the field had sprouted, for Yahweh God had not caused rain upon the
earth and there was no man to serve the soil. And a spring used to rise
from the earth and water the whole face of the soil (Gen. 2:5–6).*

GENESIS 2:5 says that "no shrub of the field had been made" and "no plant
of the field had sprouted" for two reasons. The first is that "Yahweh God had
not caused rain upon the earth," and the second is that "there was no man to
serve the soil." Then verse 6 explains that "a spring used to rise from the earth
and water the whole face of the soil," answering the first problem. Verse 7
answers the second problem by the creation of man, the gardener.

This is the first reference to rain in the Bible, and rain is not mentioned
again until the story of the Flood, where the phrasing is very similar: "For after
seven more days, I am causing rain on the earth" (Gen. 7:4). The Bible implies,

but does not state, that God never sent rain until the Flood, which has been taken by creation scientists as a clue to the nature of the antediluvian world. Whatever the value and/or limitations of such a use of Genesis 2:5–6 and 7:4, we want to ask *why* God set up the world this way. Why are we told that God did not send rain but instead caused water to spring up from the ground?

The Hebrew word *'ed*, which I have translated "spring," occurs in only one other place in the Bible besides Genesis 2:6, and that instance (Job 36:27) does not help with the translation here. While some versions give "mist," the ancient Greek and Latin versions give "spring," and that makes the most sense. Most commentators agree with Gordon Wenham, who writes that "spring" "fits in with the more likely etymology of the word from Sumerian/Akkadian, *id*, which represents the cosmic river."[8]

Very well: The Land and Garden of Eden were watered by a spring. Why call attention to the fact that God did not send rain? Why not just mention the spring and leave off the statement about rain?

The reason, I believe, is to call our minds back to Genesis 1:2–9. We find in Genesis 1:2 that there was an ocean over the original earth. Then God created the firmament and separated the waters above from the waters below. On the third day God gathered the waters below into areas below the surface of the land.

Now we have a clear distinction between waters above the firmament, which being above are parallel to rain, and waters below, which would have to come up from under the earth. Both Genesis 1:2–9 and 2:5–6 set up the distinction eschatologically; ground water comes first and then heavenly water.

With this distinction in mind, we can begin to see rather clear associations between ground water and the first creation, which is earthy and Adamic, and heavenly water and the second creation, which is heavenly and Last Adamic: "The Spiritual [world order] is not first, but the natural [world order]; then

---

8. Gordon J. Wenham, *Genesis 1–15*, Word Biblical Commentary (1987; reprint, Grand Rapids: Zondervan, 2014), 58. For a full discussion of *'ed* and its meaning as ground water, see David Toshio Tsumura, *The Earth and the Waters in Genesis 1 and 2: A Linguistic Investigation*, Journal for the Study of the Old Testament Supplement Series 83 (Sheffield: Sheffield Academic, 1989).

Mark Futato, "Because It Had Rained: A Study of Genesis 2:5–7 with Implications for Genesis 2:4–25 and Genesis 1:1–2:3," *Westminster Theological Journal* 60 (1998): 1–21, claims that *'ed* refers to rain. For a response to this claim and to Futato's interpretation of this passage, see James B. Jordan, "Appendix D. Mark Futato on Genesis 1 and 2," in *Creation in Six Days*, 235–245.

the Spiritual [world order]. The first man is from the earth, earthy; the second Man is from heaven. As is the earthy, so also are those who are earthy; and as is the heavenly, so also are those who are heavenly" (1 Cor. 15:46–48, NASB).

Ground water is associated with the first world, the world defiled by sin. Originally the Land of Promise centered on the "circle of the Jordan," which "was well watered everywhere—before Yahweh destroyed Sodom and Gomorrah—like the garden of Yahweh, like the land of Egypt as you go to Zoar" (Gen. 13:10, NASB). This Edenic spot was chosen by Lot, who went for the obvious blessing of ground water—so much more reliable than rain, which must be prayed for. Notice that Genesis 13:10 interjects the statement that God would soon destroy this area. Why is this inserted here? I submit that it is to point to the fact that ground water is not going to be the place of salvation. The waters below, the original Garden of Eden, cannot be recovered. We shall have to move forward to the eschatological waters above and the heavenly Jerusalem.

Just so, Moses contrasts the old land of Egypt, watered from the ground, with the Promised Land, which is watered by rain: "For the land, into which you are entering to possess it, is not like the land of Egypt from which you came, where you used to sow your seed and water it with your foot like a vegetable garden. But the land ... drinks water from heaven's rain" (Deut. 11:10–11). Moses quotes God's promise, "I will give the rain for your land in its season, the early and late rain" (Deut. 11:14).

The laver of the Tabernacle and the bronze ocean and water-chariots of the Temple stood off the ground on pedestals and thus represented heavenly water.[9] This was the water for cleansing and baptism. The rivers that flow from the Temple in Ezekiel 47, Zechariah 14, and Revelation 22 are flowing from these heavenly containers. Alexander Schmemann, the Russian Orthodox theologian, has argued that baptism is by immersion into the creation and joins man to the cosmos from which sin has alienated him. This is fundamentally incorrect. Baptism is by sprinkling with heavenly rain, which joins us to Christ and thereby restores us to dominion over the cosmos.

---

9. See James B. Jordan, "Chariots of Water: An Exploration of the Water-Stands of Solomon's Temple," Biblical Horizons Occasional Paper 12 (April 1991).

GROUND WATER AND HEAVENLY WATER

As we have seen, Genesis 2:5–6 makes a point out of the fact that the primeval world was not watered by rain (from the waters above) but by a spring (from the waters below). We saw that the first water is earthy, while the eschatological water is heavenly. Sin defiled the first creation, so that our hope lies in the eschatological and heavenly world to come. We need to be baptized from the heavenly ocean by sprinkling with holy rain, not to be immersed back into the first earthy ocean. Now, we'll examine this theme further.

1. Most modern commentators draw from the fact that Eden and the Garden were watered by springs the notion that Eden was low ground and that it existed in Mesopotamia. Some even suggest that the four rivers of Genesis 2:10–14 did not flow out of Eden but flowed into it, forming one great river. Exegetically, however, this is very unlikely. Also, the Ark rested in the mountains of Ararat, a high place, and routinely the other garden-sanctuaries and places of worship in the Bible are said to be mountains or high places.[10] Eden was a plateau, the highest place on earth, and the ground water was springs that came up in that place.

2. The first time it rained in the Bible was at the Flood. Perhaps it rained before this, but theologically speaking the first "rain from heaven" was at the Flood. Let us probe the significance of this. Rain comes from heaven. Too much rain is dangerous to mankind and constitutes a judgment, as does frozen rain (the plague of hail: Exod. 9:22–35). Water from above is, thus, judgmental. It is judicial. In the Levitical law, it sprinkles the righteous, judging and cleansing him of contracted ceremonial death (uncleanness). It hails upon the wicked and drowns him.

The ground waters are in subjection to the heavenly waters. Gentle rains produce streams in the desert and water the land of God. The heavy rains of the Flood were accompanied by vast amounts of ground water. "On the same day all the fountains of the great deep burst open and the windows of the heavens were opened and the rain came upon the earth for forty days and forty nights" (Gen. 7:11–12). When the Flood was announced, however, it was announced in terms of rain only (Gen. 7:4). Similarly, the hail on Egypt

---

10. I have dealt with this at more length in *Through New Eyes*, 150ff.

was followed by Pharaoh's drowning in the Red Sea, while God sprinkled baptismal rain from heaven upon the Israelites as they passed through the sea dry-shod (Ps. 77:17–19).

We saw earlier that the grains had not sprouted because it remained to be seen whether man would sin or not (Gen. 3:17–19). Similarly, part of the reason it had not rained is because it remained to be seen whether man would sin or not. Grains could have sprouted in such a way as to be relatively labor-free; instead, harvesting grain is labor-intensive (by the sweat of the nose). Similarly, the rain could have been gentle and baptismic, or it could have been stormy and full of hail. Because of sin, the latter is often the case, and the first instance we see of it is at the Flood.[11]

3. It is worth noting that there is more than one Hebrew word for "rain." The particular word used here, *malar*, focuses on God as the sender of a rain, while the other words, such as *geshem*, speak of rain more as a natural phenomenon, that is, ultimately coming from the hand of God, but not as directly and specially.

Of course, the verse itself says that Yahweh God had not sent rain upon the earth, so the choice of the verb *malar* follows naturally. Still, this fact adds strength to what is already obvious: The first world is watered from below, while water from above (pointing to the waters above the firmament) is eschatological. Man begins on earth, and is later baptized into heaven with water from above, the rain sent by God.

4. Men and plants are discussed together in Genesis 2. The *'ed* mingles with the ground to make the plants grow, and the Spirit of God mingles with the ground to make the man (2:6–7).

Moreover, Genesis 2:8, which states that God planted a garden and then that He put the man into it, is expanded in 2:9–14 and 2:15. Additionally, the discussion of the Garden in 2:9–14 concerns both plants and water, in the form of rivers.

---

11. In the film, *The Bible: In the Beginning*, it storms on Adam and Eve as they are expelled from the Garden. Good theology, even if not true historically.

Thus, Genesis 2:5–15 is organized as a whole series of conceptual parallels:

Wild plants (verse 5a)
> Man-cultivated plants (verse 5b)

No rain (verse 5c)
> No man (verse 5d)

'*ed* water for plants (verse 6)
> Spirit for man (verse 7)

Garden (verse 8a)
> Man in garden (verse 8b)

Garden and water (verses 9–14)
> Man in garden to cultivate it (verse 15)

5. Finally, we should see that the water in the ground of the Garden is associated with Eve. What Adam was to guard was the Garden, and preeminently Eve, its mistress. This is precisely what he refused to do. Later in the Bible, new Adams meet their Eves at wells and defend them there. Eliezar met Rebekah at a well and brought her home to Isaac (Gen. 24:11ff.). Jacob met Rachel at a well and unsealed it for her—a sign, as it turned out, of his coming marriage to her (Gen. 29:10–11). Good Shepherd Moses met Zipporah at a well and defended her against bad shepherds (Exod. 2:16–19).

All of these women were outsiders, who were married by representatives of the Messianic line (compare also Joseph, Samson, Solomon, etc). The spring in Eden flowed out to other lands; the messiahs of the Old Testament married foreign women. In fulfillment, Jesus spoke to an outsider Samaritan woman at a well, asked her about her husband(s), and in so doing offered Himself as True Husband to her and her people (John 4:1–22). He associated the water He offered with the Spirit whom He would give (John 4:10, 23–24; 7:37–39).[12]

Let me add that meeting earthly wives at wells (ground water) is part of the first creation. In heaven there is neither marrying nor giving in marriage, for all are married to the Divine Husband. Thus, the well at which Jesus meets us is heavenly water, the Spirit. As the spring watered the Garden and grew the fruitful trees, so the marriage of woman and man is to be fruitful on earth,

---

12. I discuss this marital imagery briefly in connection with the Laver of Cleansing in "Chariots of Water."

and the marriage of Jesus and God's Daughter (humanity) is to be fruitful unto eternity.

Lastly, the care with which a gardener directs water to cause plants to flourish should be seen as instructive of how a husband should care for his wife and family. One does not grasp or force water, and neither can a man grasp or force his wife.

4

THE CREATION OF MAN

GENESIS 2:7

Then Yahweh God formed man of dust from the ground and breathed into
his nostrils the breath of life; and man became a living soul (Gen. 2:7).

THE word for man is *'adam* and the word for ground is *'adamah*.
Commentators routinely point out the similarity between these two words,
noting that the first is masculine and the second feminine. In terms of what
we have already seen, we can see the motherhood of the earth expressed
here. Humanity is the offspring, so to speak, of heaven and earth, of God and
the soil.

Most commentators question whether there is any relation between the
words *'adam* and *'adamah*. The question of etymological relationship needs to
be reexamined presuppositionally, however. If we assume that the human race
existed for tens of thousands of years and that languages grew up gradually
over time, then we can try to understand Hebrew in terms of evolutionary
development from certain "triliteral roots," as is commonly done today. Thus,

Hebrew lexicons are organized in terms of these "three-letter roots," with specific words grouped under each root.

Even on an evolutionary presupposition, however, I wonder if languages would grow developmentally out of roots. I suggest that languages grow and develop out of usage, and usage includes puns, analogies, and other things that are not "orderly and scientific." The connections between words are more a matter of sound associations than of evolutionary development, though historical development also plays a part.

From a biblical standpoint, however, the whole question must be recast. God scattered humanity at Babel, and the Spirit of God worked rapidly, yea instantly, to create many new languages. We don't know if Hebrew was set up at that time, or if Hebrew is the primordial language of humanity before Babel. In either event, it was created virtually *ex nihilo*, either around 4000 BC or around 2150 BC (Babel; cf. Gen. 10:25, 30 and 11:2).[13] This being the case, such things as puns and other word-similarities were built into human languages by God, and where these occur in the Bible we ought not to think them adventitious. The words *'adam* and *'adamah* are indeed related, then, and the motherhood of the soil is in view.

Another word in this passage that is surely related to these two is the word *'ed* in 2:6, which refers to the water that flowed out of the earth (*'erets*) and watered the *'adamah*.[14] The *'ed*, we notice, does not flow from the *'adamah*. Rather, the *'ed* waters the *'adamah*. The *'ed* carries out the same function as the *'adam*, the man, will later. There is no *'adam* yet made to cultivate the *'adamah*, but for the time being *'ed* does so. Once the *'adam* is created, he will work with water and become the cultivator of the *'adamah*.

The *'adamah* is the mother, but she has no water in herself. She must get water from a father. The *'ed* from the earth (*'erets*) acts as the father-fluid, and later *'adam*, ruler of the earth, acts as father, to make mother *'adamah* fruitful.

---

13. I come up with 3930 BC as the date of creation in "The End of the Kingdom of Judah (Chronologies and Kings XIII)," *Biblical Chronology* 4.7 (July 1992). The Tower of Babel episode happened about 1780 years later.

14. Vowels in Hebrew are secondary; what counts are consonants. (Notice, for instance, how Old Testament Edom becomes New Testament Idumea: "ee-dom" becomes "ee-dum.") Thus, *'d*, *'dm*, and *'dmh* can be seen to be quite similar, particularly when we take note of the context and theology of this passage. Also, taking these word similarities into account helps explain the choice of the rare word *'ed* in this passage instead of one of the more common words for springs of water.

More precisely, man takes over God's function as High Father, to bring 'erets and 'adamah together in fruitful marriage.

But where does man himself come from? Is he the offspring of mother 'adamah and 'ed from father 'erets? By no means. Man is made from dust, which is dry and without water. Genesis 2:7 sets us up for the question: "Then Yahweh God formed man of dust from the 'adamah." A man-shape has been made of dust (*not* clay). Now, where will father-water come from to quicken this dust? The answer is that the "water" is the (moist) breath of the Spirit of God.

According to Genesis 2:5–6, plants are generated by water and soil, by 'ed coming from the 'erets combined with soil ('adamah). According to Genesis 1:24, the 'erets brought forth animals, and according to Genesis 2:19, God formed the animals out of 'adamah. Though God acted to make these things, they are not said to be made of a combination of heaven and earth. Only man, the ruler of the 'erets (earth) is made of God's breath and the dust of the soil. Only man is the "offspring (generations) of the heavens and the earth."

The Spirit of God, His divine Breath, is heavenly. The firmament of Genesis 1:7 separated the waters, and the firmament is called "heaven." Thus, the waters above the firmament are heavenly waters. The Spirit's breath should be seen to impart the moisture of the heavenly waters to the dust. This creates an association between wind, water, and the Spirit of God, an association that continues throughout the Bible. When God sends a dry, desiccating wind that dries up our moisture, we die (Ps. 32:4). Similarly, God's Spirit is not found in a flood of water devoid of air (Ps. 32:6). But when God sends sprinklings of water from above, mixed in air, we are baptismally revived.[15]

---

15. In Genesis 2:7, God breathes into Adam's nostrils the "breath" of life. Hamilton comments: "Instead of using *ruah* for 'breath' (a word appearing nearly 400 times in the OT), Genesis 2:7 uses *nesama* (25 times in the OT). Unlike *ruah*, which is applied to God, man, animals, and even false gods, *nesama* is applied only to Yahweh and to man" (Victor P. Hamilton, *The Book of Genesis, Chapters 1–17*, New International Commentary on the Old Testament [Grand Rapids: Eerdmans, 1990], 159). The only possible exception is Genesis 7:22, and in light of the rest of the usages, this statement also may refer only to mankind. Thus, even the breath of man is different from the breath of animals.

FROM EARTHLY TO HEAVENLY

Earlier, we reflected on the fact that the first Adam was of earth, while the last Adam is of heaven (1 Cor. 15:46–49). We associated this with the original ground waters and the later heavenly waters. Now we need to refine these reflections in the light of what we have just been considering. Even the first Adam was made of heavenly water mixed with earthly soil. Thus, the contrast is not really between waters but between "soils."

The first world-order is characterized by earthly soil and earthly waters, but it is ruled over by a man made of heavenly water and earthly soil. The last world-order, inaugurated by the resurrected and heavenly Adam (Christ), is ruled over by a Man made of heavenly water and heavenly soil. What Paul argues in 1 Corinthians 15:35–50 is that all along the implication of Genesis 2 was that humanity would move toward an eschatological transfiguration from earthly soil to heavenly "soil."[16]

This leads me to a philosophical observation. The Greek view of the universe was that everything is made of Being or Substance. Roman Catholic theologians have continued to use this confusing language, which tends toward pantheism if not carefully safeguarded, since Substance seems sometimes to embrace both the universe and God. Protestant theologians have been more careful and have rigorously defended a "two-substance" doctrine, that the universe may be composed of substance (matter-energy), while God is something Else. On the basis of Genesis 1:1 and what we have been studying here, however, we have to posit a "three-substance" doctrine. There is the substance of the earthly creation, which we may call 'adamah, and there is also another substance of the heavenly creation, of which the Spiritual body of the resurrection is composed, and then there is God Himself.

Paul's logic in 1 Corinthians 15 derives from these truths. The fact that the first Adam was made of heavenly water and earthly soil implies, for Paul, that there will come a time when humanity will be transfigured into a new being, made of heavenly "soil" and heavenly water, in some sense. In other words, in some sense the resurrected and transfigured body is heavenly and no longer earthy, in contrast to the old body. This future transfiguration is also implied by the fact that the test God put before Adam, as we shall eventually

---

16. See the full discussion of verse 44b in Richard B. Gaffin, *Resurrection and Redemption: A Study in Paul's Soteriology* (Phillipsburg, NJ: Presbyterian and Reformed, 1987), 78ff.

see, involved holding off from the Tree of Knowledge until God was ready to let him have it.

I want to make two observations on the resurrection body, based on all this. First, it is a real physical body, just as the heavens are a real physical place. I say this against the gnostics, including the "consistent preterists" of the Max King school of thought who, in their magazine, *Kingdom Counsel,* reject the notion of a physical resurrection and a final transfiguration.

Second, the fact that the new body is composed of heavenly substance answers the question of how the atoms of the decomposed dead are rejoined to make the resurrection body. They aren't. Rather, the resurrection body is something new, based on the old to be sure, but composed of a different kind of matter. The earthy body is sown, and is resurrected a heavenly body. I can't get more precise than this and the details are unclear to me, but I see this distinction between earthy and heavenly substance as the direction in which the answer to this question is found.

Our considerations also lead us to understand the difference between Old Testament baptism and New. Paul required the believers of Acts 19:1–7 to go beyond the Old Testament baptism of John and receive the New Testament baptism of Jesus.

Old Testament baptism was indeed water from heaven, but it essentially resuscitated the old Adam. Each time a person was baptized in the Old Testament and given new life, he fell into sin again, recapitulating Adam's fall. New Testament baptism, however, carries with it the guarantee of a heavenly body. It does not restore men to the Edenic condition of the first Adam by removing sin, but rather it carries men forward to the New Jerusalem condition by removing sin and also incorporating them into the heavenly soil of Christ's transfigured body. What was only implied by Old Testament baptism (salvation) is actually bestowed in New Testament baptism (salvation).

Old Testament baptism, culminating in John's, was for repentance, putting men back into the Edenic situation. That is why Jesus, on our behalf, received it: so He could stand as Second Adam in Eden and resist Satan for us. New Testament baptism is not only for repentance but also for transfiguration. It places us in union with the resurrected and transfigured Christ.

Both baptisms are heavenly, with water from above mixed with air. But Old Testament baptism simply revived the earthly soil (*'adamah*). New Testament baptism brings with it the new soil of the heavenly Adam. We are put into the new body of the Church, a down payment or pledge that we shall receive new physical, heavenly bodies in the resurrection.

NASAL THEOLOGY

Then Yahweh God ... breathed into his nostrils (Gen. 2:7).

If someone stops breathing, we try to resuscitate him by breathing our breath into his nostrils. Adam had never breathed before, and God started him breathing by breathing His own breath into Adam's nostrils. Why did God choose this particular method? Why is it important for us to understand that God started man's life through his nose? We will take a short look at Nasal Theology to seek for an answer.

It seems that the Bible regards the nose as the focal point of the face. The bride's nose is celebrated as the tower of Lebanon (Song 7:4), and her nose is adorned with a sparkling jewel (Gen. 24:47; Ezek. 16:12). The nose is defiled when a ring is put into it in order to lead captives away (2 Kgs.19:28), or when it is chopped off (Ezek. 23:25). The proud man lifts up his nose, as when Psalm 10:4 speaks of the "pride of his countenance" (literally, "pride of his nose").

As the focal point of the face, the nose expresses the attitude of the whole person. Many times when we read that a man fell down with his face to the ground, it literally says that his nose is to the ground (e.g., Gen. 19:1; 48:12; Num. 11:31; 1 Sam. 20:41).

If we look up the Hebrew word for nose (*'aph*) in a Hebrew concordance, we find that this word is used hundreds of times to mean "anger." When we read that God's anger is kindled, it literally says that His nose is kindled. When we read of the anger of Yahweh, it is literally "the nose of Yahweh" Fire blasts out of His nose (Exod. 15:8).

At the same time, phrases like "Yahweh is long suffering" literally say that Yahweh is "long-nosed" (Num. 14:18; Ps. 86:15). "Slow to anger" is literally "long-nosed" (Neh. 9:17; Ps. 103:8). God takes a long breath and holds it, "counting to ten," before taking action against sinners.

Also, if you want to draw blood out of a person's face, the place to do it is his nose. Strike a man, and his nose will bleed (Prov. 30:33).

Finally, when Elkanah gave special honor to his barren wife Hannah, he gave her "one portion of two nostrils" (1 Sam. 1:5). Lying behind this expression is the idea that honoring someone sends a sweet scent into his or her nose, and to Hannah this was doubled.

This leads us to the notion of smell and scent in the Bible. There are bad smells, such as Eglon gave off when he dirtied his trousers in Judges 3:22–24. The Hebrews stank in Pharaoh's nostrils (Exod. 5:21), but later the river and the land of Egypt stank far worse (Exod. 7:18, 21; cf. 8:14). In contrast, God's house was filled with sweet incense, and the sacrifices were a sweet smell to Him.

The fact is that our nose is the most sensitive of our facial organs. We will tolerate an unpleasant sight or a bad noise more easily than we will tolerate a bad smell. Walk into a smelly bathroom and you'll see what I mean. Or ask a policeman what it is like to investigate a three-day old suicide. The "bite" of a horrible stench goes straight into us in a way that a horrible sight or bad noise never does. We quickly depart the scene of a bad smell. The bad smell of our sin drives God away from us, which is why we need the sweet scent of the sacrificial substitute and the incense in order to please Him.

Thus, there is a certain focal character to the nose in the life of man. Not only is the breath of life taken into man through his nose, but the nose is to the face as the heart is to the whole man. The nose is the center of the face. For God to breathe life into man's nostrils is a way of emphasizing that the life of man is derived centrally from God. For man to please God, man must be a sweet smell in the nostrils of God—that is, man must please God at the center of His face, at the core of His being.

It is not surprising, then, that when God passed judgment on man, He passed judgment on the center of man's life, at his nose. Genesis 3:19 does not literally say "in the sweat of your brow" or "by the sweat of your face," but "in the sweat of your nose you shall eat bread." The nose that had breathed in God's very breath in Genesis 2:7 would now drip with sweat because of man's sin—and perhaps the agony of work and fear would cause the nose to drip a "bloody sweat."

The core of man's heart had been defiled, and the sign of this was the defilement of center of the face, the nose. Man's life should have been watered by the central spring of *'ed* that came out of the ground and watered Eden. Instead, the life of man, made of soil, will be watered by the sweat that comes out of the center of himself. Only the agony of the Savior's bloody sweat can atone for the defilement of the human nose, of the human face, and of the whole human person.

5

THE GARDEN IN EDEN

GENESIS 2:8

And Yahweh God planted a garden in Eden in the east (Gen. 2:8a).

WE now arrive at the Garden of Eden. We are told that God Himself planted it. There is no reason to take Genesis 2:8 out of chronological order, and so we should see that God planted the Garden *after* He created Adam. God set up grain plants and fruit trees all over the earth on the third day, but now on the sixth day He plants a special Garden while Adam watches.

World—Man—Garden: that's the order. We see this order also later on in history, except that in later instances, God calls His apprentice alongside Him to help in the preparation of the Garden.

Consider the exodus from Egypt. Exodus 15:17 speaks of planting Israel in the Land of Promise. Man is redeemed (re-created) first by God's redemptive act and then is brought to a land previously prepared. God emphasizes to Israel that they did not do anything to prepare the Land of Promise. God had prepared it for them: "great and splendid cities which you did not build, and houses full of all good things which you did not fill, and hewn cisterns which you did not dig, vineyards and olive trees which you did not plant" (Deut. 6:10–11, NASB). Before entering the land, however, Israel is to set up a symbolic garden, the Tabernacle. God Himself built the Tabernacle, in the sense that God's Spirit directed those who built it (Exod. 31:3). Thus the order is: Land—Man—Garden.

We also notice that man must come to grips with life in the Garden before moving into the land and into the world. Israel lived in the wilderness gathered around the Garden-Tabernacle before moving into the land. Israel was tested in this environment and failed the test. Similarly, Adam had been put into the Garden environment for testing before he moved out into the Land of Eden and into the world.

Did Adam help God make the Garden of Eden? It is safe to say no, he did not. Adam watched. Adam was to learn from God's action. Adam, as God's image, was to imitate the patterns he saw God putting into play. And this is the pattern: The first thing we do in life is worship God, and the first environment/institution to be built is the Church. Later on, this is what Israel was to learn to do, as we see not only in the exodus, but also in the book of Haggai after the return from exile.

If the sanctuary-garden comes first, why didn't God make it before He made the rest of the world? For two reasons. First, there would have been no man to watch and learn. Second, the world is the raw material for the sanctuary. The "formless and empty" creation of the first day is the raw material for the world made during creation week, and the initially completed world of the first week furnishes the raw materials for the Garden-sanctuary.

Adam watched God set up the Garden. God planted fruit trees, which rapidly grew to bear fruit. God also planted the two sacramental trees in the center of the Garden-sanctuary (Gen. 2:9). Adam was passive in all of this. Later on in history, as men mature under God, God calls His people to take a more active role in the production of places and instruments of worship.

Consider Abraham: The patriarchs worshipped at oasis sanctuaries, characterized by altars of earth, trees, and wells. Not a whole lot of work is involved in this. The sacramental meal would have consisted of part of a cooked sacrificial animal. Here again, there is not much human work involved.

Move to Moses: The Tabernacle was a far more complex garden-sanctuary, requiring great skill to build and much work to maintain. Similarly, the sacrificial/sacramental system was greatly expanded. Man was more involved. When we move forward to the Temple era, there is even more for man to do.

Finally, under the New Covenant, we find that the design and placement of garden-sanctuaries (churches) is left entirely up to us. We also find that time and effort is involved in producing the sacraments, in that the production of both bread and wine require skilled human effort at various stages. Planting and growing the Garden is given into our hands, as is preparing the sacramental meal. Yet by faith we insist that what we do is done only under the command of and in the power of God, so that ultimately the Garden is still His production.

Sacred Geography 101

Now we begin to take notice of the theme of sacred geography, which begins here. We notice that God set a Garden on the east side of the Land of Eden, and in verses 10–14 we shall find other lands that are downstream from Eden. In terms of sacred geography, there are several facts to take into account.

First, Eden and the Garden were on high ground. This follows from the fact that the rivers flowed out of the Garden, and rivers flow downstream.[17] This begins the Mountain Theme in the Bible: The holy mountain or high place or rooftop or upper room or altar-mound is the place where God meets with men.

Second, the Land of Eden was higher than the Garden. The river flowed from Eden eastward into the Garden area (Gen. 2:10). If the Garden is the sanctuary where God meets with man, Eden must be the heavenly homeland where God lives with His people. The water comes from Eden to the Garden. Thus, the water is "water above" not "water below." Access to Eden is through the Garden.

We see this theme carried out later, when Israel first builds a sanctuary in the wilderness and only afterwards takes over the Promised Land. A cultural heaven on earth can be built only if men go through the sanctuary of God. Worship renewal must come before cultural renewal.

---

17. Some have contended that the four rivers flowed together from other places to form the Edenic river. We shall discuss this interpretative possibility and show why it is wrong when we get to verse 10.

Third, the Garden is on the east side of Eden. The rivers flowed eastward out of the Garden to water the rest of the world (Ezekiel 47, by implication). Thus, the progression is eastward, and returning to the sanctuary is a westward movement. Israel came into the Promised Land not from the south (up from Egypt), but from the east, having circled around. They crossed the Jordan River in a westward movement to enter the land. Similarly, the Tabernacle and Temple were always oriented so that the doorway was on the east. One had to come from the east in order to enter.

Before we go farther with this theme, however, we have to mention the erroneous interpretation of this verse found in many modern conservative commentaries and some older ones as well. They assume that "eastward" means east of the Land of Promise, not on the east side of the Land of Eden. They assume that Eden was located in Mesopotamia, which was east of Palestine. "And Yahweh God planted a garden in Eden, off in the east." There are several problems with this reading.

First, there is absolutely no reason to believe that the "author" of Genesis was located in Palestine. We are told that Moses wrote the Pentateuch (Luke 24:27,44), and Moses was never in Palestine. From the area of the wilderness wanderings, when Moses put this book together, Mesopotamia was not due east but northeast.

Moreover, it is very likely that Moses was only the final editor of the Genesis material. So, maybe Abraham put in the phrase "eastward" to indicate Mesopotamia, because Abraham did live in Palestine. But maybe it wasn't Abraham who wrote this, but Adam or Seth.[18]

There is no evidence in the text to assume a Jewish or Palestinian perspective in Genesis 1–11. Quite the reverse: These chapters are set in a world context. At any rate, there is no reason to believe that "eastward" means east of Palestine. That is a pure assumption. Moreover, it is an assumption taken from liberal scholars who think Genesis was written centuries later by

---

18. In *Creation in Six Days*, 172–173, I wrote, "My own best guess is that Joseph wrote Genesis in its definitive form (requiring only a few additional notes from Moses and Samuel)." If this is correct, it does not affect the argument I present here. For Joseph, as much as for Moses, Mesopotamia would not be directly east but northeast. Note, too, the words "definitive form": Joseph—or Moses, or whoever wrote Genesis—may well have been using manuscripts written originally by Adam or Noah or Seth or Abraham (cf. Gen. 5:1: "The *book* of the begettings of Adam").

some priests living in Palestine during the age of the monarchy. We can safely dismiss this argument.

Second, the fact that the four rivers flowed from Eden to the lands of Havilah (Saudi Arabia today), Cush (Ethiopia), and Mesopotamia indicates that Eden must have been in the north. It was probably located in the same place the Ark of Noah landed.[19]

Third, the phrase "eastward" is in Hebrew *miqedem*, which combines *min* (from) and *qedem* (east). This phrase means "on the east side," not "in the east." For evidence, look up Genesis 3:25, which is found right in this same context and clearly means "at the east of the Garden," not "far off to the east of Palestine." See also Genesis 12:8, where the mountains "on the east" are immediately to the east of the places spoken of, not far off. Consider, as well, Numbers 34:11; Joshua 7:2; Judges 8:11; Ezekiel 11:23; Jonah 4:5; and Zechariah 14:4. Most of these verses speak of something immediately to the east of something else. In Genesis 2:8, the Garden is not to the east of Eden, but to the east inside Eden. The point is that there is no justification for importing the idea of "general eastwardness" into Genesis 2:8. *Miqedem* means "eastward" of a location mentioned in the immediate context, in this case, the Land of Eden.

EASTNESS

Now that we have discussed the fact that the Garden was located in the eastern part of the Land of Eden, we can continue with an exploration of "eastness" in the Bible.

The verb related to *qedem* ("east"), *qadam*, means "meet face to face," usually in a hostile sense (as in Deut. 23:4; 2 Kgs. 19:32; Neh. 13:3; Pss. 88:13; 95:2; Isa. 37:33; Mic. 6:6). Here again, this makes it very unlikely that Genesis 2:8 refers to something far to the east of Palestine. Rather, it refers to something in the immediate presence of the Land of Eden. The idea of "preventing" or "opposing," which *qadam* conveys, may also point back to the cherubim's preventing Adam and Eve from re-entering the Garden. God's people, His human cherubim, wind up in confrontation with the wicked "at the east."

---

19. You can see a map of this in *Through New Eyes*, 151. This map is mis-drawn in one respect; the rivers are shown coming out of the south side of the Garden.

Unlike cherubim, human beings can face only one direction at a time. The fact that man proceeds from God's throne eastward explains why the word for east (*qedem*) is also used in Hebrew to mean "before" (as in Job 23:8, Ps. 139:5). The idea is "immediately before," in the sense of close confrontation.

Qedem also means "of old, ancient," in the sense of "the good old days." God's good mountains are "ancient," and God Himself is "eternal" (Deut. 33:15,27; cf., e.g., 2 Kgs.19:25; Neh. 12:46; Job 29:2; Pss. 44:1; 55:19; 68:33; 72:2, 12). Why are ancient things considered "eastern"? My guess is that it goes back to the association of the east with the Garden, but there is no clear-cut answer to this question. Perhaps that which is ancient in a good sense is that which went "before" and which man in sin is "prevented" from having (God Himself, God's good mountains, the kingdom of God, etc.).

It is implied that Adam and his children would follow the four rivers eastward (and southward as we shall see) to the four corners of the world as they multiplied and took dominion. But because of sin, the movement eastward and southward is a movement in the direction of sin and/or judgment. Not only were Adam and Eve driven to the east, but later Cain moved farther east (Gen. 4:16).

In Genesis 10, we read that Shem was the father of the children of Eber (verse 21). This identifies the Eberites (Hebrews) as the seed-line. Eber had two sons: Peleg and Joktan. Joktan was blessed with thirteen sons (verses 25–29). We read that the priestly Joktanites moved eastward in their dwellings (verse 30). Four verses later, we read that "as they journeyed east," they came to Shinar and built the tower of Babel. In context, this "they" has to refer to the Joktanites. Thus, the Joktanites, as the priestly seed-people, were leaders in the Babelic enterprise, which by representation included all nations. The Babel event is the "fall of the Joktanites" and meant that the seed-line would go through Peleg, "in whose days the earth was divided" (10:25). From Peleg came Abram the Hebrew.

Lot journeyed east to separate himself from Abram (Gen. 13:11).

The wise men came from the east in a westward motion to see the baby Jesus (Matt. 2:1).

East is not bad. East is the direction man goes when he initially proceeds out from God's throne. At times of worship, he comes from the east, since the only gateway into the Tabernacle and Temple courts is on the east side.

This sacred geography would operate whether he is in sin or not. If he is in sin and is being driven out from God eastward, then his eastward movement is farther and farther into sin. In that case—which of course is the case for all men after Adam—his westward motion involves repentance. It is probably a bad sign that Lot went east of Abraham, but it is simply a sign of proceeding outward that Abraham blessed his sons and sent them to the east (Gen. 25:6).

When Jesus speaks of His coming, He says that He will come from the east (Matt. 24:27). Thus, the Church historically has spoken of herself as facing east in worship. The eastern wall of a church building is the one we face in worship; the western wall is the door through which we enter. If we kneel and bow down, we are not bowing to anything on the altar-table, but we are bowing to the east in expectation of Christ's coming to be with us in worship. Notice that this reverses the directions in the Bible before Christ. We assume that we as believers have moved through the Garden and into the Land of Eden, and now the place of worship is east of us instead of west.

BACK TO EDEN

The fact that Adam was kicked out of the Garden to the east and that cherubim guarded that eastern door means that Adam and Eve never lived in the Land of Eden. Their homeland was east of Eden and east of the Garden. Like the priests and the Judahites in the camp of Israel, the godly seed of Adam guarded the door to the Garden before it was washed away in the Flood (compare Num. 2:3; 3:38).

The first person to dwell in Eden was Abraham. The Land of Promise is called Eden in Ezekiel 36:35 (cf. Ezek. 31:9ff.; Joel 2:3). God called Abram in Ur, and Abram learned to worship God in Haran for many years before entering the land (Acts 7:2–5). The first thing Abram did in the land was set up sanctuaries (Gen. 12:7, 8; 13:4). The door to Eden was again the Garden. Similarly, Israel set up the Tabernacle in the wilderness after they left Egypt; only afterwards did they enter the land. Also, God gave the returning exiles no rest in the land until after they had restored the Temple (Hag. 1–2).

In the new creation, sacred geography has become spiritualized in Christ, but the same principles apply. Unless we rebuild the Church, we will not live in a holy land.

Now let us expand on these thoughts by taking note of the sacred geography of the Tabernacle and Temple. The river flowed out of the Garden, making it the highest place on the earth next to the Land of Eden itself, where the river arose. This geography is recapitulated in the Tabernacle in two ways.

First, the Tabernacle courtyard's highest point was the altar of earth raised up in the middle of it. The entire courtyard is called the "doorway" to the Tabernacle itself. We see this from Leviticus 1:3, where the animal is said to be offered in the "doorway of the tent of meeting," and the later verses in this chapter make it clear that this "doorway" included the whole area between the altar and the actual gate of the court.

Positioned between the altar and the Tabernacle was the laver of cleansing—in the Temple, the bronze sea. Here are waters that are associated with the Tabernacle but that are used (and thus flow forth) to cleanse the priests and the sacrifices that are put on the altar. Thus, this water flows from the Tabernacle to the altar, from Eden to the Garden.

Therefore, the Tabernacle where God dwells is the symbolic equivalent of the Land of Eden, God's homeland. The Israelite was not given access to the actual Tabernacle, but living in the Land of Promise was the equivalent. The sins of men defiled the Garden-altar, and thus called forth God's anger. This would mean that Israelites would be cast out of the Land of Promise, as in fact happened at the exile. Accordingly, the altar had to be satisfied by means of sacrifices, which appeased God's wrath and enabled Israel to live in the land.

In the new creation, where we presently dwell, we are given access to the heavenly tabernacle. Thus, any land where we live is potentially a Land of Promise. We can keep it only if we guard the holiness of God in our worship, church discipline, and daily lives.

To sum up so far: The courtyard is the Garden; the altar as the highest place in the courtyard is the two trees where God meets with man; and the Tabernacle is the Land of Eden, God's dwelling.

Second, the items placed on the altar formed a representation of the Tabernacle.[20] The real Tabernacle is God Himself and His consuming fire. The curtains of the Tabernacle represented, in part, that fire; they were flame colored and woven with fiery cherubim (seraphim; "fiery ones"). When the animal entered the fire, it was entering God's house as the representative of the offerer.

Thus, in this way the symbolism is set out vertically: The courtyard is the Garden; the altar as the highest place in the courtyard is the place where God

---

20. James B. Jordan, "The Whole Burnt Sacrifice: Its Liturgy and Meaning," Biblical Horizons Occasional Paper 11 (March 1991).

meets with man; and the fiery sacrifices on top of the altar represent God's home, the Land of Eden.

The reason for having both of these symbolic models is not hard to see. Eden was both eastward and upward from the Garden. Thus, the Tabernacle points to the fact that God's home is to the east, and the fire on the altar points to the fact that God's home is upward from the mountaintop (the altar mound).

In our new creation worship, we don't have to move to the east or go to a mountaintop. In Christ, we are already there. Thus, sacred geography has been transformed in the new creation.

THE FOUR DIRECTIONS

Before moving to another topic, let's consider some of the other aspects of sacred geography in terms of the four directions. Not every mention of north, south, east, and west in the Bible carries the symbolic weight of sacred geography, but many of them do.

According to Genesis 2:10–14, the river that flowed east out of Eden turned south as it broke up into four rivers. The first mentioned is the Pishon that flows to the land of Havilah. Havilah is the Sinai Peninsula in the post-Flood world.[21] This seems to be the Jordan valley before the destruction of Sodom and the creation of the Dead Sea. The second river, Gihon, flows to Ethiopia. The other two are the Tigris and the Euphrates. All flow from the north, the area of Ararat. Thus, the outward motion of Adam and Eve would have been south as well as east.

God's throne is said to be in the north in Isaiah 14:13. His throne on Mount Zion is symbolically in the far north (Ps. 48:2). God comes from the north in Job 37:22; Ezekiel 1:4ff.; and Ezekiel 8.

In the old creation, when sacred geography was in play, men proceed out from God's house and throne in an eastward and southward direction and return from the east and south. East and south are the directions in which both curse and blessing flow.

Thus, Abraham moved in a southward direction through the Promised Land and down into Egypt. Then he came up from Egypt back into the Land

---

21. The map in *Through New Eyes*, 151, has Havilah too far south.

of Promise. Jacob moved east into Mesopotamia and then came back to the Land of Promise. The Israelites went south into Egypt and then came back up into the land, circling around so that they entered from the east.

When David was driven from Jerusalem by Absalom, he went to the east and then returned. Elijah fled south to Sinai and returned. In exile, Israel was taken to the east to Assyria and Babylon and then returned. Meanwhile, Jeremiah and those with him went down to Egypt. We never see people exiled to lands in the north or west or returning from them.

The river of Ezekiel 47 comes from the south side of the Temple and flows due east to the Dead Sea.

When God comes, He comes from the north, as in Ezekiel 8. The area of the Tabernacle courtyard north of the altar has a particular association with God's coming in judgment.[22] In line with this, it is interesting to see that when Abraham first came into the Promised Land from the east, he stopped at Haran in the north on the way. Thus, his invasion of the land was from the north (northeast). In this, Abraham imaged God's own coming. Similarly, Israel's invasion of the land after her departure from Egypt was from the east, and God came back into the Temple from the east in Ezekiel 43 after departing in an eastward direction in Ezekiel 11.

God's coming from the north is matched by the armies He sends to punish His people. Though they come from Mesopotamia in the east, they follow the route used by Abraham and arrive from the north (northeast; Jer. 1:13–15). When Israel returns from eastern exile, she arrives via the north (Jer. 3:12,18). This follows the march of God and seems to underlie what we find in Ezekiel 44 and 47. In Ezekiel 43, God returns to the Temple through the east gate, and then it is blocked off (Ezek. 44:1–3). Because the river flows south of the altar in an eastward direction, it forms a watery barrier between the altar and anyone approaching from the south. Thus, access to the altar and to the visionary temple is possible only from the north (Ezek. 44:4). The people must come in from the north. This is an interesting change from the earlier Tabernacle and Temple, when the people came in from the east.

When we get to the book of Acts, we find a surprising change. For the first time there is a primarily westward movement. First, in Acts 8, we find

---

22. See my "The Lamb of God," *Biblical Horizons* 39–40 (July–August 1992). Online: http://www.biblicalhorizons.com/biblical-horizons/no-39-the-lamb-of-god-part-1/ and http://www.biblicalhorizons.com/biblical-horizons/no-40-the-lamb-of-god-part-2/.

Philip going north to Samaria and then south to encounter the Ethiopian eunuch. Then in Acts 9:32–43 we find Peter moving west to Lydda and then to the seacoast town of Joppa. From there he moves north to Caesarea (Acts 10). In Acts 11:19, we find the gospel going west to Phoenicia, Cyprus, and Antioch (this is a northwesterly direction). Nobody is pictured going east.

Of course, most of the rest of Acts is concerned with Paul's journeys, each of which moves farther west, until Paul expresses his hope to reach Spain before he dies (Rom. 15:24). These parts of the world simply do not figure in the history of the sacred geography before Christ. I suggest that this westward movement symbolizes the fact that men have moved into Eden, which was west of the Garden.

With the destruction of Jerusalem, the old creation was finally wiped away and the new creation was fully revealed. In this new world, the symbolism of sacred geography no longer matters. "In Christ there is no east or west, in Him no north or south."[23]

MAN PLACED IN THE GARDEN

And Yahweh God planted a garden in Eden in the east; and He placed there the man whom He had formed (Gen. 2:8).

The two phrases in Genesis 2:8 summarize and introduce the next two paragraphs of the narrative. Verse 9, which describes the planting of the Garden of Eden, expands verse 8a. Verses 15–17, which describe how God put Adam into the Garden, expand verse 8b. Sandwiched in between are verses 10–14, which describe the setting of Eden in the world.

Back in chapter 1, we saw part of the reason for this literary order, which is that it recapitulates Genesis 1:

Day 1 (2:5–7) — world covered by water; formation of man as Light.

Day 2 (2:8–9) — the Garden-firmament for the Man-Light.

Day 3 (2:10–14) — separation of land and water in the lands below the Garden-firmament.

Day 4 (2:15–17) — the firmament governed by the Man-Light, separating light and darkness, permitted tree and forbidden tree, good and evil.

---

23. John Oxenham [William A. Dunkerly], "In Christ There Is No East or West," online: https://hymnary.org/text/in_christ_there_is_no_east_or_west_oxenh.

At the beginning of this chapter, we took note of the fact that Adam was already on the scene and so watched God plant the Garden of Eden. This was part of Adam's primeval pedagogy: As God's image he would learn how to act by observing and imitating God's work.

But more than this, the Garden is the sanctuary, the place of worship. God always builds His own place of worship, for it is His house in the midst of men. Thus, though men are involved in building the later houses of worship in the Bible, we are always given to understand that God is really doing the work.

Remember that the Tabernacle was made out of the spoils of the Egyptians, that Solomon's Temple was made out of the spoils of the Philistines, and that the Restoration Temple was built out of the spoils of the Persian Empire (an event recorded in Esther 9). Thus, God provided the raw materials. Also, we are told that the Spirit of God inspired Bezalel to make the Tabernacle (Exod. 31:3), making it clear that God was really building His own house through men. All of this comes to a climax when we see that the Church is built not by us but by Jesus, the God-man. God builds His Church, and puts us into it. We don't build it.

So, God sets up the Garden-sanctuary and puts Adam into it, just as God sets up the Church and puts us into it. Adam watched God build His garden-house and learned something about building his own garden-house. Similarly, from studying how God has set up the Church—her structure, government, financing, etc.—we learn how to set up our own domestic and national governments. This is why the Bible spends so much time on church government and law, and comparatively little on national government and law. The Church is the nursery of the Kingdom, and the principles we learn in the Church are to be carried forth in the transformation of family, state, and other institutions.

For instance, the governmental patterns that have emerged in Western Civilization are direct copies of church government. Constitutional monarchies imitate the constitutional episcopacy; republics imitate presbyterianism. Or again, the Church tax is an un-graduated income tax (the tithe), and Peter Leithart has shown that this is the proper form of taxation for the civil government as well.[24] We could multiply examples, but let's move on to another observation.

---

24. Peter J. Leithart, "The Objects of Taxation," Biblical Horizons Occasional Paper 9 (1990).

I think there is another dimension to the order of events here in Genesis 2. The events in Genesis 2 recapitulate for the image of God the events of Genesis 1. Consider Genesis 2: first we have the man, then we have the Garden, then the man moves into the Garden, and finally the man is given a wife from his side. Now consider Genesis 1: first we have God, then we have the world, then God moves into the world, and finally God creates a Bride (humanity) from His side.

To amplify: First, we have God in Genesis 1:1. Second, God makes a Temple for Himself in Genesis 1:1. Third, God moves into the Temple and works with it in Genesis 1:2–25. Finally, God makes a Bride (humanity) in Genesis 1:26–30. Genesis 2:7 says that God formed man of the ground but quickened him by His Spirit. The Spirit is called the Paraclete, one who comes alongside. The Paraclete comes alongside man, but He comes from being alongside the Father and the Son. Thus, in a powerful sense humanity is quickened by God's Rib (the Spirit) to become God's Bride.

So we see the same order in Genesis 2. First man is made (2:7). Second, God makes a house for Him to share with man, His bride (2:8–9). Third, man moves into the house and works with it (2:15–20). Finally, God makes a paraclete for the man, taking her from his side to work alongside him (2:21–24).

THE GARDEN

We have already considered the second half of verse 8, but I have neglected to discuss the *garden* in the first half of that verse. We have discussed the geography of the garden in the Land of Eden, in the midst of the world. What we have not yet done is take up the general meaning of *garden* itself. So, let's drop back to verse 8a and consider gardens this time.

The Hebrew word for "garden" is *gan* (masculine) or *gannah* (feminine). It is related to the verb *ganan*, which means, "defend." James Smith writes, "*Ganan* is used only in reference to the protective guardianship of God. Of its eight occurrences, six have to do with the Assyrian crisis in the days of Hezekiah. Isaiah assured the king that God would care for Jerusalem like a mother bird hovering with wings spread over her young in the nest (Isa. 31:5)." The verb is used twice in that verse (cf. 2 Kgs. 19:34; 20:6; Isa. 37:35; 38:6). Smith continues, "Zechariah twice uses the same verb to describe the divine protection of God's people in their wars against the sons of Greece (Zech. 9:15) and of Jerusalem in the last days (12:8)."[25]

Not only do all eight occurrences of this verb refer to God's defending His people, but they also all refer to the defense of Jerusalem or Zion. Zion, like the Garden of Eden, is God's holy mountain. Jerusalem is the developed form of the Garden of Eden, as the raw materials are transformed into a more glorious condition. Thus, we might paraphrase all eight uses of this verb by saying that God promises to "garden" Jerusalem.

Not only in Hebrew is the word "garden" related to the verb "to guard." It is true in English as well (as you can see). The Garden of Eden is God's holy place, which He guards. Adam was to be God's priestly assistant. Adam failed to guard the Garden, to *ganan* the *gannah*; in fact, Adam became something the Garden needed to be guarded from, so God kicked him out and put the cherubim to guard the Garden.

The noun *magen*, meaning, "shield," is also related to *ganan*. We are most familiar with this word in the phrase Magen David or Mogen David, the "Shield of David," a reference to the six-pointed star that became a Jewish symbol during the so-called Middle Ages. Smith writes: "In view of the fact that God is always the one who protects (*ganan*) His people, it is no surprise that He is so often called the shield (*magen*) of Israel. He is the shield about His servants (Gen. 15:1), the house of Aaron (Ps. 115:10), the nation of Israel (Dt. 33:29), and all those who walk uprightly and put their trust in Him (Prov. 2:7; 30:5)."[26] God is called a shield many times in the Psalms.

God is Lord of hosts, and the host around God is an army of angels (and men). Such warriors carry shields. Shiny shields held in an array around God create not only a ceremonial boundary but also a glorious one. The image of God may also have such a glory-shield around him. Thus, Solomon made three hundred golden shields for ceremonial use, which were carried around him by his guards when he walked from the Palace to the Temple for worship (2 Chron. 9:16; 12:9–11).

We've seen that the ideas of a guarded place and of a walled (shielded) enclosure are related to the biblical idea of a garden. Mackie writes:

---

25. James E. Smith, in R. Laird Harris, et al., eds., *Theological Wordbook of the Old Testament*, 2 vols. (Chicago: Moody, 1980), #367.

26. *Ibid.*

In its most precise application the term refers to a level piece of ground enclosed by a wall or hedge, in which plants, shrubs, and trees are cultivated by irrigation.... While not excluding the idea of garden familiar in the West, its meaning in general is often nearer to that of our *nursery-garden* or *orchard*.... The fact of its being artificially and continually watered, distinguished the garden proper from the ordinary grain field, the vineyard, and the plantation of olive or fig trees.[27]

This more precise meaning of "garden" is seen in passages like Deuteronomy 11:10 and 1 Kings 21:2, which speak of an irrigated vegetable or herb garden. The Garden of Eden was a more elaborate kind of garden. The Hebrew had another word, apparently taken from the Persian, to refer to an enclosed orchard, the word *pardes*, from which "paradise" comes. The paradises of the later Persian Empire were enclosed park-like gardens large enough to accommodate herds of deer and other animals.[28]

In a sense, *pardes* might seem more appropriate for the Garden of Eden, but since *gan* is used, we must see that the Hebrew *gan* can mean either a small vegetable garden or a large, enclosed orchard with animals. *Pardes* is used only three times in the Hebrew Scriptures. It is used for the paradise of a Persian king (Neh. 2:8). It is used in Ecclesiastes 2:5, next to *gan*, to indicate that Solomon had both gardens and orchards. And it is used in Song of Songs 4:13 to refer to the bride and is parallel to "garden" (*gan*) and "enclosed spring" in verse 12.

When we get to the Greek translation of the Old Testament, however, we find that two different words are used to translate the Hebrew *gan* and *gannah*. When it is a small vegetable garden that is in view, the Greek *kepos* is used, but wherever the Garden of Eden is alluded to, and wherever "garden" is used figuratively, the Greek word is *paradeisos*. Thus, the Greek usage tends to make more specific the range of meaning encompassed by the one Hebrew word.

When we get to the New Testament, we find that "paradise" is used to refer to God's garden, while *kepos* is used for other smaller gardens, like the Garden of Gethsemane. Revelation 2:7 refers to the Tree of Life in paradise, an

---

27. G. M. Mackie, "Garden," in James Hastings, ed., *Dictionary of Christ and the Gospels*, 2 vols. (Edinburgh: T. & T. Clark, 1906) 1:635.

28. M. P. Johnstone, "Paradise," in Hastings, ed., *Dictionary*, 2:318.

allusion back to the Garden of Eden. In Luke 23:43, Jesus assured the converted criminal that he would be with Him in paradise that very day, implying that Jesus is the true Emperor and that His heavenly palace includes a glorified Garden of Eden. Finally, Paul identifies the "third heaven," the place where God dwells, with paradise in 2 Corinthians 12:4.

Let's now survey briefly the use of "garden" in the Bible. First, of course, the Garden of Eden is mentioned thirteen times in Genesis 2 and 3. The next garden reference is Genesis 13:10, where we are told that both the land of Egypt and the circle of the Jordan were like the Garden of Yahweh.

This leads me to two observations. First, the area of Sodom and Gomorrah, which is now under the Dead Sea, was like the Garden of Eden in a negative sense. This area was a sanctuary for evil, even though it was delightfully provisioned with water and vegetation.

Second, if the land of Egypt was like the Garden of Eden in being well watered, the best part of Egypt, Goshen, was the best of that garden, and that is where God put His priestly people. Thus, when the Hebrews settle in Goshen at the end of Genesis, we are to see God's people being allowed back into the Garden, where they can, Joseph-like, minister to all the nations of the world.

Numbers 24:6 refers to Israel as God's garden, which surely implies His protection. When God restores Israel, it will be, figuratively, a restoration of the Garden of Eden. So says Isa. 51:3; 58:11. So also says Jeremiah 31:12. Ezekiel uses the garden as a symbol for Israel in Ezekiel 31:8–9. And, if the people are the garden, so is the holy land (Joel 2:3; Ezek. 36:35).

2 Kings 21:18 and 26 tell us that Manasseh and Amon were buried in a garden tomb. Later, the True King of Israel will also be buried in a garden tomb.

The Song of Songs compares the Bride to a garden seven times. The equation of the Bride with a garden takes its rise from Genesis 2, for Eve was put into the Garden with Adam for Adam to guard. She was the highest expression of the Garden and the thing Adam had to be most careful to cultivate and guard. The Bride in Song of Songs is a walled garden, enclosing a spring of water, and full of delightful smells (Song 4:12–16; cf. Song 5:1; 6:2). An enclosed garden would keep the scents of the flowers and herbs inside, making it a delight. In Song of Songs 8:13, the Bride is not the garden but is sitting in the garden, as Eve originally did and as the Church does with her Lord.

Since the original garden was God's sanctuary, and since the Tabernacle and Temple represented glorified gardens, it is no surprise that false worship took place in false garden-sanctuaries. Isaiah speaks of such in Isaiah 1:29–30; 65:3; 66:17.

There are two gardens mentioned in the New Testament, and only by John. We can consider first the garden of Joseph of Arimathea (John 19:41), a member of the Sanhedrin and a disciple of Jesus (Mark 15:43; Matt. 27:57). Jesus' body was place in the tomb in the garden. Tombs for the well-to-do were often located in gardens. "His grave was assigned to be with wicked men, yet with a rich man in His death" (Isa. 53:9). As we have seen, the only other mention of a garden tomb associates it with royalty.

John tells us that when Jesus arose, Mary Magdalene thought He was the gardener (John 20:15). Of course, she was right. Jesus is both the new Adam and the God of the new garden, which is the bride.

The other garden is a grove of olives centered on an olive press. John simply speaks of it as "the garden" (John 18:1, 26). The other Gospels don't call it a garden but Gethsemane, "the oil press." Evidently the garden was an enclosed place inside the olive grove on the Mount of Olives. Both Matthew and Mark give the impression that Gethsemane was a place arrived at only after traversing part of the orchard hillside (Matt. 26:30,36; Mark 14:26,32).

The Garden of Gethsemane is presented as a new Garden of Eden. First, we have a grove of food-trees. Second, God is present. This is dramatically confirmed when, in John 18:6, Jesus uses the name of God for Himself—Yahweh, "I am"—and everyone falls to the ground. Third, the garden is a place of temptation. When Jesus advised the disciples to pray that they not be led into temptation, we see what He was about to go through (Luke 22:40, 46). Fourth, the bloody sweat of Jesus could only have been seen on His brow, a reference to Genesis 3:19. Fifth, Jesus' prayer in the garden is His clinging to the Tree of Life, which Adam rejected when he rejected God.

From the Garden of Gethsemane Jesus left to be crucified outside the gate, thus taking upon Himself the exile Adam had earned in Genesis 3. Then Jesus was buried in a garden and arose to be the new Gardener. From Garden to exile to New Garden—that is the history of humanity.

6

THE TREES OF THE GARDEN

GENESIS 2:9

And Yahweh God caused to grow from the ground every tree, being pleasant to sight and good for food; and the tree of life was in the middle of the garden, and the tree of the knowledge of good and evil (Gen. 2:9).

ACCORDING to Genesis 1:11–12, God had already caused the "earth" to "produce" seed-bearing plants and fruit-bearing trees. As we saw earlier, these are the foundations respectively of grain and grapes, bread and wine. Other kinds of plants waited until after the fall of man for their creation (Gen. 2:5 + 3:18). Now we find, after the creation of Adam from the ground, that God plants some more trees in the Garden of Eden while Adam watches. This is to teach Adam, as we have seen.

In Genesis 1:11–12 the "earth" produces vegetation, while in Genesis 2 it is the "land" (*'adamah*) that brings forth vegetation. As we saw in an earlier essay, the *'adamah* is feminine, and brings forth humanity under the ("masculine") power of God. The word for "earth" (*'erets*) is not pictured as a mother for humanity, or as "mother earth" in any sense. The *'erets*, we saw, gives forth water and (so to speak) marries the *'adamah* to produce plants and animals. By way of contrast, God sends forth His Spirit to "marry" the *'adamah* and make man. As we are about to see, the trees that come forth from the *'adamah* can be symbols for human works and offspring.

In Genesis 1:11, the *'erets* "produces" or "sprouts" vegetation. The verb is *dasha'*, which literally means "to grass." Genesis 1:11 literally reads "Let the earth grass forth grass." The verb is used only twice in the Bible, here and in Joel 2:22. The noun "grass" (*deshe'*) is used for tender grass and herbs. The idea is new, tender grains. As we saw in our consideration of Genesis 2:5, these newly-sprung grasses had not yet sprouted ears of edible grains before the fall of man. By way of contrast, the trees had fruit already on them.

In Genesis 1:12 the verb is different. There the earth "brings forth" the plants. The verb, *yatsa'*, is one of the most common Hebrew verbs, used over a thousand times to mean "come forth, depart, go out, bring out, etc." It is a very ordinary word with no special connotations.

Now we come back to Genesis 2:9. Here the trees "grow up" out of the *'adamah*. The verb for "grow up" is *tsamach*. It is not all that commonly used, but significantly it is used in connection with human life. Not only do plants grow up out of the ground, but human plants do as well. The descendants of the righteous will grow up like poplars (Isa. 44:4). The Messiah will grow up out of the human soil of God's people (Ps. 132:17; Jer. 33:15; Ezek. 29:21; and Zech. 6:12).

Most interesting is that this verb is used for the growing of hair out of the human body (Lev. 13:37; Judg. 16:22; 2 Sam. 10:5; 1 Chron. 19:5; Ezek. 16:7). Man, remember, is made of soil, and so just as the soil grows plants, the human body grows hair. This analogy is also found with other words in Leviticus 25:5, 11, which says that the plants that grow wild during the sabbath and Jubilee years are "nazirite" vines (translated "untrimmed"). In other words, the land's holiness in those years is shown in the luxuriant growth of plants out of its soil, just as the Nazirite's holiness during the time of his vow is shown by the luxuriant growth of his hair (Num. 6).

The hair of the Nazirite represents the works that he accomplishes during the season of his vow, and so it is put on the altar for God. It is his glory, and hair is associated with glory in 1 Corinthians 11:15. The hair on the head is the woman's glory, while the hair of the face is the man's. Having your beard pulled out wrecks that glory (2 Sam. 10:5), just as shaving a woman's head destroys hers. The war bride cut her hair off, removing the glory of her old life, and grew a new glory within the covenant of God (Deut. 21:12–13).

Glory in the Bible is social. God's glory cloud consists of myriads of angels and men gathered around Him. We are His "hair" and "beard," the halo around Him. Thus, the people that Paul evangelized in his second and third missionary journeys were symbolized by his Nazirite hair, and he offered them to God on the altar in Jerusalem (Acts 18:18; 21:24).

All of this imagery fits together. Our children are our offspring. We are the soil from which they, as trees or (sadly) thorns grow. They are like the hair that grows out of us and forms a glory cloud around our face (male) or head (female). Rearing our children is very much a holy war, a Nazirite task, and we hope to offer them to the Lord as the Nazirite offered his hair, once our task is completed.

With all this in mind, we can understand better why Genesis 2:9 is worded precisely as it is. Out of the ground God caused the trees to grow up. Out of the human body God causes hair to grow up. Out of human life God causes our children to grow up. Out of the soil of humanity God caused the Messiah to grow up. The choice of words in Genesis 2:9 thus helps set the stage for one of the images of human life used pervasively throughout the Bible.

FROM PLANTS TO WATER TO MAN

Genesis 2:8 begins an expanded recapitulation of the same themes as are found in 2:5–7. The order of presentation in 2:5–7 is this:

In the World (verse 4):

1. Plants: no shrubs exist; no grains have sprouted (5a).

   2. Water: no rain to water the earth (5b).

      3. Man: no man to cultivate the earth (5c).

   2'. Water: springs water the earth (6).

3'. Man: man is formed (7).

Now we find the same concerns repeated at the next stage of development:

In the Garden (verse 8):
1. Plants: fruit trees grow in the Garden (9).
2. Water: river flows from Eden to the Garden to the world (10–14).
3. Man: man is put into the Garden to cultivate it (15).[29]

This triadic repetition jumps out at us once we see it. And it is not very difficult to see that once again we have an image of the trinity here. As so often is the case in the Bible, the Kingdom of God is presented in three dimensions: glory, knowledge, life; or person, word, and sacrament. Here the personal dimension (Father focus) is the man, obviously. The sacramental dimension is first of all the water (Spirit focus). And the word dimension is the plants, of which the climactic is the Tree of Knowledge (Son/Word focus). Of course, these associations are very "fuzzy," but since the world has been created by a triune God, we should not be surprised that the world reflects that tri-unity in many ways, some clearer than others.

The associations are also multi-dimensional, in that the two primary trees (life and knowledge) can be associated with the Spirit and the Word respectively, as the two gifts that proceed from the hand of God the Father and are offered to build up the person-life of the images of God.

Let's meditate on the relationships in the Garden and see how they correspond to and display God's relationship with man. In each section the plants are mentioned first, then the water, and finally the man. In the history of redemption, the Son (plant) came first, then the Spirit (water), to re-create humanity.

But the Plant cannot grow without Water and a "Man" to till the soil. So the Water comes, and then God (the archetype of man) tills the soil to produce the initial Trees, including the two special ones. Just so, the Spirit and the Father brought the Son into the world and made Him the Tree of Life for us.

The Plant (the Branch, the Shoot of Jesse, etc.) offers two things, Life and Knowledge, the former associated more with the Spirit. The juicy water-filled fruits communicate Life to us, Life provided by the Tree (the Son). They also,

---

29. Notice that verse 15 virtually repeats verse 8. This identifies the opening and close of the paragraph. Compare verses 18 & 24 and 2:25 & 3:7.

for those who are mature and ready for it, provide Knowledge (in the sense of rule, participation with the Father).

Also, as we shall see, the water of the Spirit proceeds from the heavenly Land of Eden to the earthly Garden of Eden and from there out to all the world.[30] As the water goes, so man goes, taking the trees with him, so that Ezekiel 47 pictures trees of life all along the river that flows from the sanctuary. Such trees heal the nations and feed and restore men (Rev. 22:2).

I am not arguing that all these trinitarian and covenant-historical ideas are *taught* in Genesis 2:5–15. Rather, what I am saying is that the reason these relationships exist in Genesis 2, and what accounts for the specific literary organization of the passage, is that this world and this Word both reflect the intra-trinitarian life of God, especially as that life is manifested in His creation. That is why the passage focuses on plants, water, and man. That is why plants, water, and man interact the way they do. That is why the passage moves in its literary structure from plants to water to man, from Word to Life to Person.

THE TREES IN THE CENTER OF THE GARDEN

Genesis 2:9 tells us that the trees of life and knowledge were in the midst of the Garden. Because of the careful geometry of the Tabernacle and Temple, we are probably authorized to assume that these two trees were side by side in the center of the Garden, but all the text actually states is that they were among the trees in the midst of the Garden.

Obviously we don't know what the fruits of these trees were, and that's a good thing. If we knew what fruits they were, there would be all kinds of superstitions surrounding them. As we go along, I shall argue that we can associate (not identify) the Tree of Life with bread and the Tree of Knowledge with wine.

The Garden is the place God put Adam to start with and the place where God meets with man. By calling attention to these two trees, the Bible associates them with God's meeting with man. That is, these trees take on a special "sacramental" aspect. We have general trees and two special trees; we have general fruits and special fruits. Of course the history of the covenant will

---

30. Positioned between the heavenly Eden and the world, the Garden is the firmament, the mediating boundary. See the discussion in chapter 1.

fill out more and more how these two, the special and the general, interact. For now, we just need to see that this bipolarity exists.

Both these special trees were "pleasant to sight and good for food." Thus, when Eve judged that the fruits of the Tree of Knowledge was pleasant to sight and good for food, she was judging correctly.

In Genesis 2:16–17 God said to Adam that he might eat freely of every tree in the Garden except the Tree of Knowledge. This clearly and unmistakably means that Adam was invited to eat of the Tree of Life, especially since that tree was marked out in some special way.

God mediates life to us through food and water. If we don't eat, we die. Now, the food we eat is actually dead. Animal flesh will rot if we don't cook it and will decay even when cooked if we don't eat it. Similarly, fruit taken off of a tree will rot if we don't eat it. Thus, we are eating non-living, dead things. How, then, do we get life from eating these dead things? The answer is that we don't get life simply from food; we get life from God the Holy Spirit *mediated* through food.

The same thing is true of the new Kingdom/Melchizedekal life that is mediated to us through the sacramental food of the Lord's Supper. Just as life is not contained in dead fruits, so the body and blood of Jesus are not contained in bread and wine. Just as the Spirit imparts life to us through food, so the Spirit imparts the sacrifice and resurrection of Jesus to us in the eating of the sacrament. Giving thanks for ordinary food does not somehow bring it to life, so that then when we eat it we are getting life. Neither does giving thanks for the bread and wine have the effect of putting Jesus inside of them. Rather, in both cases the Spirit works through the action of eating.

With this in mind, we can see that every tree in the Garden was a tree of life. What, then, was the specific purpose of the Tree of Life? That tree was a sign of the true nature of all the other trees in the Garden. By going to the Tree of Life, Adam would be confessing that he did not have life in himself and that he needed to get it from God's provision. There was nothing inherently special about this tree, though it had a special function. It was like all other trees, except that it had been marked off as the place of a test. Similarly, there was nothing special about the Land of Eden or the sabbath day, but they were marked off arbitrarily by God to serve special purposes.

When Adam chose to bypass the Tree of Life and go to the Tree of Knowledge, he was saying that he did not need to go to God for life. He was presuming on God's gift of life. He was asserting that he had life in himself. He was asserting that he was independent of God, autonomous. He was asserting that he was the source of his own life, that he was a God in the same sense as his Creator is.

Once Adam sinned, however, God blocked his way to the Tree of Life. This indicates to us that the Tree of Life carried a special, focused measure of the life God imparts to us. Adam might still get life from the other trees, but the special energy of the Tree of Life would have the effect of strengthening him in a fuller way. If he were righteous, it would strengthen him in righteousness, but as it was it would strengthen him in his sin. It would have the effect of sealing him more and more in his sin. Thus, for Adam's own good God cut him off from the Tree of Life. By holding back the Tree of Life, God gave Adam and humanity time to repent. God made room in history for a plan of redemption. Eventually, however, all men will eat of the Tree of Life, and some will be sealed into damnation while others will be sealed into eternal life.[31]

THE TREE OF THE KNOWLEDGE OF GOOD AND EVIL

What was the Tree of the Knowledge of Good and Evil? It was a real tree with real fruit, and somehow man's interaction with that tree and fruit would produce in him knowledge of good and evil. There are three aspects of this situation we need to understand.

First, Adam and Eve already knew the difference between good and evil, right and wrong, in a moral and spiritual sense. They were made in God's image and had His moral character imprinted on their persons. They were not somehow ethically neutral. Genesis 1:28 says that God blessed Adam and Eve, and verse 31 says that they were very good. The fact that they were blessed and pronounced good certainly eliminates the possibility that they were somehow in a state of ethical neutrality. The Tree of the Knowledge of Good and Evil was *not* designed to teach Adam and Eve right from wrong.

Second, some have suggested that man would mature in his understanding of good and evil, of right and wrong, by refraining from eating of the tree. The discipline of agreeing with God and saying "no" to something that is in itself

---

31. Compare the quickening power of water in Leviticus 11:32–38: water cleanses, but it also quickens and spreads impurity. Compare also 1 Corinthians 11:28–31, which identifies the ultimate Tree of Life.

"a delight to the eyes and good for food" would have the effect of gradually bringing man into an ever more self-conscious understanding of what good and evil, in the sense of right and wrong, are. God's initial programming of goodness into man would be reinforced by man's conscious decision to pursue the good, which would deepen his moral consciousness and bring him into a greater state of maturity. I agree that this is part of the meaning of the Tree of Knowledge, but there are two errors sometimes connected with this interpretation.

The first error is the idea that the fruit of the tree had nothing to do with good and evil; rather, it was simply the avoidance of the fruit that would bring about an increased understanding of good and evil, of right and wrong. As we shall see, however, "knowledge of good and evil" has a particular meaning that must be associated with actually eating the fruit. The prohibition was temporary. Holding off from the Tree of Knowledge was a form of fasting. When God was ready, man would be allowed to eat and acquire "knowledge of good and evil" in a special sense. This will be developed as we go along.

The second error, found in Geerhardus Vos's *Biblical Theology* (and thus widely influential), is that man somehow knew that he was not to eat of the Tree of Life until God was ready to let him do so.[32] For Vos, passing the test of the Tree of Knowledge would lead to the reward of the Tree of Life. This is based on sheer supposition. Other Reformed expositors, most notably G. Ch. Aalders, have pointed out that Adam had a choice of trees, and was clearly to choose the Tree of Life and forbear the Tree of Knowledge.[33] Vos fails to see that the fruit of the Tree of Knowledge is the reward.

The third thing to understand concerning the Tree of Knowledge is that eating the fruit of this tree was designed to effect a change in man's position. The phrase "knowledge of good and evil" has to do with rule and authority, the right to pass judgments, to the right to act as a god under the authority of God. Evidence for this interpretation comes right from the context itself, for in Genesis 1 and 2 it is God who repeatedly passes judgments: "God saw that it was good," "God saw that it was very good," "It is not good for the man

---

32. Geerhardus Vos, *Biblical Theology: Old and New Testaments* (1948; reprint, Eugene, OR: Wipf and Stock, 2003), 28.

33. G. Ch. Aalders, *Genesis*, trans. W. Heynen, Bible Student's Commentary, 2 vols. (Grand Rapids: Zondervan, 1981), 1:113.

to be alone." Thus, for man to acquire knowledge of good and evil means, in context, that man has the privilege of making judicial pronouncements.

Indeed, the rest of Scripture confirms this. Solomon, the first fulfillment of the Davidic Son-covenant and a most splendid type of Christ, prays to be given "an understanding heart to judge Your people, to discern between good and evil. For who is able to judge this Your weighty people?" (1 Kgs. 3:9). God grants this kingly request—we notice that Solomon does not assume that he already possesses this discernment—and immediately we see Solomon exercise just judgment (1 Kgs. 3:28).

Similarly, the wise woman of Tekoa said to David, "For as the angel of God, so is my lord the king to discern good and evil" (2 Sam. 14:17, NASB). In other words, man's judicial authority is a copy of God's. The angel of God has wisdom to "know all that is in the earth" (2 Sam. 14:20, NASB), and such knowing entails seeing: "My lord the king is like the angel of God, therefore do what is good in your sight" (2 Sam. 19:27, NASB). When Laban pursued Jacob, God appeared to him and told him not to pass judgment on Jacob: "Take heed to yourself that you do not speak to Jacob either good or evil" (Gen. 31:24).

Infants, such as Adam and Eve were, do not have the wisdom to know good and evil in this judicial sense (Deut. 1:39), and sometimes the aged lose this capacity due to senility (2 Sam. 19:35).[34]

Thus, the Tree of the Knowledge of Good and Evil does not have primarily to do with moral knowledge but with judicial knowledge. According to Genesis 1:29, the fruit of every tree was made for man to eat of. Hence, the prohibition on the Tree of Knowledge was temporary. Refraining from it involved fasting from something for which they were not ready, and this term of fasting was designed to work into their hearts the dispositions needed for proper exercise of judicial authority.

The author of Hebrews puts it this way: "For everyone who partakes of milk is not accustomed to the word of righteousness, for he is a babe; but solid food is for the mature, who because of practice have their senses trained to discern good and evil" (Heb. 5:14, NASB).[35]

---

34. Additional passages that support this interpretation are found in Cornelis van der Waal, *The Covenantal Gospel*, trans. Dr. & Mrs. G. L. Bertram (Neerlandia, AB: Inheritance, 1990), 49–51.

35. See also James B. Jordan, "The Glory of the Man: Women, Psalms, and Worship," in P.

TREES OF LIFE

As Adam and Eve passed by the Tree of Knowledge day after day (or sabbath after sabbath) and refused the lure of the serpent, they would acquire a deepening sense of good and evil. What Hebrews says is applicable to Adam and Eve. Being newly created, as babies, they were naked. They had not yet had any experiences at all. But "through experience" in the garden they would gradually "have their senses trained to know good and evil" (Heb. 5:14). They would not be learning right from wrong, but how to make good judgments.

At the same time, sabbath after sabbath they would eat of the Tree of Life, the virtue of which would be to seal them more and more into the life of God. At some point, when they were ready, God would announce that the fast was over and the feast had come. They would be invited to eat of the Tree of Knowledge and become enthroned as co-regents with God, junior partners in the divine community of rule.

As it happened, however, they chose to eat of the Tree of Knowledge without permission. They seized the mantle of rulership, of godhood, in a perverse manner.[36] Instead of letting God elevate them to the status of junior godhood, they tried to make themselves "Gods" on the same level as God. If God had permitted them to eat of the Tree of Life, they would have been sealed into this evil estate.

We have seen that the trees of the Garden, growing out of the soil, represent human beings gathered in God's presence, for man also is made of soil. Indeed, the parallels between the third day and the sixth day in Genesis 1 establish the same point:

Third Day: first paragraph: dry land appears.

    second paragraph: grain and wine plants appear on land.

Andrew Sandlin and John Barach, eds., *Obedient Faith: A Festschrift for Norman Shepherd* (Mount Hermon, CA: Kerygma, 2012), 171: "Knowledge of good and evil, then, is godlike authority. It is what the early church called deification. We can also call it glorification. It is maturity in the likeness of God. A vast amount of what is in the Bible is there to help us to grow up in maturity and godlikeness, but not much attention is paid to it these days."

36. On seizing the mantle of rulership, see James B. Jordan, "Rebellion, Tyranny, and Dominion in the Book of Genesis," in Gary North, ed., *Tactics of Christian Resistance*, Christianity and Civilization 3 (Tyler, TX: Geneva Divinity School Press, 1983), 38–80.

Sixth Day: first paragraph: animals (*behemah*) as throne (*bamah*) for man's kingship.

　　　　second paragraph: man made of land, enthroned on animals.[37]

How are men and women to be trees of life to one another? Proverbs 3:18 says of Lady Wisdom that "she is a tree of life to those who take hold of her, and blessed are all who hold her fast." Recall the trinitarian man—plant—water subtext of Genesis 2 that we studied earlier. Plants focus on the Second Person of God, the Word of God. Here it is Wisdom who is called a tree of life. The Word of God is a tree of life to us, and as we speak it to one another, we are trees of life to each other.

Proverbs 11:30 seems to speak of both trees: "The fruit of the righteous is a tree of life, and he who is wise captures souls." Insofar as we are trees of life to one another, we bear fruit that sustains others. As we mature into age and wisdom, we become trees of knowledge, able to exercise God-like dominion and capture persons, ruling them so to speak, and leading them to God.

Proverbs 13:12 speaks more abstractly: "Hope deferred sickens the heart, but the arrival of a desired thing is a tree of life." When God, in whom we hope, withdraws from us, leaving us "deserted" in a "dark night of the soul," we become sick of heart; but when He whom we desire returns to us, He is a tree of life to us. Since we are the images of God, the same is true in interpersonal relationships. We need the fellowship of one another lest we become sick of heart.

Proverbs 15:4 says, "a healing tongue is a tree of life, but perversion in it is the crushing of the spirit." Here again notice the association of words, and the Word of God, with the tree of life. A sharp or contemptuous or mocking tongue crushes the spirit of other people, while an aptly spoken word of encouragement is a fruit of the tree of life for them.

Revelation 22:2 pictures the glorified city-garden of New Jerusalem, and in it the Tree of Life, bearing fruit for the healing of the nations. This is a picture, of course, of Jesus.

This healing is not something that is promised primarily for the end of history, but rather is something that is given to the saints at the beginning of their walk. The Tree of Life is the Alpha Tree. We are invited to it as soon as we come into the Garden. Thus, Revelation 22:14 says, "Blessed are those who

---

37. Compare God enthroned on cherubim.

wash their robes, that they may have the right to the Tree of Life, and may enter by the gates into the city." Baptism puts us back into the Garden, for we are re-created by water even as the world was created by water. As soon as we are back in the Garden, or have arrived at the city-garden of the Church, we are invited to eat of the Tree of Life. Access to the Tree of Life is by faith, not by works. It is not a gift given to those who have matured, as is the Tree of Knowledge.

Thus, Revelation 2:7 says, "To him who overcomes, I will grant to eat of the Tree of Life, which is in the paradise of God." Overcoming is not some great work that we must do year after year until we are ready for the Tree of Life. Rather, we overcome when we resist the words of the beast that crouches at the door to the Garden (Gen. 4:7) and in union with Christ enter the Garden through faith (Rev. 5:5; 21:7). This is something that happens every day. The Tree of Life is not a symbol of maturity and rule but is a blessing given to those who have the kind of childlike faith that Adam and Eve were called to have.

TREES OF KNOWLEDGE

While the Bible uses the phrase "tree of life" several times, pointing to its meaning as the blessings that Christ gives us and we give each other, the phrase "tree of knowledge" or "tree of the knowledge of good and evil" is not encountered directly elsewhere in the Bible. Still, based on what we have seen so far, we can suggest what it means for us to be trees of knowledge to each other.

The tree of knowledge is the man who has matured to the point of being granted the robe of authority and rule. He has matured in the likeness of God to the point where he can be called a god himself. The word for "god," *'elohim,* is used for judges and rulers several times in the Bible (Exod. 21:6; 22:8–9, 28; Pss. 58:1; 82:1–8; John 10:34). Thus, rulers are trees of knowledge.

I have discussed tree imagery in the Bible in general elsewhere.[38] Here our interest is in seeing trees associated with rule and rulers. The staff used by Moses to bring the plagues would be a form of the Tree of Knowledge, insofar as it portrays the rule of God Himself (Exod. 4:2–5; 7:15, 17). Aaron's

---

38. Jordan, *Through New Eyes,* ch. 7.

staff that blossoms is a picture of his own rule over the house of God (Num. 17).

David's line of rulers is spoken of as a tree, the root and shoot of Jesse, in several places, pointing to the Messiah (e.g., Isa. 4:2; 6:13; 11:10,12; Jer. 23:5; 33:15; Zech. 4:3).

The rule of Nebuchadnezzar is displayed as a great tree, "beautiful of appearance and good for food" in Daniel 4:11–12. This false tree of knowledge (rule) was cut down and replaced by a true one.

Trees are associated with thrones. Deborah set up her chair of judgment at the Palm Tree of Deborah (Judg. 4:4–5). Joash the Abiezrite held court and conducted false worship at an oak (Judg. 6:11–32). Saul held court at a pomegranate tree (1 Sam. 14:2) and at a tamarisk tree (1 Sam. 22:6).

Once we see that association of some trees with rulers, we can see that the grove of trees that constitutes the Church consists of trees of life and knowledge. All of us are, in union with the Tree of Life (Jesus), trees of life to one another. Similarly, those who exercise rule and oversight in the Church (elders), in union with the true Tree of Knowledge (Jesus), are trees of knowledge to those under their authority. Just as Adam was not to seize the fruit of the Tree of Knowledge until he was mature and seasoned, so we are not seize the eldership in the Church until we are old enough and have been recognized by God and the congregation as ready for this heavy responsibility.

After His baptism, Jesus partook regularly of the Tree of Life from God, but never took of the Tree of Knowledge. He told His disciples that He was eating food that they did not know about (John 4:32), but when asked to pass judgment, He refused to do so, and He rejected Satan's attempts to get Him to seize the throne. At His ascension, Jesus was enthroned and partook of the Tree of Knowledge. Now for the first time there was a man who had achieved true Spiritual maturity and become enabled to rule God's Kingdom.

During the Old Covenant, God gave people to eat of the Tree of Life whenever they came into His Kingdom. That is what the many meals of the Old Testament were all about. In the house of God, however, the priests were never permitted to drink wine; the wine was poured out. The wine represented the Omega Food of the Tree of Knowledge and is associated with rule. We can see this displayed in the book of Esther, where the righteous king Ahasuerus always pronounces his just decrees at a "feast of wine."[39] When we get to the

---

39. See my lectures on Esther entitled "Witness or Perish" (available at http://www.

New Covenant, however, Jesus passes from the bread to the wine, from the Tree of Life to the Tree of Knowledge. Now for the first time, His people are allowed to consume not just bread but also wine in His direct presence (in the Lord's Supper).[40]

The fact that we are given both bread and wine in the Lord's Supper teaches us that we have been given to eat of both trees, for both are in Christ. At the experiential level, however, each of us still has to grow to maturity. We start out feeding on Christ the Tree of Life until we "have our senses exercised to discern good and evil," and we become more mature. Then we are ready to engage in some aspects of ruling—over small things at first—having "become teachers" and leaders, able to help others move through the pilgrimage of this life (Heb. 5:11–14, in the context of the pilgrimage theme of Hebrews 4).

Sadly, all too often young men are made "elders" long before they are mature. They are given access to the Tree of Knowledge prematurely, and this can be as destructive to them as it was to Adam. They become unstable men, create chaos in the Church, and eventually lead many to destruction, as Adam did. Let us pursue the Tree of Life, and when God is ready, He will give us the Tree of Knowledge. Rule is a heavy responsibility, and only a fool tries to seize it.

TREES FOR FOOD

One of the must fundamental teachings of the Bible and of the Christian religion is that man does not have life in himself. Man must get life from outside of himself in order to maintain his life. The way this is done is through eating and drinking. Apart from life, communicated through food and drink, men die. Hunger communicates to man his lack of independence, his total dependence on something outside himself for life.

Accordingly, the question is: Who or what is man dependent on for life? As we have noted, men need food for life, but where does food come from? An evolutionary, this-worldly perspective says that the human person is like a machine that runs on fuel provided by food. Implicit in this perspective is a denial of life, an assertion that there is finally and ultimately no qualitative

---

wordmp3.com/product-group.aspx?id=21).

40. See Jordan, *From Bread to Wine.*

difference between a man and a rock. Men are no more alive than a robot made of steel. The robot runs on electrical energy, and man runs on food.

Even where the older mechanistic worldview breaks down and some kind of vitalism takes its place, the notion of being "alive" is still fundamentally pantheistic: Man is a "living" animal that stays "alive" by eating food. From a Christian standpoint, there is not much difference between the mechanistic and the vitalistic standpoints. Both deny that life is an injection of God's grace from outside the universe, and that food is merely a channel of that grace.

The biblical perspective is far different from either mechanism or vitalism. According to the Bible, man is given life by the Holy Spirit, the Lord and Giver of Life. The Spirit proceeds from the Father and also from the Son, out of eternity into time at every moment of time, to communicate this life. When the Spirit withdraws, men die.

Christian biochemist Rupert Sheldrake has suggested an analogy that is helpful. Asked about the possibility of creating life in the laboratory, Sheldrake said this:

Imagine that someone who didn't know anything about transistor radios was shown one and he was amazed at the music that came from it and tried to understand it.

He might think that the music originates entirely within the set as a result of complicated interactions among its parts. If somebody suggested [that the music was] coming from outside through a transmission ... into the set from somewhere else, he might deny it on the grounds that he could see nothing coming in. Nor could he measure anything because the set weighed the same switched on and switched off, and although he couldn't understand the set in terms of its parts and their interaction, he might think that as a result of further research, he would be able to do so. So, he might think he understood the set, or could understand the set in principle, even though, in fact, he knows nothing about radio waves, etc. He might even try to prove he understood it. He could take it to pieces. He could find out the things it was made of, silicon crystals, copper wires and so on. He might then think he could prove that he understood the set by making a replica. By getting copper, crystals and all that he could make a radio set which would work in the same way as the original. When switched on, music would come out of it. He could say, "Look, I've fully understood this thing. I've synthesized one of these things entirely from known materials."

But still, you see, he wouldn't really understand how it worked. He still wouldn't understand about radio waves in spite of the fact he'd been able to make a radio set. I think that's just the position we're in in relation to life. I think the mechanists are like people who try to understand radio sets ignoring radio waves and concentrating only on copper wires, components and the way they're wired together. Those are important of course, and they're really there and if you destroy a component or take one away the radio won't work properly. But it's only part of the picture. What's wrong with the mechanistic view is that it's a limited view; like most errors, it is based on a half-truth.[41]

What Sheldrake is setting forth by analogy is the Christian view. It is the vitalizing energy of the Holy Spirit that causes living things to be alive.

LIFE THROUGH FOOD

Does life come from food, then? No. How can it, since food is dead? The flesh we eat is that of dead animals; the vegetables are dead vegetables. There is no way that we can eat life directly from any other living thing. The belief that this is possible through wizardry underlies all vampire myths. The vampire supposedly steals life by drinking the living blood of a living animal or person. Practically speaking, such behavior would be fruitless. Symbolically speaking, however, vampirism is very important. The Bible tells us that the life of the flesh is the blood. Accordingly, it is the height of idolatrous presumption for man to attempt to circumvent God's Spirit and get life by drinking blood. God told Noah that man might eat meat only if he renounced the blood (Gen. 9:4). This stipulation was reiterated to Moses (Lev. 17) and again to the New Testament Church (Acts 15:28–29).

It is God's Spirit who makes these dead substances work with our bodies to renew our lives. The action of the Spirit in communicating general life through food is parallel in concept to His communicating the life of the New Creation through the dead bread and wine that form the Lord's Supper.

Reformed theology has wavered between the position of Calvin and that of Bullinger on this question. The position of John Calvin and Martin

---

41. Rupert Sheldrake, "Modern Bio-chemistry and the Collapse of Mechanism," in Roy Abraham Varghese, ed., *The Intellectuals Speak Out About God* (Chicago: Regnery, 1984), 56–57.

Bucer has been termed "symbolic instrumentalism," the idea that Christ (and kingdom life) is communicated to the faithful recipient of the Supper *by means of* his eating the bread and drinking the wine. The position of Heinrich Bullinger and John Knox has been called "symbolic parallelism," the idea that Christ (and kingdom life) is received by faith *while* the faithful partakes of bread and wine.[42]

Calvin's position is obviously closer to what we think of concerning an ordinary meal. We don't mentally divorce the act of eating from the expectation of renewed life; rather we expect the Holy Spirit to work *through* the food, and so we ask God to "bless this food to the nourishment of our bodies, through Christ our Lord." Such traditional prayers express the Christian belief that dead animal and vegetable matter by themselves cannot give life. They are rather the instruments by which the Spirit gives life.

At creation, God set two trees in the center of the Garden-sanctuary, the Tree of Life and the Tree of the Knowledge of Good and Evil. He told Adam that he might eat freely of every tree except the latter. Clearly this was an encouragement to Adam to eat of the Tree of Life. Adam decided that he had life in himself, however, and that he did not need to seek life from God. He seized the forbidden fruit and lost Eden.

To teach Adam and his heirs that they do not have life in themselves, God caused men to hunger. Adam would have to labor hard to eat, by the sweat of his brow. Repeatedly throughout the Bible, especially in the wilderness wanderings, God made His people hungry so that they would cry to Him as the only source of life. Similarly, Jesus let the crowds that followed Him become hungry, and then He fed them.

Men do not have life in themselves, then, and the only place they can get it is from God. God has appointed food as the means by which He communicates life to man.

---

42. Cf. B. A. Gerrish, "The Lord's Supper in the Reformed Confessions," *The Old Protestantism and the New: Essays on the Reformation Heritage* (Edinburgh: T. & T. Clark, 1982), 118–130.

Food and History

A second aspect of eating is that food is both fuel and reward. We need food to get going, but good food is also our blessing for a job well done. Food is, thus, both alpha and omega, and our lives are encircled by food.

Adam's first full day was God's seventh. Adam began in rest. He began with a day of worship. He began, or was supposed to begin, at the Tree of Life. This would be his week's "breakfast," his first meal, his alpha fuel.

Adam's labors would make him hungry, however. He would look forward to coming home for dinner. Thus, his dinner would be a reward for his labors, his omega food. And, in terms of the weekly sabbatical cycle, Adam would look forward to eating of the Tree of Life once again with God.

Alpha food—do you start off the day with a glass of wine? I hope not. Alpha food is bread, not wine. But how about omega food? Is mere bread a wonderful reward? For a starving man, yes, but not for the royal family of the King of kings. No, our reward is such wine as makes men marvel. As at the wedding feast at Cana, it was the best wine that was saved for the *last*. Christ, our Bread and Wine, is both our alpha fuel and our omega reward.

It is possible to carry this reflection back into the original Garden-sanctuary. The Tree of Life was alpha fuel, and the Tree of the Knowledge of Good and Evil—which had to do with enthronement and investiture—was the omega reward. The first was like bread, and the second like wine. By seizing the reward, Adam demonstrated impatience. After all, God had promised that eventually he would be given it (Gen. 1:29).

I am not identifying the Tree of Knowledge with the grape, except in a sense of symbolic correspondence. Note however, that man's first food was grain and fruit (Gen. 1:29), and this carries over to the bread and wine offered Abram by Melchizedek, the baker and cupbearer in prison with Joseph (both of whom he replaced), the bread and wine on the table of showbread, and the bread and wine of the Lord's Supper. Thus, it is not too far-fetched to suggest that the Tree of Life is functionally equivalent to bread and the Tree of Knowledge to wine.

Both bread and wine take time to produce, and both involve leaving the original substance alone to mature for a while. Bread, however, rises from leaven in only a matter of an hour so, while wine takes much longer to ferment and is more difficult to produce. Thus, bread always comes first.

For instance, we read in Exodus of the Table of Presence-Bread and in Leviticus 24 of the bread put upon that Table. We read in Leviticus 2 about the various kinds of grain and bread used in the Tribute Offering. Not until Numbers 15 do we read that a libation of wine is to accompany these once they enter the land. This command, coming after Numbers 13–14, implicitly promises that eventually the wayward Israelites will indeed enter the land.

The book of Hebrews associates entering the land with entering sabbath rest, and we can see that this would be the appropriate time for drinking wine. Recall that Noah, the Bringer of Rest, drank wine after finishing his work (Gen. 5:29; 9:21). Entering sabbath is equivalent to enthronement; thus the wine of sabbath is associated with the enthronement-rule of the "knowledge of good and evil."[43]

In the Sinaitic Calendar, the feasts of the first part of the year focus on bread: the Feast of Unleavened Bread and the Feast of Harvest, at which two leavened loaves were offered. The Feast of the Ingathering (of grapes[44]) was in the seventh month. At this feast, all Israel tabernacled with God in rest and festivity.

The association of wine and proper sabbath rule is nowhere better seen than in the book of Esther. There are seven feasts of wine in this book, at each of which righteous king Ahasuerus decrees a just judgment. Ahasuerus has "knowledge of good and evil," and this seems to be signified by his partaking responsibly of wine.

A final thought: The year begins with unleavened bread, bread eaten before it matures at all. There are two eschatologies that grow from this one beginning. The first, calculated from the sabbath after Passover, is Pentecost, the Feast of Harvest, when two leavened loaves are offered. The second, calculated as the seventh month from the first (Passover) month, is the Feast of Ingathering, which involves wine and strong drink (Lev. 23; Deut. 14:26). Thus from one beginning are two eschatologies, one near and one far. In the New Testament we see this also. The Pentecostal period begins at Pentecost and ends at the destruction of Jerusalem, when the leavened loaf of

---

43. On the connection between sabbath and enthronement, see James B. Jordan, *Sabbath Breaking and the Death Penalty: A Theological Investigation*, Geneva Papers 2.3–6 (June 1986), ch. 3.

44. Cf. Deuteronomy 16:13: "when you have gathered from your threshing floor *and from your winepress.*"

the Firstfruits Church is offered to God in the massacre of the 144,000. The Tabernacles period begins then, for that massacre is also a harvest of grapes, and makes possible the dominion that the Church has exercised ever since (see Rev. 7:4–8; 14:13–20; 15:2; 16:3–4; 17:6; 19:14–15; 20:4).

7

WATER FROM EDEN

GENESIS 2:10–14

Now a river was going out of Eden to water the garden; and from there it divided and became four heads (Gen. 2:10).

THE notion that the Land of Eden was Mesopotamia, located near the mouths of the Tigris and Euphrates rivers, is widespread but has no biblical foundation. We are supposed to believe that Genesis 2:10 is pointing backwards. Eden, we are told, was the delta of the Tigris and Euphrates, and looking back upstream we will come to four headwaters that have flowed together first into these two rivers and then into the Edenic delta.

This is impossible for several reasons. First of all, the sanctuaries of God are always on high ground in the Bible. The notion that Eden was a lowland delta is out of accord with every other picture of a sanctuary in Scripture.

Second, the four rivers that supposedly flowed together to form the Edenic delta include the Pishon, which flowed around Havilah (the peninsula between the Gulf of Aqaba and the Red Sea, between Egypt and Israel; cf. Gen.

73

25:18; 1 Sam. 15:7) and the Gihon, which flowed around Ethiopia (Cush). No such rivers flow into the Mesopotamian delta.

Third, the text clearly implies that the river arose in the Edenic *plateau*, flowed down into the Garden, and from there broke up into the headwaters of four rivers.

Finally, the Ark of Noah rested on Ararat in Armenia, a good location also for Eden.[45]

What the text is saying is that in the antediluvian world there were four rivers that flowed from the center of the world out to other lands, symbolically to the four corners of the earth. If we draw a line back from the present-day Tigris and Euphrates, we come to the mountains of Armenia.[46]

Verse 14 says that the Hiddeqel River flows east of Assyria, by which we know that the Tigris is meant (cf. Dan. 10:4). The fourth river, Perath, is the Euphrates, as is clear from many biblical passages. Moses did not need to add any further information about these two, for they were clearly known.

The Pishon and Gihon, however, are unknown. Thus, we are given more information so that we know where they were and what their post-diluvial equivalents are. Since the Pishon flows south from Armenia to Havilah, it must be the same as the Jordan River, which in the world after the Flood starts in northern Palestine and, after the destruction of Sodom, stops at the Dead Sea. Originally it flowed into the wilderness area where Israel wandered for forty years.

Similarly, since the Gihon flows around Ethiopia, it is the same as the post-diluvial Nile. Of course, after the Flood the Nile flows in the opposite direction, arising in central Africa and flowing north, but apparently in the same basic bed as the pre-Flood Gihon.

Four rivers and three lands: Ethiopia, Havilah, and Assyria. The central land is Havilah, directly south, it seems, of Eden. The river between Eden and Havilah is the central river: the Jordan. Biblical history takes place in this geographical setting. Abram came from Mesopotamia to Palestine,

---

45. See the map in *Through New Eyes*, 151. (This map mis-identifies Havilah as the Arabian Peninsula.)

46. John Sailhamer (*Genesis Unbound: A Provocative New Look at the Creation Account* [Portland, OR: Multnomah, 1996], ch. 6) sees these four rivers as the borders of the Land of Eden, which he takes to be the Promised Land. For a response, see Jordan, *Creation in Six Days*, 143–145.

and then to Egypt, and then back to Palestine. The Hebrews went to Egypt and the Israelites came back to Palestine. The Israelites went into captivity in Mesopotamia and the Jews came back to Palestine. The Pishon/Jordan, mentioned first in Genesis 2, is central.

Ethiopia is south of Egypt, and Havilah south of Palestine and Eden. Thus, this passage sets up a north-south dynamic and also an east-west dynamic. Moving to the east, away from the Pishon/Jordan in the direction of Mesopotamia, is a movement away from God in the book of Genesis (Gen. 4:16, 10:30 + 11:2, 13:11). Similarly, moving south toward Ethiopia through Egypt is also a movement away from blessing. Coming up from Egypt, the Israelites stayed in Havilah for a time, building the Tabernacle, and then moved north into Palestine where the Pishon/Jordan was by then located.[47]

Four rivers: streams to the four ends of the earth.

Four lands: the central one Havilah, immediately south of Eden and connected by the central river.

The Pishon (Jordan) and Gihon rivers are said to wind through their lands, while the Tigris is said to flow (go, walk, move) east of Assyria. Hamilton writes, "I am not able to discern the reason for the change in verb."[48] Allow me to suggest a possible reason. Later on, in Genesis 13:10, the lands of Canaan and Egypt are said to be "well watered throughout" like the Garden of Eden, which was watered by the original stream from the Land of Eden. The implication is that the waters coiled around in the Garden of Eden to water it, and that there was something similar in Canaan and Egypt in Abram's day. The waters of the Nile "well watered" Egypt by becoming a delta, and presumably so did the waters of the Jordan before they were dammed up to form the Dead Sea at the time Sodom was destroyed. The Pishon is the pre-Flood Jordan, and the Gihon flowed down to the area of Egypt and Ethiopia, thus symbolically (though not literally) corresponding to the Nile.

---

47. I discussed these geographical dynamics somewhat in *Through New Eyes*, 148ff., 183, 228, 246. I erred on p. 183 (bottom) by writing that exoduses come from the south and the north. I should have written that they come from the south and east. The movement toward God is westward and northward in the first covenant world.

Students with access to a theological library may wish to consult an interesting article related to this symbolical geography: D. F. Pocock, "North and South in the Book of Genesis," in I. H. M. Beattie and R. G. Lienhardt, *Studies in Social Anthropology: Essays in Memory of E. E. Evans-Pritchard by his former Oxford Colleagues* (Oxford: Clarendon, 1975), 273–284.

48. Hamilton, *Genesis 1–17*, 167n4.

While the Tigris and Euphrates also form a well watered land, it is not part of the theology of Genesis to call attention to that fact. In Genesis, the two other gardens are Canaan and Goshen, the "best part" of well watered Egypt (47:6). Thus, I suggest that here in Genesis 2 the rivers and Canaan and Egypt are said to coil around in order to anticipate that their lands will be somewhat like the Garden of Eden itself.

GOLD IN HAVILAH

The name of the first is Pishon; it surrounds the whole land of Havilah,
where there is gold. And the gold of that land is good; the bdellium and
the onyx stone are there (Gen. 2:11–12).

We are not told much about the Land of Eden in Genesis 2, but the fact that there was a garden of trees there associates Eden with food. The later Eden is Palestine, the land of Canaan, the Land of Promise. It is definitely Foodland: a land that flows with milk and honey, where there are grapes and pomegranates. Every Israelite had a vine and a fig tree. He had a field for bread and a vineyard for wine, which were not to be mixed, and also an olive tree for oil. When Hiram supplied Solomon with cedar for the Temple, Solomon provided Hiram with food (1 Kgs. 5).

Before entering New Eden, the Israelites sojourned in Havilah for (originally) one year (later extended to forty years). During this time they built the Tabernacle and made the garments of the High Priest. Here they encountered gold, bdellium, and onyx.

In Genesis 2:11–12, gold is most important, for more attention is paid to it. After the gold are the onyx and the bdellium. We know that onyx is black. Bdellium is white (though we have no idea what actual stone is referred to by the term "bdellium"). Numbers 11:7 tells us that the manna that fed Israel in Havilah was like coriander seed and the color of bdellium, which Exodus 16:31 says is white. Coriander seeds are white. The white, manna-esque stone of Revelation 2:17 is bdellium.

Between white and black are all other colors; between white and black stones are all other jewels. In a more potent sense, white includes all other colors. Aaron's garments, made in Havilah, were decorated with these three basic stones.

Aaron's garb identified him as a son of man, a son of Adam, a second Adam, the representative of Israel. His glory was the first glory of an Adamic priest, not the last glory of a Melchizedekal one. Adam was made of earth. Stones are hard earth. Gems and gold are glorious hard earth. Such stones represent humanity in an initial stage of glorification. The glorified body of the Melchizedekal priest needs no such garb because his transfigured flesh shines with its own light. The last Adam is of the Spirit, and the Spirit provides a direct glory (see 1 Cor. 15:40–49).

In Aaron's garb, the outermost and thus the most glorious aspect of his clothing consisted of three stones: the golden plate, inscribed "Holy to Yahweh"; the onyx stones, inscribed with the names of the sons of Jacob in birth order; and the twelve gemstones (amplifications of the white bdellium) of the breastpiece, inscribed with the names of the tribes of Israel. Thus, these beautiful stones have to do with glorification, and with representation, for by means of the engravings on these stones Aaron represented Israel.[49]

Now consider Adam. He was created naked, without any glory or maturity. In time, he would create garments for himself and Eve, to beautify her and him. In time he would follow the central river out to Havilah and find the gold, black, and white (and all other color) stones that would be the final touches of his priestly glorious garments as God's son. This glorification would be prophetic of his eventual transfiguration by the Spirit into a greater kind of glory.

The onyx stones had the twelve sons of Jacob on them in birth order. These stones represent our beginning as children of God: all the same, all equal. The "bdellium" breastpiece consisted of twelve gemstones with the twelve tribes on them (which are not exactly the same as the twelve sons). Thus, the breastpiece represents us as mature, glorified persons, each different, each of a different quality of glory, each with a different position and calling.

What this indicates to me is that the black stone is primordial, while the white stone, with its rainbow efflorescence, is eschatological. In the clothing of the Adamic priest there is black, white (color), and gold. When we see the glorified Melchizedekal priest in Revelation 1, there is no black: only white and gold (and later rainbow colors, Rev. 10:1). We grow from darkness to light (Gen. 1:2–3), from evening to morning. This is not first and foremost a

---

49. Note that in Exodus 28 the stones are discussed in reverse order: first onyx, then the gemstones (amplifications of bdellium), and finally gold.

moral analogy, but an analogy of glory: We grow from having no glory and light to being light and glorious. Only after the fall do white and light take on connotations of righteousness as well as glory.

Finally, we see that Adam could be a baby priest in the Garden without visiting Havilah, but to mature into a full Adamic priest he would have to go downstream. He would have to exercise dominion and bring the fruits of that dominion back to the sanctuary to adorn it. The church is not to be a plain, bare-bones place in all ages but is to mature in glory in terms of the glories of this world, anticipating the glories of the next. Beautifying ourselves, our clergymen, and our churches with the stones of Havilah and with other arts is a sign of maturation and glory.

THE GENTILE SEA

At this point I want to review and supplement some material presented in the previous chapters. We discussed the parallels between Genesis 1 and Genesis 2. We can set these out in the following chart:

1. Garden formless, empty, given lightbearer (man) (2:4–7).

   "And YHWH God formed man"

   Spirit hovered, made light // breathing into dust, made man

2. Garden-sanctuary (2:8).

   "And YHWH God planted a garden"

   Parallel to firmament

3. Trees grow out of land (2:9); centrality of land (2:10–14).

   "And YHWH God caused to grow"

   Reverse parallel to land and trees of Day 3

4. Man established as ruler (2:15).

   "And YHWH God took the man and put him"

   Parallel to luminaries "put" and established as rulers on Day 4

5. Commands, regarding trees (2:16–17).

   "And YHWH God commanded the man"

   Parallel to command on Day 5

6. Community (2:18–24).

   "And YHWH God said"

   Parallel to community of man and animals, man and wife

7. Sabbath sin and judgment (2:25–3:23).

   Parallel to sabbath, Day 7

It is clear that the Garden parallels the firmament between heaven and earth. According to Genesis 1, God took some of the waters of the earth and put them into heaven, on the other side of the firmament. These are parallel to the river that arose in Eden, and so Eden is parallel to heaven. Accordingly, the four rivers that flow out of the Garden into all the world are parallel to the sea, for they are waters below the firmament.

These rivers "encompass" or surround the lands they flow through (Gen. 2:11,13). Perhaps the best way to understand this is that these rivers *define* these lands: the Pishon/Jordan defines the lands of Canaan and Havilah; the Gihon/Nile defines the lands of Egypt and Ethiopia; the Tigris and Euphrates define the land of Assyria or Mesopotamia. In each case, the rivers actually flow through the centers of these lands.

These are the outlying lands ruled by the priests of the firmament-sanctuary-garden. Man was originally put on high ground, ruling over the world. Later, God's priestly people are given the Tabernacle and Temple as symbols of their sanctuary role as rulers of the world. The Bible makes it abundantly clear that God's people always rule the world, and if the world is going to hell, it is because we are ruling badly through prayer and good works.[50] It is for this reason that the book of Revelation can speak of Jerusalem-Babylon as ruling over the kings of the earth and as directing the actions of the Beast.

As I pointed out in *Through New Eyes*, the Bible presents the gentiles as dwelling amidst many waters, and gentile nations as beasts of the sea.[51] This symbol for understanding the first creation world is set up here in Genesis 2.

One aspect of the overall discussion in *Through New Eyes* that needs refinement is my discussion of the three kinds of lands as three places where humanity lives. I pointed to the Garden as the place of worship, the homeland as the place of rest and relaxation, and the world as the place of work. I now see a fourth place: the place of rule and judgment. I think this is implied by the Land of Eden, which Adam and Eve never entered because they were driven

---

50. See James B. Jordan, "Who Rules the Land? The Meaning of the Noahic Covenant," *Biblical Horizons* 19–20 (November–December 1990). Online: http://www.biblicalhorizons.com/biblical-horizons/no-19-who-rules-the-land-the-meaning-of-the-noahic-covenant-part-1/ and http://www.biblicalhorizons.com/biblical-horizons/no-20-who-rules-the-land-the-meaning-of-the-noahic-covenant-part-2/.

51. *Through New Eyes*, ch. 12.

away from the doorway into Eden, the Garden. Yet, unlike Cain who found no place for a home, Adam and Eve found a home outside of Eden (Gen. 4:14). All of this implies to me that entry into the Throneland of Eden would have been given to Adam when he was mature enough to eat of the Tree of Knowledge of Good and Evil, which as we have seen has to do with elevation to a position of rule and judgment.

Abraham is concerned with the sanctuary, Jacob with the land, and Joseph with the world. The Mosaic period is concerned mainly with the sanctuary and worship; the Kingdom period is concerned mainly with the homeland; and the Restoration period is mainly concerned with witness in the gentile world. Only when we come to Jesus is a man found fit to eat of the Tree of Knowledge and enter into the Edenic Throneland of heaven itself.

In a more general way, then, human beings exist in four worlds:

Eden – the state, rule and authority

Garden – the church

Home – the household, community, and nation

World – the place of work and of other homes, communities, and nations; intercourse between all these

8

MAN IN EDEN

GENESIS 2:15–17

And Yahweh God took the man and put him into the Garden of Eden...
  (Gen. 2:15).

ADAM was put into the Garden, not into the Land of Eden. The Garden is the Firmament-chamber that leads to the Throneland, where Adam would sit enthroned in sabbath rest as a junior god under God Most High.[52]

The Bible tells us a lot more about the meaning of this event in Leviticus 8–10. To understand it, we have to understand the symbolic parallels between the Tabernacle and the Garden.

---

52. See James B. Jordan, "The First Word," *Rite Reasons* 31 (February 1994). Online: http://www.biblicalhorizons.com/rite-reasons/no-31-the-first-word/.

We have already seen the following parallels:

Land of Eden	Heaven
Garden of Eden	Firmament
Forecourt Area	Mountains
Forecourt Land[53]	Earth
Watered Lands	Sea

It is clear from Genesis 2 that Eden and its Garden were on very high ground; thus the immediate forecourt of the Garden would also be high ground: a mountain. Mountains, being the highest places on earth, would also be the immediate forecourts of the Firmament heavens. After Israel left Egypt, God set up a symbolic parallel to this arrangement, which also reflected the actual arrangement of Israel in the world; to wit:

Land of Eden	Heaven	Holy of Holies	Shadow Throneland(Canaan)
Garden of Eden	Firmament	Holy Place	Holy Place
Forecourt Area	Mountains	Tabernacle Court	High Places for Altars
Forecourt Land	Earth	Israelite Camp	Land of Promise (Canaan)
Watered Lands	Sea	Wilderness	Outside the Land

Consider first of all the third column. In the Holy of Holies God Himself was enthroned. Nobody was allowed to go in there and remain, because no man had yet passed the test of patience set before Adam and thus no man had the right to enter into enthroned sabbath rest next to God. The High Priest might go in once a year for a few seconds, and then he had to leave (Lev. 16). Into the Holy Place only the priests might go, for they were anointed and consecrated (made holy); thus, they also might eat holy food. This area is equivalent to the Firmament and to the Garden of Eden.

Continuing, we come to the Tabernacle Court, called the Forecourt of the Tabernacle. Only a clean person might enter the courtyard, in which were the Altar of Ascensions and the Laver of (Priestly) Cleansing. Thus, the boundary between the Tabernacle and the Court was holiness, and the boundary between the Court and the Camp or Land was cleanness. Uncleanness is

---

53. This is the land where Adam lived after expulsion, the land Cain was expelled from; it is the land of the river Pishon, the central river.

symbolic death, and a person under the judgment of symbolic death (Gen. 3; Lev. 11–15) was not permitted to draw near to the Tabernacle by entering its Courtyard. The area of the Israelite Camp, including the Surrounding Encampment of converted gentiles (the "mixed multitude"), was a place where the issue was clean versus unclean. The area outside the Camp as a whole was clean, for the principle of symbolic death (uncleanness) did not apply except within the boundaries of the total Camp.

All of this symbolized Israel's position in the world (column 4). The area outside the Camp represented the gentile world. The Camp represented the Land of Promise, as a Forecourt Land. The Tabernacle Courtyard, with its mountain-altar in the midst and its cloudy white curtains all around, represented the mountainous "high places" in the Land, where the Tabernacle and Temple would be placed and where Israel would worship through sacrifice at those times when Tabernacle and Temple were not in operation. The Holy Place, as before, represented the Firmament, the Garden of Eden.

And finally, the Holy of Holies represented the Land of Promise as a Shadow Throneland, a land of milk, honey, and wine (grapes), all forms of glorified water. We can see this clearly if we remember that Israel did not leave Egypt and go directly to the Land of Promise. They had to build the Tabernacle first. They had to have access to the Mountain Altar in the Tabernacle Courtyard, and their priests had to be given access to the Holy Place, the Garden of Eden. Only when they had "passed through" these two environments were they able to enter the Land, which means that the Land was a shadow of the Edenic Throneland. As Hebrews 3–4 points out, of course, entrance into that Shadow Eden did not give Israel the fullness of entering into enthroned rest; only when Jesus entered Heaven, and thus entered the Edenic Throneland, did we with Him enter the Throneland of Rest.[54]

All of this leads us to see that the ritual of the investiture and ordination of Aaron, which enabled him to enter and conduct labors in the Holy Place, is parallel to the placement of Adam in the Garden of Eden.

---

54. On the connection between sabbath and enthronement, see *Sabbath Breaking and the Death Penalty*, ch. 3.

AARON AND ADAM

We come now to the investiture and consecration of Aaron as a New Adam, a "son of Man." First of all, God rebuilds the Land and Garden of Eden by issuing His creative Word to Moses; in other words, *God* sets up the Holy of Holies and the Holy Place, as well as the Forecourt area of the mountaintop (the Altar of Ascensions; Exod. 25–40). When God enters the Tabernacle, no man may be with Him; even Moses has to leave (Exod. 40:35).

We are now ready to put a new man into the Garden (the Holy Place). Since access back to God must come through the sacrifice of a Son, we find first of all in Leviticus 1–7 the laws of sacrifice. The animal sacrifices substituted for the son, as we see in Genesis 22 when God provided a ram in the place of Isaac. We also see the animals as sons in Leviticus 1:5, where it is literally a "son of the herd" that is to be offered.[55]

In Leviticus 8, we find the beginning of Aaron's entrance into the Holy Place. First, Aaron, his sons, and the representatives of the congregation are brought into the forecourt of the Tabernacle, the area in the Courtyard around the Altar of Ascensions (mistranslated as Altar of Burnt Offerings in English versions). Then Aaron and his sons are brought near and washed with water (Lev. 8:6): The new birth is with water; in Genesis 2:7 God formed Adam and breathed into him the breath of life, for the first birth consists of air breathed into dust (not clay).

"And the man became a living being" (Gen. 2:7). Equivalent to this, and showing what it meant, Aaron is given his garments of glory and beauty (Lev. 8:7–9). A study of Aaron's garments is, thus, a study of Adam's position and privilege.

"And God planted a garden in Eden" (Gen. 2:8). Equivalent to this, Moses anointed the Tabernacle. Immediately after Moses anointed the Tabernacle with the liquid light of oil, symbolizing the presence of God through His Spirit, God's glory entered the Tabernacle and Moses had to leave (Exod. 40:9–12, 34–35).

"And there He placed the man whom He had formed" (Gen. 2:8). Now, however, there is a problem: Aaron is a sinner, and like Moses, he cannot enter the new Garden. Moses anoints Aaron (Lev. 8:12) and links him to the

---

55. See James B. Jordan, "Leviticus 1: Translation and Commentary," Biblical Horizons Occasional Paper 34 (June 2003).

Tabernacle, but Aaron cannot yet enter. Meanwhile, skipping to the parallel with the end of Genesis 2, Aaron's helpers are clothed so that they can be consecrated with him. Aaron's first helpers are his sons. As Eve with Adam, the sons will help Aaron "dress and guard" the new Garden, the Holy Place.

For Aaron to get into the Garden, the Holy Place, he must first ascend up the Holy Mountain, the Altar of Ascensions. Moses offers the sacrifices of access for Aaron. The Sin Offering opens a ladder to heaven, cleansing the way to the top of the Mountain (Lev. 8:14–17; especially verse 15: blood on the horns or top of the altar). Then the Ascension Offering (mistranslated Burnt Offering) creates an "elevator" to heaven from the top of the Altar-Mountain, carrying Christ (the clean and unwashed head and fat) first, and then His people (the baptized legs and guts) (Lev. 8:18–21). Finally, the Ordination Offering (a variety of Peace Offering) transports Aaron before God up the elevator provided by the Ascension Offering (by being placed on the Ascension Offering). Standing before God, symbolically, Aaron receives his commission: Blood is taken from the Altar and put on him, for it will be his job to offer the blood (Lev. 8:22–32). Before Aaron can enter the Garden, though, he must guard the Forecourt Area (the Altar-Mountain Top) for seven days (Lev. 8:33–36).

Now Aaron is ready for the next big step: into the Garden or Holy Place itself. But he cannot go alone. Adam was put into the Garden alone, but now there is a great nation of people who must also be brought in by being represented by Aaron. So, in Leviticus 9 we find Aaron offering sacrifices for himself for the first time. He opens the ladder to the top of the mountain by the Sin Offering and creates the elevator to heaven with the Ascension Offering (Lev. 9:8–14).

Then he brings his second group of helpers along with him, for Aaron's second group of helpers "meet for him" is the congregation itself. He opens the ladder to heaven for them with the Sin Offering. He then carries them up into heaven in the Ascension Offering, where they present their tribute in the Tribute Offering (mistranslated as Cereal or Grain Offering) (Lev. 9:15–17). Then Aaron offers a Peace Offering for the people that signifies that they have peace with God and also provides them with their official commissioning (Lev. 9:18–21). Aaron then blesses the people from the Altar, the Mountaintop (Lev. 9:22).

The column of smoke over the Altar is equivalent to the Holy Place, the Garden. The animals have entered the smoke, the Garden, representing

Aaron and Israel. Now Aaron can go into the Holy Place, itself made of smoky blue-gray curtains and dark goat's hair. He and Moses do so, and then come out to bless the people, who shout for joy (Lev. 9:23–24).

But as Adam sinned by presuming to eat of the Tree of Rule and thereby seize entrance into the Throneland of Eden, so Aaron's sons bring their own presumptuous fire to the Altar of Incense, the gateway into the Holy of Holies Throneroom. As Adam "died," so the sons of Aaron die (Lev. 10:1–2). The Holy Place Garden is defiled by the corpses of the sons. Aaron is forced to stay in the Forecourt and may not enter the Garden until sacrifice has been made once again (Lev. 4:16).

TASKS IN THE HOLY PLACE

And Yahweh God took the man and put him into the Garden of Eden, to serve it and to guard it (Gen. 2:15).

Adam was to "dress and keep" (KJV) or serve (cultivate) and guard the Garden. We shall look more at these two tasks later, but now let us consider what light Aaron's tasks in the Holy Place shed on Adam's original tasks.

In the Holy Place were three items: the Table of Presence Bread, the Golden Lampstand, and the Altar of Incense. Aaron was to maintain these. Since the Holy Place symbolizes the Garden of Eden (and the Firmament), Aaron's tasks show us something of Adam's.

On the Table of Showbread (literally Bread of the Face, Face-Bread, or Presence Bread) were twelve loaves of bread representing the twelve tribes of Israel. Aaron and the priests, the supervisors and semi-inhabitants of the Garden, were allowed to eat these when they were changed out once a week; nobody else was allowed to eat them except temporary Nazirite priests in a Holy War Camp situation (2 Sam. 21:1–6). Thus, this food shows us something of the holy food of the trees of the Garden of Eden.

In particular, this bread points to the Tree of Life. We see this from the fact that wine was also put on or at this table, but it might not be drunk by the priests (Lev. 10:9). Similarly, the Tree of Knowledge was in the Garden, but Adam was not to eat of it. This is because wine is associated with rule and sabbath enthronement. Noah drank wine after the Flood, for Noah had given rest. In Esther, the king drinks wine whenever he makes a pronouncement.[56] The Nazirite, a temporary warrior priest, does not drink wine (Num. 6:3). The fact that we now drink wine as well as eat bread with God shows that Jesus has completed the task of Adam and Aaron, entered the Throneland of Eden, and now shares wine with us. Notice that it is immediately after the sons of Aaron commit the sin of presumption, equivalent to Adam's seizing the forbidden "wine," that Aaron is told never to drink the wine and beer that he brings into the Holy Place (Lev. 10:9).

As regards the wine on or at the Table of Presence Bread, the comments of Kurtz are instructive:

> A libation of wine in connection with them [the loaves] is not mentioned in any of the passages which treat professedly of the arrangement of the shew-bread...; but it must certainly be taken for granted, on account of the frequent allusion to the bowls and cans belonging to the table of shew-bread (cf. Exod. 25:29; 37:16; Num. 4:7).[57]

The Golden Lampstand was itself made as a symbolic almond tree. The word "almond" in Hebrew is the same as "watching," as in Jeremiah 1:11–12. The lamps on the Lampstand were set to face the Table of Presence Bread, watching over it (Exod. 25:37). This symbolized the priests' duty to watch over and guard Israel. This is, of course, parallel to Adam's task to guard the Garden, and especially to guard Eve (which he did not do). The lamps were to burn continually (Lev. 24:2–3), for the Greater Aaron who watches over Israel neither slumbers nor sleeps.

The fruit of the Lampstand consisted of seven lamps set on bowls at the tops of the branches of the Lampstand. Aaron had tools—tweezers and trays—with which he trimmed the wicks and then re-lighted the lamps daily (Exod. 25:38; 30:7–8). Thus, Aaron cultivated this tree in a way parallel to Adam's cultivating the trees of the Garden.

Finally, Aaron was to offer up incense on the Altar of Incense each morning and evening. This represented prayer, which ascended from the

---

56. See my lectures on Esther entitled "Witness or Perish" (available at http://www. wordmp3.com/product-group.aspx?id=21).

57. J. H. Kurtz, *Sacrificial Worship of the Old Testament*, trans. James Martin (Edinburgh: T.& T. Clark, 1863), 318.

Garden through the Veil into the Throneroom to God. This was also Adam's clear duty, for he was to worship God morning and evening and thereby stay close to God, praying for himself and his people.

Aaron entered the Holy Place Garden only twice a day, unless he had to offer a Sin Offering for himself and/ or the congregation (Lev. 4:16). Otherwise, each morning he ascended through the morning Ascension Offering to pour out a libation of beer, to trim the lamps, and offer incense, and each evening he did the same (Num. 28:3–8; Exod. 30:7–8). Once a week, probably in the morning, he also swapped out the bread (and likely the wine) on the Table of Presence Bread. Aaron might eat the bread in "a holy place," but not in "the Holy Place"—that is, in the Forecourt (Lev. 24:9; 6:16).

Thus, though Aaron's work displays Adam's for us, Aaron was not in the same privileged estate as Adam. Until the Last Adam entered Heaven at His ascension, nobody was allowed to remain perpetually in the Holy Place. When the Last Adam entered Heaven, the veil between the Throneroom and the Garden was ripped, so that they became one place where bread and wine, the fruit of both Trees, might be eaten near together.

TO SERVE AND GUARD

We come now to the specific commands given to Adam, to serve the Garden and to guard it. In the past I have identified these as man's kingly and priestly (basilic and hieratic) tasks respectively. As Peter Leithart has shown, however, a priest is not simply a guard, nor is a king simply a supreme servant.[58] In both cases, both actions are important.

The Hebrew word *kohen*, which we translate "priest" in English, has the general meaning of "special servant" or even "royal servant." Leithart summarizes its meaning as "administrator of a royal household."

Unfortunately, we in English face both linguistic and theological confusions when it comes to "priest." The English word "priest" is a contraction of "presbyter," which means "elder" or "old man." The concept of eldership is,

---

58. Peter J. Leithart, "What Is a Priest?" *Biblical Horizons* 33 (January 1992). Online: http://www.biblicalhorizons.com/biblical-horizons/no-33-what-is-a-priest/ and https://theopolisinstitute.com/what-is-a-priest/. For a more in-depth treatment, cf. Peter J. Leithart, *The Priesthood of the Plebs: A Theology of Baptism* (Eugene, OR: Wipf and Stock, 2003), ch. 2: "Attendants in Yahweh's House: Priesthood in the Old Testament."

in fact, much more kingly than priestly. Thus, the history of the English word "priest" is misleading and unhelpful.

Moreover, our theology identifies a priest as a mediator between God and man. Surely it is true that in the Old Creation, the Aaronic priests, being God's special household servants, acted as mediators between Him and the people, and it is surely true that each of us as priests act as mediators for other believers today. But mediation is not the central idea of being a *kohen*. In fact, a *kohen* is a special servant, and the word "deacon" might be a more accurate English translation of it. We shall, however, stick with "priest."

Our studies thus far have created some associations that will help us understand these two functions better. The Garden of Eden is associated with the Tree of Life, which may be eaten there, and later with bread and with the sanctuary in Israel. The Land of Eden, to which Adam and Eve had not yet been admitted, is associated with the Tree of the Knowledge of Good and Evil, and later with wine and with the land of Israel. Since Adam and Eve were cast east of the Garden, they never entered the Land of Eden.

Now, the Tree of the Knowledge of Good and Evil is kingly, a sign of mature wisdom and maturation in godlikeness. It indicates the right to sit enthroned in sabbath rest and pass judgments, under God. It is symbolized by wine later in the Bible, as we see in the cases of Pharaoh's cupbearer, Nehemiah as cupbearer to Artaxerxes, Noah's drinking wine after being given the right to exercise capital punishment, Ahasuerus in Esther drinking wine ceremonially each time he issues a decree, and Proverbs 31:4 telling us that it is not for kings to drink *much* wine. Priests, however, were never to drink wine on the job *at all* (Lev. 10) and, as the book of Hebrews reminds us, the priests never got to sit down and never came to sabbath enthronement and rest.

The priestly comes first, then the kingly. Man matures from deacon (priest) to elder (king). Man begins in the Garden, worshipping God, and then moves to the Land, exercising rule. Man begins life with bread, alpha food, the Tree of Life. At the end of the day he rests with wine, omega food, the Tree of Rule.

Thus, Adam must first learn to serve and to guard. In a real sense, guarding is primary for the priest. The priest superintends the garden-sanctuary and, as we have seen, the Hebrew word for "garden" means a "guarded place." The sanctuary is the guarded place, while the land is the place of dominion. The priest must guard his heart and guard the kingdom against the lies of Satan. The kingly power is not able do this, for no sword can defeat Satan's lies; only the true priestly Word can defeat him. Serving, however, is the beginning of the kingly aspect, for it is through service that we learn to rule. As Jesus said, we learn to rule not by lording it over others, but by serving all (Mark 9:42–45). Through service we acquire wisdom, and become fitted for rule when we become elders (old people; age 55–60 and older).

Guarding is guarding, but service matures through warriorhood into governance. Thus, when we are mature enough to become kings, we continue to be guards, but our primary task is leading and judging. The king must, like Solomon, be wise enough to lead and judge God's people. Thus, for the king the main thing is the serving function, though the king as guard of the land will maintain the army and the fortress cities around the border of the land.

In summary, both priest and king are involved in both guarding and serving. The priest, however, is primarily concerned with guarding, while the king is primarily concerned with serving.

To expand this model: the priest guards as a servant. The issue is obedience, doing what he hears. The primary issue for him is the circumcised ear. The warrior guards as a fighter. He has more independence of action, because he has acquired some wisdom, but he is still a journeyman. The primary issue for him is the circumcised thumb. Finally, the king guards as a ruler. He has the greatest human degree of independence of action. He is an elder, a master. He exercises dominion over a land, so the primary issue for him is the circumcised foot.[59]

PERMISSION AND PROHIBITION

And Yahweh God commanded the man, saying, "From any tree of the garden, eating you may eat. But from the tree of the knowledge of good and evil, you shall not eat from it, for in the day that you eat from it, dying you shall die" (Gen. 2:16–17).

---

59. Later, the Bible expands the priest—warrior—king paradigm to a priest—king—prophet paradigm in which the priest is associated with the circumcised ear, the king with the circumcised hand/thumb, and the prophet with the circumcised big toe/foot. See my discussion of maturation through these stages in *From Bread to Wine*.

At the end of chapter 7, we laid out the seven actions of Yahweh God here in Genesis 2. These parallel the seven days of Genesis 1. We have now arrived at the fifth action, parallel to the fifth day.

In the chiastic structure of Genesis 1 and also of Genesis 2, the fifth event is parallel to the third. On the third day the land and sea were established, and grain plants and fruit trees were made; on the fifth day, birds were made to fill the land (and nest in trees) and fishes to fill the sea. Similarly, the third action of Yahweh God here in Genesis 2 was to plant a garden with trees and separate it from the outlying watered lands (the "sea"). Thus, we have land, sea, and trees (Gen. 2:8–14). Now, in the fifth action, we have commands regarding trees (2:16–17).

On the fifth day, God blessed the birds and fish with a semi-command: "Be fruitful and multiply." Here, Yahweh God provides a more focused kind of command to Adam: "Do not eat, lest you die." This is simply the other side of a blessing, to wit, the threat of curse.

In my translation I have brought out the poetic parallelism of the Hebrew original, which is usually lost in English. The first sentence ends "eating you shall eat," while the second ends "dying you shall die." I believe that the repetition of the verb in Hebrew, which is for emphasis, also reflects the nature of God's revelation. God confirms His word with an oath, saying things twice as it were and thereby providing a testimony of two witnesses. See Hebrews 6:13–14, where adding the oath is explained by the repetition of the verbs: "blessing I will bless you; multiplying I will multiply you."

I have already discussed the fact that eating of the Tree of the Knowledge of Good and Evil was designed to be part of a transition from a pre-glorious to a glorious estate for man, a transition from priestly service to regal rule. Ultimately, such a transition would have involved the glorification of the very flesh of humanity.

Thus, might we say that God's statement here was "neutral" or "two-sided"? In other words, might we say that if Adam and Eve had remained faithful, God would eventually have let them eat of the fruit, and they would have "died," but in a painless fashion, being transfigured? In that case, dying would be a neutral event; whether it involved judgment and pain would depend on whether it was a sinner or an unfallen righteous person who died.

While such an interpretation is tempting philosophically, the fact is that as far as I know, the biblical words for death are never used in such a positive way. In fact, Satan's challenge to God's words were to the effect that they would not die, but would be transformed into gods themselves. Thus, it would seem that death is the promised curse for eating the tree the wrong way and is the opposite of glorification.[60]

The serpent was right, of course, as he often is; he simply used the truth to communicate a lie. The purpose of the tree was indeed to reward faithful humanity with the status of junior godhood under God. Thus, the tree magnified, transformed, and glorified humanity. If a sinner ate the tree, however, it would be a sinner who was magnified, transformed, and intensified. The "glorification" of sin is death.

This transformation into death would happen in the day Adam ate of the tree. It is sometimes assumed that God postponed the judgment of death because Adam and Eve did not die physically when they ate the fruit, but this is based on too narrow a view of death. Death embraces all the consequences of covenant breaking, just as glory embraces all the consequences of covenant keeping. The covenant-keeper moves from glory to glory, from reward to reward, and similarly the covenant-breaker moves from death to death. His covenant-breaking separation from God produces the rending of all other covenants: himself with other people; himself with the world; and himself with himself (physical death). His physical death is just the last step, even as our physical glorification will be our last stage of maturation.

Adam should have gone to the Tree of Life. Life is the bond of the covenant, for life is produced by the Spirit, who is the Bond of love in the Trinity. Thus, Adam would have affirmed the bond of the covenant and would have begun to mature in terms of that bond, beginning to become glorified. At some point God would have let him eat of the Tree of Knowledge and become a king, a ruler, and move out of the Garden into the Land of Eden. Eventually, Adam would have been physically transfigured, moving from earth to heaven.

---

60. In a later essay, "Merit Versus Maturity," 166ff., I argue the view that I set aside here, namely, that if Adam had been faithful, he would have been allowed to eat of the Tree of the Knowledge of Good and Evil and would have passed through a "good death," something like the "deep-sleep" he went through in connection with the creation of Woman, and would have emerged more glorious.

See also my, "The Glory of the Man," 170: "When they were ready, God would allow them to eat and they would fall into a deep sleep and arise to a new life. An examination of the details in Genesis 3 shows that this new life meant moving outside the garden, with its free food, into the land, where they would need skill to make bread."

Finally, the barrier between heaven and earth would have been removed, and the celestial marriage of the Son and the Daughter would have taken place.

By rejecting the Tree of Life, Adam rejected the bond of the covenant. He became a covenant-breaker. By eating of the Tree of Knowledge, Adam tried to glorify himself as a covenant-breaker, but instead of glorifying himself, he simply moved into the process of death. All the other covenants began to unravel. He accused his wife. He was estranged from the soil. Finally his own body betrayed him and he died physically.

History is real: we move forward as impatient, self-willed covenant-breakers or as patient, submissive covenant-keepers. We move from death to death or from glory to glory. Moving into greater and greater glory, into greater and greater responsibility and oversight, is what the Tree of Knowledge is all about. The righteous cling to the covenant bond and wait for God to give glory when He is ready. The wicked seize glory, and in doing so, despise the covenant bond and find only death.

9

Man Alone

Genesis 2:18–20

And Yahweh God said, "It is not good for the man to be alone; I will make
him a helper suitable for him." (Gen. 2:18)

ON the sixth day of Genesis 1, God created man in His own image and
likeness. Now, the sixth action of Yahweh God will be to make a second man
in the image and likeness of the first.

The woman is to be a helper suitable or fitted to the man. Obviously,
then, humanity was created to be a helper suitable or fitted to God Himself.
Humanity is God's destined bride, the Father's daughter who is to grow up to
be the Son's wife.

The matching helper concept is most fully realized, within humanity,
in marriage, which is doubtless why Satan attacks marriage so vigorously.
Outside of the church, our relationship to God, Satan assaults marriage
with the most effort and success. Outside of Christianity—indeed, outside
of Protestant Christianity—men are almost never virgins on their wedding

night. Post-marital fidelity is scoffed at. Hostility and silence overcome marriages; divorce and hatred result.

There are, however, other matching-helper relationships that flow out from this fundamental one. At the ordination of Aaron in Leviticus 8, a passage that builds structurally on this one,[61] we find that Aaron's sons are his matching helpers. In 1 Samuel 26, a passage that builds on the architecture of garden-mountain and land and on other themes from Genesis 2 and 3, David presents himself as a proper matching helper for Saul, better than Abner, showing that the commander of the army is one kind of matching helper for the king (and Joab was a bad helper for David). The deacon is the matching helper for the elder in the Church, as Joshua was for Moses, Elisha was for Elijah, and Gehazi was for Elisha.

But why was such a matching helper needed? Weren't the three persons of the Godhead enough fellowship for Adam?

The passage says that it is "not good" for the man to be alone. This was on the sixth day. Before God can see that it is good at the end of the day, this problem must be corrected. But is the man alone? Doesn't he have God? And if humanity is created to be God's bride, is that not enough?

In approaching this problem, we have to take time and eschatology into account. The celestial marriage will not take place until the firmament seal over the earth is broken; then will the bride be married to the Groom. Until then there is distance between God and man, not a distance caused by sin (because there was as yet no sin), but a distance set up by God as part of His program of maturation for us. During this time we are to learn about our role-relationship with God by means of role-relationships in this world, under the firmament. In marriage, the woman's firmament-seal is broken and the man and woman are no longer alone, but one flesh. This is a type or foreshadowing of the celestial marriage.

So it is not enough to say, "I fellowship with the three persons of God; I don't need human companionship." God has said that in this life He does not intend to manifest Himself as a complete companion, and thus we need other companions, especially a spouse.

Since Adam was a priest—and as priest of the Garden, spiritual leader of humanity—the fact that he needed a wife means that the requirement of clerical celibacy is Satanic to the core. If there is any kind of man who needs

---

61. See the treatment of this passage in chapter 8.

a wife, it is a clergy-man. A man is in a profound sense "alone" unless he is married. Of course, God calls some men to be "alone" all their lives, but this is not the normal calling, nor is it the normal situation for a parish minister. Such a man is "alone" unless he is married. In this life, before the last day, God will not be our spouse, and He says we should have one. It is "not good" if we don't. He may call us to live a life that is "not good," and thus to undergo suffering for Him, but for the Church to require such a life is a great evil.

Nuns, you may know, wear a wedding ring as spouses of Christ. That is a nice idea, and of course has some biblical justification. To prize celibacy in this life is, however, perverse and disobedient. All Christian women, and men too, are espoused to Christ. Our baptism is our espousal. God has said that it is "not good" to be alone in this life and that He is not going to be our spouse in this life. Thus, the unmarried state is a tragedy, or a sacrifice. It is not a "way of life." Celibacy may be thrust upon us, but it is not something we should choose. The Reformers were right to reject vows of celibacy.

THE FORMATION OF THE BEASTS

And Yahweh God formed from the ground every beast of the field and every bird of the heavens, and brought to the man to see what he would call them; and whatever the man called a living being, that was its name. And the man called names to all the cattle, and to the birds of the heavens, and to every beast of the field, but as for the man there was not found a helper suitable for him (Gen. 2:19–20).

There is something of a puzzle in these two verses. According to Genesis 1, the birds had been made on the fifth day, before man, and the land animals also were made before man on the sixth day. Four ways of dealing with this problem have been proposed.

First, many neo-evangelical commentators simply take this is an indication that the days of Genesis 1 are not literal. This solution creates far more problems than it solves, of course, and so we must reject it.

Second, according to Hirsch, the rabbis held that "formed" here is used in the sense of "pushed together."[62] This is a credible suggestion on the face

---

62. Samson Raphael Hirsch, *Genesis*, trans. Isaac Levy (1966; reprint, Gateshead: Judaica,

of it, for the verb *yatsar* is almost always used in the sense of "forming" something by pushing it together, as in pottery. God pushed together the dust to make man; a potter pushes together clay to make a pot. So because the birds and wild animals would not come to Adam on their own, God pushes them together to him, while the domestic animals were already present with him in the Garden. Clever as this suggestion is, we notice that the verse goes on to say that God brought the wild animals and birds to the man, which would be redundant if the idea of compelling them toward Adam had already been expressed. Hirsch states with respect to 2:19 that God did not "form" the beasts and birds from the ground, but "drove" them from the ground to the Garden.[63] They had already been made. There is no need to suggest that God created new specimens. The verb, yatsar, means, "fashion, form, shape" in the sense of compressing together. The previous use of this verb in verses 7–8 has this sense, that God compressed together the dust of the ground to form Adam.

Thus, Hirsch suggests that the sense of 2:19 is that God drove together into a group a bunch of wild animals and birds from the outlying 'adamah ground and brought them into the Garden to Adam. In my opinion, this makes eminent good sense and resolves quite nicely the problem that the verse seems to pose. Thus, the verse should be translated: "Now Yahweh God collected from the ground every beast of the field and every bird of the air, and He brought them to the man."

This translation makes sense not only in context and grammatically, but it also provides a closer connection to God's bringing the animals to Noah before the Flood (6:20).

A third explanation is that while God had already made lots of beasts and birds, here on this occasion He made one more pair of each to bring before Adam. If this is the right explanation, however, why are cattle excluded? Why would God make a new pair of the other animals and not of cattle?

Thus, I think that the traditional explanation is best: the Hebrew here simply summarizes action that has already taken place. We would render it in English with the pluperfect tense, which does not exist as such in Hebrew: "And Yahweh God *had* formed." He had also formed the cattle, but they are

---

1989), 66.

63   Hirsch, *Genesis*, 66.

not mentioned here because they did not need to be brought to Adam; they already had access to the Garden.

This being the case, why does the verse not just read, "And Yahweh God brought every beast of the field and every bird of the heavens to the man"? Why does it say that God had "formed" them? The reason seems to be that just as Yahweh God "formed" the man in verse 7, so here He "formed" the animals. This points to a connection between man and the animals, and on the basis of that connection or similarity, Adam is able to reason from animal life to human life.

The analogy between men and animals underlies the sacrificial system, the laws of unclean foods, the book of Proverbs, etc. Here, of course, Adam reasons from the fact that the animals come in sexual pairs to the notion that he also should have a female complement. Adam does not reason that he is different from the animals, and thus needs no helper. Rather, he instinctively knows that the analogy exists.

The medieval Jewish commentator Nachmanides notes that when Adam named the animals, he gave different names to the males and females. He notes this in connection with the Hebrew language, which he (rightly, I believe) thinks was Adam's language. It is also true in English: bull and cow, ram and ewe, etc. Nachmanides says that this aspect of the naming procedure is what drove him to see that he was alone. Thus, it is not that Adam named the animals and just also happened to notice that they came in sexual pairs, but that his actual naming focused his attention on their sexuality.[64]

The analogy between humans and animals is heightened by the fact that verse 7 says that after God *formed from the ground* Adam, he became a *living being*. Here in verse 19, *God formed from the ground* the animals, and Adam named every *living being*. Thus, the animals are like man in being "formed" by God and in being "living beings."

Now one more question can be raised: Verse 19 connects humanity with beasts and birds only, while Adam named *cattle*, beasts, and birds. Aren't domestic animals even closer to humanity than beasts and birds? Yes, of course. Then why aren't they also mentioned as "formed" in verse 19?

---

64. I have moved away from the view that Adam saw that all the animals he named came in sexual pairs, male and female, and reasoned from that that there ought to be a partner corresponding to him as well.

I think the answer to that lies in a common sense approach to language. For everything to be spelled out, the verse would have to read like this: "And Yahweh God formed from the ground all cattle and every beast of the field and every bird of the heavens, and brought every beast of the field and every bird of the heavens to the man to see what he would call them; and whatever the man called a living being, that was its name." The text is simply written more compactly. It is obvious that cattle are also "formed" and are also "living beings." What verse 19 wants to point out in addition is that the beasts and birds had to be brought to Adam in the Garden, for they were not ordinarily found there.

ANIMALS AND HUMANITY

If the only purpose God had in bringing the animals before Adam was for him to learn that he needed a mate, it would not have been necessary for Adam to name them. Naming something is a way of laying hold of it. If you do not have a name for something, you cannot deal with it. Adam was told to serve and to guard the Garden. Now, all these animals are in the Garden, and he must serve and guard them.

In "The Glory of the Man," 180–181, I write:

> Now, we do not read that God brought two of every kind of animal to Adam, so that he perceived that they came in sexual pairs and learned that he needed a mate. I preached it this way for many years, but one day woke up and realized that this is not what the text is about. The woman is to be far more than a sexual partner, and the concept of "helper suited" is far broader than only marriage.... What Adam learned was that he was the only human being, the only image of God.
>
> And, significantly, Adam learned that there was no one to dialogue with him in worship. The garden is the sanctuary area, the place where God meets with man at the two special trees.... What God meant by saying it is not good for the man to be alone was that it is not good for people to worship alone. Worship involves community and dialogue. There must be a second person to respond to the words of the first.

Elsewhere, I say, "Animals were brought to Adam and he named them, but none of them spoke back. The text does not say that the animals came in pairs, and what Adam learned was not that he needed a wife. What he learned was that he needed a conversation partner, someone who could speak in response to him in the liturgical situation of the garden sanctuary" (James B. Jordan, "Restoring the Office of Woman in the Church, I," online: https://theopolisinstitute.com/restoring-the-office-of-woman-in-the-church-i-2/).

The use of the verb "serve" is important. The fact is that we cannot have dominion over anything unless we serve it; we cannot rule anything we do not serve.

This is clearly seen in our relationship with the lower creation. For instance, you can throw out seeds to grow vegetables, but unless you act as a servant of the young plants, you will not get any vegetables. You have to nurture the plants, thin them out, weed the patch, water if necessary, etc. (If you don't believe me, try to grow roses.)

The same is true with animals: If you do not serve them in the sense of meeting their needs and spending time with them, they will never serve you. With regard to human beings the matter is less obvious because you can bully human beings into obeying you, but this never lasts very long and never produces lasting dominion. Thus, we are to learn the nature of true dominion by dealing with plants and animals, which we cannot successfully bully.

In a sense, before you can guard you have to serve; that is, you have to know what it is you are called to guard. Thus, while the fullness of man's kingly task comes only after he has learned to guard, the beginning of his kingly task precedes his guarding. The order is: serve, guard, rule.

God created animals to teach man. We can see it immediately here. First, to teach man about his serving function, God brought the animals to Adam for him to name. Adam gave them descriptive names, based on his observation of them. Then, to teach man about his guarding function, God permitted an animal to come to Adam to test him.

Man began his service (naming) on the sixth day and his guarding at the beginning of the seventh, before God came to the Garden for worship. Thus, man does not worship God in isolation from his calling, but with his calling "in hand." The Law states that we are never to come before God empty-handed (Exod. 34:20; Deut. 16:16). This is signified by the various offerings, but particularly by the "filling of the hand" of the priests, a phrase that refers to their ordination but that also takes place literally in the Lifted or Waved Offering, when various vegetables and animal portions are piled on the hands of the priest and offered to God. Thus, man as priest offers the world to God.

And so, when Adam came before God on that first sabbath day, he was to have the world in his hand to offer to God, affirming that he was merely a steward. The Garden, being the center and first place in the world, would be offered by Adam metonymously, the part for the whole. Adam, however, had tried to take over the world for himself and in the process lost it altogether.

Animals come before man. The animals were made a few hours before Adam, but afterwards the animals spread out over all the earth much sooner than humanity did. Wherever men went, animals were there first. They could follow the animal trails to find water. They could observe which plants animals ate to know what was good to eat. They could observe which plants sick animals ate and learn possibly what could be used in healing. Moreover, as the book of Proverbs shows us, we can learn much from animals in other ways as well.

In order for man to learn, however, he has to put language on top of his observations. This means he has to become self-conscious about what he learns. He has to name things. We have seen God name things in Genesis 1; now for the first time we see man also naming things. How did Adam learn to speak, to name? By hearing God speak.

So Adam learned about the world by naming the animals. And he also learned that each came in a sexual pair, and from this he reasoned that God intended him to have a mate as well. The animals were indeed helpers, but not the helper "fitted" for him.

The relationship of animals to humanity is primordial, not eschatological. It is in the childhood of the race, when we live in the countryside close to the soil, that we learn from animals. As we move into cities, which is God's plan for humanity, we move away from the soil and away from our animal tutors. In the city, where people live close together away from animals, intricate human relationships replace the earlier relationships with animals. In the course of history, human culture loses its animal analogies and becomes more humano-centric. The three animal faces of the cherubim (ox, lion, and eagle), which characterized humanity before the coming of Christ, give way before the fourth face, the human face, the face of God's image.

Here we see already all four faces. Adam, the man, names cattle (ox), beasts (lion), and birds (eagle).

WHAT'S IN A NAME?

The Hebrew verb "call" (qara') is used both nominatively (to name something) and vocatively (to call someone's name). It is used five times in Genesis 1:1–2:3 for five things that God names (Day, Night, Heaven, Earth, Seas). It is used ten times in our passage (2:4–4:26).

It is interesting to note that there is a kind of literary rhythm in the usage of this verb, which brings out a significant point:

1. Adam calls names for animals (2:19): nominative
2. Adam calls names for animals (2:19): nominative
3. Adam calls names for animals (2:20): nominative
4. Adam calls name for woman (2:23): nominative
5. Yahweh God calls the man to appear (3:9): vocative

6. Adam calls Eve's name (3:20): nominative
7. Cain calls Enoch's name (4:17): nominative
8. Eve calls Seth's name (4:25): nominative
9. Seth calls Enosh's name (4:26): nominative
10. Men call to Yahweh in worship (4:26): vocative

In the first set there are no personal names, only generic ones. In the second set all the names are personal or specific ("Eve," not "woman"; "Enoch," not "city"). A man knows about women before he comes to know which particular woman he is to serve. (The woman is put in the Garden; therefore, she is to be served and guarded.) Moreover, most men give their wives a secret pet name. First we know "woman"; then we know "darling." The same is true in all of life: We know categories by observation, but personalization takes time and therefore comes later. If you move to a new city, it is just a city until you have lived there long enough to feel the personality of its name.

The exception to this process is God Himself. I think it is significant that we do not have a "generic" type of name for God anywhere in this entire section. From the beginning, He is not just "God" but "Yahweh God." We cannot know God generically without also knowing Him personally because God is unique. There is no other god, no class of "gods," into which Yahweh fits. Adam knew that his woman was a female, like the female animals he had observed; later he knew her specifically as Eve. But with God it is not so.

Both of the vocatives have to do with God and man. In the first, God calls to sinful man; in the second, sinful man calls to God. This is the order of grace.

The vocative case, which in English we call "direct address," does not exist for all nouns. It exists only for names. We cannot call out "Oh, lamp," or "Oh, book," the same way we can call our children home for dinner: "Oh, Johnny!

Susan!" Similarly, the imperative and interrogative moods cannot be used with all nouns, only with names. We can say, "Adam, do not eat! Adam, where are you?" We cannot say, "Lamp, do not eat! Book, where are you?" (Well, we can say the latter when we are looking for a lost book, but we are being funny and personifying the book, treating it as a person with a name.)

Eugen Rosenstock-Huessy has some powerful thoughts on the concept of naming:

> *The name is the right address of a person under which he or she will respond.* The original meaning of language was the very fact that it could be used to make people respond. The very word "responsiveness" today is less popular than its often invoked variation—"responsibility." I am responsible for something objective. The complaint is heard often that people are not responsible enough. However, may it not be true that we cannot be responsible when we are not allowed to be responsive first? If no soul calls upon our name, we perhaps are too weak to shoulder responsibilities. As long as we are only taught and addressed in the mass, our name never falls upon us as the power that dresses our wounds, lifts our hearts, and makes us rise and walk.
>
> The right words, i.e. "names," guarantees responsiveness. Responsiveness is the lying open for being empowered. We have long spoken of an open mind. But the mind is open for conceptual understanding of the things outside. The other openness of any human being is an appeal made to him in the power of his name. "As an American, as a human being, as a Christian, as a believer, as a child of God, you must listen," this appeal might say....
>
> Now, the power of a name lies in the fact that it eases our conscience The simple fact, that the mother calls the child by the right name, makes the child smile. The cry, which is the first utterance of the child when it enters the world, is transformed into the smile of response through the intermediary of the name. The name pacifies the child and gives it ease in this new and cold world which it did not enjoy before. Names give orientation. As long as we are addressed with a name that has power we feel that we are led. We may smile, because, even when an enemy calls our name, we still are not confused. We know where we are. In as far as our society is imperiled today it is because people are not addressed in the powerful manner which might give them orientation....

Because we need orientation, we wait for our soul to call upon our name. This fact leads to one other difference between words [nouns] and names. All nouns can be used by everybody and can be carried over to any number of things and objects either by definition or metaphorically. But the same element of speech when used as a name is neither a metaphor nor a classification. It is exclusively used between you and me. If the child was not sure that the mother meant him, Johnny only, and nobody else, the child would not smile. The name is personal, or it is no name. Personifications are possible only as long as language is name-giving. Because name is personification. The word [noun] is generic; the name is specific. Names are exclusive speech between a person and somebody whom he tries to make into a person by calling him with the right name. Whereas a description of the outer world can be given in nouns, the orientation of you or me in the world can only be given us by a specific name-giving process to which we then respond. Orientation and response are two aspects of one and the same process. The child which hears itself called by the same name again and again, responds and thereby gains orientation.

"Orientation" is the objective aspect and "response" is the subjective aspect of one and the same social process of giving or using the right name. Nouns classify, but names orient. Nouns generalize, but names personify. Nouns dismiss living subjects into the realm of objectivity. Names pick up the little baby or the flower or the sun, and incorporate them into one society of communication. Without names, communication would be impossible. For before two individuals may talk to each other in words about things, they must be mutually responsive, they must recognize each other as persons. Each must make more and more of a person out of his interlocutor by giving each other names.[65]

Thus, naming is the first part of speech. God names us, and thereby calls us into personhood. God does not do this directly, however, but does it through other people. Parents call us by name and bring us into personhood. When we marry, our spouse calls us by name, perhaps a new pet name, and brings us into a new stage of personhood. We are also called by names according to our occupations (farmer, pastor, etc.) and associations (freemason, Christian,

---

65. Eugen Rosenstock-Huessy, *I Am an Impure Thinker* (1970; reprint, Eugene, OR: Wipf and Stock, 2013), 42–44. The italics on the first sentence are mine for emphasis.

etc.). As we grow, we take on more and more new names, adjusting toward our new eschatological name that God gives us and that no one knows but we ourselves (Rev. 2:17).

Since God calls us into personhood by naming us, we should not be surprised that the image of God acts in the same way. Adam, the image of God, called his helper "woman" and then "Eve." Thus he oriented her in the world and in his life.

There may be a message in the fact that the general names came before the fall, while the personal names came after it. Adam rightly named the animals and the woman, but have fallen people always given the right personal names to their children? Texas Governor Hogg named his daughter Ima. This cutesy prank was cruel and unconscionable, and this woman certainly had a right to reject this name and pick another.[66] People all too often give their children unsuitable or bizarre names. Such names can warp the child's personality, and constitute a trespass that the child must learn to forgive.[67]

Also, we may start out with one name and grow into another. Jacob was rightly named, for he was the Replacement for sinful Isaac, a type of the Second Adam. But he grew to become Israel, God's Wrestler. This did not involve rejecting the name Jacob, for God calls him by both names, but it does show that the Second Adam grows to become God's Warrior. On the other hand, Paul seems to have dropped the name Saul. King Saul was from Benjamin, as was the apostle. Dropping the name Saul was a way of rejecting the sinful associations of the old name, associated with the apostle's early, Saul-like life of persecuting the Christians, the new Davids. His new name clarified his life and oriented him to his new mission.

---

66. This wording may give the impression that Ima Hogg changed her name, but in fact she did not. She wrote her first name illegibly or just used the initial I. It is not clear that Big Jim Hogg named her Ima as a prank. The name "Ima" came from a character in a poem by his brother, and Jim Hogg was quoted as saying that it was his *wife* who named their baby. Cf. https://en.wikipedia.org/wiki/Ima_Hogg. Thanks to John Barach for this information.

67   I took this example from Rosenstock-Huessy, "Lectures on Universal History" (1954), Lecture 22, transcript available at http://www.erhfund.org/lectures/volume-12-universal-history-1954/lecture-22/.

10

DEEP-SLEEP

GENESIS 2:21A

And Yahweh God caused to fall a deep-sleep [tardema] *upon the man, and he slept* [yashan] (Gen. 2:21a).

AS you can see, the Hebrew verb and noun for deep-sleep (*radam* and *tardema*) are not related at all to the ordinary verb for sleep (*yashan*). We might render "deep-sleep" as unconsciousness but, as we shall see, such a translation will not work. We ask the question then, why does the Hebrew use a completely different word? Why not just say "deep sleep," using the adjective "deep" to modify the ordinary noun for sleep?

An investigation of the usage of the peculiar verb translated "deep-sleep" will reveal that it has a special meaning associated with de-creation or death, especially in covenant-making acts of God. The first instance of it is here, where we see God separate the woman from the man and then join them in covenant.

Deep-sleep is close to death and is the place where covenants are made, preceding either total death or resurrection. The term occurs in Judges 4:21, where Sisera falls into deep-sleep just before his head is crushed. Building upon this incident is 1 Samuel 26:12, when David finds Saul in deep-sleep and is given opportunity to crush his head, but merely removes items from around his head instead. Coming back to life from deep-sleep, Saul renews covenant with David (1 Sam. 26:13–25).

Jonah, fleeing from God, is found in deep-sleep in Jonah 1:5–6 (the word is found in both verses). Soon he will be cast overboard and experience death and resurrection in the belly of the great fish, renewing his covenant with God therein.

Some, like Sisera, move from deep-sleep to the total sleep of death. The Egyptian army was, like Jonah, in deep-sleep in the Red Sea, but they were not raised to life again:

> The stouthearted were plundered;
> They slumbered their sleep;
> And none of the men of might have found their hands.
> At Your rebuke, O God of Jacob,
> Both chariot and horse were cast into deep-sleep (Ps. 76:5–6).

Such is the case also in Isaiah 29:10: "For Yahweh has poured over you a spirit of deep-sleep." Similarly, the sluggard in his laziness is moving into a deep-sleep condition near death and may starve to death (Prov. 19:15). The same fate awaits him who deep-sleeps during harvest (Prov. 10:5).

The man who is in deep-sleep and is headed for death is not conscious, but the man who is in deep-sleep and is headed for resurrection may be in a vision. Eliphaz claims to have had a vision while in deep-sleep (Job 4:13), and Elihu states that God visits men with visions while they are in deep-sleep (Job 33:15). As we shall see, Abram also experienced a vision in deep-sleep.

The association of deep-sleep with death and resurrection is clearly seen in Daniel. In Daniel 8:18, Daniel is told that he is going to be shown the end. Immediately he falls into deep-sleep, but then he is raised to stand on his feet to be shown the vision. Similarly, as soon as Daniel hears the Angel of Yahweh speaking to him in Daniel 10:9, he falls into deep-sleep, from which he is raised to hear the message. This event is a type of the death and resurrection of Israel that is prophesied throughout the message, and especially in Daniel

12:2; compare 10:9 and 15. An identical death-resurrection sequence is found in Revelation 1:17, where John falls at Jesus' feet "as a dead man" and then is raised again. John's death and resurrection is a type of the death and resurrection of the Church described in Revelation.

THE COVENANT WITH ABRAM

In our survey we skipped Genesis 15, because it gives perhaps the fullest picture of this kind of event. At the beginning of this chapter, Abram has become aware that though God has promised him the land, he does not possess it. The land had refused to yield anything to him, forcing him by famine into Egypt. Then, when he finally returned to the land, a civil war raged over it, during which is became clear to him that he was not in charge of the land at all. Yet, Abram had defeated Chedorlaomer and had delivered Lot. Now Abram is afraid Chedorlaomer will return, and God appears to comfort him. During the night God tells him that his seed will be like the stars and that he will possess the land.

Abram asks for assurance, and God tells him to cut three animals in half and to kill two birds. During the next day, Abram does this. Birds of prey seek to devour the carcasses, but Abram drives them away. Notice this: the animals are dead, but not devoured. They are, symbolically speaking, in deep-sleep, but not yet dead. They are dead, but not under the curse-judgment of the covenant. Then Abram himself falls into deep-sleep (Gen. 15:12). While in this condition, Abram sees God pass between the parts of the animals.

This event is often misunderstood today. God is not saying, "May I be ripped in half and devoured by the birds if I don't keep this covenant." Rather, God is making a covenant between the two parts of the animals, which signify Abram on the one hand and the land on the other. This symbolism is possible because both man and the animals are made of soil, so animals can represent both soil and man. God's fiery Spirit will reunite the two halves of the broken covenant. Adam was cursed from the soil, and up to now Abram has experienced that curse. Now, however, God will resurrect that relationship by His Spirit and on the basis of the death-sacrifice of a representative. The land will remain uncooperative for four hundred years, but then will become a new and more glorious "land flowing with milk and honey."

Thus, the covenant is made through death and resurrection. When we apply this sequence to Jesus, we can see immediately what it means. Jesus is the animal torn in half but not cursed in His death. He died, but did not undergo corruption. The birds did not devour Him, though He was hanged up and made available to them by His crucifixion (compare 2 Sam. 21:9–10). As the dead animals represented the estrangement between Abram and the land, so the death of Jesus is necessary because of the estrangement between God and mankind. Being both God and man, Jesus in His death takes upon Himself both sides of the estrangement.

Then, God's Spirit raised Jesus from the dead, passing between the two halves and granting covenant renewal. Jesus' spirit was reunited with His flesh. As the Spirit moved between the divided animals in Abram's vision, creating a bond between Abram and the land, so now after Pentecost the Spirit moves between God and mankind, creating a bond between them. Just as Abram and the land were both glorified after this death and resurrection event (Abram's being multiplied like the stars, and the land's becoming a land flowing with milk and honey), so also a new and glorious covenant comes about between God and man through the resurrection of Jesus, so that humanity no longer lives under the curse of the law but in the glories of the Kingdom of God.

For Abram to appreciate this, Abram too must die. He must enter deep-sleep and then awaken. So must we. We must die to the old broken, cursed, shattered covenant in Adam and be raised into the New Covenant in Christ. Then we are restored to God, to one another, and to the world. Then the soil no longer curses us. God Himself is the bond of the New Covenant.

The instances we have looked at all happened after the fall of man, and thus deep-sleep carries with it the possibility of final death or of resurrection to the new creation. Before the fall, however, it did not carry this precise meaning. Adam goes into deep-sleep and "dies" to his state of being alone.[68] Then, from his side, God makes a partner for him. When Adam awakes, he is in covenant union with his wife. This covenant is made through blood, for it is not just a rib but a whole flesh-and-bone (and hence blood) piece of Adam that is made into Eve. As Adam says, "This is flesh of my flesh, bone of my bone." And Adam also says that man must "die" to his old family to make a

---

68. Consider Adam's personal experience. Arguably he has never fallen asleep before. He begins to lose consciousness. "What is happening to me?" he wonders. But Adam at this point trusts God. Surely God knows what is happening to him. He is able to fall asleep, confident that God knows what He is doing in bringing this strange event upon him.

new one: "For this cause a man shall leave his father and mother and cleave to his wife."

Thus, dying to the old and moving by resurrection into the new is not just something that comes into being because of the fall of man. Human life involves such passages even apart from sin. After the fall, of course, such transitions become much more traumatic, and in the greatest passage what must be left behind is an old world of sin and what we are raised to is a new world in God's kingdom.

The formation of Eve from Adam's side is fulfilled when the soldier pierces Jesus' side and blood and water come out of it. Jesus has died but is not to be cursed. In that place of deep-sleep, His bride is formed. The Church is created on the basis of the blood of Christ and by the water of baptism that comes from His side. It is the Spirit, the para-clete, the "side-comer," who comes from Jesus' side in baptismal water, and it is the Spirit who forms the bride.

11

FROM ADAM'S SIDE

GENESIS 2:21B–22

And Yahweh God caused to fall a deep-sleep upon the man, and he slept. And He took one of his sides, and He closed the flesh in its place. And Yahweh God built the side that He took from the man into woman, and He brought her to the man (Gen. 2:21–22).

THE Hebrew word *tsela'*, usually translated "rib" here, does not mean "rib." It means "side." This is the only place in the Bible where this word is used in connection with human beings. It is used once for the side of a mountain, and all other usages refer to sides of buildings or appear in other architectural settings.

The woman was not made from the man's rib. He states that she is "bone of my bones and flesh of my flesh." Thus, a whole complex of flesh and bone was withdrawn from Adam and used to make Eve. How much, we are not told.

God then closed up the flesh in that place. "Closed" is the word used for shutting doors. It does not say that God "filled in" the place that He had taken from Adam, though we may assume that He did that as well. The idea is that Adam is now incomplete. He is not made complete again by God's "filling in" his flesh. Rather, he is to be made complete by joining with the woman.

The woman is not made from the soil, as Adam had been and as the animals had been. Thus man's relationship with the animals cannot have a "one flesh" dimension. It is purely interactive. But with the woman there can be a mystical joining, because man and woman were originally one substance. As Hirsch puts it, "Man, as it were, was divided, and the one part formed into Woman." Hirsch goes on to note that she was not *bara'* (created), *yatsar* (formed, Gen. 2:8), *'asah* (made), but *banah* (built), "only built out, arranged as Woman. So that what was previously one creature was now two, and thereby the complete equality of women for ever attested."[69]

Then we read that God brought the woman to the man. He put them back together. A man is incomplete without a wife. The physical joining of man and woman points to their one-flesh relationship, which is unique. Celibacy is thus a special calling and should be rare.

Now, we need to consider this in terms of the relationship of God to humanity. Man was not made out of God's side, and thus man does not have any "God-stuff" in himself. There is no physical link between man and God. Accordingly, God's relationship to man is like man's relationship with the animals. It is purely interactive. There is no mystical connection between God and man.

Until Christ comes. By assuming human nature, the second Person of God makes possible a mystical connection to humanity. The blood and water that flowed from His side, after His death on the cross, create the Bride for Him. His blood (death) extends to us, and so does His water (new life). Resurrected in Christ, we are mystically joined to him.

God has no inadequacy in Himself. The Father and the Son are always mystically joined by the Spirit. But by becoming man, the Son placed Himself in a position of inadequacy. He now needs completion. He needs a woman to be a complete Man. If He has no bride, He remains forever incomplete. Thus, once He became a Man, Christ had to find a bride, and this meant that He had to die for her sins.

Notice that throughout the Old Creation, humanity was symbolized by animals. God related to humanity as to an animal. The sacrifices were animal

---

69. Hirsch, *Genesis*, 68.

sacrifices. The faces of the cherubim that applied in the Old Creation were the ox, lion, and eagle faces. The book of Proverbs relates human life to animal life. This is life under the Law. The Law is God's means of interactive communication with us.

But now, in the New Creation, there is a higher dimension at work. The Spirit comes as the bond between Christ and His bride. The Spirit creates the mystical union, with "groanings too deep to be uttered" (Rom. 8:26). The Law is still of value, but secondary now to this mystical union. The Spirit re-contextualizes the Law. The Law is no longer on the outside of man, speaking to him from without only, but is now also on the inside, because of the mystical union. God speaks to us now not as animals but as a wife to whom He is united.[70]

As God led the woman to the man, so the Spirit leads the Bride to Christ.

What we have just seen raises the question: Would Christ have come into the world if Adam had not sinned? The answer is clearly "yes." Adam would not have always been the federal head of humanity. There would come a time when a Son of Adam would be born, who would be God Himself in the flesh. The Spirit would make of God and man "one flesh" through the gift of the Son. But in this case, Christ's passage from Old Creation life to New Creation (resurrection) life would not have involved taking upon Himself the curse of the cross.

The fact that there was an eschatology for Adam, apart from sin, is clearly stated in 1 Corinthians 15:44, where Paul argues that "if there is a natural body, there is also a spiritual one." Paul goes on to state that "the spiritual is not first, but the natural; then the spiritual. The first man is from the earth, made of dust; the second man is from heaven" (1 Cor. 15:46–47). All this Paul argues from creation, not from redemption.

There is nothing humiliating about God's becoming man. It is like making a beautiful set of clothes and then putting it on. The creation and humanity (the apex of creation) are good and beautiful. For God to become man was an act of self-glorification. Thus, even apart from sin, there would have come a time when God would take upon Himself human flesh and join in marriage with humanity through the bond of the Spirit. As it happened, this wonderful

---

70. Of course, by anticipation, this relationship was also in play during the Old Creation; but now it has come in its fullness.

event took place in a context of sin and curse, but it would have come to pass anyway.

THE DEIFICATION OF HUMANITY

I commented just now that by becoming man, the Second Person of the Godhead now becomes "one flesh" with humanity. That is, He now is incomplete; He is missing a "side." He needs a bride, but the only bride available is dead under the judgment of God. Thus, the Son must die in her place. Then she can be made fit for Him, to complete Him.

I also pointed out that humanity is not made of "God-stuff" but of dust energized by the Spirit. I do not want to be read as saying that now, because of the incarnation, humanity can be deified in the sense of being merged with the "God-stuff" of the Son. By no means. Jesus is God and man. As God He is in no sense incomplete. And as God, He does not become "one flesh" with us. That cannot be, for it would break the Creator/creature distinction, which is impossible. All the heresies of the early church revolved around attempts to merge God and humanity, and all must be rejected for that reason.

No, it is as man that Jesus becomes one flesh with us. We are not made part of God when we are joined to Him in marriage; rather, we are united to His glorified humanity. Salvation involves the restoration and glorification of our humanity. The Bible speaks of glorified human beings as "gods," so the early church rightly spoke of our being "deified" or "divinized" in the sense of becoming glorified in Christ. But the doctrine of the "deification of man" means that we are glorified creatures, not that we become merged with the Creator in some metaphysical sense.

But we have to go one step further. It is Jesus Himself, not just His "abstract humanity," that we are united to. The doctrine of the "Communication of Properties" (*communicatio idiomatum*) means that the properties of both of Jesus' natures are properties of His one Person. We marry Jesus, not just His human nature. In that sense, we are married to God, and become "one flesh" with God, but without any infusion of "God-stuff."

The physical connection between man and the world is real, for man is made of dust. The physical connection between man and woman is real, for woman was built from man's side, out of his "stuff." Similarly, the meta-physical connection between the Father and the Son is real, for they are of the same uncreated "Stuff." There is not, nor can there be, any kind of physical or meta-physical connection between God and man.

But also, the Spirit connects the Father and the Son. This is a personal connection that goes beyond "mere" language communication. This is the connection that is extended to humanity as a result of Christ's incarnation and His work. The Spirit proceeds from Christ's side and connects us to Him in our marriage to Him. It is a connection that involves "groanings too deep to be uttered," that is, it is deeper than (or other than) language communication (Rom. 8:26).

The Spirit is the Bond of this inter-personal Oneness. Jesus prayed that we might be one with Him as He is one with the Father. This oneness is a connection brought about by the Spirit. This Spiritual oneness also extends to our relationship to one another in the body of Christ, the Church (John 17:21).

With this in mind, we can refine further what it means to be "deified in Christ," as the early church sought to understand it. The glory with which Jesus is glorified is the Spirit, and we are glorified by the same Spirit. The halo of glory around us is the Spirit Himself. We also have our own glory, as God's perfected images, for we also are spirits, but our primary glory is God's own glory. We remain creatures, but we are surrounded by the glory of God. Thus, in our maturity we appear as "gods," as the Bible puts it.

The Spirit's halo of glory extends around both Christ and us. The Spirit is one Garment around us both. Within that Garment, we are naked and not ashamed before Him. He has spread His cloak (the Spirit-glory) around us, and we are wed to Him.

Thus, we can summarize the doctrine of the deification of humanity as follows:

1. God's plan all along was for the Second Person of the Trinity to become a Son of Adam (the Son of Man) and join us to God in a higher, more glorious way than was originally the case.

2. In our marriage to Jesus, we are married to God Himself and deified in that sense.

3. The Spirit is the glory of God, who joins Father and Son and now joins us to the Son and us to one another. The Spirit flows from Jesus to us, deifying us in that sense.

4. The Spirit is the halo of glory around God and now is our halo as well, deifying us in that sense.

5. The Spirit's halo of glory is around us and Jesus together, and within that Garment we are "one flesh" and thus deified in that sense.

6. In none of this is there any merging of "stuff" between the creature and the Creator.

One Flesh

We have discussed how Jesus becomes "one flesh" with His bride by means of the Spirit, which flows from Him to her. Now we can make one more (bold) step forward. The "one flesh" relationship between a man and a woman does not involve physical merging, but it involves the closest kind of physical contact, involving penetration of the woman by the man and the issuance of seed from the man to the woman. This is an *analogy* to the relationship of Christ to the Church. Christ comes into us as His bride. The Spirit issues from Him to us, and we become fruitful.

But—and it is a big, big *but*—the manifestation of this penetration of our flesh by Christ is not sexual, but culinary. The bride takes Christ into herself not by having sex with Him, but by eating Him. The mystical union of Christ and His bride comes through eating the flesh and drinking the blood of Jesus in the Lord's Supper. As Bible-believing Protestants know, it is the Spirit who flows from Jesus to us in the Supper, bringing Him to us.

In my essay, "The Meaning of Eating in the Bible," I have shown that both sexual relations and eating are "one flesh" phenomena.[71] When we eat the same food, we are recreated from the same substance and we start to smell the same. If we all eat Garlic Chicken at a Chinese restaurant, we will all smell like garlic. If we all eat Christ, we will all smell like Christ to the Father.

Thus, the Bible everywhere puts sex and eating together in its symbolism. The most obvious place is the Marriage Supper of the Lamb.

We unite with one another in the Church in the same way. We don't have sex with each other, but we greet one another with a holy kiss. Kissing is symbolic eating. If this is not clear to you, think of a father getting down on his knees and "gobbling up" his little child with kisses.

John 7:38–39 says that out of our innermost parts flows living water, and that this refers to the Spirit. What is true of us is most true of Christ. From Him flows the Spirit to us. But it is also true that the Spirit flows from us to each other.

The Spirit is a "water" that flows from our innermost parts. The background for this statement is Leviticus 15, which deals with defiling issues. The issues come from the private parts, from the sexual organs. Even the act

---

71. James B. Jordan, "The Meaning of Eating in the Bible," *Studies in Food and Faith* 7 (January 1990).

of marriage itself involved a defiling issue (Lev. 15:18). Now, however, our issues are cleansed. More than that, the Spirit flows from our innermost parts to one another.

Obviously, we "one-another" each other in a variety of ways. A study of the phrase "one another" in the Epistles shows the ways the Spirit flows from us to each other. But the physical expression of this "one flesh" relationship is, as we have seen, eating. We eat Christ, and we kiss one another.

Our relationship to Christ is verbal (the Word) and non-verbal (the sacrament of the Spirit). Our relationship to one another is the same. We speak to one another, and we kiss one another. When the Church restores the holy kiss (men with men; women with women), the Church will regain much spiritual health.

We should not be afraid of the sacraments. Bible-believing Christians (that is, Protestants), speak of the sacraments only as "visible Words." Yet they are not visible, but edible; and they are not primarily words, but the act of the Spirit, which is "groaning too deep to be uttered." The sacraments involve mystical union with Christ.

We want the Word first and sacraments second. This is right in that Christ precedes the Spirit. But sometimes the order is reversed. Sometimes you are not getting along with your spouse. You've been fighting. You barely speak to one another. And of course, you have not been sleeping together in the full sense. A wise counselor tells you, "Go home and go to bed together." Often this physical union has the effect of breaking the logjam of communication, at least to some extent.

The same is true in worship. Sometimes we are so upset about what God has brought into our lives that we do not really hear the sermon. But we can join with Christ in the sacramental meal. We can eat Him into ourselves. We can engage in this "act of love." And that can be the point at which our relationship with Him begins to be restored.

And sometimes we don't get along with each other in the Church. But if we have to kiss each other, we shall be forced to overcome the tension that exists between us.

THE BRIDE-BUILDING

We've been discussing the larger implications of these primordial statements, and this time I want to discuss their architectural implications. The woman was built from the "side" of the man, and we have seen this word often refers to the sides of buildings (and occasionally mountains).

Moreover, she was "built" from his side. This is the only time this verb is used in the creation narrative. The verb is used hundreds of times in the Bible, almost always for building cities, altars, buildings, and the like. The next reference is in Genesis 4:17, where Cain built a city. "City" is feminine and implies that the city is the bride (as the New Jerusalem is Christ's bride). Cain had a son and then built a bride for him, naming them both "Enoch." This shows (a) man as the image of God, having sons and then marrying them off, and (b) Cain as playing God, having a son and then building a bride for him. But we shall eventually get to this verse in our commentary on Genesis 2–4.

Here I want to point out that these verses speak of individual human beings as buildings. We are familiar with this from 1 Corinthians, where our bodies are said to be temples of the Holy Spirit. Here is the first mention of this concept.

The notion that the man and the woman are two separate buildings is carried forward in the Bible in this way: We ordinarily find that men and their wives dwell in separate tents or have separate rooms in the house. It is only when the act of marriage takes place that the woman is taken into the husband's tent/room or he comes to visit her in hers (e.g., Gen. 24:67; Esth. 4:11; Song 3:1–2).

I do not draw from this that it is wrong for husband and wife to sleep in the same large bed night after night. (See below.) But I think we should see that the Bible gives to the wife a considerable property of her own. In a prosperous household, she has her own rooms or tent, her own servants, and so forth. This fact points to the high and somewhat independent place of the woman in a biblical society.

God has His own tent, the Tabernacle, and His own house, the Temple. This is the place where the act of marriage between God and His people should take place. It is no accident that the Temple was built on a threshing floor, the place where Ruth's marriage was arranged (2 Sam. 24:24–25 + 2 Chron. 3:1, and Ruth 3).

In the temples of the pagans, men had sex with sacred prostitutes and women had sex with sacred gigolos. This signified being married to the god of the temple. In biblical religion, there is no such sexual outworking of the analogy. Instead, as we have seen, God eats us and we eat Him.[72] Yahweh eats the sacrifices, which represent us. We and the priests eat various meals made up of the same sacrifices, which represent eating Christ. This is how the "act of marriage" is manifested.

But because of man's sin, God never allowed His bride into His marital bower. The priests might enter the Holy Place only twice a day, morning and evening. Only the High Priest might enter the Holy of Holies, and only once a year, under a threat of death. Clearly, the bride was not ready, not fit for the Divine Husband. God did not eat-marry the sinful people, but only ate-married their animal substitutes, the sacrifices.

Things are different now. The Book of Revelation says that the bride is now fit for the Groom. The New Jerusalem, which is the house/tent/room/city of the bride, is entered by the Groom, who sets His throne there (Revelation 21–22). Here the Marriage Supper of the Lamb takes place week by week. But since the New Jerusalem comes out of heaven, it is also God's house/tent/room/city, and the bride is taken into it. Heaven and earth are one. There is one permanent house/tent/room/city. The age of having a separate tent for the wife and the husband is over.

But in that earlier time, there were two tents. Around the Tabernacle were encamped the tents of the bride-to-be. Each year this encampment was reenacted at the Feast of Tabernacles. The tents/houses of the bride were to be kept holy in a way analogous to the holiness of God's tent/house. Dead animals were to be kept out (Lev. 11). "Leprosy" was to be dealt with (Lev. 14). Annually, all leaven was to be purged for a week (just as no leaven was put on God's altar and no leaven taken into His house). And so forth. But there were still two houses, with a veil between them.

The veil between God's house and the human houses spoke of the fact that the marriage was not yet consummated. See Genesis 24:56, where Rebekah veils herself so that Isaac may remove the veil. We still have this custom in many marriage ceremonies today. The veil represented the firmament boundary-seal over the earth. In the New Jerusalem, that veil is removed, and heaven and earth are one. The virginal seal of the bride of Christ has been pierced at last and the marriage has begun.

---

72. See Revelation 3:16 for a picture of Jesus eating us.

12

THE MARRIAGE OF MAN AND WOMAN

GENESIS 2:23–24

And the man said,

  This time, at last!

  Bone of my bones,

  And flesh of my flesh!

   ᴬ *This one*

    ᴮ *shall be called*

     ᶜ *woman* ['ishshah]*,*

     ᶜ' *For from man* ['ish]

    ᴮ' *was taken*

   ᴬ' *this one* (Gen. 2:23).

EUGEN Rosenstock-Huessy has said that God is the power that compels human beings to speak. Ultimately only the true God can do this, for all the other gods are silent. Thus far in Genesis, God has spoken twelve times (1:3,

6, 9, 11, 14, 20, 22, 24, 26, 28–30; 2:16–17, 18). Now for the first time, man speaks in direct response to God.

To be sure, Adam has been naming and categorizing the animals, reflecting God's work of naming in Genesis 1. But the Bible only tells us *about* this; no actual speech blazes forth from the text. Now, however, Adam is compelled to speak. Words explode from him.

If Adam had merely named the woman, only the second half of his poem would be needed. But God compels speech from Adam that goes beyond merely naming the woman, and this in at least two respects: First, Adam begins with an exclamation, "This, at last!" and follows it up with another exclamation. Second, Adam speaks poetically. His speech takes on an exalted, musical quality, which is what happens when a person is "inspired."[73]

God is the One who brings new things in history. Indeed, history is the record of new things. We don't regard "history" as being produced when people go about the same things they have always done. Rather, "history" moves "forward" when new things come on the scene.

For instance, the separation of church and state in the Middle Ages created something new, something we take for granted now. At the end of the Middle Ages, a few men became discoverers and explorers; now all children play at being explorers. In the nineteenth century a few men became inventors; now all children dream of being inventors. These are new qualities brought out of the human psyche, which after all is as rich and deep as the image of God Himself. Thus, we study the United States Constitution, not all the imitations that came after. All nations now must maintain the pretense of having constitutions. Even the old USSR had one.

God is new every morning, and thus the Christian is future-oriented. Christians must learn to expect new things from God. Christians must not look to the past and try to recover past ways, because God is always bringing new things. The solutions to the problems of today do not lie in the past but in the new things that God will do, which will cause us to burst forth with exclamations of surprise. If we are faithful, we will praise God when we are surprised; if we are unfaithful, we will praise some false god.

Adam had a problem. If he had looked to the past, he would have expected God to give him some special animal as a helper. Instead he was

---

73. For a discussion of these new terms—'ish and 'ishshah—and their relation to the words 'esh (fire) and 'ishsheh (fire-offering), see my, "The Glory of the Man," 177, 181–182.

surprised, because God did a new thing. The animals were indeed helpers, but the woman was a helper *fitted* for the man.

David had a problem. The Tabernacle had been wrecked in Eli's day. If David looked to the past, he would expect the Tabernacle to be set back up. Instead, God revealed the Temple to him, something new and greatly transfigured from the old Tabernacle.

At every point in history, God brings reformation not by restoring old things, but by providing something new that resembles the old but is a transfiguration of it. That is what we must look for today. Those who want to go back to Eastern Orthodoxy, or to seventeenth century Calvinism, are to a serious extent out of touch with the God of the Bible.

When God does His new, surprising work, we are excited and sing. When a man falls in love, he sings and hums and whistles. So does his sweetheart. That is because this is a new and serendipitous thing that has come into their lives. Just so, Adam sings here. The first three lines of his song have two beats each (in Hebrew and in our translation), and the last two lines have three beats each (ditto). Notice also the chiastic structure of the last two lines.

The expression "flesh of flesh, bone of bone" does not refer to marriage but to kinship (Gen. 29:14; Judg. 9:2; and 2 Sam. 19:13—Amasa was David's nephew). Eve was Adam's sister, and we are Jesus' sister, God's daughter to marry His Son. Thus, the Song of Solomon always says "my sister, my bride." But in 2 Samuel 5:1, all the tribes come to David and say that they are his bone and flesh, which indicates kinship by covenant. That is, they are kin, being descended from Jacob, but they choose to make that kinship operative by covenanting with David as king.

Why "flesh and bone"? Some, like Victor Hamilton in his commentary, have suggested that flesh is weakness and bone is strength.[74] I believe it is more to the point that bone is scaffolding and flesh is tent. We have already seen that the woman was "built" architecturally from the man's rib. The curtains and coverings of the Tabernacle correspond to skin and flesh, while the pillars and boards correspond to bones. Man and woman remain two sets of bones, but they become one flesh. Thus, they are naked to each other, and covered by one cloth when the man spreads his garment over the woman.

---

74. Hamilton, *Genesis 1–17*, 179.

One Flesh

For this reason, a man forsakes his father and his mother, and he sticks to
his woman, and they are as one flesh (Gen. 2:24).

This comment is not part of Adam's speech, but is a comment in the word of God on the situation God had brought to pass between the man and the woman.

The biblical concept of marriage is nuclear, not clannish. The woman forsakes her family (Ps. 45:10), but so does the man. Indeed, in Genesis we find that Isaac did not live near Abraham, nor did Jacob live near Isaac. Yet the idea of forsaking does not mandate living apart. What it definitely does mean is that the young man is now the head of his own marriage and family. He is not governed by his father any longer.

The father may still be the political head of the tribe, but not of the new marriage. The man forsakes his father and his mother; that is, he forsakes the old marriage and family. He starts a new marriage and family, independent and separate from the old. Patriarchy and familism are not biblical perspectives.

It is interesting to note that Adam's father was God Himself. We find that God departs the scene here and returns the next day (Gen. 3:8). Even God honors the privacy of the wedding night and honors the relative separation of the new family. He leaves Adam alone with his new wife, to see if Adam will follow what He has taught him. The father instructs his son until the son is married; after that, the son is "on his own," so to speak. When God returns to judge Adam, He returns not as Adam's immediate Father, but as his heavenly Father and Lord.

The custom of having a honeymoon is designed to establish this separation. The young couple goes away from their parents for a while. If they later return to the same locale, they return as a new family in their own right.

The man is to stick or cling to his wife. This is the creation ordinance, and it is important to see what it means. The same word is used with reference to the covenant between God and Israel: The people are to stick or cling to Him (Deut. 4:4; 10:20; 11:22; 30:20).

If a man clings to his wife, he will not be able to commit adultery, for he is stuck to his wife. This clinging does not refer only to mere sexual relations, but to the whole of life. A married person must be careful about his or her affections and friendships with members of the other sex.

If a man clings to his wife, he will not be able to commit sinful divorce.

If a man clings to his wife, he will not be able to commit the sin of bigamy or polygamy. Note that polygamy is outlawed from the beginning. It is never permitted in the Bible. It is always an evil situation, usually entered through sin.[75] But if you sinfully chop off your arm, you don't get a new arm when you repent; and if you sinfully take a second wife, you're going to have to live with two wives.

The Bible goes so far as to say that if a man visits a prostitute, she becomes his wife, implying surely that he has responsibility for her from that time on (1 Cor. 6:16).

Along these lines, notice that the helper suited to the man is a woman, not an animal. Bestiality is prohibited by Genesis 2.

Notice as well that the helper is not another man. Homosexual relationships are also forbidden by Genesis 2. I mention these two things because many people think that not until the Mosaic law, in Leviticus 18 and 20, do we find a prohibition on homosexuality. Not so. It is clearly outlawed as a creation ordinance.

SEPARATION AND REJOINING

Recall that Genesis 2:4–3:24 are a microcosmic recapitulation of the seven days of creation. Chapter 2:18–24 is the "sixth day," when animals are brought to Adam, and Eve is made. There are some things that emerge from a literary analysis of this unit that we should notice.

This section is not a chiasm, but rather an example of straight parallelism. We can gain wisdom and insight from examining the parallels.

The opening statement stands alone: "And Yahweh God said, "It is not good for the man to be alone; I will make him a helper suitable for him."

Then follow two parallel paragraphs. In both paragraphs, God forms something and brings it to the man, the man names it, and then there is a separation. The point that is not usually noticed is the parallel between Eve's separation from Adam and a man's separation from his parents.

---

75. The exception is Jacob, who was contractually married to Rachel, but who acquired Leah by being tricked into lying with her.

Let us now lay out the parallels:

[19] And *Yahweh God formed* from the ground every beast of the field and every bird of the heavens,	[22] And *Yahweh God built* the side that He took from the man into woman,
and *brought* to the man to see what he would call them; and whatever the man called a living being, that was its name.	and *He brought* her to the man.
[20] And the man *called names* to all the cattle, and to the birds of the heavens, and to every beast of the field, but as for the man there was not found a helper suitable for him.	[23] And the man said, "This time, at last! Bone of my bones, and flesh of my flesh! This one shall be *called* woman, for from man was taken this one."
[21] And Yahweh God caused to fall a deep-sleep upon the man, and he slept. And He *took one of his sides,*	[24] For this reason, a man *forsakes* his father and his mother, and he sticks to his woman,
and He closed the *flesh* in its place.	and they are as one *flesh.*

There are two "new" things to notice from the parallelism. First is the reiteration of the word "flesh." There is a paradox here, in that the woman is taken from the man's flesh and then his flesh is closed up, sealing him off from the woman and her from him, as unique and separate persons; but then the two are said to be as one flesh. There is separation and then a rejoining.

Second, the parallels cause us to meditate upon childbearing. A child emerges from his mother's flesh, and then is cut off from her when the umbilical cord is cut. Before that, the child comes into being through the marital union of his father and mother. Yet, the child remains united to his mother's flesh through nursing, and after weaning continues to be part of his parents' "flesh" in the larger sense of being in their family.

With this in mind, we can rightly say that a man "sleeps" in the flesh of his mother and father until he awakens when he marries. And since the woman is taken from the man, the same is true of her, as the story of the Sleeping Beauty affirms.[76]

We noted earlier that a man as well as a woman leaves his old family behind when he marries, a doctrine that strikes a death blow to all "patriarchy." We can now see further dimensions of this teaching. When a man and a woman "sleep" together, then from their "sides" a new person emerges. When the son or daughter leaves to be married, God closes up the flesh of the parents and seals them off from the new marriage.

---

76. And while she sleeps, a "forest" grows around her "castle," which is penetrated on her wedding night, an obvious allegory that is properly expressed in the story by her being awakened by a loving kiss.

13

Naked and Not Shamed

Genesis 2:25

Now the two of them were naked, the man and his woman, and they did
not sense shame (Gen. 2:25).

WHILE this statement follows from the previous statement that the man
and woman were to become one flesh, and thus be shamelessly naked to one
another, it actually begins the next paragraph, which ends with the addition
of shame to their nakedness (3:7). Thus, this sentence should actually begin
Genesis 3 instead of ending Genesis 2.

Moreover, in terms of the literary structure of this section of Genesis,
this statement begins the seventh event, corresponding to the seventh day
of creation.[77] From here to the end of chapter 3 is the broken sabbath of
humanity. Because of sin, mankind did not enter into God's sabbath and thus
could not set out on the course of working toward their own sabbath. Only

---

77. See chapter 7, in the section with the heading "The Gentile Sea."

when Jesus ascended into heaven did God's people enter into God's own rest and in union with Christ also enter into the rest Adam would have enjoyed had he persevered in faithfulness.

In other words, God entered His rest after His week and invited humanity into His rest. After the second week, so to speak, Adam would have entered into a secondary, but real, human rest, as his works were approved by God. Thus, the third week of human existence would have sprung jointly from Divine rest and the rest of God's image. The third week (and third hour, third day, third month, third year) sequence encountered so many other times in the Bible finds an implied foundation here in Genesis 1–3.

Jesus (a) satisfied God's wrath for the breaking of His sabbath by Adam and (b) completed the faithful patience that Adam broke, thus bringing humanity (a) back into God's sabbath rest and (b) into human rest as well. See Romans 5.

As we enter into Genesis 3, all of which happens on the sabbath day (the day after Adam and Eve were created), it may be important to note that there is another shadow of the creation sequence in this section of Genesis, though unlike the two previous sequences, we do not find specific discourse boundary markers here. This shadow, unlike the shadow sequence of Genesis 2, is not a positive specification of God's creative work, but a negative judgment upon it. To wit:

Day 1: God makes light.
>Genesis 2: The empty, formless earth is given a light, humanity (2:4–7).
>Genesis 3: The eyes of Adam and Eve are opened (3:7a).[78]

Day 2: God makes the firmament chamber between heaven and earth.
>Genesis 2: God makes the Garden-sanctuary (2:8).
>Genesis 3: Adam and Eve put a separation (clothing // firmament) between them (3:7b–10); compare the layers of cloth between Yahweh and Israel at the Tabernacle.

Day 3: God makes land, and trees and grain.
>Genesis 2: Trees grow out of the garden; centrality of the garden (2:9–14).

---

78. Cf. Matthew 6:22: "The lamp of the body is the eye; if, therefore, your eye is clear, your whole body will be full of light." This passage will be discussed in more detail in chapter 18.

Genesis 3: God comes to the Garden and accuses them of eating from the forbidden tree (3:11).

Day 4: God establishes heavenly lights to rule.
Genesis 2: Adam established as ruler (2:15).
Genesis 3: Adam, and then Eve, renounces ruling authority (3:12–13).

Day 5: God creates swarms and sea monsters, commanding and blessing them.
Genesis 2: God commands Adam regarding trees and threatens a curse (2:16–17).
Genesis 3: God curses the serpent (3:14–15).

Day 6: God creates animals and humanity, blessing them with (a) fruitfulness and (b) food from the soil.
Genesis 2: God establishes community between men and animals, and between man and woman (2:18–24).
Genesis 3: God diminishes the blessing of (a) fruitfulness and (b) food from the soil (3:16–19).

Day 7: God enters His rest.
Genesis 2–3: Adam and Eve are united, but fail to enter God's rest, and make clothes for themselves.
Genesis 3: Adam and Eve are reunited, and God makes clothes for them (3:20–21). Then God excludes them from His sabbath (3:22–24).

JUDGMENT UPON THE CREATION

As we have seen, Genesis 3 parallels Genesis 1 and 2 in structure. Let us proceed a bit farther and notice that once again we have a chiastic structure in these events, which helps us grasp the theology of the passage more fully. To wit:

1. Adam and Eve are at rest with God and united with one another as one flesh. Their sin brings about disunity (2:25–3:7a).

2. The disunity is signified by the barrier of clothing they place between each other and between themselves and God, and they flee from the blessed presence of God (3:7b–10).

3. God accuses them of eating from the forbidden tree (3:11).

    4. The height of disunity is seen as Adam blames God and Eve, and both humans reject their position as heavenly rulers over the earth (3:12–13).

5. God curses the serpent to eat dust (3:14–15).

    6. God's judgment upon the woman and the man signifies that they are no longer to experience the same kind of blessed nearness to Him and that they are alienated from Him (3:16–19).

7. Adam and Eve are excluded from God's sabbath, but they are reunited with each other and God gives them clothing (3:20–24).

By linking the structure of Genesis 3 to the structures of Genesis 1 and 2, we can see that a major theme of Genesis 3 is that of disunity or alienation. It is not merely a matter of judgment upon humanity for disobedience that is in focus here, nor is it punishment in general. Rather, the punishment is specifically related to the blessings of Genesis 1 and 2, the blessing of a free relationship with God and the blessing of close and productive relationships in this world. The immediate consequence of sin is alienation from God and social alienation, and this alienation is made fully visible at the heart of the passage. Then it is partially healed as the passage moves toward its conclusion.

God had joined humanity to Himself. Adam alienated that relationship, but God put it back together in a preliminary way by making an animal skin for Adam and Eve.

God had joined Adam and Eve. That relationship was completely broken and alienated, but God put it back together in a preliminary way by making the woman desire her husband (3:16b).

God had joined Adam to the world as gardener. Adam had destroyed that relationship, but God put it back together in a preliminary way by saying that the soil would indeed yield fruits to Adam, but only through his sweat. Adam would have to water the soil with his own sweat and eventually feed it with his own dead body (3:19).

Finally, and in a slightly different vein, God had joined Adam to the world as shepherd over the animals. Adam had perverted that relationship by identifying with the animals and rejecting God. God healed that perversion slightly by putting enmity between the serpent and the woman, announcing that the Seed of the woman would restore dominion over the animals by crushing the serpent. All difficulties between human beings and animals are reminders that we must not identify with them but rule over them. The difficulties force us to rule over them, whether we want to or not; otherwise, they will eat us.

Note that those who try to eat of the Tree of Rule are cursed to eat dust (points 3 and 5 above). Human beings who identify with animals (as idolaters and environmentalists do) and who reject the call to rule over them will receive the curse placed upon the serpent.

Sin, thus, is not only a matter of rebellion against God and estrangement from God. It has the immediate effect of estranging us from one another, from the animal realm, and from the physical cosmos. Thus, salvation cannot merely be a matter of "me and Jesus." The hyper-individualism of post-Reformation theology must be corrected on this point. Salvation means the community of the Church, the restoration of "nakedness" between those who are in Christ, signified by the holy kiss (men with men, women with women). Salvation also restores us to a right relationship with animals and the cosmos. Where this restored community is not present, neither is a true relationship with God.

NAKEDNESS

The nakedness of Adam and Eve requires several comments. First of all, against those who think that nakedness is what God intended for humanity as a permanent estate, we have to notice that God Himself is robed in a glory cloud whenever He appears in the Bible. Human beings, as the images of God, would also wear garments of glory and beauty. After all, we do not dress only to cover our private parts. We wear clothes of color and design (beauty) to express ourselves, signify our office or work, and to impress others (glory). Eventually, Adam and Eve would also wear garments for these purposes. When they became "like God" in the fuller sense, they would, like God, be robed in office and glory.

Second, Adam was naked because he was a newborn baby. As we have seen, the concept of the "knowledge of good and evil" is associated with the robe of office, of rule and authority. Adam did not yet have the capacity for this. He was a newborn babe, partaking only of milk, as Paul writes in Hebrews 5:13–14. The fact that Adam sinned as a baby, and not as a mature adult having full knowledge of the truth, is what made it possible for God to redeem him (Gen. 3:22; Heb. 6:4–6).

Third, Adam and Eve were naked to each other because they were married. The married couple are clothed together in one garment, not two separate ones. There were no barriers between them because they were not ashamed before one another. If a married couple cannot get openly naked with each other, there is a problem that needs to be resolved.

Once Adam and Eve had sinned, they felt shame before God (and so they hid from Him) and before one another (and so they created clothing to put a barrier between themselves). Formerly they had been surrounded together by leaves. Now each makes his own garment. Formerly they walked openly in the garden. Now they hide from God under the leaves of a tree.

A sense of shame and guilt is a tremendous barrier to proper sexuality. The sectarian forms of Christianity, such as Orthodoxy and Roman Catholicism, have a major problem with sexuality precisely because these religions do not have a proper doctrine of justification. They are never able to assure people that they are clear before God. As a result, they affirm such perversions as the perpetual virginity of Mary, require clerical celibacy, and grossly misinterpret the Song of Solomon. Suppressed sexuality finds an outlet in annual chaos festivals like Mardi Gras and in rampant prostitution. Sexual bliss between married couples is regarded as dangerous and must always be linked with procreation. In paganism, the perversion of sexuality is even worse. Only in Protestant countries can there be any significant recovery of the liberation of sexual joy in marriage.

When God interviewed Adam, the man said that he was afraid because he was naked and therefore hid himself. Clothing is a barrier, and thus reduces fear. Lecturers prefer usually to stand behind a podium because it protects them from their hearers, whom they fear. Only an accomplished speaker can do without one.

God asked, "Who told you that you were naked?" (3:11). This question, in a sense, is rhetorical. It seems to mean, "So what if you are naked?" If anybody had told Adam that he was naked, it was God Himself. So why should Adam fear God? Adam's problem was not that he was naked, but that he was estranged from God. Thus, God moves Adam away from his false excuse to the real issue: "Did you eat from the tree of which I commanded you not to eat?"

Using nakedness as an excuse for estrangement from God is mankind's universal response. Human beings will not admit that sin is the issue. They want to make nakedness the issue. Practically, this means that people blame their powerlessness for their problems. They see themselves as victims, powerless, naked, instead of as sinners. They say that they cannot face the world because they don't have money or strength, instead of admitting that they are sinners before God who need forgiveness. They want power, not forgiveness. Thus, those who have power and money always want more; they can never have enough, because deep down inside they feel naked before the omnipresent God.

Shame is not guilt. Shame means a feeling of weakness and impotence. But why do we feel that way? We say it is because we do not have enough power, enough clothing—that is, because we are naked. But God says we feel that way because we are alienated from Him and we need forgiveness. Then, even if we are poor and "naked," we shall not be ashamed.

Sinners try to cover their shame (impotence) by accumulating power and wealth. They hope that they can play the same game with God, accumulating good deeds so that they can appear before God clothed and negotiate with Him. But God does not play this game, because shame is not the issue. Sin is the issue. We must come before God in our shame, nakedness, and impotence, and receive salvation as a completely free gift. Then our shame can be removed completely, and we can rejoice with Him and face the world unafraid.

GUILT, DEATH, AND SHAME

In the previous section, I discussed shame in terms of impotence. Now, I want to explore the concept of shame more fully. In his book, *Naked and Not Ashamed*, Lowell Noble writes:

> Insight into the meaning of shame can be gained by contrasting it with honor. Honor and shame are two sides of the same coin. Dishonor is a synonym of shame. Honor refers to upright character, integrity, glory. While honor may be involved in acts of right and wrong, it goes far beyond what the law requires. Honor involves the integrity of one's being in the way he lives and in the way he respects others.

The loss of honor is disgraceful, shameful. Therefore, a person attempts to cover up, to hide, so as to avoid painful exposure. The shameless person has no sense of honor; he engages in disgraceful behavior openly.

Even though there is a painful negative element in an experience of shame, the importance of shame must not be restricted to the negative aspect. An experience of shame exposes what is wrong with the goal of showing what is right and moving a person in that direction. A person can refuse to move towards honorable behavior and again revert to hiding behind his mask to try to cover his shame. The function of anticipated shame is to keep a person doing that which is honorable. Anticipated shame serves as a powerful force for social control.[79]

As Noble notes, shame involves loss of glory. In the Bible, glory is beautiful clothing; consider the glory cloud around God. Thus, when a person loses glory or "face" and experiences shame, he moves instantly to cover or re-cover himself as fast as possible.

Since the glory covering exists as people as well as physical clothing (as the glory cloud around God consists of myriads of angels and saints), a person loses glory or face when he is betrayed and/or abandoned by those around him. If he is excommunicated from the Church, or otherwise isolated, he must act to find a new social group to act as his clothing. Thus Cain, expelled from God's community, went forth and created a city for himself. Thus those who leave the true Church become active in founding or promoting false ones.[80]

Shame also involves the loss of a sense of integrity. Integrity is the inner side (what Noble calls "honor"), while glory is the outer side.[81] The biblical word for integrity is "holiness." God is holy (has integrity), and so we must be holy as He is holy. Holiness does not mean "set apartness," because it makes no sense for God to command, "You be set apart as I am set apart." Rather, holiness means inner integrity, both the metaphysical integrity of being a

---

79. Lowell L. Noble, *Naked and Not Ashamed: An Anthropological, Biblical, and Psychological Study of Shame* (self-published, 1975), 7.

80. For example, virtually every apostate Calvinist I have ever known who has gone into Rome or Orthodoxy immediately became involved in apologetical labors designed to win others to his newfound heresy. This is an act of self-justification designed to cover up the shame of abandoning the truth.

81. Note that the priests of Israel were dressed in holy linen garments under their outer garments of glory.

unique person and being personally inviolate and the moral integrity of being in conformity to God's image.

Thus, when a person's integrity is violated, he feels shame. If his beard is torn off, or if his clothing is ripped, or if people praise others more than they do him, he loses glory and feels shame (2 Sam. 10:4–5; 1 Sam. 15:27–30 [Samuel tore Saul's robe here]; 1 Sam. 18:6–9). If his or her body is raped (2 Sam. 13:12–19), or his house is broken into and robbed, or if he commits a sin, or if he does a poor job of something, he loses integrity and feels shame.

Both sides of this experience (loss of glory, loss of integrity) are expressed by the term "nakedness." A person feels naked and exposed if any of these things happen to him. Thus, in Leviticus, it is a violation of a person's holiness to expose his or her nakedness. Forbidden sexual invasions of another person's body defile holiness and expose nakedness.

When we feel naked and ashamed, we can do either of two things. We can draw close to God and let Him restore our inner integrity, so that we feel clothed and confident in our new situation, or we can try to re-cover ourselves, try to keep with the old situation by getting our glory back.

Consider an example. When the people sang, "Saul has slain his thousands, but David his myriads," Saul lost glory and felt burning shame. He could have gone before God, poured out his heart, and adjusted to the new situation. Then he would have felt good that God had given him a young warrior—indeed, his adopted son—to help the kingdom. He would have recovered a sense of personhood and worth—integrity—and would not have felt ashamed and exposed. But this is not what Saul chose to do. Instead, he tried to kill David and thereby get the original glory back for himself. He tried to turn the clock back, instead of moving into God's future.

Oddly enough, we feel shame sometimes even when we have done nothing wrong. Ravished women, for instance, usually feel intense shame. Why is this? It is because we are sinners; that is, we carry original sin, basic sin, in our inner parts (flesh) always. When we are overcome with guiltless shame, this is a sign that we need to "make our calling and election sure" by returning to the fact that we are fully justified. "There is therefore now no condemnation"—no shame—"to those who are in Christ Jesus" (Rom. 8:1). God graciously provides times of guiltless shame in order to draw us closer to Him, so that we become more secure in the knowledge of our justified position with Him.

When God restores us, He first declares us just before Him (justification), and then restores our holiness and integrity (sanctification), in order that He might then give us glory and glorious covering (glorification). Sinful man, however, seeks glory without first seeking justification and sanctification (integrity).

To seek one's own glory results in that glory's turning into shame (Hos. 4:7; Jer. 9:23–24 + 1 Cor. 1:26–29). This is what happened to Adam and Eve. The Tree of Knowledge, as we have seen, is the Tree of Eldership, Rule, and Glory. By seizing it, they sought their own glory and found only shame. Instead of drawing near to God, admitting fault, and receiving integrity from Him in their new situation, they tried to re-cover themselves. The Garden had been their common garment, and they sought to reinforce that covering with the leaves of the trees of the Garden. Thus, *they sought to deal with shame without dealing with guilt and sin.* When God slew an animal and gave them animal skin to clothe them, He was moving them into a new future. God dealt with their guilt and provided glory to them, but a new glory—a new covering appropriate to their new situation.

As we have seen, the Bible has a huge amount to say about shame, and we have only touched on it here. Paul writes, "All have sinned and fallen short of the glory of God" (Rom. 3:23). He did not write, "fallen short of the righteousness of God." Paul refers back to Adam and Eve and to the basic problem of integrity and glory.

Our theology deals largely with justification and sanctification and hardly at all with glorification. We tend to postpone glorification until the resurrection. This is a serious defect in our theology, which blinds us to a great deal that is in the Bible. Consider the following three lists of terms and concepts:

Justification	*Sanctification*	*Glorification*
Legal	Moral	Personal
Right standing	Right behavior	No shame
Guilt	Corruption	Glory, praise, influence
Condemnation	Death	Exposure of nakedness
Righteousness	Life	Holiness (integrity)
Justified in God's court	Sanctified by God's Spirit	Glorified with God's garment
The *Son*	The *Spirit*	The *Father*

Thus, shame is not the root but the fruit of sin. Shame is pain that alerts us that something is wrong, but we must not try to deal directly with shame by trying to re-cover ourselves and recover our glory. Rather, we must deal with our guilt and sin, and then the shame is removed, enabling us to move into a *new* life-situation.

When we sin, as did Adam, we feel condemned, and we experience a sense of death (loss of life). This leads to a feeling of nakedness. When a person was condemned to death in Israel, his dead body was exposed naked on a tree for the birds to eat (Gal. 3:13; 2 Sam. 21). Nakedness, thus, comes after death.

Adam tried to deal with his sin by covering his shame. That did not work. His next step would have been to try to deal with his sin by getting life from the Tree of Life. God prevented this also, because it also would have been a false way of dealing with the problem. Adam needed to deal with his guilt and receive forgiveness. Then he would be admitted to the Tree of Life (to which he was pointed in the beginning) and eventually be led to the Tree of Greater Glory.

The grave error of Eastern Orthodoxy is that it seeks to provide glory for sinners without providing a sound judicial basis. Orthodoxy covers shame with glorious robes and beautiful, iconic-community filled churches. But because there is no judicial theology in Orthodoxy—no doctrine of justification by faith alone—their glory remains purely aesthetic and decorative. They make no real cultural impact.

The grave error of Roman Catholicism is that it seeks to provide sanctification and life for sinners without a sound judicial basis. Catholicism focuses on death and life, filling its churches with bleeding crucifixes and statues. Catholicism moves to the Tree of Life without first settling the issue of guilt and forgiveness. As a result, the life that Catholicism promises through the sacraments, and the morality it enjoins on its people, falls flat and does not work.

Only Protestantism, with its sound transactional and judicial theology, can provide a proper basis for both life and glory. For this reason, Protestantism has provided the greatest new power and cultural impact (life and glory), in spite of the fact that Lutheranism does not have a well-developed doctrine of life and sanctification and in spite of the fact that Calvinism does not have a well-developed doctrine of shame and glorification.

THE STRUCTURE OF GENESIS 2:25–3:7A

As we have seen, the narrative of the fall of mankind begins and ends with statements about nakedness. Humanity moved from shameless nakedness to shameful nakedness. A striking aspect of this, hidden from English readers, is the fact that the word "crafty" ('arum) is almost identical in Hebrew to the word "naked" ('arummim, from the root 'arom). Thus, the craftiness of the serpent is, by means of this God-ordained pun, associated with nakedness. Humanity loses the sinless nakedness that God gave us and adopts the crafty nakedness of the serpent.

The passage has seven sections, which are chiastically arranged, to wit:

1. Shameless nakedness (2:25).
2. Crafty "nakedness" of serpent (3:1a).
3. Serpent asks about eating (3:1b).
4. Woman speaks of death (3:2–3).
5. Serpent promises about eating (3:4–5).
6. False wisdom sought: serpent's "crafty *nakedness*" (3:6).
7. Shameful nakedness (3:7a).

At the center of the passage is God's statement that eating the fruit of the Tree of Knowledge will lead to death and Satan's open contradiction of God's warning. God's warning was phrased as a series of "not" commands, and Satan's contradiction is stated the same way. This is indicated by the typefaces below.

1. *Nakedness*
   2:25 Now the two of them were naked ('*arummim*), the man and his woman, and they did not sense shame.
2. *Serpent's nature*
   3:1 And the serpent: He was crafty ('*arum*), more than all the beasts of the field that Yahweh God made.
3. *Serpent speaks*
   And he said to the woman, "Indeed, did God really say, 'NOT shall you eat from any tree of the garden'?"
4. *Woman speaks*

² And the woman said to the serpent, "From the fruit of the trees
of the garden we may eat. ³ And from the fruit of the tree
that is in the center of the garden, God said, 'NOT shall you
eat from it, and NOT shall you touch it, or YOU WILL DIE"

5. *Serpent speaks*

⁴ And the serpent said to the woman, "NOT DYING YOU SHALL DIE.
⁵ For God is knowing that in the day of your eating from it
your eyes will be opened
and you will be like God, knowing good and evil."

6. *Humanity adopts serpent's nature*

⁶ And the woman saw
that good was the tree for food,
and that pleasant was it to the eyes,
and desirable was the tree for gaining wisdom,
and she took from its fruit,
and she ate,
and she gave also to her husband with her,
and he ate.

7. *Nakedness*

⁷ᵃ And the eyes of both of them were opened,
and they knew that they were naked.

14

THE SERPENT'S TEMPTATION

GENESIS 3:1–5

And the serpent: He was crafty, more than all the beasts of the field that
Yahweh God made (Gen. 3:1a).

ADAM'S first educational event occurred when God brought the beasts of
the field and the birds of the sky for him to examine and name (2:19). From
this examination Adam learned that he was unlike the animals: He was alone.
Based on analogy with the animals, Adam could reason that he needed a
female complement. At that point, God provided this complement.

Adam's first course of education came in the area of "dressing" the
Garden. He needed a helper suited to him. The animals were indeed helpers,
but not the helper peculiarly fit for him as a partner in dominion.[82]

----

82. In "Liturgical Man, Liturgical Woman," *Rite Reasons* 86 (May 2004), online: http://www.
biblicalhorizons.com/rite-reasons/no-86-liturgical-man-liturgical-women-part-1/ or https://

Now comes Adam's second course of education. Once again, God providentially brought an animal to him. This second animal test was in the area of "guarding" the Garden. Adam would need to resist the animal's words and affirm his God-given dominion over the animals.

The first course showed Adam that he could learn from the animals about his dominion task in the world. The second course was to show Adam that he could not learn from animals about ethics and his relationship with God.

Animals are the highest point of "nature." Throughout history, pagans have asserted that we learn *everything* from nature. Nature, we are told, shows us how to live rightly. Arguments from nature show what is true about God. Generally, this information goes by the name "natural law."

Christianity has sought to tame this "natural law" approach. This endeavor has proven problematic. Very often, "natural law" information, mediated through paganism (particularly Greek and Roman sources), has been used to add to what God has spoken in His Word concerning ethics and our relationship to Him. Indeed, "natural law" has been allowed to lead Christians to disobey Scripture altogether. For instance, from the Greeks the Eastern Church learned (falsely) that information coming through the eye is more certain than information coming through language. Thus, they hold that icons and pictures are a more certain mode of communication to and from God than is the Bible. Icons come first and are for everybody, while the Bible is only for the educated. Or, to take another example, the Roman Catholic Church bans all use of contraception on the basis of supposed "natural law."

Genesis 2 and 3 provide a corrective and a rebuke to those who use nature this way. There is a great deal we can learn from nature and from animals, but not in the area of ethics and of our relationship with God. In that area, we are to take God's Word and only God's Word as our guide.

The issue is clearly joined in Genesis 3. God had spoken, and now the serpent ("natural law") speaks. The serpent flatly contradicts God's command and then twists what God said to fit it into a new framework.

The eschatological development of humanity has meant that this issue has become more subtle and involved since the first encounter of Eve with the serpent. The crafty serpent has become more and more crafty. Ancient pagans went forth and made gods directly in the image of animals and served the wolf or the bear or the eagle. With the coming of the latter days, philosophy emerged in the world to war against the prophets God raised up at this time (the time of the Babylonian Captivity to the destruction of Jerusalem). Philosophy took "nature" as a whole and created far more comprehensive forms of nature-worship. Greek Philosophy, Buddhism, and the Tao, for instance, emerged at this time. In the Christian Era, the issue has become more subtle still, with the development of "natural law" theologies in the Eastern and Roman Churches.

Our Protestant fathers reasserted the supremacy of the Bible, but then all too often turned naively to Greek and Roman sources for notions of human society. Human beings are not animals but are images of God. Thus, from a Christian standpoint, human society must be ordered by the Word of God and not by "nature." I believe Calvin saw this rather clearly, but until Rushdoony virtually nobody operated self-consciously in terms of it.

We can see things in nature that correspond to biblical teachings. Perhaps in some animals, the male will lay down his life to defend his mate. But we don't learn the principle that the husband should die for his wife from the animals; we learn it from Ephesians 5 and then we see an example of it in the case of particular animals. Similarly, we must not learn law and ethics from Cicero but from the Bible. If Cicero said something true, that is all well and good, but it is only an example, not an authority.

By bringing the serpent to Adam, God teaches us a lesson that the Church has been learning over and over for millennia and that she has not yet fully learned. We must not try to learn ethics from the lower creation. Matters of right and wrong, which always ultimately concern our relationship with God, must be determined by God's Word and His Word alone.

---

theopolisinstitute.com/liturgical-man-liturgical-women-part-1/, I expanded the view presented here and argued that the help Adam needed was not primarily in the area of dominion but rather in the area of worship: "We have to note that the context is the Garden of Eden, the first sanctuary, wherein were placed two sacramental trees. The setting is not the land or the wider world. If it were, then the idea would be that the woman is needed to help with various dominion tasks— which is indeed partly true, but secondary and not the point of the passage. The point of the passage is that animals could not help Adam worship God in the sanctuary. Adam needed a liturgical helper, someone who could join him in liturgical speech and action."

THE COMING OF THE SERPENT

And the serpent: He was crafty, more than all the beasts of the field that Yahweh God made (Gen. 3:1a).

Several aspects of this statement call for brief comment. First, the verse states that Yahweh God made the serpent. Modern commentators pretty universally take this statement as directed against any kind of autonomy for evil powers. That is, Moses writes with paganism in mind and wants his people to know that God's enemies are not self-existent like God Himself but are mere creatures of God in revolt against Him. While unquestionably this is a valid use or application of the statement found here, it imports into the text considerations that are not patently there.

I suggest that the phrase "that Yahweh God made" is included for at least two purposes. One, it shows that the serpent is not self-existent but is a creature of God in revolt against Him. But this is not said with the foil of paganism as its background. Rather, it is to show that no autonomy is possible for any creature. Adam will seek autonomy by following the advice of a clearly non-autonomous creature, an act of supreme folly.[83]

And two, the phrase indicates that the serpent's approach to Adam and Eve was part of Yahweh God's plan. Yahweh God had brought animals to Adam to name. Now, though He does not bring the serpent, Yahweh God allows the serpent to challenge His word as part of His pedagogy and test of Adam. Had this phrase been omitted from the text, it might appear that it was only accidental that the serpent appeared to test Adam.

Second, the serpent is one of the beasts of the field. He is not compared with all animals in general, nor is he positioned with the cattle. To understand the importance of this we go back to Genesis 2:19–20, where God brought birds and beasts to Adam, and Adam named cattle, birds, and beasts. The contrast makes it clear that the cattle were already present with Adam in the Garden. Indeed, as Hirsch points out, the word for cattle, *behemah*, is related to the word for seat or throne, *bamah*, in that domestic animals form a throne for

---

83. Adam's belief in his own autonomy is seen in his failure to go to the Tree of Life first; he assumed that he possessed life in himself and did not need to seek it through the medium of God-given food.

human life.[84] Humanity will eventually tame all wild animals, converting them from beasts to cattle, but in the beginning there were these two categories.

Thus, the serpent does not properly dwell in the domestic arrangement of the Garden. He is, therefore, an invader. He comes from the outside. Later on, one of the characteristics of unclean animals in Leviticus 11 is that they swarm into the home from outside and thus break the boundary. As a boundary-breaker, the serpent leads Adam into breaking the law-boundary God has established. And so again, later on in the Law the breaking of geographical boundaries is regularly linked symbolically to the breaking of moral boundaries.

Third, the tempter is an animal. As we have seen, God has already used animals to teach Adam, and so the use of an animal here is not surprising. But more generally, we are told that the Law was given by angels, and that angels were the tutors of humanity in our childhood (Gal. 3:19; 4:2; Acts 7:53; Heb. 2:2). The angels used animals to teach us, as we see from the sacrificial system, the laws of unclean animals, the proverbs, and other matters as well, such as David's killing the bear and the lion as preparation for his warriorship and kingship. Thus, for Satan as Arch-cherub to use an animal to mis-teach and mislead Adam is entirely in keeping with the situation God had set up.

Fourth, the tempter is a serpent. Here again, modern commentators often seek to try and relate this to snake-cults in the ancient world and assume that Moses is attacking them by positioning the serpent as evil. This approach is to be rejected. In Genesis 1:21 we read that God *created* the great sea monsters (*tannin*). The verb "create" implies a wondrous work. Job 40:15–24 and 41:1– 34 describe Behemoth and Leviathan in language that fits the use of this verb. Behemoth, a land dinosaur, is "first of the ways of God" (Job 40:19) and as for the aquatic dinosaur Leviathan, "nothing of dust is like him" (Job 41:33).[85]

Now, from Genesis 1 it appears that land dinosaurs and serpents were made on the sixth day, but clearly land dinosaurs are linked with water dinosaurs (as in Job 40–41). The word for serpent, *nachash*, is linked with the word for dinosaur, *tannin*, in Isaiah 27:1: "In that day Yahweh will punish

---

84. Hirsch, *Genesis*, 29.

85. The suggestion that Behemoth and Leviathan were the hippopotamus and crocodile is ridiculous on the face of it—just read the text of Job. Moreover, every ancient world culture has stories and iconography of dragons and dinosaurs. Clearly they were around for some time after the Flood.

Leviathan the fleeing serpent with His fierce and great and mighty sword, even Leviathan the twisted *serpent*; and He will kill the *dinosaur* that is in the sea."

We should also note that the word for serpent, *nachash*, is also the word for bronze, thus associating the shining scaly skin of the serpent with shining metal.

From this we see that the choice of the land serpent, or land dinosaur, is entirely appropriate. It was the greatest of the land animals, and its appearance shines like the angels it represented. Because the curse on the serpent in Genesis 1 is to crawl on its belly, we may assume that the serpent who approached Adam and Eve walked upright as many of the dinosaurs did (though being newly created, it was probably not as large as some of them grew to be). The best picture I can imagine is of Adam and Eve conversing with a man-sized dinosaur standing erect on its hind legs like an allosaur.

Fifth, Adam and Eve would not be surprised to hear the dinosaur speak, because they had no background of experience to the contrary. For all they knew, all animals could speak.

To the Woman

And he [the serpent] *said to the woman...* (Gen. 3:1b).

Adam and Eve were together at the two trees. The statement in Genesis 3:6 that the woman gave "to her husband with her, and he ate," can only mean that Adam was present during the conversation. The phrase "with her" is meaningless otherwise. Moreover, the paragraph that narrates the fall is bookended by the statement in 2:24, "and the man and his wife were both naked and were not ashamed," and 3:7, "and the eyes of them both were opened and they knew that they were naked." From this structure we also see that Adam was present throughout the event.

Why did the serpent address the woman? Why didn't the serpent address Adam? There are several aspects or dimensions to the answer to this question.

First, the serpent knew that Adam had heard the command directly from God, while Eve had heard of it from Adam. God had spoken to Adam and Eve together and had told them that all the trees were for them to eat. Thus, the serpent could play on a possible confusion in Eve's mind. The Greater Speaker had told her that all the trees were for eating, while the lesser speaker had told her that before she was made, God had excepted the Tree of Knowledge. Eve would have been more impressed with God than with Adam. The serpent subtly asked her to choose between the two. Of course, if Adam had done his job and intervened, things would doubtless have gone differently; but he did not do so.

Second, the serpent could see from Genesis 2 that man is primordial while woman is eschatological. The man comes first and thus is initiator and teacher; the woman comes last and thus is receiver and glorifier. The Bible fills this out at length: Humanity starts in Adam and re-starts in the Last Adam, but ends as Bride. By replacing Adam as teacher, Satan could pervert the destiny of humanity. The Bride would become his, made in his likeness, instead of Adam's and God's, made in their likeness.

Thus, the serpent acts to seduce Eve with a view to perverting her descendants and creating his own eschaton. Spiritual seduction, and spiritual bestiality, is exactly what Paul calls this in 2 Corinthians 11:2–3: "For I am jealous for you with a godly jealousy; for I betrothed you to one Husband, that to the Messiah I might present you a pure virgin; but I am afraid, lest as the serpent deceived Eve by his craftiness, your minds should be led astray from the simplicity and purity to the Messiah." Notice that Paul mixes the language of sexuality and of thinking. By following the serpent's line of thought, Eve was seduced by the serpent. As a result, her offspring would be guided by the serpent and would be his seed. This came true in Cain, Esau, and many others. It took God's intervention, later in this passage, to make possible a godly seed as well.

Third, these events imply something that is a disputed theological point. I believe that the Second Person of the Trinity was destined to be born into the world whether humanity sinned or not. There is nothing humiliating about God's becoming a man. Humanity is the most glorious aspect of God's glorious creation. Putting on the creation, by putting on human flesh, would be like putting on a glorious robe that you have made for yourself. Humanity's destiny was always to mature into a Bride for the Son. If we don't say this, then (a) we denigrate the creation and (b) we are forced to a doctrine of the "felicitous fall." Supposedly the fall was a happy event, for because of it the Son came into the world and now we can be the Bride of Christ. I find this a seriously problematic notion.

I believe Satan knew that the Son was to be born into the world to complete the maturation of humanity. By perverting humanity, especially the mother, Satan could prevent the Celestial Marriage—or so he thought.

Finally, by striking at the woman, Satan sought to reverse the true order or hierarchy of life. That order, as we have noted, is eschatological: man first, bride second. But in history, the order is also hierarchical: man teacher, woman recipient. Thus, a consequence of Satan's destroying the eschatological order was also the destruction of social order.

Adam passed God's word on to Eve. Satan comes to challenge Adam's word, and indirectly God's. This is still true today. The pastor is to pass God's word to the Bride, the Church, but Satan comes into the Church and encourages people to ignore the pastor and submit only to God. "I submit to God, and to the Bible; but I don't submit to any clergy!" That is the attitude of many within the Church. Of course, many pastors are not very faithful, just as Adam was not very faithful. Like Adam, they stand back and don't intervene when people ignore them.

What should Eve have done? She should have turned to Adam and asked him about it, discussing it with him. This is what we should do in the Church. If we think that the pastor is not teaching things correctly, we should go to him privately and discuss it with him. If we continue to disagree, we should "go along" with his teaching in the public life of the Church and disagree only in private.

God does speak to us, as He spoke to Eve, and we must submit to Him. But God also speaks in a special way to pastors, who are set apart by the Spirit to be servants of the Word, and we must also submit to them. This dual submission is required by God, so in submitting to the pastor, we are submitting to God. This dual submission may be hard on occasion, but God wants to see us doing it. Otherwise, we wind up like Eve.

ADAM'S DUTY

Adam was to guard the garden, and Eve is now in the garden. He is to guard her. That, of course, is what he fails to do. We remember that Eve has gotten her knowledge about the forbidden fruit from Adam. The serpent challenges Eve, and then explicitly denies God's word. The conversation has been nothing more than an educational experience up to that point, as the serpent asks Eve to think about things. But when he contradicts God, it is clearly Adam's duty to step in. He must rebuke the serpent and protect his wife.

This is the holy war. Adam's weapon will be his words, as we see in Jude 9: Michael fought with Satan by saying "The Lord rebuke you." Adam could say that and score a temporary victory. But Adam could not drive the serpent from the garden, and he was certainly not ready to combat the serpent in the outer world.

The reason is that during our childhood, humanity was under angelic tutors (Heb. 1–2; Acts 7:53; Gal. 3:19) and was lower than the angels (Ps. 8:5). From this weak position, Adam would not have been able to deal with the serpent, for Satan was behind the serpent. It is at this point that Adam would have begun to realize that just as he needed a helper to do his work of cultivation, so now he needed power and glory to do his work of guarding. He must be elevated over the angels, crowned with glory and honor (Ps. 8:5b; 1 Cor. 6:3).

We may readily suppose that it would have been at this point that Adam would become conscious of his nakedness and of the need for glorious and judicially-empowering clothing. Adam would bring his problem before Yahweh, and Yahweh would point him to the Tree of the Knowledge of Good and Evil.

Jesus rebukes Satan, but Satan returns again and again. After His resurrection, however, Jesus can both bind Satan and also give the power to crush Satan to all His people in union with His glorification (Rom. 16:20). Jesus, as New Adam, shows what Adam's own situation was. Unlike Adam, Jesus constantly protected His Bride: "I guarded them, and not one of them perished but the son of Perdition [Satan]" (John 17:12). When the son of Perdition came with soldiers to the garden (note!) of Gethsemane, Jesus protected the disciples: "If you seek Me, let these go their way" (John 18:8). But in order to give full and complete protection to His Bride, Jesus would have to go to the Tree of Knowledge and die.

Such, then, was the process of education before Adam. We cannot know explicitly what steps might have been involved. Perhaps after protecting his wife, Adam would instantly have known that he needed the kingly and glorifying gift of the Tree of Knowledge. Perhaps he would have asked Yahweh for that gift and "died" and been glorified on that same day.

It seems more likely, however, that a time of maturation in awareness would be involved. Satan would continue to attack Eve, and Adam would continue to have to defend her. The attacks might become physical, for Satan's attacks are certainly physical in the rest of the Bible. Adam would fight as a warrior prince and become more and more aware that he needed full kingly powers. He would need not only the power of the Word, to rebuke Satan, but the power of the Spirit, to overcome and crush him.

At some point, perhaps, Satan would try to kill Eve, and Adam would have to sacrifice himself to save her. He would go to God and say, "I now know what death means. I am willing to die to save Eve. Not my will, but Yours be done." I think we can say that at that point, God would give Adam permission to eat of the Tree of Knowledge. Not Satan but God would put Adam to death, and then raise him glorified and empowered to cast Satan from the garden forever.

Or perhaps better, the hypothetical conversation would have gone like this:

Adam: I must destroy this serpent, or at least drive him from the garden. I fear for Eve. I feel weak and naked. I'm desperate. I love Eve, and will do anything to protect her.

Yahweh: Yes, and I can provide you what you need. You need a royal garment, and then you can exercise judgment, and exile the serpent from the garden.

Adam: How will You do this for me?

Yahweh: I now hereby give you permission to eat from the Tree of the Knowledge of Good and Evil. It will make you into a judge and ruler, and I will invest you with robes of authority.

Adam: But You have said that I will surely die when I eat from it?

Yahweh: Yes, you will.

Adam: Will I rise again? Is that what You have in mind?

Yahweh: Think about it, my son. What has happened to you already?

Adam: Well, I did go into a deep-sleep when I became aware that I needed a helper fit for me. But if I go into deep-sleep again, or down even deeper into this "death" state, I'll be unconscious. How can I protect Eve if the serpent attacks her again while I'm in this "death" state?

Yahweh: Do you trust Me? Do you trust Me fully, my son? Are you ready and willing to commit your spirit into My care, and also commend Eve into My care?

154

Adam: Yes.

Yahweh: Then eat, and do not doubt.

Adam must mature in faith to the point where he is ready to die for Eve. We see a perfect example of this in Romans 9:3, where Paul writes, "For I could pray that I myself were accursed away from Christ for the sake of my brethren, my kinsmen according to the flesh." In order to defeat Satan, who had Israel in his grip, Paul is ready to die and be separated from God, confident we may be sure of eventual resurrection, since he had the example of what happened to Jesus before him. Moses had prayed the same way in Exodus 32:32. When Adam was ready to die for Eve, God would bring him to the Tree of Death and Glory.

When God saw that Adam was ready, God would allow him to eat of the Tree of Knowledge. Adam would eat of the Tree, fall into death, and be raised empowered to deal with the serpent. He would kill the serpent, and the skin of the serpent would become part of his glorious clothing. He would then be ready to move into the outer world as a king.

I believe that at this point, Eve would also be given the fruit of the Tree of Knowledge and would join her husband as world ruler. Jesus said, "Greater love has no one than this, that he lay down his life for his friends." Adam would come the point of laying down his life in order to protect and guard Eve. We see from the New Testament that first Jesus and afterward His Bride are glorified. This is the true order that Adam allowed to be reversed in the fall, when he allowed Eve to eat first.[86]

THE SERPENT'S QUESTION

And he [the serpent] *said to the woman, "Indeed, did God really say, 'Not shall you eat from every tree in the garden?" And the woman said to the serpent, "From the fruit of the trees of the garden we may eat.*

---

86. I improved these thoughts in "Merit Versus Maturity," 182–184, 186, and this represents my recent understanding of the subject. Later in that essay, after arguing that God the Son would have become incarnate even apart from the fall into sin (187–189), On page 189, I write:

And from the fruit of the tree that is in the center of the garden, God said, 'Not shall you eat from it, and not shall you touch it, or you will die'" (Gen. 3:1b–2).

The translation of the serpent's initial question to Eve is in some doubt. Our Bibles render it as a question: "Indeed, did God really say: 'Not shall you eat from every tree in the garden'?" Victor Hamilton notes that the opening Hebrew words *'aph ki* ("indeed" and "really" above) never carry interrogative force anywhere else in the Bible. Thus, he suggests as an alternative that the serpent is feigning surprise: "Indeed! To think that God said...!"[87]

However we translate it, the general meaning is clear: The serpent questions God's word as mediated to Eve through Adam. Thus, another translation might be: "Was it really God who said...?"

Eve shows her unfallen powers of deduction and reasoning in her reply. She had heard God say, "Behold, I give to you ... every tree which has on it fruit of a tree seeding seed; for you it will be for food" (Gen. 1:29). God had told Adam not to eat of the Tree of Knowledge (2:16–17), omitting the word "fruit." Satan also omitted the word "fruit," alluding therefore to God's statement to Adam, which the latter had transmitted to Eve. But the woman puts the two statements together: "From the fruit of the trees of the garden we may eat."

For this reason, I doubt that Adam would have received a glorified body at the Tree of Knowledge. Rather, he would have received power to kill the serpent and exile Satan from the garden, and he would have received animal garments of glory as a sign of his new kingly position.

But the conflict would continue in the new outer world into which Adam would now be sent. Satan would continue to attack, perhaps not through animal (serpent) agents, but directly through his host of fallen angels. The conflict would be intensified. As the generations went by, humanity would become more and more aware of the need for a full and final disposition of the problem of evil.

The ultimate Holy Warrior would need to come in order to bring about full transfiguration into glory; that coming one would be the son of Adam, the seed of Eve. It would be His passage through the good-death of the Tree of Knowledge that would bring "many sons to glory" and complete the victory in the holy war.

87. Hamilton, *Genesis 1–17*, 186.

Then the woman continues: "And from the fruit of the tree that is in the center of the garden, God said, 'Not shall you eat from it, and not shall you touch it, or you will die.'" This statement is usually taken as an unwarranted addition to God's prohibition. If, however, we consult Leviticus 11 we find that anything that is not to be eaten is also not to be touched. To put it more clearly: One becomes unclean by touching anything that one becomes unclean by eating (Lev. 11:8, 11, 24–28, 31, 39–40). Uncleanness is symbolic death. Thus, it seems that the woman's theological instincts were better than those of her critics. She[88] had rightly reasoned that things not to be eaten should also not be touched or handled. Thus, this was part of what God had "said."

It seems pretty clear that Eve was not trying to reproduce word for word what Adam had told her God had said. Compare:

> Not shall you (s.) eat from it, for in the day of your eating of it, dying you (s.) shall die (2:17).

> Not shall you (pl.) eat from it or you (pl.) will die (3:3).

Note that Eve rightly changes the singular of the original command to the plural when she paraphrases it, for it applied to her as well as to Adam.

Others have faulted Eve for saying "the tree that is in the center of the garden" instead of "one of the two trees in the center of the garden." But here again, such commentators are reaching too far. The woman's meaning was clear and her language unobjectionable.

What may indicate the beginning of a problem was that Eve used the same word for God that the serpent used: God. It was not "God" who prohibited eating of the Tree of Knowledge, but "Yahweh God." Satan had skillfully removed half of God's self-revelation from the discussion. The name Elohim ("God") refers to God's kingship; thus judges and rulers are also called elohim (Exod. 21:6; 22:8–9; Ps. 82:1,6). Satan will tempt Adam and Eve to try and become elohim, in an unspecified sense.

The name Yahweh refers to God as the faithful, covenant-keeping God. This description of the meaning of the name is found in Exodus 6:2–8. The full meaning of this name can be seen only after God makes promises as El Shaddai (The All-Powerful) and then keeps them. The use of Yahweh Elohim in Genesis 2 points to God as the faithful God. But Satan cannot use this

---

88. I have expanded, in "Restoring the Office of Women in the Church, I" (https://theopolisinstitute.com/restoring-the-office-of-woman-in-the-church-i-2/)

name, because he is trying to get Adam and Eve to be unfaithful. He wants them to become unfaithful elohim, not faithful elohim.

Thus, the focus of discussion becomes clear. The only proper way for Adam and Eve to mature to the point of eating of the Tree of Knowledge is through faithfulness. As images of God, when they have become like Yahweh, the Faithful One, they will become like gods, elohim, rulers. Satan seeks to get them to seize the prerogatives of being gods, elohim, rulers, in a context of unfaithfulness.

Accordingly, we see Eve slip when she allowed Satan to set the terms of the discussion. Had she responded, "Yahweh God has said," then she would have controlled the discussion better. This has always been a problem in the Church, especially in apologetics. We allow the adversary to set up the terms of debate and the parameters of discussion, and then we lose. While it is important to answer a fool according to his folly, that he not be wise in his own eyes (Prov. 26:5), we are first told *not* to answer a fool according to his folly, that we not be like him (Prov. 26:4). Eve began to lose the argument when she allowed the adversary to set the terms of discussion.

God could have made man and woman at the same time and told both of them together not to eat of the fruit. He did not. He told the man, who then told the woman. This established the pattern that the man speaks first. He speaks a pioneering, directing word. He and other men, however, cannot be the only speakers. It is necessary for the woman to speak second, to speak a word that advances beyond that of the man, a glorifying word. The woman will be stimulated to new insights by the word of the man, insights that the man will never have by himself.

What the woman would speak would be the second word, the glorifying word. We see this right away in the narrative of Genesis 2 and 3. Before the woman was made, God told Adam that he was not to eat the fruit of the Tree of Knowledge. Later, when the serpent challenged the woman to eat of that fruit, she replied that God had said not to eat of it. How did she learn this? From Adam....

In "The Glory of the Man," 182–183, I note that "the woman is made to talk back to the man (!) by adding a glorifying word in the midst of sanctuary liturgy." I point out that in Leviticus 11 "we read that those things that make one unclean (symbolically dead) by eating also make one unclean by touching and handling." Likewise, in Colossians 2:21, "touch not, taste not, handle not" "go together. According to Paul, Eve was reasoning correctly."

THE SERPENT'S LIE

And the serpent said to the woman, "Not dying you shall die. For God is knowing that in the day of your eating from it your eyes will be opened and you will be like God, knowing good and evil" (Gen. 2:4–5).

At this point, the woman should have turned to her husband and pastor for confirmation and help, but she did not. At this point, Adam should have intervened to protect his wife and parishioner, but he did not. It is easy to understand Eve's position: She has been trapped into an argument. The Bible says that she was deceived and misled (2 Cor. 11:3; 1 Tim. 2:14).

Adam's failure to intervene is much more serious. We have the contrast of Paul, who in 1 and 2 Corinthians desperately intervenes in the life of the Bride in order to prevent her from being seduced by Satan through deception (2 Cor. 11:2–3). Adam's motivation is clear: He wanted Eve to eat so he could see what happened. When she ate and did not die, he joined her. Had she fallen dead, he would say that she had not followed his instructions ("I've got more ribs. How about another one?").

At any rate, the serpent continues to address the woman. He directly contradicts what Adam had told her. Then he follows it up with a statement that is perfectly true, but taken out of context. He tells her that their eyes would be opened, which indeed happened (2:7), and that they would become like gods themselves, knowing good and evil, which also happened (2:22).

They would become like God, for they would become rulers.[89] But they would be unfaithful rulers, naked of the glory-garments that become true rulers.

And they would be "knowers of good and evil," for as we have seen already, this phrase refers to rule and discernment and judgment. But they would be confused and unwise judges, because they had not matured in faithfulness earlier. They would have the office and duties of elders, while still but infants themselves.

And finally, their eyes would be opened. Physically, of course, their eyes were already open, but in the context of Genesis 1, sight has to do with

---

89. Concerning God-likeness, we find that rulers and judges are called gods (*elohim*) in Exod. 21:6; 22:8, 28; Psalm 82, and John 10:34.

judgment: "God saw what He had made and it was good." The opening of the eyes here is, in a word, kingly sight.[90]

Thus, Satan was right. God did indeed know that they would receive the gift and responsibility of kingship if they ate of the Tree of Knowledge, and because they were not mature enough to bear this burden, God had told them to wait.

Where Satan lied was in saying that they would not die. Note again that this is only indirectly an assault on God's word, since Eve knew of this threat only from Adam—and Adam was keeping quiet. For all she knew, Adam had indeed lied to her, since he was not saying anything in his own defense. But Adam knew.

Satan lied. When they ate of the tree they did indeed die. They died in several senses. First, they died in the sense that death is separation from God, for they hid themselves. Second, they died in the sense of being cast out of the Garden, as lepers were to act as mourners, cast out of cities (Lev. 13:45; Num. 5:2–3; 2 Kgs. 7:3–4; 2 Chron. 26:21). Third, it follows that they died to the Kingdom of God, as Samuel mourned for Saul, who died to kingship even though he was still alive (1 Sam. 15:35–16:1). Fourth, they died in being estranged from the world that was to be life to them (Gen. 3:17–19).

The Tree of Knowledge was a Tree of Transfiguration. Had they been faithful, they would have eaten it and been glorified as true kings. As sinners, however, their eating transfigured them downward, toward degradation. Ultimately, they died physically as well, and over that death hung the threat of the eternal death of hell.

As we leave the serpent—for he has nothing else to say to Eve—let us summarize his tactics as we have seen them in this passage:

1. He craftily stirs human beings up against their teachers, pastors, husbands, parents, authorities.

2. He sets the terms of the discussion, so that we are bound to lose.

3a. He twists the truth, putting it into a false context.

3b. He directly lies about God's threats and promises.

---

90. Compare also 2 Samuel 19:27; Psalm 11:4; Isaiah 44:9; Jeremiah 32:18–19; Ezekiel 5:11; 7:4; 20:17 as instances of eyes passing judgment.

Though these factors have emerged inductively from our examination of the text, it is a fact that they fit nicely into the Framean ethical paradigm,[91] to wit:

    1. Dispositional Motivation: Satan stirs up doubt, mistrust, and rebellion.

    2. Situational Context: Satan sets the terms of the discussion.

    3. Normative Law: Satan abuses truth and lies.

---

91. Frame's ethical triad appears in a number of his works. In particular, see John M. Frame, *The Doctrine of the Christian Life,* A Theology of Lordship (Phillipsburg, NJ: P&R, 2008).

15

THE WOMAN'S EVALUATION

GENESIS 3:6

And the woman saw
that good was the tree for food,
and that pleasant was it to the eyes,
and desirable was the tree for gaining wisdom,
> *and she took from its fruit and ate;*
> *and she gave also to her husband with her and he ate* (Gen. 3:6).

ALL human beings lust for three things: life, glory, and knowledge. All of us want life, even if we are not aware of it until we are threatened or ill. All of us want glory. We want others to listen to us. We want praise. We want to be thought of as beautiful (especially if we are women). We want a good self-image. And third, all of us want knowledge. We want to understand what is going on, even if we don't realize this until we get into a situation in which we don't know what is going on. We want wisdom and insight into reality so that we can plan and act according to our desires.

These are the three treasures. They are offered by all gnostic religions, by all ideologies. In the ancient world, the myth was that the treasure was guarded by a serpent, preferably an oroborotic one (a serpent with its tail in its mouth). The hero kills the serpent and gets the treasure. In Tolkien, Bilbo gets the treasure without killing Smaug (smog).

Gnosticism offers philosopher's gold, an elixir that makes you golden in the sense that you have wisdom, glory, and will live forever. You get this threefold gift by going through initiation, passing under the blood of a slain bull or something else that represents the dragon, and coming into the inner circle.[92]

Now, what I'm calling gnosticism is the great counterfeit. The reality is that God has these three gifts in His Garden. That is where they are located. And, until Jesus came, the three gifts were guarded by cherubim, who are conflated with dinosaurs in the dragon myths. In the garden-replica of the Tabernacle and Temple, we find these three gifts portrayed in three descending locations.

First, in the Holy of Holies we find Aaron's rod, symbol of rule and authority. This is a glorified almond rod (Num. 17:8). The Hebrew word for "almond" also means "watcher," so that almond trees always signify oversight and rule. This is the glory aspect, the "delight to the eyes." With it is the golden pot of manna. Here is the true "theologian's gold," which is "good for food." Jesus says that people ate manna and died, but those who eat Him will live forever; thus the manna is a picture of food that gives eternal life. And finally there are the tables of the Law as well as the complete Torah, the former of which is lodged in the Ark-Throne-Altar. This is where God talks to us, giving us His secrets and His insights, and where we converse with him as council-members who have His law in our hearts. And so this is "desirable to make one wise."

Second, in the Holy Place we have the golden Lampstand, which is a styled Watcher ("almond") Tree and shines light. This is glory, desirable to the eyes. Also we have the golden Table of Facebread, more "theologian's gold" of eternal life. And finally we have the golden Altar of Incense, where God and man converse, where we become wise.

---

92. In Greece, the Minotaur and the Bull guarded the treasure in the Labyrinth and thus were "dragons." This version emerged late, after dinosaurs had died off and were no longer familiar. Earlier versions were based on dinosaurs. Every culture in the world has stories of (a) a Flood and (b) dragons.

Third, in the Courtyard we have more general and overlapping signs of the same three gifts. The pillars represent God's glorious host. The Laver of Cleansing washes us and makes us glorious. (Man was created of dust; the application of water from heaven is glorification). We have the fire on the altar, which is God's glory presence and which glorifies the animals placed into it, which represent us. Then, in the area of food, we have the sacrifices, which God eats with us. And finally, in terms of wisdom and communication, we have once again the altar itself, where God meets with us.

All of these were there in the beginning: The gift of the Father (glory), the gift of the Spirit (life), and the gift of the Son (wisdom). But the sin of Adam means that these gifts were locked away, guarded by cherubim. Cherubim guarded them in the Holy of Holies also, while priestly cherubim guarded them in the Holy Place and Courtyard. These constituted the essence of the mystery that was hidden away for ages until Christ came, the mystery that Paul explicates in his writings.

Wisdom and Glory

All the trees of the Garden were good for food and a delight to the eyes, and the captain of this host of trees was the Tree of Life. Only the Tree of Knowledge, however, was desirable for gaining wisdom. When we bring this into more theologically abstract language, we say that all the Trees were life-giving or sacramental and all the trees were glorious, but only the Tree of Knowledge is associated with the Word and only it bestows wisdom and glory. All the trees were glorious, but only one Tree bestowed glory upon those who ate of its fruit.

If we translate this situation into ordinary human life, we can see quite clearly what it entailed. A baby encounters the glory of his parents, and they feed him. Initially, however, a baby is not able to hear words and acquire wisdom; this is something that comes over time and leads to maturity. Eating food does not lead to maturity, though it sustains life. Being around glorious people does not lead to maturity; in fact it can be a trap if a child tries to be like a glorious adult without acquiring wisdom first. It is the Word that produces wisdom and glory, gradually, in us.

The Tree of Knowledge is associated with that wisdom-producing Word, and the word is "No" or "Not yet." Passing by the Tree of Knowledge, realizing that it is good, but obeying God and holding off would develop patience.

Patience works in us the ability to take a long view of time and history, and thereby makes us more God-like. We grow into masters of time, elohim. Then we are ready to be given the right to rule and pass judgments, because we have learned cause and effect and we have learned how history moves and what the ripple effects of our judgments will be.

We have seen that the phrase "Knowledge of Good and Evil" is equivalent to rule and authority and glory. This glory (or its degrading inversion) is bestowed by the fruit of this tree, according to God's arrangement. Here, however, the tree is said to bestow wisdom. Wisdom is the precondition for receiving glory and rule. It is not the fruit that bestows wisdom, but rather the presence of the fruit in the Garden that can bestow it (or better, stimulate it). As Adam and Eve obey God and hold off from this fruit, they grow wise.

In chapter 2, we noted that Adam and Eve were to eat unprocessed fruit, which is first day food. In time, grain would sprout and be made into bread. Last of all, after a longer process, fruit would be made into wine.

We can now make some more associations here. The trees of the Garden offered fruit, baby-food with no wisdom-inducing word associated with it. The Tree of Life, next to the Tree of Knowledge, offered bread. Bread is a symbol of the Word quite often in the Bible. As Adam and Eve stood by the two trees and obeyed God, eating of the Tree of Life and leaving the Tree of Knowledge alone, they would be eating God's *No!*-Word and learning wisdom—and this would be associated with the "bread" of the Tree of Life. Finally, when they had learned the Word well enough, they would be given the "wine" of the Tree of Knowledge. Wine in the Bible is always associated with enthroned rule and rest, and thus is eschatological.

The fact that fruit was given by God to Adam and Eve right from the beginning, and that food accompanies God's work with us all along the way, fits with the overall biblical teaching that baptized children belong at the Lord's Supper as soon as they are able to eat and drink. At the early stage, the Supper is general fruit to them, strengthening their life in Christ. As they grow up, the Supper becomes general bread and Tree of Life to them, strengthening their life and knowledge in Christ. When they are mature and have dominical responsibilities of their own, the Supper becomes general wine and Tree of Knowledge to them, strengthening their life and knowledge and glory in Christ.

TABERNACLE AND TREES

The trees of the Garden are replicated in the Tabernacle and Temple, and these replications shed light on their original meaning. First of all, in the Holy of Holies Aaron's rod was of wood glorified with blossoms and food. Notice that Aaron's rod is a tree that is a delight to the eye (blossoms) and good for food (almonds) and represents his authority (knowledge, in the sense of rule). The glory-aspect of the trees is paramount here. Like God Himself, Aaron is vested in glorious robes and dispenses sacrificial food to the people. Aaron is humanity matured (somewhat) into the likeness of God, and thus given (somewhat) of the Tree of Knowledge.

The Ark was made of wood overlaid with gold. Its "fruit" is the Cover with its cherubim. This is the place where God communicates with us, and so it is "desirable for wisdom." That is, when we communicate with God through the altar, we become wise and thus eligible for the Tree of Knowledge. Here the word-aspect of the trees is paramount.

Then there is the golden pot of manna, which is not made of wood at all. The tree aspect is missing here, though manna corresponds to the life-aspect of the trees. Why? I suggest that it is because the manna came from heaven, not from trees on the earth.

In the Holy Place we have the Altar of Incense, which was of wood overlaid with gold. Here the "fruit" is the incense. Again, like the Ark, this represents the communication of glorifying wisdom.

The Table of Facebread was also made of wood overlaid with gold. The fruit of this tree is the bread, which correlates with being good for food.

But the Lampstand, though in the form of a tree, was made of pure gold. There is no wood in it. Why? I suggest it is because the Lampstand represents the heavenly lights, not an earthly tree.

Finally, in the Courtyard the Bronze Altar was made of wood overlaid with bronze. The fruit of this tree is the fire-glorified sacrifices. This tree bears food that is good to eat: Jesus Himself.

The pillars in the Courtyard represent God's host, grounded in bronze and crowned with silver. As a guardian host, this army has God's wisdom and projects a delight to the eyes. But since the wood is not overlaid with gold, this is a host of persons not yet glorified.

But the Laver is not made of wood at all. Why? I suggest it is because the Laver represents the waters above the firmament, not earthly waters. The

Laver confers watery glorification, the cleansing water of the Word. Thus, the Laver "makes wise."

Summary:

Garden	Holy of Holies	Holy Place	Courtyard
All trees glorious	Aaron's Rod	Lampstand	Pillars
Tree of Life (food)	Manna	Facebread	Sacrificial Altar
Tree of Knowledge[93]	Ark/Throne	Incense Altar	Laver

Each of these sets is one large tree:

Holy of Holies tree:	life	Golden Pot of Manna (fruit, in heavenlies)
	word	Ark/Throne (holding up God, the Ultimate Manna)
	glory	Aaron's Rod (humanity lifting up the Throne)
Holy Place tree:	glory	Lampstand (heavenly lights)
	word	Incense Altar
	life	Table of Facebread (incense on top of bread)
Courtyard tree:	word	Laver (heavenly ocean)
	person	Pillars (standing on bronze)
	life	Bronze Altar (of earth)

If we look at the growth of these three trees, which are one super-tree, we see the course of spiritual life. As we saw in the previous section, the baby is given the fruit-food aspect to make him grow. Thus the Altar produces Pillars. These encounter the Word baptismally and this initiates them on their

---

93. i.e., as the tree where wisdom is gained and glory bestowed.

course of learning wisdom. The Word comes to them first, and they don't have anything to say back. They listen without conversing.

Then they move into the second story of the Tree. Life continues to come to them through food, but now in the bread aspect discussed last time. They grow at the Incense Altar, where they converse with God and acquire wisdom. And this leads to glory, so that they become Lampstands.

Finally, the glorified person stands as Aaron's Rod. The Word that he now holds is what he teaches as a teacher, no longer a mere learner or interlocutor. Moreover, that Word provides the manna of life to those just starting out in the Courtyard and maturing in the Holy Place.

A final note: Associating the Laver with the Word clears up a mystery, which is why the ritual of the Tabernacle and Temple was silent. We hold to the order: Word, then sacrament. Where are the words in the Tabernacle ritual? Well, what corresponds to the Word ritually is that the priest had to wash hands and feet, and the sacrifice in the laver, before approaching the food-producing altar. Thus: Word, and then sacrament.

UNCLEANNESS

God had said that in the day that they ate the fruit of the Tree of Knowledge (without permission), they would die. We have seen that death takes a variety of forms and expressions, for death is the opposite of life. Thus, death is exile from God's presence; death is pain; death is toil; etc. "Unclean" in the Bible means "symbolically dead," and in the present section our concern is to consider uncleanness as it relates to the three characteristics of the fruit of the Tree of Knowledge.

When we get to the judgments God pronounces in Genesis 3, we shall see that the laws of uncleanness in Leviticus 11–15 follow these judgments in series. The judgments, and the laws of uncleanness, also follow in series the three aspects of the Tree of Knowledge.

First is life, associated with food. We have seen already that in the triplexes of the Tabernacle, food (life) is associated with the golden pot of manna, the table of face-bread, and the altar of ascensions. In the laws of uncleanness, food comes first, in the form of the laws of diet in Leviticus 11.

These foods are said to be "unclean for you." That is, they bring symbolic death to "you," which means the Israelites. These foods did not have this effect on God-fearing gentiles. Moreover, the prohibition on these foods was clearly temporary, for in the New Covenant they would be eliminated. Israel knew this, because God had given all foods to Noah and they knew that their call as a priestly nation was only temporary, until the coming of the Messiah. These good foods, intended for life, caused death instead, just like the fruit of the Tree of Knowledge.

Second is glory, associated with transfiguration and rule and authority. It appears that, in Leviticus, we must set aside Leviticus 12 and go to Leviticus 13–14 in order to pick up the theme of glory. This is because Leviticus 11–15 also tracks the judgments of Genesis 3. The first judgment is against the serpent and relates to Leviticus 11. The second concerns childbearing and relates to Leviticus 12. The third relates to the sweat that flows from the dust of man's body and correlates to Leviticus 13–14. So Leviticus 11–15 inserts the judgments concerning childbearing into the sequence, but we shall ignore this for now.

Glory is the light and splendor that shines from God and that is to shine from His images when they are glorified. The glory comes to human beings over time. The "leprosy" in Leviticus 13–14 is anti-glory. The skin becomes white, but deathly white, because of the underlying "flesh." The walls of tents and houses become rainbow-colored (red and green), but in a deathly way, not a glorious way. These conditions are not "pleasant to the eyes." And in fact, attention is drawn repeatedly throughout Leviticus 13–14 to the eyes of the priest, who must evaluate the condition and determine whether it is true "leprosy" (counterfeit glory) or not.

Third is knowledge or wisdom. Eve saw that one gains wisdom from the tree, though as we have seen, she sought that wisdom the wrong way. The laws of unclean issues in Leviticus 15 correlate with this feature. This is not immediately clear, and we can simply shortcut the argument by going to John 7:38–39. There Jesus says that living water will flow from the innermost parts of the saints, and this is the reverse of the defiling issues of Leviticus 15. He says that this living water is the Spirit, who flows from believer to believer as they one-another one another. Later He says that the Spirit leads us to all truth (John 14:17; 15:26; 16:13). Thus, these outflows speak of communication from one person to another. As we have seen, the waters of the laver of cleansing also speak of the communication of the Word.

Thus, issues from the defiled flesh in Leviticus 15 correspond to the flow of anti-wisdom from the Tree of Knowledge. Instead of leading one another to wisdom and knowledge, we lead one another into error and folly. That is what our "flesh" does. And this outflow of folly from the flesh causes death (uncleanness).

Let us now summarize:

Manna/face-bread gives life	Detestable meats give uncleanness (death)
Aaron's rod/lampstand gives glory	"Leprosy" as anti-glory
Ark/altar/laver gives knowledge	Human lavers give forth defilement

16

BEHEMOTH

IN Genesis 3, it is not said to be the fallen angel Satan himself who tempts Eve and Adam, but the greatest of the beasts of the field. No one questions that Satan lies behind this animal, but we need to explore what this animal is and why it is he and not some other.

Let me begin by suggesting a progression in Genesis 1 that seems to illuminate the data we must consider. On the fourth day, God established light-signs in the firmament to rule day and night, appointed times, and years. Symbolically, these are rulers. They can be human rulers, but in the First Covenant they are angels, and the greatest of these is Lucifer. Let us immediately link this with Revelation's Sky Dragon.

On the fifth day, God *created* (the word used for wondrous works) the great sea dinosaurs, as well as all creatures of sea and air. Clearly the Leviathan (Job 41) is the greatest of the fifth-day creatures, and let us immediately link him with the Sea Beast of Revelation.

At the beginning of the sixth day, God made cattle and other land creatures. The Hebrew word for cattle is *behemah*, and the greatest of these is Behemoth (Job 40), whom we must link with Revelation's Land Beast.

Finally, in the middle of the sixth day God created humanity as His image, and we can link this with the creation of the Beast-Image in Revelation.

Thus, the sequence is:

> Sky dragon
> Sea beast
> Land beast
> Image of God

Now, in Revelation 13, the Sea Beast is the apostate gentile guardian power, the Land Beast is the apostate Herodian and High Priestly power, and the Beast Image is the false priesthood and sanctuary. The "image of the Beast" speaks and causes all who do not worship him to be killed. Recall that Adam and Eve wanted to be gods. Now these false priests claim to be gods and insist on being worshipped.

Who set up the Beast Image? The Land Beast. Who tempted Adam and Eve (God-Images) to make themselves into gods? The Land Beast. Thus, I suggest that temptation in the Garden comes from the land.

Who set up the Land Beast? The Sea Beast. Let us assume that temptation in the land comes from the sea.

And who set up the Sea Beast? The Sky Dragon. Let us assume that temptation in the world comes from the demonic realm.

If this scheme be correct, we should see it in the triadic spirals of covenant history. Let me suggest that we do.

First, the priestly period (Sinai to Saul). This is the Age of the Ox, symbol of the priest, of man as image of God guarding the Garden. Where do the temptations come from? They come from the gods of the land into which the people have come to live, the land surrounding the Tabernacle-garden-sanctuary. These gods are Land Beasts, who tempt the people to reject God and make themselves gods, so that "there was no king in Israel and every man did what was right in his own eyes" (Judg. 17:6; 21:25). That is, every man ate of the Tree of the Knowledge of Good and Evil and did what was good or evil in his own eyes.

Second, the kingly period (Saul to Exile). This is the Age of the Lion, symbol of man as king guarding the land. Note that this moves us backward from Day 6b to Day 6a. Where do the temptations come from? They come from the gods of the surrounding lands, the "sea" around Israel. The temptation is to incorporate the worship practices of these lands into the worship of

Yahweh. These false gods are Sea Beasts, who set up icons (Land Beasts) in Israel, which in turn seduce the people to make themselves into gods.

Notice that in the book of Job, which as wisdom literature is associated with the inception of the kingly period, Job is attacked by Satan, but the symbol of Satan's power is Leviathan, who is said to be under God's control in Job 41. Compare Job to a king: rich and powerful and respected.[94] His three friends correspond to the king's three mighty men. King Job is disgraced publicly, as David was when David was exiled, though in Job's case there were no grounds for it. Disgraced (defeated in battle), the king is tempted to throw in the towel and deny God. This points to the sociopolitical nature of temptation during the kingly period.

Before moving forward, notice that the kingly land beast, the Lion, tempts the priestly Ox people during the priestly period. The Lion parallels Behemoth. Also, the worldly sea beast, of the fifth day, corresponds to the Eagle, also of the fifth day, and is the tempter in the kingly period. With this in mind, we are ready to proceed to the next period.

Third, the ecumenical period (Exile to Jesus). This is the Age of the Eagle, symbolic of emperor guarding the world and of prophet teaching the emperor. This moves us back to the fifth day. And where do the temptations come from? They come from the fourth day, which is angelic (demonic) and human. That is, the fourth face of the cherub is the human face, the fullness of man as God's image, now ascended to the position formerly held by the angelic rulers. The temptation is to adopt philosophy rather than history as salvation. Instead of seeing salvation as something God does through historical acts, salvation is seen as something we do through the adoption of philosophy, which may mean contemplation and asceticism, or active obedience to rules.

Philosophy, in this evil sense, is humanistic and demonic. The ecumenical period, when God's people were living in the world context, was characterized by philosophy: Buddhism and Taoism in the east; the Greeks in the west. The Oral Law of the Jews is their adoption of philosophy, wedding it to a perversion of the purpose of God's law. The Sadducees, Zealots, Essenes, and Pharisees, each in different ways, fell under the seductive sway of alien philosophy. Thus, the False Man tempts the Eagle people.

---

94. Cf. James B. Jordan, "Was Job an Edomite King?," *Biblical Horizons* 130–131 (June–July 2000).

But it is also an age of demonism. This is not clearly seen until we come to the Gospels, but there (for the first time, really), the demonic is openly revealed as behind human temptations.[95] Thus, just as the Land Beast sought to seduce the people in the sanctuary, and the Sea Beast sought to disgrace the people in the land, so the Sky Dragon seeks to overwhelm the people in the world. Once again, the people are tempted, this time through philosophy, to set up their own standards of good and evil and make themselves gods.

Thus each era is tempted to move falsely into the next. When God makes the people oxen (priests), they are tempted to become kings in the wrong way. When God makes the people lions (kings), they are tempted to take power over the rest of the world in the wrong way. When God puts the people in the world as eagles (prophets), they are tempted to elevate themselves completely over the universe through philosophy instead of waiting for God to do it through the historical event of the ascension of Jesus Christ to the throne. Thus, the qualities of each coming age are used by Satan to seduce the people of the present age into grasping them prematurely. In each case, the sin of the people means they lose the gift of the present age.

According to Revelation 13, Satan's gift to the Beast-Image is Power-Horn, the gift to the Land Beast is Authority-Diadem, and the gift to the Sea Beast is Throne-Head. If we reflect on these, we can see how each operates.

If a man has power, he cannot be shamed. The Land Beast came to Adam and caused him to seize the Authority-Diadem associated with the Knowledge of Good and Evil (kingship), but the consequence was that Adam lost power and became ashamed. He no longer had the sense of full confidence and well being that would enable him to stand naked. Similarly, when Israel sinned in the period of the Judges by seeking kingship prematurely, God removed the sanctuary from them (1 Sam. 1–4), and they fled from battle in shame.

God gave Israel Authority-Diadem in the days of the Kingdom. The Sea Beast comes to the kings and tempts them to seize Throne-Headship over many nations. Not content to live and prosper in their own land, the Israelites were constantly at war with other nations round about. They rejected the prophets, whose influence was felt in the other nations, and sought to dominate the nations themselves. They sought the glory that was a Delight to the Eyes, and instead lost their kingship altogether. Consider Cain also: Cain

---

95. The Gospels are the climax of the third age; the fourth age begins when Jesus ascends to the Throne.

was angry (not shamed) because he lost the glory of being the worship leader as firstborn, and he committed murder to get even.

God gave true Throne-Headship to Israel in the days of the Empire, because they became a nation of prophets scattered among the nations and were given influence. But they sought more. The Sky Dragon came to them and persuaded them to make themselves gods in the sense of being creators. As such gods, they would create their own garden-sanctuaries. Thus, each group of Jews set up its own false synagogue garden: Sadducees, Pharisees, Essenes. In so doing, they lost their position as international prophets, setting up barriers to the gentiles, and came under Christ's condemnation. This is the picture provided in Revelation 13: The Sky Dragon operates through the Sea Beast to set up the Land Beast, who in turn creates a false church/synagogue/garden, the Beast-Image.

Here again, the temptation was to seize prematurely what in time would be given. In the New Covenant, the believers do indeed set up churches and determine times and places of meeting, apart from any geographical and calendrical rules set up by God through the angels. We are, in Christ, indeed come of age at last.

17

THE TREE OF DEATH

EYE for eye, tooth for tooth—that is the standard of justice, according to God's law. And fruit for fruit. Having taken the fruit from the Tree, Adam and Eve had to replace it. Since Adam was mainly at fault, he was the one who would have to replace it.

We can imagine ways of replacing it, which would involve double restitution. Adam might have gone to another Tree of Knowledge and taken two fruits and tied them to the original Tree—except that there were no such other fruits. Moreover, the fruit, taken wrongly, communicated death, and whatever is tied to the tree would have to be dead.

We don't have to use our imagination, however, because tying dead people to trees is a penalty found in the Law:

> And if he is a man guilty of a judgment of death, and he is killed,
>> and you hang him on a tree:
> You shall not leave his body overnight on the tree,
>> but burying you shall bury him on that day,
> for he that is hanged is a curse of God;
> and you shall not render unclean your land that Yahweh your God is giving you as an inheritance (Deut. 21:22–23).

We notice a couple of things here. First, the man was killed and then hanged up. Second, the man thus hanged was a curse, and if left overnight, would bring a curse down on the land. What is implied but not stated is that the man's corpse lay under God's curse until sundown. The specific character of this curse is the well-known "curse of the covenant": to be exposed and devoured by the birds. Third, we notice that no specific crime is mentioned as calling for this judgment.

We do have a few examples in the Bible. In Joshua 8:28–29, we find that Joshua completely burned up the city Ai and hanged up the king of Ai after killing him. In Joshua 10:26–27, five Canaanite kings were slain and hanged. In both cases, the men hanged were Canaanite leaders, Canaanite "Adams."

In 2 Samuel 4, we find that David slew and hanged the two men who murdered King Ishbosheth. They had raised their hands against Yahweh's anointed. Similarly, in Esther those who rebelled against the king are hanged (Esth. 2:23; 7:9–10; 8:7; 9:14).

Thus, we can see two related aspects of being hanged. First, if one's rebellion against God has reached its fullness, as with the Canaanites. Second, if one rebels against the king (the King). Adam sinned, yes, but the "iniquity of the Adamites was not yet full," so Adam was not hanged immediately.

All of this finds its fulfillment, of course, in the hanging of Jesus Christ upon the tree. Jesus was hanged alive, so that He experienced the curse of God while still living, but this is the only apparent difference. Since Jesus fulfilled all the Law, in some sense He was killed before being hanged. Possibly the judgment of death pronounced on Him fulfills that aspect of the Law.[96]

Adam broke a fruit off of God's tree. Jesus was the replacement. Thus, the hymn writer Venantius Fortunatus (AD 530–609) rightly sang:

Faithful cross, above all other,
One and only noble Tree!
None in foliage, none in blossom,
None in Fruit thy peer may be;
Sweetest wood and sweetest iron,
Sweetest weight is hung on thee!

---

96. It is interesting to reflect upon the possibility that Joseph of Arimathaea's burying Jesus before sundown actually averted a curse upon the land of Israel, for a time.

And:

Blest tree, whose chosen branches bore
The wealth that did the world restore,
The price of humankind to pay,
And spoil the spoiler of his prey.

18

Eyes Opened

Genesis 2:7a

And the eyes of both of them were opened, and they knew that they were naked (Gen. 2:7a).

BACK in chapter 13, we saw that this statement correlates with Day 1 in Genesis 1 and the first act in Genesis 2:

Day 1: God makes light.
Genesis 2: The empty, formless land is given a light: humanity (2:4–7).
Genesis 3: The eyes of Adam and Eve are opened (3:7a).

Matthew 6:22 says "the lamp of the body is the eye." Thus, the opening of the eye has everything to do with light.

Jesus' comments on the effects of the fall on the eye are noteworthy. First of all, from Matthew 6:22–7:2. This entire discourse reflects on the fall in Genesis 3.

²² The lamp of the body is the eye;

If, therefore, your eye is clear, your whole body will be full of light.

²³ But if your eye is bad, your whole body will be full of darkness.

If, therefore, the light that is in you is darkness, how great is the darkness!

On another occasion, Jesus spoke to the same effect, as recorded in Luke 11:33–36,

A. ³³ No one, after lighting a lamp, puts it away in a cellar,

Or under a peck-measure,

But on a lampstand,

In order that those who enter may see the light.

B. ³⁴ The lamp of your body is your eye.

When your eye is clear, your whole body also is full of light;

C. But when it is bad, your body also is full of darkness.

³⁵ Then watch out that the light in you may not be darkness.

B'. ³⁶ If, therefore, your whole body is full of light,

With no dark part in it,

It will be wholly illumined,

A'. As when the lamp illumines you with its rays.

This statement of Jesus is peculiar to us. It looks as if He is saying that light shines from our eyes. And that is, in fact, what He is saying. The light, however, does not shine outward, but inward. Two considerations will help us understand this better.

First, as we have studied before, the eye is an organ of judgment. This is established in Genesis 1, where repeatedly God saw what He had made and passed judgment on it. The opening of the eyes of Adam and Eve means that they have become judges, and right away they are called upon to pass judgment. Here in the Sermon on the Mount, Jesus closes the section on the eye by warning about passing judgments (7:1–2). So, then, if the eye gives good judgments, then our whole person and our whole life, our "body," will act in terms of these good judgments. Our life will be illuminated. If, however, the eye gives bad judgments, then our life is darkened and we shall act foolishly.

The second consideration arises from the symbolism of the Tabernacle. We cannot take the time to develop this in full here, but briefly: Considered as a symbol of the human person, the Tabernacle and Courtyard are the head and body respectively. The bronze altar is the body up to the neck. The Holy of Holies is the heart and mind. The Holy Place is the face: Lampstand as eyes, Incense Altar as nose, and Bread Table as mouth. Recall that the Lampstand is a stylized Watcher Tree (almond) and watches over the Table. Thus, the lamp is the light inside this symbolic body. Jesus, of course, was familiar with the Tabernacle, since as Yahweh He had given the instructions concerning it to Moses centuries earlier. Thus, it was quite natural for Jesus to allude to the Tabernacle and call the eye of the body a lamp.

The notion of the eye as a lamp for the body forces us to consider that light comes into the body from outside through the eye. The eye is "fueled" from outside. In the Tabernacle, that fuel was the lamp-oil, which is a symbol of the Holy Spirit. When the eyes are opened properly to pass judgments concerning good and evil, the light comes streaming into the body through the eyes from the Glory-Light of God, from the fuel of the Spirit's influence and guidance. If, on the other hand, men reject God's light and fuel, then what comes in through the eye is Satanic darkness, which spreads darkness throughout the body. To be sure, the sinner will indeed pass judgments concerning good and evil, and his body will act in terms of these eye-mediated judgments, but they will be dark and evil judgments, perverse and twisted.

Continuing with Jesus' remarks from Matthew 6, we read:

[24] No one can serve two masters.
For either he will hate the one and love the other,
Or he will hold to one and despise the other.
You cannot serve God and mammon.

Once we realize that Genesis 3 is the broad background of Jesus' statement, we can see that the two masters here are God and Satan. Adam was presented with this choice, and he chose the wrong master. Because Jesus is doing more than merely commenting on Genesis 3, of course, He substitutes "mammon" (money viewed as an idol) for Satan here.

[25] For this reason I say to you:
Stop being anxious for your life,
What you shall eat,
Or what you shall drink;
Nor for your body,
What you shall put on.
Is not life more than food,

And the body more than clothing?
[26] Look at the birds of the heaven:
That they do not sow,
Nor do they reap,
Nor gather into barns;
And your heavenly Father feeds them.
Are you not worth much more than they?

Eating and clothing: exactly the things in view in Genesis 3. Adam seized forbidden food and then became anxious about clothing. Unlike the birds, Adam was not willing to receive the generous foods God had authorized for him. As a result, Adam was cut off from the Tree of Life, and part of what this meant was that he would eat only "by the sweat of your nostrils." God made him anxious about food, the food of life. This was so that he would turn back to God in faith and ask for his daily bread. But the anxiety about life and food, and the shame-filled concern for clothing, arose in Genesis 3.

[27] And which of you by being anxious can add a cubit to his height?

Jesus says nothing further about this, which has caused some to speculate that the apostles were short men who wished they were taller! Actually, the notion of becoming taller and more glorious is part of the original fall of mankind. Glorious headdresses and crowns are worn by rulers, and that is what Adam wanted to become. Jesus' point is that when we strive for such added cubits, we are repeating Adam's sin. We are not to be anxious about height and glory. Rather, we are to be faithful, and when God is ready, He will give us the crowns we deserve.

[28] And why are you anxious about clothing?
Observe how the lilies of the field grow:
They do not toil,
Nor do they spin,
[29] Yet I say to you that even Solomon in all his glory did not clothe himself
  like one of these.
[30] But if God so arrays the grass of the field,
Which exists today
And tomorrow is thrown into the furnace,
How much more you?
O man of little faith!

186

As we have seen in earlier studies, the sin of Adam is equivalent to seizing robes of official glory. God was robed in glory, and naked Adam sought to make himself a god. Ambitious people have sought glory-robes ever since. Jesus' point is that God is the one who gives true robes of glory. The glory-robes given by God are far more beautiful than anything we could ever make.[97]

> [31]Do not be anxious then,
> Saying, "What shall we eat?"
> Or, "What shall we drink?"
> Or, "With what shall we clothe ourselves?"
> [32] For all these things the gentiles eagerly seek;
> For your heavenly Father knows that you need all these things.
> [33] But seek first His kingdom and His righteousness,
> And all these things shall be added to you.

Jesus continues to play off of Adam's original sin. He says that the gentiles, here meaning the unbelievers, eagerly seek food and glorious raiment. In this way, they act in terms of Adam's sin. Jesus assures us that our Father knows we need these things and will give us exactly what we need of daily bread—just as God provided all kinds of fruits for Adam in the Garden and made clothing for him after he sinned.

Then Jesus says in other words exactly what God had said to Adam in the beginning. We are to seek God's kingdom and righteousness, and when God is ready, He will give us glory-robes and access to the Tree of Judicial Knowledge/Rule. That was the test before Adam as well. He knew that the prohibition on the Tree of Knowledge was only temporary. If he had sought God's kingdom and righteousness, he would have been given to eat of it in time. Instead, Adam sought to establish his own kingdom and his own standards of good and evil (his own righteousness).

> [34] Therefore do not be anxious for tomorrow;
> For tomorrow will care for itself.
> Each day has enough trouble of its own.

---

97. We should note that in Solomon's Temple, both the Pillars and the Bronze Ocean were of lily-design.

And now we have an added insight that is all-important in understanding the original sin and fall of mankind. Adam was seeking to control the future. Eating the Tree of Knowledge and making himself a god, as he supposed, would enable him to determine what would come after him.

This is the ultimate folly. God and God alone controls the future, and the future is always surprising because God is "new every morning." God is infinite, and as He unfolds His infinity to mankind in history, new things constantly come into play. For this reason, the wise man knows that he can control only the things put under his hand at present. But sinful man wants to control the future. Fathers want to control their children's destinies. Rulers want to control dynasties and the future of their realms.

> [7:1] Do not judge
> Lest you be judged.
> [2] For in the way you judge,
> You will be judged,
> And by what measure you measure,
> It shall be measured to you.

The final statement in this section of the Sermon on the Mount is, unfortunately, put into the next chapter. Thus, many readers fail to see that it is intimately linked with what has gone before, especially 6:22–25 about the eye. The eye is the organ of judgment, as we have seen.[98]

Once we understand the context, these sayings cease to be so puzzling. Jesus is not saying that we may never pass judgment. Obviously not, since He established rulers both in the state and in the church throughout the history of the Bible. Rather, His warning is in terms of Genesis 3. Adam had seized the prerogatives of rule, and God called on him immediately to pass judgment. His eyes were opened, yes, but also darkened; he judged wickedly (blaming his wife) and was judged accordingly.

Jesus is addressing the disciples as men who still think and act like Adam. He tells them to "stop being anxious." As long as they are Adamic in their thinking and are anxious for glory and food, they are not ready to rule. Until they come to trust the Father and to seek His kingdom first and foremost,

---

98. Note that 7:3–5 are also about the eye and about seeing clearly, which ties in with 6:22–25.

they are not ready to pass judgments. Only when they have matured in faith, as Adam would have done if he had not fallen, will they be ready to judge righteous judgments.

FIG LEAVES

And the eyes of both of them were opened, and they knew that they were naked. And they sewed fig leaves and made for themselves girdings (Gen. 3:7).

The preceding section has led us to the possibility that the opening of the eyes does not have so much to do with the inspection of things outside of Adam and Eve as with the inspection of themselves within. The lamp of the body is the eye, which gives light to the interior.

Obviously, Adam and Eve already knew that they were naked physically. They had seen their own and each other's genitalia already and had doubtless consummated their marriage. External nakedness is, thus, only peripherally in view in this event. Their eyes were opened to an *inner* nakedness, which then they tried to clothe.

We analyzed this inner nakedness, or shame, in chapter 13. We saw that it is associated with impotence and powerlessness. It is associated with a loss of glory and a loss of integrity or wholeness.

When a person feels he has lost glory or standing or position, he seeks to recover himself. "Re-cover" is the right word, because special clothing is associated with glory and position. When Adam seized the glory and position or office-bearing that was the gift of the Tree of Judicial Authority, he immediately sensed his nakedness. He felt exposed. He felt exposed before God, and before other people, who are images of God. Thus, he needed to cover himself before God and his wife, and she needed to do the same.

As naked babies, Adam and Eve had felt secure in the arms of their heavenly Father. As an innocent married couple, they had felt secure with each other. Now those securities were gone. They sensed a need for protection, at least some kind of visible barrier between themselves and each other and God. So they made garments of fig leaves.

How did they "sew" these leaves together? We are not told. Perhaps they just wound them around their bodies to form a covering.

What did they make? The Hebrew term means a girdle. It is used for fancy belts worn outside the robe by men and women and for the military belt that holds weapons. In this case, we should see two implications. First, it is clear that this girdle covered the genitals, for this is where the sense of shame is located. Second, it is also clear that some sense of glory is implied by the use of this term. "Apron" or "loincloth" could have been used. Adam and Eve sought to cover their sense of shame and impotence with a garment of glory and power.

Why fig leaves? Well, practically speaking, the Garden had fruit trees in it, and the leaves of the fig are among the largest. All the same, if "fig" and "leaves" were not important, we would not be told these specifics.

First of all, we can say that Adam and Eve sought to cover themselves with vegetables, while God covered them with an animal skin, after shedding its blood. It is clear that for sinful man to be covered before God, a life must be taken—because the curse is death. For man to live and have glory, some living thing must take his death for him. Biblically speaking, plants are not alive; they do not have the "breath of life," but animals do.

Second, the fig is associated with the land of milk and honey, as a glance at a concordance will show. In Judges 9, the fig, with the olive and grape, is one of the three truly noble trees. Because of these associations, the fig becomes a symbol of Israel, and Jesus' cursing of the barren fig tree is a picture of the coming judgment on the Jews. I suggest that the fig's association with Eden and with Canaan is one of the many links between the two. Moreover, since Jesus curses a fig rather than an olive or a vine or some other tree that might have symbolized Israel, we see that His curse reaches all the way back to the beginning of the First Creation.[99]

---

99. Compare Matthew 23:35, where the blood of all the righteous from *Abel* forward was to be visited upon that generation.

19

Yahweh Returns to the Garden

Genesis 3:7b–10

A. *3:7b* *And they sewed fig leaves and made for themselves girdings.*

 B. *8a* *And they heard the sound/voice of Yahweh God walking about in the garden as the Spirit of the day.*

  C. *8b* *And they hid—the man and his woman—from the face of Yahweh God among the garden's trees.*

   D. *9a* *And Yahweh God called to the man.*

  C'. *9b* *And He said to him "Where are you?"*

 B'. *10a* *And he said "Your sound/voice I heard in the garden,*

A'. *10b* *"And I was afraid because I was naked and I hid."*

THIS second paragraph in the story of the initial rebellion of humanity is structured chiastically. At the center is God's call to Adam, a call that reverses the situation. To this point, Adam and Eve have been seeking to avoid God; now God brings Adam near and confronts him. The outermost sections concern nakedness (and also are the only two phrases with two finite verbs). The B sections concern God's sound in the Garden as heard by the pair. In C Adam hides, and in C' God asks where Adam is.

Back in chapter 13, we discussed the chiastic structure of 2:25–3:7a. That structure is duplicated here by contrast. To review:

A. Naked and not ashamed.
  B. Serpent arrives.
    C. Adam and Eve listen to the serpent.
      D. Woman speaks instead of Adam.
    C'. Serpent teaches falsely.
  B'. Adam and Eve accept serpent's words.
A'. Naked and ashamed.

Compare the two paragraphs:

A and A'. Notice that both paragraphs have the theme of nakedness as the opening and closing elements.

B. In the first paragraph it is the serpent who comes, while in the second it is God who comes.

C. Adam and Eve do not flee from the serpent (they had no reason to), but they do flee from God.

D. The woman's speech is at the center of the first paragraph, while God's call is at the center of the second.

C'. The serpent's false teaching versus God's probing question.

B'. Adam and Eve accept the serpent's teaching, while they flee from God's voice.

This second paragraph deals with man's creation of a firmament between himself and God. The firmament made on the second day of Genesis 1 is a place between the visible cosmos and the heavenly cosmos where God is enthroned among His angels. It is not a place that can be reached by spatial travel but is a sort of dimensional barrier between these two dimensions. Moreover, as later passages of Scripture reveal, the firmament is a chamber between heaven and earth, with its earthly side visible as the hard shell or veil of the sky over the earth. Considered as a veil or shell over the earth, the firmament or visible heaven has the sun, moon, and stars in it. Accordingly, the symbolic firmament chamber of the Holy Place has the seven astral lights of the Golden Lampstand within it.[100]

In Genesis 2, we found that verse 8 corresponds to the creation of the firmament and is the planting of the Garden of Eden. The Garden is located between the highest ground of the Promised Land, the Land of Eden, and the lower parts of the world, to which the Edenic rivers flow. It is clear from Genesis 1–3, as well as from the rest of the Bible, that if Adam had remained faithful he would not only have been given to eat of the Tree of the Knowledge of Good and Evil, but he would also have moved upstream into the Land of Eden. Because of his sin, he was cast downstream. We have looked at all this in some detail already.

For our purposes here in Genesis 3, we have to consider the firmament in its other aspect, that of a veil or barrier. The original veil was set up by God between heaven and the earthly cosmos as a bridal veil, to be removed when the marriage of the Son and humanity is consummated at the end of history. That event is still before us, as we can see from the blue sky above us. This original firmament heaven was not a "heavens of bronze" cutting man off from God, but a permeable veil allowing contact and interaction within the firmament location.

The garments made by Adam and Eve were designed to add another layer between them and God, a layer that would protect them from God. Their fig leaves did not accomplish this, as the subsequent events showed. But the fig leaves did cut Adam and Eve off from each other. The prenuptial veil God set up between His intended bride and Himself has now been reproduced at the human level, but in a perverse way. Husband and wife are now at odds, as will shortly become apparent when Adam seeks to blame his wife for his own sin.

As noted, these garments did nothing to protect humanity from God's consuming fire. The firmament veil over the earth was not intended for that purpose either. Thus, God will give men new garments, garments of blood (shed when the animal skin was made), which alone can protect humanity from His fire. Accordingly, the blue firmament veils of the Tabernacle and Temple, separating the Holy of Holies from the people, will have to be sprinkled with blood to be effectual in protecting the people.

---

100. For a fuller treatment of the firmament, see Jordan, *Creation in Six Days*, 176–181.

WALKING IN THE GARDEN

And they heard the sound/voice of Yahweh God walking about in the garden as the Spirit of the day (Gen. 3:8a).

The first half of verse eight is dense with Hebrew words that can be translated more than one way, and how we translate them matters a great deal. There is really no way that English can completely reproduce the meaning of verse 8a, so we have to unpack it word by word.

The familiar AV says, "And they heard the voice of Yahweh God walking in the garden in the cool of the day." Something like this is found in most, if not all, later versions. There are three obscurities in this translation.

The first is the translation "voice." How does a "voice" walk? The Hebrew word means either voice or sound. Here the translator must make a choice, and "sound" is certainly preferable: Adam and Eve heard the sound of Yahweh God moving about among the trees in the Garden. Yet, because the Hebrew word also means "voice," we cannot ignore the possibility that more than mere sound is meant. The second Person of the Godhead, who reveals God, is the Person who is coming on this occasion and He is also called the Word of God. Thus, the "sound" of the second Person is also a "word." In a real sense, then, it is the "voice" of God that is moving about in the Garden.

The second obscurity is the translation "walking." The Hebrew verb form used here means "walking to and fro; walking about." What this implies is that God was not purposely coming straight for Adam. God provides signs that He is on the way. This is Adam's judgment day, but judgment does not come suddenly without any warning. Judgment is preceded by indications that God is about to come.

The third and most important obscurity is the word "cool." The Hebrew word is *ruach*, which means "spirit, wind." To render it as "cool" is simply a mistranslation, a paraphrase of what the translator thinks is meant. The translator imagines that at a certain time of the day there was a breeze in the Garden, and so renders the phrase "cool of the day." But this may not be what is meant at all.

It is to Meredith G. Kline's credit that he noticed the connection between this "judgment day" event and other "days of the Lord" in the Bible and that the appearance of God's glory in His Spirit accompanies such events. He points out that when God comes to visit and walk about among His people, or to address them, He comes in a mighty wind, in a cloud of glory, with a tremendous sound, surrounded by cherubim, and that His chariot is energized by the Spirit of God.[101] There is no reason to think that matters were otherwise in Genesis 3. God arrived, the great sound was heard, and cherubim were present. It was a Spirit-Day, a Day of the Lord.

The phrase should be translated "as the Spirit of the day." If the Hebrew text read "as the Spirit of judgment," the meaning would be clear, but God wants us to associate judgment with the Day of the Lord at this early place in history.

In Genesis 1, the first day sees the Spirit come into the world and reproduce Himself as light, creating "day." Thus, "day" is always a manifestation of the Spirit. Also, on each day, God passed judgment, seeing what He had made and calling it good. The climax of this day-judging comes on the sabbath, when God sees all that He has made and calls it very good. Thus, while every day is a Spirit-day and a judgment day, the sabbath is the fullness of judgment day, the sevenfold judgment day.

Through His hovering Spirit and incisive Word God made the first day-light, and through His Spirit and Word God passes judgment on the last day.

As the sabbath Spirit-day began, God pronounced judgment on all things, declaring them very good. Now, later in the day, He comes and pronounces judgment on Adam and Eve for their sin.

The scene is set. God did not come wandering up to Adam and Eve during the cool breeze of the evening of that first sabbath. Rather, He arrived in all His glory, with His angels, with a mighty voice/sound and the rushing wind of the Spirit. It was to be a time of worship and festivity, but it turned into a time of judgment.

FACE TO FACE

And they hid—the man and his woman—from the face of Yahweh God among the garden's trees (Gen. 3:8b).

When God's face comes face-to-face with sinful man's face, man hides his face. As we meditate on the design of creation and the structure of God's word, the interaction of faces draws our attention.

---

101. Meredith G. Kline, *Images of the Spirit* (1980; reprint, Eugene, OR: Wipf and Stock, 1999), ch. 4.

In Genesis 1:2, darkness was upon the face of the deep, and the Spirit of God was hovering over the face of the waters. The original earth, thus, had a face, a face that by implication was matched by the face of the heaven looking back.

The firmament was a transparent boundary put between heaven and earth. Birds are said to fly across the open face of the firmament in Genesis 1:20. This verse does not say that birds fly "in" the firmament, but "upon" it. That is, they fly in front of the face of the firmament, with the sky behind them.[102]

Meanwhile, plants have grown up on the face of the earth (1:29), and rivers water the face of the ground (2:6). Since the earth is a face, it is no surprise that the sources of rivers are eyes and that the plants are like hair. The Hebrew word for a spring of water is "eye" (Gen. 16:7; 24:13, 16, 29, 30; Exod. 15:27; etc.). The "untrimmed" vines of Leviticus 25:5, 11 are literally *nazir*, the word used for the Nazirite, whose hair was untrimmed. During the holy year, the face of the land became a "nazirite." The earth has a mouth (Gen. 4:11; Num. 16:30; etc.), and if there had been volcanoes in Israel, I imagine the earth would have had a nose as well!

Humanity is the leader of the earth; more, humanity embodies the earth. Human beings eat the earth and make the earth self-conscious before God. We eat plants, made of a combination of earth, air, water, and light; we eat animals that have eaten plants. Thus, when man's face is turned away from God, so is the earth's. The firmament between heaven and earth changes, so to speak, from a transparent veil to a hard shell of bronze.

When we are guilty before someone, we cannot look him in the face. We look down when we are shamed or guilty. Only those whose conscience is seared can brazenly face those they have wronged. I have seen those who have wronged me literally put their hands in front of parts of their face when they spoke with me, while with effort they kept eye contact with me. Perhaps you have had the same experience, from one side or the other! We want a barrier between ourselves and those we have wronged.

The more intimate we are with someone, the more possibilities of shame and guilt exist. Often, after years of marriage and many small conflicts, a husband and wife will no longer look each other in the face for long periods of time. They may look at the same things together, but not at each other.

---

102. Behind the firmament is heaven, and the things that appear in or in front of the firmament (winged creatures, stars, clouds, etc.) point to heavenly realities.

If the marriage is in really bad shape, they no longer even look at the same things together.

Adam and Eve could no longer look each other in the face, and they certainly could not look God in the face. They averted their gaze and put up barriers. Between themselves they put up clothing, and between themselves and God they put the trees of the Garden. But God forced them to look at Him.

In Jesus, however, heaven and earth are united. The face of creation is turned back to the face of God, and the Bride's face is turned back to her Husband's.

Thus, God became a "monster." He became a medusa, a power that men fear to look upon. It is no surprise that the gods of the heathen are monsters, because men hate and fear coming face to face with God. Only when this monster is slain, men believe, can men be free. The threatening monsters of paganism, thus, are not images of Satan, but of God, as fearful dragons are images of the cherubim. Or, better, the monster-gods of paganism combine the true enemy (Satan) with the Judge of all the earth (God).

HIDING AMONG THE TREES

Adam and Eve hid from God. That is all the text needs to contain in order to make the point that our first parents sought to conceal themselves from God's arriving presence. The text, however, adds something that is generally treated as superfluous: that they hid among the trees.

It would have made more sense, possibly, to have hidden among bushes, but perhaps there were no bushes. Perhaps there were only trees in the Garden. Yet, we already know about the trees from the preceding verses. Why reiterate the matter? Why take extra words, in this very compact narrative, that Adam and Eve hid "among the trees"?

I suggest that we can answer this by looking forward in the Bible to see what a grove of trees means. A stand of trees is a symbol for a community of people. Since there were no other people in the Garden, Adam and Eve could not have hidden among people; but later on the equivalent of hiding among trees would be hiding in society.

Trees as symbols of people should be familiar to any Bible reader. Both trees and men come out of the soil (Gen. 2:7, 9). Psalm 1 and Judges 9 speak of men as trees. In Mark 8:24, the healed blind man first perceived men as trees walking. Moreover, groves of trees were places of worship in the patriarchal era, and such groves became the pillars and boards of the Tabernacle and Temple—all representing God's garden of people gathered around Him.[103]

So, then, it is likely that Adam's hiding among trees is equivalent to hiding in society. To be a shield against God is one of the deep foundational purposes of every human society untransformed by the Kingdom of God. Men seek to create societies in which their sins can be hidden from God's view.

Men will of course admit that nothing can be hidden from God, but since they seldom think about God directly, they also seldom think directly about the nature of their own societal structures. After all, as long as the firmament remains between earth and heaven, God seldom interacts with men directly. He acts through mediators. Every human being knows God in his or her own heart and thus seeks to hide from himself, so that self-deception rather than self-knowledge is the goal of every man. Other people manifest God to us, and so we seek to hide from them. Judges and rulers and religious leaders pointedly manifest God's presence to us, and so we seek to hide from them. Thus, the practical way to conceal ourselves and our sins from God is to conceal ourselves and hide our sins from other people.

This concealment can take the form of isolation: We keep our sins hidden from other people; or in extreme cases, we separate from people so they won't see our sins. Ultimately, in hell, everyone separates from everyone else. In history, however, the preferred way to conceal our sins is "among the trees," in the crowd. If "everybody is doing it," perhaps we won't be noticed when we do it.

To take a mundane example: Most of us drive faster than the needlessly (though lucratively) low speed limits on our highways. If you are like me, you make sure that you aren't going as fast as the fastest people. If the fastest cars are going 85 mph, I stick to a safe 79 mph. Thus, if the highway patrol arrests anyone (seeking to increase its revenue), it will not likely be me. Thus I hide among the trees.

This principle is true of society as a whole. People want a society in which sin is tolerated to a large extent, because in such a society they can hide. People like having a scumbag like Bill Clinton in the White House, because they can consider themselves superior to a man like him. Somewhere deep inside they

---

103. For a fuller discussion, see *Through New Eyes*, 90ff.

figure that if God arrests them, they will point to Bill Clinton and say, "I was not as bad as he was."

Moreover, people readily pressure the righteous to conform to their unrighteousness. The unmarried virgin male; the man who does not drink to excess; the man who rejects degrading conversation: He will be ridiculed and pressured to join the crowd. Such a man makes it difficult for other men to hide among the trees.

All men know right from wrong, and all men want to engage in wrongful things from time to time. If "everybody is doing it," men can fool themselves that "it is not all that bad." Thus, they have a deep drive to create societies that reinforce wrongful behavior. The groves that men plant all have this characteristic, whether pagan cultures or churches like the Roman Catholic and Orthodox, which "hide" the sins of iconolatry and necromancy in the trees of "holy tradition" and "everybody does it."

Godly societies, such as true churches and the families and nations that nurse at her breast, are groves planted by God. Such orchards do not hide sin any more than the Garden of Eden hid Adam and Eve.

TRUE ORDER RESTORED

A few brief comments will bring us to the end of the "firmament" section (corresponding to Day 2) of the sabbath day fall and judgment of humanity. First, to review:

A. [3:7b] And they sewed fig leaves and made for themselves girdings.

B. [8a] And they heard the sound/voice of Yahweh God walking about in the garden as the Spirit of the day.

C. [8b] And they hid—the man and his woman—
from the face of Yahweh God among the garden's trees.

D. [9a] And Yahweh God called to the man.

C'. [9b] And He said to him "Where are you?"

B'. [10a] And he said "Your sound/voice I heard in the garden,

A'. [10b] "And I was afraid because I was naked and I hid."

As we saw at the beginning of this chapter, the chiastic structure of 2:25–3:7a is duplicated here by contrast.

    A. Naked and not ashamed.
      B. Serpent arrives.
        C. Adam and Eve listen to the serpent.
          D. Woman speaks instead of Adam.
        C'. Serpent teaches falsely.
      B'. Adam and Eve accept serpent's words.
    A'. Naked and ashamed.

The woman's speech (D.) is at the center of the first paragraph, while God's call is at the center of the second. The woman is officially below the man, while God is officially above him. The contrast shows that while a man must listen to the helper suited to him, he must always hearken to God first and foremost. By letting his wife engage in the defensive warfare that was his own job, Adam had begun a reversal of true order, which climaxed when he put himself under the animals (serpent) he was supposed to rule. Now God reasserts true order.

Adam's order, which we find all through human history, is this:

1. On top: the demonic realm, mediated through the lower creation.
2. The feminine principle: "mother nature."
3. The masculine principle: humanity.
4. God, made over into whatever humanity wishes him to be.

God restores true order by:

1. Judging the man, woman, and serpent, putting Himself over all.
2. Putting the woman (and "mother nature") back under the man.
3. Putting the serpent (animal kingdom) and demonic realm in the dust under humanity, and particularly under the woman.

The serpent's false teaching (C') stands against God's probing question. The serpent offers wisdom, but does not provide any. We shall take this up in the next chapter in more depth, but the serpent moves Adam and Eve by asking them a confusing question and then following with a flat assertion. There is no possibility of gaining wisdom. Satan's question leads to helplessness and confusion, and his teaching is pure domination. By way of contrast, God asks a probing question, which forces the deepening meditation that leads to wisdom. Similarly, God's revelation in the Bible is filled with paradoxes and difficulties that provoke wisdom. Salvation and the basics of godly living are uttered clearly, but beyond those basic matters God reveals things in ways that force us to gain wisdom as we wrestle with them.

Also, note that by comparing C and C', we see man hiding from God, and God forcing him out into the open.

Adam and Eve accept the serpent's teaching (B'), while they flee from God's voice. Our previous studies have dealt at length with the matter of nakedness, openness, and fear. True glory garments leave human beings open and transparent before God. As Meredith Kline has shown, the glory robes of the High Priest were a mirror image of the Tabernacle,[104] and thus a perfect interface with God's personage. The heart of God (the Holy of Holies) was imaged by the outer Ephod box of the High Priest's garments, so that man stood heart-to-heart with God. Adam's garments were designed to do the opposite: not to glorify his nakedness (openness) before God, but to hide it.

---

104. Kline, *Images of the Spirit*, ch. 2.

20

GOD'S INSPECTION

GENESIS 3:9, 11–13

And He said, "Who told you that naked you are? From the tree that I commanded you not to eat from it, did you eat?" (Gen. 3:11)

WITH this statement we move to Day 3 of the sabbath day events. On the third day of Genesis 1, God clothed the land with grass and trees, and at the Day 3 event of Genesis 2, God caused trees to grow in the Garden and established rivers to flow from it (2:9–14). Now at the Day 3 event of Genesis 3, God asks Adam about the Tree of Knowledge and about his nakedness.

Let us take all three questions Yahweh God asks. First, from verse 9, "Where are you?" There are those who insist that the Bible must be interpreted only in a "plain sense" manner and who castigate and ridicule those who seek for deeper levels of meaning. These exegetes are very suspicious of typology and symbolism, literary structures, deep structures, and the like. Yet against them are not only common sense and the obvious statements of the Bible, but the whole history of the Church as well. No preacher, teacher, or commentator has ever taken this question "Where are you?" in some "plain sense." Did God not know where Adam actually was? Obviously God did indeed know exactly where Adam was, in every sense of the words. He knew where Adam was hiding in the Garden, and He knew where Adam was located spiritually.

I suppose that according to "plain sense" interpretation, Adam should have answered, "I'm over here, Lord. This way. Look. Follow my voice." But who in his right mind has ever taken the text to mean that?

No, Adam understands quite clearly that God's question was a probing one, not a superficial one. Adam answers honestly: "I'm hiding from You because I'm scared of You." Whether Adam is hiding in trees or fig leaves, or in caves or in a crowd, does not matter. "Where" he is, is alienated from God. That's the answer.

And so, preachers and teachers and commentators have always seen that this question is universal: "Reader, where are you? Are you alienated from God? Are you holding something back from Him? Are you scared of Him because you've done something you know He does not like?"

Let us now turn to the second question: "Who told you that naked you are?" Good question. In a sense, nobody had told Adam that. This is a second kind of question, one that does not have a right or wrong answer. Rather, it is designed to provoke thought.

As we think about it, one answer is that God "told" Adam that he was naked. God had made Adam naked. Assuming God had built into Adam a knowledge of the first human language, Adam knew that the word "naked" applied to him. From this fact, Adam could know that God had clothed the land with flowering grains and lovely trees. Since Adam was made of soil, he could expect to be clothed similarly. The lilies of the field are more glorious than Solomon in all his array, and Adam could expect to be clothed in a similar glory. And just in case we miss the analogy, this question comes in a "third day" slot in Genesis 3, so that we are forced to consider the analogy with land and plants.

Another "answer" to the question would come from taking the question a different way: "Who made you aware of a shameful nakedness, so that you hide from Me?" Taking the question that way, the "answer" has several levels. Adam's inner conscience told him that he was naked and needed to hide. But since it is God who works through our inner awareness of reality, it was God who made Adam aware that his nakedness had now become shameful. And, at another level, it was the Seducer and Accuser who was making Adam feel guilty and shamefully naked, as we see in Zechariah 3:1–5.

Then a third question, and a third kind of question: "From the tree that I commanded you not to eat from it, did you eat?" This question requires a simple yes or no answer. The first question required an answer at a deep level, not at the level of "plain sense." The second question really has no "answer" and is designed solely to provoke thought. The third question alone operates first at the level of "plain sense."

Even here, however, we should not rest at the level of simple sense, because it is easy to see that this question probes us as well. We have devoted a lot of attention to the theology of the two trees and their meaning, but in back of all this and in front of it as well is one simple matter: God said not to eat of the forbidden tree. Period. Note that God does not ask, "Did you eat of the fruit of the Tree of the Knowledge of Good and Evil?" He might have asked it that way, but if He had, we would be moved once again to consider the larger eschatological meaning of that tree. But He does not ask it that way. He asks, "Did you obey or disobey? Did you believe My words, or did you not believe them?" Before all theologizing, that is the first question we have to deal with; and at the end of all theologizing, that is the question we must come back to, for we shall answer it again on the Day of Judgment.

GOD'S QUESTIONS AND SATAN'S

The order of the questions in Genesis 2:9–11 is important. God might simply have come straight to Adam and asked him if he had disobeyed. He did not do so. First, God brought to Adam's consciousness the fact that Adam was alienated from Him. Then, God reminded Adam that He had made him naked in the first place, which reminded Adam of who God really is and encouraged Adam to understand that he could not hide from God and would have to answer to Him. Then and only then did God ask Adam directly about his sin. To boil it down more: God did not ask Adam about his sin until He had first reminded Adam of their relationship, now estranged, and had secondly reminded Him of who He is. In this context, God asked Adam to confess his sin.

There is sheer grace here, and also a pattern of evangelism. God gets Adam in a "mood" to speak with Him and to confess his sins. God does not simply barge in and demand a confession without first establishing a context for doing so. Just so, it is important for people to face their estrangement from God and then see who God really is, before they will deal with particular sins.

Moreover, the fact that God used questions rather than "preaching" to establish this context is very important. God might have said: "Okay, Adam, I know you are hiding from Me because you are afraid of Me. And Adam, I know you feel that nakedness is shameful, but remember who I am: I made you naked, and I can clothe you. I'm God; you're not. So, Adam, let's hear your confession: Did you disobey Me?" But God did not do it that way. Rather, He asked questions that brought up to the forefront of Adam's consciousness the facts of his alienation from the Almighty Creator.

When we "preach" to people, often they retreat into their minds and into their sinful fantasies and won't hear. "I'm not hiding from God," they say. "God did not make the world the way it is; and if He did, He's a monster." But when we use questions, we draw up into people's minds the reality of their situation:

1. "Where are you in your life right now? Is this really where you want to be? Are you lonely?"

2. "What about God? Somebody is in charge of all this 'mess' around you, right? Somebody made it all, right?"

These kinds of questions set the stage for bringing people to God through confession of their sins.

It is quite the opposite with the question(s) raised by the Deceiver. Recall that the serpent asked Eve a seemingly profound question, which was designed to cause meditation: "Who told you not to eat of this fruit?" We discussed the confusing answer to that question earlier in this series.

On the one hand, Adam had told her not to; but Adam claimed to be speaking for God. The words of the Deceiver, and the context in which he asks them, were designed to lead Adam and Eve into a position of helplessness and confusion. Once they were in that position, the Devil could simply assert his lie. They had become confused and now were open to domination. This is the root of philosophy and statism. Mystery cults and philosophies ask questions that put people in a position of confusion, because no answers are really possible. Helpless people are open to domination.

Satan's questions are like this always. Note the question in Job: "Does Job love God for nothing?" Either way you answer that question tends to be unsatisfactory. No, Job does not love God for nothing; rather, he loves God because God created and redeemed him. Yes, Job does love God for nothing, because his love is not dependent upon specific gifts. All the same, the question tends to mess with our minds, and we notice that God simply ignores it. Consider also Satan's questions to Jesus in the wilderness temptations and how Jesus simply ignores and rejects them. Jesus refuses to be drawn into a conversation on Satan's terms.

God's questions are designed to make us think so that we gain wisdom and salvation and grow in grace and glory. Satan's questions are designed to make us think so that we become confused and open to his evil suggestions.

THE SIN OF ADAM

And He said, "Who told you that naked you are? From the tree that I commanded you not to eat from it, did you eat?"

And the man said, "The woman whom You gave with me, she it was who gave me of the tree, and I ate."

And Yahweh God said to the woman, "What is this that you have done?"

And the woman said, "The serpent deceived me, and I ate" (Gen. 3:11–13).

The Bible speaks of original sin as the sin of Adam, most clearly in Romans 5. As long as expositors stick with systematic theology and with the various New Testament passages, they remain sound on this matter. These same men, however, when expounding Genesis 3 are very likely to pass the blame to Eve. Indeed, there is a very long and horrible tradition in the Christian religion of blaming the woman for the sin of man, seeing the woman as evil, a seductress, a danger, etc.

On two occasions, however, the Bible tells us that Eve did not sin deliberately but was indeed deceived, just as she said she was. In 2 Corinthians 11:3 we read, "as the serpent deceived Eve," and in 1 Timothy 2:14 we read, "Not Adam was deceived, but the woman, being wholly deceived, fell into transgression." How often do we hear, though, that "Adam tried to blame Eve, and Eve passed the blame to the serpent"? Both Wenham and Hamilton, the two major recent evangelical expositors, repeat this shibboleth.[105]

It just ain't so. In our studies thus far, we have already discussed the fact that Eve was misled by Adam and the serpent into tasting the fruit. As Paul

---

105. Hamilton, Genesis 1–17, 194; Wenham, *Genesis 1–15*, 78

wrote, she was "deceived" and merely "fell" into transgression. Adam was not deceived and transgressed with full awareness of what he was doing. Yes, Eve's sin was a trespass, and somewhere in her consciousness she knew better; but the Bible clearly distinguishes between sins of being led astray and sins committed with full knowledge and competence.[106]

Still, it is possible that Eve is trying to pass the blame here in Genesis 3:13. The text, however, does not give grounds for any certainty on the matter. What she says is quite simple and quite true: "The serpent deceived me, and I ate." This statement could just as easily be a confession of sin. Noting in the statement allows us to analyze Eve's intention, and to do so is an illegitimate psychologizing of the text.

The case is quite otherwise with Adam, and the contrast between Adam's statement and Eve's is instructive. Adam does not in fact blame Eve. He blames God: "The woman *you* gave [to be] with me." Eve does not say, "The serpent *you* put in the garden." Moreover, and this is not usually made clear in translation, Adam emphasizes that it was the woman who gave him the fruit: "The woman You gave with me, *she* gave me of the tree." In Hebrew, it is not necessary or common to write out the nominative pronoun ("she"), because the verbal form makes it clear. Whenever the pronoun is actually included, it is for stress and emphasis. Adam says, "*You* brought me this woman, and it was *she* who led me into sin."

Adam spits in God's face. He accuses God of causing him to sin. Originally Adam loved Eve as a wonderful gift from God, but now he accuses God of poisoning him. "Hey, God, if You didn't want me to sin, why'd you give me this temptress?" But we know that Adam was standing by all along (Gen. 3:6), and by his silence put Eve up to eating the fruit.

Adam had clearly chosen sides with the serpent, and when Eve says, "The serpent deceived me," her statement likely includes Adam along with Satan, for Adam had joined with Satan.

In conclusion: Adam's statement quite forcefully reinforces his sin as he blames God and Eve. Eve's statement lacks these qualities, and we are not given the information to know what overtones her statement carried. Likely she was still confused. Adam was not.

---

106. Cf. C. Van Dam, "The Meaning of *Bishgagah*," in Riemer Faber, ed., *Unity in Diversity: Studies Presented to Prof. Dr. Jelle Faber On the Occasion of his Retirement* (Hamilton, ON: Senate of the Theological College of the Canadian Reformed Churches, 1989), 13–23.

THE DARKENING OF THE SUN AND MOON

As we have seen, the creation of man and the Garden in Genesis 2 is a microcosm of the creation of the world and cosmos in Genesis 1. The creation of Adam corresponds to the sending forth of light on Day 1, and his placement as guardian and ruler over and within the Garden corresponds to placing the sun in the firmament on Day 4. The two great lights placed in the firmament on Day 4 symbolize the man and woman. Now, in 3:12–13 we come to the Day 4 event in Genesis 3. Here is a review of some of the material we have looked at above:

1. Adam and Eve are at rest with God and united with one another as one flesh. Their sin brings about disunity (2:25–3:7a).

   2. The disunity is signified by the barrier of clothing they place between each other and between themselves and God, and they flee from the blessed presence of God (3:7b–10).

   3. God accuses them of eating from the forbidden tree (3:11).

      4. The height of disunity is seen as Adam blames God and Eve, and both humans reject their position as heavenly rulers over the earth (3:12–13).

   5. God curses the serpent to eat dust (3:14–15).

   6. God's judgment upon the woman and the man signifies that they are no longer to experience the same kind of blessed nearness to Him and that they are alienated from Him (3:16–19).

7. Adam and Eve are excluded from God's sabbath, but they are reunited with each other and God gives them clothing, (3:20–24).

The sins of Adam and Eve are the darkening of the sun and moon in the firmament. Man, placed in the garden-firmament between heaven and earth, no longer gives forth light and truth to the world. Additionally, to anticipate an event shortly to take place, the casting out of Adam and Eve from the Garden is the falling of the sun and moon (and stars, their children) from the firmament.

This sort of symbolism is found later in Scripture. Especially in Genesis 37:5–10, the sun is Joseph's father, the moon is his mother, and the twelve stars (or, more likely, zodiacal constellations) are his brothers, all of which submit to him as the proto-Messiah.

In the light of these associations, we can see even more clearly why the Bible uses the darkening and fall of astral bodies as a symbol of the collapse of human civilizations.[107]

Further meditation on this symbolic structure yields additional insights. As the moon reflects the light of the sun, so Eve was to receive truth from Adam. Instead, she listened to the voice of the serpent and reflected his darkness. As a reflector, however, she was merely deceived. The greater evil is Adam's, for he was the sun, the human source of truth, the Word of God, to Eve. His failure to instruct her meant that he, as sun, was not putting forth the light. Additionally, as God will shortly charge, Adam listened to his wife when she was clearly wrong, and thus tried the pervert the order of nature, making the sun reflect the moon!

The Church is the Bride. She is to be lunar, reflecting the light of the Messianic Sun of Righteousness, the New Sun predicted in Malachi 4:2.

---

107. For a further study, see *Through New Eyes*, ch. 5, on Isaiah 13:9–10; Ezek. 32:7–8; Joel 2:31; Matthew 21:9; 24:32–34; and Revelation 6:12–13.

21

JUDGMENTS: OVERVIEW

THE judgment on the serpent (3:14) shadows the fifth day of creation, while the judgment on the woman and the man shadows the sixth day (3:14–15,16–19), for the serpent is associated both with the dinosaurs (Day 5) and the beasts (Day 6a). Though this is so at one level, at a more formal literary level the oracles against serpent, woman, and man form one unit:

A. The serpent and dust; "Cursed" (14).

B. The woman's seed; "I am putting" (15).

B'. The woman's seed; "I am increasing" (16).

A'. The man and dust; "Cursed" (17–19).

Let us begin with the B sections. In both B sections, Yahweh God says that He Himself will act: "I am putting enmity"; "I am greatly increasing." This is not the way the A sections are phrased. Secondly, both B sections have to do with hierarchy and rule: the rule of the woman and of her seed over the serpent, and the rule of the husband over the wife. Third, the B sections form a chiasm thematically:

  c. Serpent and woman: Who will rule?

   d. Serpent and child: Child will crush. Child will suffer.

   d'. Woman and child: Child will be born. Woman will suffer.

  c'. Husband and woman: Who will rule?

Turning to the A sections, the opening statement against the man (verse 17b) is parallel to the curse upon the serpent (verse 14), though the man is not cursed directly:

1. Cursed are you above all	Cursed is the ground with reference to you
2. Crawl on belly	In severe labor
3. Dust you will eat	You will eat of ground
4. All the days of your life	All the days of your life

The judgment on the man is then expanded (verses 18–19), following the same order and themes:

  1. Ground produces thorns

  2. Sweat of the nose

  3. Eat food

  4. End of life

Thus, in the A sections the themes are death and food, while in the B sections the themes are conflict and hierarchy.

The parallels between the serpent and the man serve to highlight something we have already clearly seen, that the man has chosen to identify with the serpent and to exchange being the son of God for being the son of Satan. Thus, the enmity between the serpent and the woman will often be expressed as enmity between man and woman, with men raping women throughout history and with women desiring to rule over men.

Moreover, having chosen to identify with the serpent, the man now experiences the same judgment as the serpent: to live with his nose to the ground, struggling for food, destined for death. In addition, the reminder that man is made of dust, and the fact that the serpent eats dust, implies that man will be eaten by the devil in the end, instead of being taken (eaten) into God's heavenly fellowship. It is the new man, the second Adam, born painfully of the woman, who will provide an alternative to this dismal fate.

RETHINKING THE STRUCTURE

Up until now—and most recently at the end of the previous chapter—we have been working with a particular approach to the structure of Genesis 3. But that structure needs some revision.

In Genesis 1, we are told first that God made the heavens and the earth, and then that the original earth needed some work. Then God comes and does the work of Day 1, giving light. In Genesis 2:4b, which begins the second passage, we are told that it is the day when God made earth and heaven, but that at the time in question (which turns out to be Day 6), the earth still needs some work. Parallel to 1:2, we are told of water over the earth in 2:6. Then Yahweh God comes and does the work of making man, the new Light. From this point, Genesis 2 recapitulates Genesis 1 thematically, as we have seen:

Day 2	2:8	the Garden-firmament
Day 3	2:9–14	trees on land, separation of land and waters
Day 4	2:15	placement of Man-light in Garden-firmament
Day 5	2:16–17	instructions, blessings and curses (cf. 1:22)
Day 6a	2:18–20	animals
Day 6b	2:21–24	man and woman

What I should have noticed before but failed to: Following God's work making earth and man is another introductory statement describing a condition that God comes to correct. As the earth was dark, chaotic, and empty in Genesis 1, and as it was devoid of man in Genesis 2, so now the problem is the fall of man. Perhaps the opening statement of the Genesis 3 story (which is found in 2:25) provides the first hint of the parallel:

Genesis 1: heavens and earth
Genesis 2: earth and heaven
Genesis 3: man and wife; naked and without shame

What follows immediately is the fall of man. Since man was identified in Genesis 2 as the new Light for the world, his fall is the darkening of that light. The world is now dark again.

Now God must act, as Yahweh God, to deal with this new darkness. Yahweh God does seven things in Genesis 3:8–24, which recapitulate His two preceding sevenfold actions. Just as God's actions on the sixth day involved a recapitulation of creation week, so do God's actions on the seventh day, the day of sabbath worship and judgment.

1.   *Genesis 3:8.* Yahweh God arrives in a Day 1 mode, in the *Spirit* of the *Day.* The insertion of the Spirit into the world in 1:2 and the manifestation of Day-Light in 1:3–5 is rather clearly alluded to. (How did I miss this?) Moreover, as the now-dark Adam and Eve hide, we see again the separation of light and darkness, of day and night.

2.   *Genesis 3:9–12.* Yahweh God interrogates Adam in the Garden firmament.

3.   *Genesis 3:13.* Yahweh God interrogates the woman. What does this have to do with Day 3, or with 2:9–14? Several things. First, the woman in the Garden, being beautiful, corresponds to the beautiful trees. Second, the outflowing streams from the Garden correspond to the streams of children that flow from the woman. Later on, the menstrual flow from the woman's body will be called a "fountain" (Lev. 12:7; 20:18). Understanding this parallel adds depth to the fact that when the woman ate the seeded fruit given by the serpent, she was committing spiritual bestiality and would carry the child of the serpent (2 Cor. 11:2–3). Thus, sinful men would be "of your father, the devil," and indeed, Eve's first child was such a one. As a fruit's seed is buried in the soil and grows to be a tree, so Satan's corrupt seed was planted in the woman, and her children would be corrupt trees.

4.   *Genesis 3:14–19.* Yahweh God passes judgment on the firmament lights, which He had placed to rule the world. These judgments follow out three days within this section:

   A. 3:14–15. Lucifer, being mankind's tutor, was the highest light, and thus most closely associated with Day 4.

   B. 3:16. Eve with her children swarming around her is associated with Day 5, the day of swarms.

   C. 3:17–19. Adam, made to cultivate the soil (2:15, the "fourth day" of chapter 2), is most closely associated with Day 6.

5.   *Genesis 3:21.* Yahweh God makes garments to clothe Adam and Eve, garments being swarms around a person in biblical imagery.

6.   *Genesis 3:22.* Yahweh God announces that man, made on Day 6, the image of God, has become "like one of Us," though in an evil sense.

7.   *Genesis 3:23–24.* Yahweh God pronounces a sabbath judgment on Adam and Eve, excluding them from the sabbath sanctuary.

MORE ON STRUCTURE

While numerics is not a structuring device, the use of numbers does often relate to themes. Moreover, observing how the text uses numerical devices helps us appreciate just how skillfully God has caused His book to be written.

Genesis 1–4 is one section of the Bible. Genesis 1 (through 2:4a) relates the creation of the world in seven days, using the word "God." Genesis 2:4a–24 relates the events of the sixth day, while Genesis 2:25–3:24 relates the events of the seventh day. Since these days are part of creation week, "God" is used, but since they relate to man's covenant with God, the word "Yahweh" is also used. Genesis 4 records a second fall, after the completion of creation week, showing how human history moved after God set it up. In fact, this passage shows the corruption of the first "week" of mankind, which is the second week of creation (and thus leads us to "passover," which begins the third week of the first month). There, since not creation but covenant is exclusively in view, "God" is not used, but "Yahweh" is.

Genesis 1:1–2:4a uses "God" 35 times, which is 5 times 7. The number five in the Bible has to do with power and strength, the number of fingers on the hand—here God's mighty hand. The number of seven, of course, has to do with the original fullness of things as God does them. Seven is three (God) plus four (the world, 2:10, etc.). This is the number of the original creation. The new creation is three times four, or twelve. Seven is the number of God and man (world) side by side, while twelve is the number of God and man (creation) married and interpenetrating.

Genesis 2:4b–3:25 uses "Yahweh God" twenty times, which is 2 times 10. Ten is another number of totality or fullness. There are ten actions of God on the seven days of creation: [1] Creation; [2] Day 1; [3] Day 2; [4] Day 3a (land); [5] Day 3b (plants); [6] Day 4; [7] Day 5; [8] Day 6a (animals); [9] Day 6b (man); [10] Day 7.

Genesis 4 uses "Yahweh" ten times.

This gives us a total of 65 uses of the name of God, one way or another. It remains to be noted that "God" also appears four times in Eve's conversation with the serpent (3:1–5) and once at the end of the passage (4:25), for a total of seventy times, which is ten times seven.

All of this is no accident. Sometimes, instead of "God" or "Yahweh," we simply read "He." The few times that this happens serve to reduce the number of named references to God, so that the numerics come out properly. This is also true as regards the matters we turn to now. Proper nouns are replaced by pronouns exactly enough times to cause the number of the proper nouns to be significant.

It is also not an accident that "garden" is used seven times in Genesis 3. The Garden is the microcosm of the cosmos set up on the seven days of creation in Genesis 1. The corruption of the Garden in Genesis 3 carries with it the corruption of the whole larger cosmos of Genesis 1.

There is more. In 2:4b–17, the creation of man and the Garden, "garden" is used five times. This is not immediately significant until we realize that the man is to guard the Garden and the woman is the preeminent thing in the Garden he must guard. The passage that delineates the failure of the man to guard the Garden, that is, the woman, is 2:25–3:7, and there "woman" is used five times. The total is ten, but the two sets of five serve to strengthen the link between the woman and the Garden, the Bride and the Kingdom who are to be guarded by the Son (Luke 3:38).

Matching this numerical link, perhaps, is the fact that in 2:18–24, where the woman is made from the man and given to the man to guard, "man" ('adam) occurs ten times. (At the end of 2:23, the word is not 'adam but 'ish.)

In 4:1–15, the story of Cain and Abel, "Abel" occurs seven times, "Yahweh" eight times, and "Cain," interestingly, twelve times. Cain establishes a new covenant, a twelve to replace the original seven, 3 x 4 replacing 3 + 4, but it is a wicked new covenant. He establishes it on the blood of his brother, anticipating in a negative way what will be needed for the true new covenant. That fact that "Yahweh" occurs eight times seems also significant, for eight is also a number of a new covenant, the beginning of a new week. Yahweh acts to cancel what Cain had done to defile the week of humanity, making possible the return of worship at the end of chapter 4.

A DOUBLE CHIASM

As we have seen, if we look at the actions of Yahweh God in the judgment scene of Genesis 3:8–24, we find another recapitulation of Genesis 1 and 2. Since the arrangement of Days and actions on those two passages is chiastic, this one will perforce be also, and we can see it as follows:

Day 1: Garden; Yahweh God comes in Spirit and Day (verse 8).

  Day 2: Man, the firmament mediator; Yahweh God addresses him (verses 9–12).

    Day 3: Woman, the Garden tree and source of life (verse 13).

      Day 4: Judgments on the heavenly rulers (verses 14–20).

    Day 5: Woman and man given garments as shroud-cloud (verse 21).

  Day 6: Man judged (verse 22).

Day 7: Garden; man exiled (verses 23–24).

If we look carefully, however, we see that verse 20 does not quite fit the pattern. If we look again, then, we can see that this chiastic skeleton supports a body that is a fuller chiasm covering the same verses. If we let the bones of the framework recede a bit from view, we can see the following chiastic flow:

A. Garden (verses 8–10a).

  B. Nakedness and Tree (verses 10b–11).

    C. Woman (verses 12–13).

      D. Curse and Dust (verse 14).

        E. Woman and Serpent (verse 15a).

          F. Seed and Serpent (verse 15b).

          F'. Seed and Woman (verse 16a).

        E'. Woman and Man (verses 16b–17a).

      D'. Curse and Dust (verses 17b–19).

    C'. Woman (verse 20).

  B'. Nakedness and Tree (verses 21–22).

A'. Garden (verses 23–24).

The value of this fuller chiasm is that it clearly puts the birth of the Seed Messiah at the center of the passage.

An overlapping structure for the central judgment section, which we pointed to above, highlights how the curse on the serpent is extended in a softened way to the woman and the man:

SERPENT   D. Banishment (verse 14a).

        E. Dust (verse 14b).

          F. Enmity of seeds (verse 15a).

            G. Hierarchy of human and demon (verse 15b).

WOMAN   F' Enmity of seeds causes pain in childbearing (verse 16a).

          G' Hierarchy of man and woman (verse 16b).

MAN   *D'* Banishment from soil (verses 17–19a).
       E' Dust (verse 17b).

With this background established, we are now in a position to move into the details of the judgments in the next chapter.

22

THE JUDGMENT ON THE SERPENT

GENESIS 3:14–15

And Yahweh God said to the serpent, "Because you have done this:
  Cursed (banned) *are you*
    from all cattle
  and from all beasts of the field;
  upon your belly you shall go (Gen. 3:14).

THE first two of the four curses upon the serpent are found in Genesis 3:14. Only the serpent is directly cursed, and the word *you* is emphatic in Hebrew. The man and the woman are not cursed directly, but mediately through the soil, an important distinction that we shall address in due course.

English Bibles render the first phrase, "Cursed are you more than (or above) all the other animals." Yet in fact the other animals are not cursed at all, so there is a problem, and the problem is in the translation. There are several words for "curse" in Hebrew, and unfortunately our English Bibles wind up translating all of them with the one word "curse." The word here, 'arur, means "banish, separate," in the sense of being isolated from what is good. To curse a person in this sense is to wish that he be cut off from God and from the covenant and from all the good things of the covenant.

The meaning here is that the serpent is isolated from or banished from being part of the cattle and the beasts of the field. Originally, the serpent was one of the beasts of the field (3:1). Now he is cut out from that category. He is not repositioned among the cattle, but among the creeping things. Genesis 1:24–26 identified these three categories. Cattle are the domestic animals that live with human beings. Beasts of the field are wild, free, undomesticated animals. Creeping things crawl along the ground, and now the serpent is put with them: He will crawl on his belly.[108]

In Leviticus 11 the character of swarmers-creepers is fleshed out. The chapter begins by distinguishing clean and unclean cattle and beasts of the field, fishes, birds, and hopping insects. In verse 29, attention is called to the larger swarming-crawling creatures. These are described as creatures that break the boundaries of human life and invade the human house, defiling the house. This is precisely what the serpent did in Genesis 3, for as a beast of the field he did not belong in the Garden uninvited, as we saw when we dealt with Genesis 2:19–20 (to wit: the cattle are not brought into the Garden because they were already there). The serpent crossed the boundary and brought uncleanness (which is symbolic death).

The list of eight big swarmers in Leviticus 11:29 mentions mole and mouse and then six serpents. These animals move on their belly. The word for "belly" here occurs only one other place, Leviticus 11:42. It is not the word for "stomach," also translated "belly" in some English Bibles, but a word that means the bottom part of the animal's abdomen.

Another aspect of this curse is that the serpent loses his name. Adam had named the birds, the domestic animals, and the wild animals, but not the fish and not the crawlers. By putting the serpent in with the crawlers, the serpent moves into the lower category of animals that are not named. They don't rate high enough to be given names.[109]

---

108. The statement, "On your belly you shall go," does not go with the next phrase about eating dust, but with the preceding phrases about being banished from being among the beasts of the field.

109. Of course, as time has gone along, men have named fish and insects and lizards also,

Behind the serpent is, of course, Lucifer. The word for serpent, *nachash*, is related to the word for bronze, *nechosheth*. Moses made a bronze serpent in Numbers 21:9, a *nachash nechosheth*. Bronze is a symbol for a lesser but real kind of glory. The altar and laver were made of bronze, while the items associated with the more glorious tent and temple were made of silver or gold.

Goliath, girded in bronze,[110] was not just a political but also a religious figure, which is why David calls him "uncircumcised" and why David rightly saw the conflict as primarily religious (1 Sam. 17:5–6). The Angel of Yahweh, who replaces Lucifer, appears as bronze in Daniel 10:6 and Revelation 2:18. We may perhaps surmise that the serpent's original name was Bronze One, and that he forfeited that name to the Angel of Yahweh, the Son of Man.

DUST YOU SHALL EAT

And dust you shall eat all the days of your life (Gen. 3:14b).

Serpents do not literally eat dirt, but "dust" here does not mean dry dirt. Rather, since man was made of dust (Gen. 2:7), by extension all the animals are made of it as well (Gen. 1:24; 2:19; and explicitly in Ps. 104:29). Serpents eat other things that crawl along the ground, such as insects and small animals, and that is what the "dust" means here.

Symbolically, eating dust is a picture of humiliation. The enemies of the Messianic King lick the dust in Psalm 72:9, which associates them with the serpent of course, but also is a picture of their heads under the feet of the Victorious One. The same picture is found in Isaiah 49:23 and Micah 7:17. The symbol of eating dust under the feet of one's enemy actually begins in Genesis 3:15, which reads, "He will bruise your head, and you will bruise his heel," and continues through the Bible in places like Psalm 7:5.

The serpent, the devil, will eat dust "all the days of your life." Man will eat in toil and hardship "all the days of your life" as well (Gen. 3:17), but men die and the punishment comes to an end. Since Satan can never die, he will eat dust forever, forever defeated. Isaiah 65 portrays the glories of the coming

---

but nobody thinks these animals have the kind of personality that mammals have.

110. Not only is Goliath's armor made of bronze (*nehosheth*); it is also described, literally, as a coat of "scales." Cf. Peter J. Leithart, *A Son to Me: An Exposition of 1 & 2 Samuel* [Moscow, ID: Canon, 2003], 107–108.

kingdom by saying that "the wolf and the lamb will graze together, and the lion will eat straw like the ox"—good, peaceful food for all—"while dust will be the serpent's food." Even in the fullness of the kingdom, the curse on the serpent will not be lifted.

Man, however, is made of dust, and we are reminded of that fact in this very passage (Gen. 3:19). Clearly, some of the dust that the serpent will eat consists of sinful men, those not raised from the dust. Agreeably to this, Peter tells us that our "adversary, the devil, prowls about like a roaring lion, seeking someone to devour" (1 Pet. 5:8).

In the sacrificial system, the sacrifices are repeatedly said to be food for God. The offerings represent the people, who are eaten by God, taken into His "consuming" fire (Heb. 12:29) and symbolically incorporated into His fellowship.[111] Satan also seeks a kingdom and wants to eat men into it.

God created man from dust, and the Bible speaks of this more generally when God tells King Baasha, "I exalted you from the dust" (1 Kgs. 16:2 NASB). Often we are reminded that men are but dust, as in Genesis 18:27; Job 8:19; and Psalm 103:14. Thus, it is not only dead men, bound for hell, that the serpent may eat, but living men as well.

Because man returns to dust, of course, it is most often as a picture of death that we encounter the symbolic meaning of dust (e.g., Job 7:21;14:8, 19;16:15; 20:11; 21:26; 30:19; 34:15; Pss. 22:29; 44:25; Dan. 12:2). When people cast dust on their heads, or dust is thrown on them, they are saying that they are experiencing death (Josh. 7:6; 2 Sam. 16:13, Job 2:12; Ezek. 27:30; Acts 22:23; Rev. 18:19).

But God is one who raises men up from the dust of death (e.g., 1 Sam. 2:8; Job 19:25; Ps. 113:7; Isa. 26:19). The resurrection body is not earthy, but spiritual (1 Cor. 15:42–49). The serpent cannot eat the dust that rises to live again. Only those who go to hell, resurrected in their merely earthy and dusty bodies, are his portion.

---

111. The repeated phrase "offering by fire" should be translated "food offering," as Gordon Wenham points out in his commentary on Leviticus. Cf. Gordon J. Wenham, *The Book of Leviticus*, New International Commentary on the Old Testament (Grand Rapids: Eerdmans, 1979), 56n8.

ENMITY

And enmity will I put... (Gen. 3:15a).

The Hebrew word for "enmity" means "enemy-hood." Another form of the word is often set in contrast to "neighbor." The concept is closely associated with hatred, in the covenantal sense of hatred: "to view as an enemy." Believers bear in mind that we are commanded to love our enemies, so that, covenantally speaking, hatred and love are not quite opposites. To hate means to regard as an enemy, but the person we hate is the person we must also love, by seeking his ultimate welfare as a convert. Thus, the old prayer, "Lord, please either kill them or convert them," is quite accurate and summarizes the thinking of the many cursing prayers in the psalms.

While we are to love our human enemies, even while hating them with a perfect hatred (Ps. 139:22), we are not to try and love the rebel angels, for there is no possibility of their conversion and salvation. The evil principalities and powers are our pure enemies, and their captain is Lucifer, the one who energized the serpent to seduce Eve and corrupt Adam.

Because fallen man is a sinner and naturally hates God, man would naturally love Satan. Thus, God acts to put or place enmity between mankind and Satan. This is because fallen man is a fool (Ps. 14:1) who thinks he can be Satan's pal and friend. Satan, however, hates all mankind, even fallen man, because Satan knows that even fallen man is still the image of God, and Satan hates God. Satan is not confused. Satan seeks the destruction of all human beings, whether converted back to God or not.

This is why all non-Christian religions view their gods as both good and evil, as both friendly and capriciously evil. One need only read Homer to see this. The gods are good some of the time and friendly to men, but the same gods can change their minds and do wicked things, sporting with helpless men. The gods cannot be trusted; they can only be appeased and bought off with gifts. We find this same view of the gods in all pagan cultures.

Thus, God has acted to protect us from foolishly thinking Satan is our friend. We may hate God, but we find that we cannot really trust Lucifer. If God had not done this, no pagan culture would survive very long. All pagan cultures would wind up in pure evil and strife and kill each other off or commit cultural suicide, if God had not acted to prevent them from doing so. This is why pagan cultures are so frozen and traditional; their traditions and taboos keep them from going off the deep end. These "archaic structures," as they are often called, keep the pagan cultures alive until the coming of the gospel.

When the gospel comes, however, "things fall apart," as Nigerian Christian novelist Chinua Achebe points out in *Things Fall Apart*.[112] The old structures immediately shatter, and now men must choose either God or death. Those who do not choose the gospel must come up with a new way to keep their cultures alive, since the traditions have been shattered. What they devise is statism. The power of the state is used to keep the culture alive. Fear of taboos and demons is replaced by fear of the state. Paganism is replaced by humanism.

The enmity is still there, however, for men both love and hate the state. Americans, for instance, want the government to provide them with security and welfare, while resenting the government and its taxation and secret police. The God-given enmity persists; man's ambiguous relationship with his false gods continues in operation.

The first history in the Bible provides a short picture of this change. God put enmity between man and Satan in the beginning, but not between man and man. The result was that the Sethite sons of God intermarried with the Cainite daughters of men, creating a unified wicked culture that God destroyed at the Flood. After the Flood the same thing happened, as the Joktanites (Hebrews from Shem) joined with Nimrod to build Babel. Then God acted to put enmity between man and man, so that never again will men be able to unite. The change from the Adamic world to the Noahic world is the same as the shift from paganism to humanism, for Noah was given to eat of the Tree of Knowledge by being made a ruler.

This change of affairs is a type, a prefiguring, of the change from the Old Creation as a whole to the New Creation (2 Pet. 3:3–7). In Revelation we find the daughters of God (Harlot Babylon) joining with the sons of men (Beast) in a short-lived war against the Church (Rev. 13–14). This is the last time men will ever be able to join together completely against the believers, until the very end of history when all nations will rise together one last time under Gog (Rev. 20). The alliance of Beast and Harlot ended when the Beast turned against the Harlot and destroyed her in the Roman-Jewish War.

One more point should be made, and that is that God did not just put enmity one time between Satan and humanity, and between one group of evil

---

112. Chinua Achebe, *Things Fall Apart* (1958; reprint, New York: Penguin, 1994).

men and other groups. That would be reason enough to praise Him. But God actively stirs up the evil hearts of men to mistrust their gods and to hate one another. God keeps putting enmity, over and over again. We see this in that He hardened Pharaoh's heart. We also see it in the fact that when the gospel goes forth and God is drawn near to a given culture, the people in that culture (who reject the gospel) wind up at each other's throats. They kill each other off. When Gideon and his men shouted Yahweh's name into the camp of the Midianites, they turned against each other (Judg. 7; cf. also 2 Sam. 14:20; 2 Chron. 20:23; Ezek. 38:21; Hag. 2:22; Zech. 14:13; and Rev. 17:16).

ENMITY WITH ADAM?

And enmity will I put between you and the woman... (Gen. 3:15a).

As we have seen, God acts to put antagonism between Lucifer and humanity, to prevent humanity from blindly following Satan to destruction. Interestingly, Genesis 3:15 does not say that God puts enmity between the serpent and Adam, but only between the serpent and the woman and between the serpent's seed and the woman's seed. This means that Eve and all human beings descended from her will be stimulated to distrust Satan. But why not Adam also?

One possibility is that Adam has become one with Satan, and so it is "too late" to put enmity between them. This would mean that there is no hope for Adam's salvation, and there have been some theologians who argue that Adam was in fact damned. I think, however, that there are two reasons to think Adam was saved.

First is the fact that God clothes him as well as Eve in an animal skin. True, this means partly that Adam and Eve have identified with the beasts of the field and thus will appear as such. But given that the beast is slain to provide the covering, it is impossible to exclude the idea of substitutionary judgment from this event. Surely part of the meaning of the passage is that God kills a beast as a substitute for the death Adam has brought on himself and Eve.

Second is the fact that Cain and Abel knew to bring sacrifices to God, and they learned this from Adam and Eve—unless angels taught them. Or we might assume that Eve taught her sons to bring sacrifices, while Adam was out spending time with his buddy Satan. Neither of these options strikes me as very credible. Nothing hints that Adam and Eve were seeking to bring their sons up to worship Satan and that angels had to interpose to teach the sons to worship the Lord. And as for the suggestion that Eve was righteous while Adam was wicked, God put the skin on both of them, which to my mind links them in the same status.

Thus, I submit that Adam was put to death for his sin on the day that he ate of the forbidden fruit, just as God promised, except that his death was taken by an animal substitute. In this way, redemption was offered to Adam, and God put him back into fellowship with Himself. Adam was spared the full judgment due for his sin, but not spared the consequences of his sin: He was driven from the Garden to a life of pain and (lesser forms of) death.

Which brings us back to our question: If Adam was put back on God's side, then why didn't God put enmity between the serpent and Adam? I see two possible answers:

1. Since Adam is one flesh with Eve, her enmity is his enmity. This may be part of the answer, but I think the following understanding is the primary one:

2. The woman was deceived, and children growing up in a sinful world learn deceptive ideas of reality from the womb forward. Thus, all human beings who have ever lived, except for Adam and Jesus, are deceived. They all start out in a state of weakness, susceptible to deceptive influences. As we have seen, this was also true of Eve. Thus, to match that weakness, God acts to place antagonism toward Satan in our hearts. Adam, however, was not deceived. He sinned with clear self-consciousness, which implies that he also now understands clearly that Satan is his enemy. There is no need for God to put enmity between Satan and Adam. Indeed, Adam as the representative man needs to oppose Satan *without* any extra miraculous enmity provided by God.

What this means, I think, is that God acts to put enmity against Satan into the hearts of children and the childish. This is for their protection, since they are relatively weak and thus liable to deception. Those who mature to full age, however, must stand against Satan without this extra measure of psychological enmity. They must move from instinctual enmity to self-conscious enmity: from emotion to will.

ENMITY WITH THE WOMAN

And enmity will I put between you and the woman, and between your seed and her seed (Gen. 3:15a).

Christians are so accustomed to thinking of the warfare between the serpent and the seed of the woman that they often overlook the conflict between Satan and the woman. But the latter is in some ways more fundamental. Satan seeks to destroy humanity, the bride of Christ, the woman. When the Seed comes forth to defend the woman, Satan seeks to destroy him also. The Seed is the woman's champion, so Satan must fight him; but Satan's goal is the destruction of the woman.

As a result of the prophecies in Genesis 3, Satan knows that the woman is destined to produce this champion. Thus, as we look at Satan's warfare against the woman we find that on some occasions he is attacking her directly, while on other occasions his assault is designed to prevent her from giving birth to the champion. In Genesis 12, for instance, Satan moves against Sarai simply because she is the woman, while in Genesis 20, he moves against her because God had just told her that she was about to become pregnant with the seed of Abraham.

The curse on the serpent goes on to say that God will put enmity between the seed of the serpent and the seed of the woman. A "literal" reading of this statement would mean that small children don't like snakes; and indeed, such a "literal" reading seems to lie behind the prophecy that in the kingdom of God the nursing child will play safely next to a cobra's hole, and a weaned child will be able to put his hand safely on a viper's den (Isa. 11:8).

The curse means much more than such a "literal" reading provides, however. The serpent, meaning Lucifer, has offspring, who will war with the offspring of the woman. This means several things.

First, notice that one child is said to be the seed of the woman. Arguing that men have seeds and women have eggs is irrelevant; the Hebrew word does not have that kind of clinical specificity. The reference is to offspring. The language comes from the plant kingdom: In Genesis 1, plants produce seeds. The woman, as a flower, produces a seed that falls to the ground and grows up to be another plant. This language is completely in line with the fact that the woman is part of the Garden that Adam was to cultivate and guard.

Second, notice that the child of the woman is at enmity with Satan. Because of the depravity of man, as a result of the fall, we might wonder that any human being can give birth to a child that is on God's side. But such goodness is not *immediately* implied here. Rather, as we have seen previously, the text is saying that God will interpose to prevent evil men (the seed of the woman) from cooperating with Satan and his evil seed.

Third, the whole statement, however, which says that the woman's seed will crush the serpent's head, points to a good seed to come from the woman. We know that this points ultimately to Jesus. Why from the woman? Because the sin was Adam's, not Eve's. She was deceived and led astray, while Adam sinned self-consciously. The seed of the man, by implication, would be corrupt. But there is hope for the seed of the woman. For a seed to be good, he has to have no human father, only a human mother.

How does good seed come from the woman? After all, she must be married (one way or another) to a corrupt man. The answer is that God interposes between the man and the woman to provide a good offspring. God graciously prevents the Adams from having children, until He is ready to act and bring about a miraculous birth. Thus, God miraculously opened the wombs of Sarah, Rebekah, Rachel, Hannah, Samson's mother, and Elizabeth, in each case producing an anointed seed who was called to stand against Satan's seed (Isaac, Jacob, Joseph, Samuel, Samson, John).

Nothing in this prophecy and its implications means that women are "less depraved" then men. Rather, the prophecy is covenantal and partly symbolic (as we shall see, since Satan cannot have children). The Bible neither teaches nor implies that depravity is carried through male sperm, or anything like that. In fact, later on the messianic seed is spoken of as the seed of Abraham, of Jacob, of David. It is here in Genesis 3 that the seed is considered the woman's seed, because of Adam's sin. Covenantally speaking, nothing good can come from Adam as father. Only if the woman is married to God will she have good seed.

Which brings us to a fourth consideration: Since angels don't multiply, Satan cannot have angelic seed. The seed of the serpent must come through the woman also. Thus, in Bible history we repeatedly see Satan try to capture the Bride in order to raise up wicked seed through her. The physical assaults on women by men in league with Satan, recorded in Bible history, represent the larger spiritual assaults on them by Satan and his army.

Thus, the woman's seed can come from God or from Satan, but not from Adam. Adam, and men in general, provide the physical mechanism for conception (except in the case of Jesus), but the child either has God or the devil as his father.

For this reason a man must give up his child to God, as the story of Abraham and Isaac dramatizes for us. In baptism, the father gives his child over to God as Father, confessing that he is not good enough to be a father. In this way our children become seeds not of Adam, but of the woman, with God as father.

THE WAR AGAINST THE WOMAN AND HER SEED: EVE TO EGYPT

Hearing the curse spoken against him, the serpent (Lucifer) knew that eventually the woman would give birth to a Seed who would destroy him. As we have mentioned, Satan's initial attack was against the woman as such, seeking to seduce her from Adam and from God. He was initially successful because Adam connived with him, virtually pushing Eve into his arms so to speak. Now, however, Lucifer not only will seek to corrupt and destroy the Bride of the Son of God (the woman), but also will seek to prevent her Seed from coming to maturity.

Revelation 12:4 tells us that throughout the Old Creation history, Satan (the Dragon) stood poised to kill the Seed of the woman as soon as He was born. Let us now briefly survey the Bible history and see the various battles in this ongoing conflict.

In Genesis 4:1, we are told that Eve gave birth to a son, Cain, and stated that she had borne him with the help of Yahweh. Right away she confesses the truth we investigated briefly in the previous section, that any true seed of the woman must have God as his Father. Cain grew up to take Satan's side, while his younger brother Abel was godly. Thus, Satan knew which son was likely to grow up and crush him, so he took measures to kill Abel.

In Genesis 4:25, we are told again that Eve gave birth to a son to replace Abel and that she named him Seth, "Appointed," for God had appointed this new son for her. Again, the child is spoken of as the seed of the woman, with God as ultimate Father. Also, we see the woman as the one who names the seed. His son, Enosh, became the first to organize corporate worship of Yahweh (4:26).

Satan's initial attempt to destroy the seed by killing them had failed. Now he acted to corrupt them by intermarriage (Gen. 6), which provoked God to destroy the entire human race. But Satan's seeming success was thwarted because there was one godly man, and he and his family were preserved to re-found humanity.

We move now to Genesis 12:10–20. Satan has seen God call Abram and declare that through his line the Seed would come. Immediately Satan acts to take Abram's wife Sarai away from him, as Pharaoh seizes her for his harem. The focus here is less on preventing the seed, however, and more on Satan's hatred for God's Bride, for the attack on Sarai is said to be not because she had a fruitful womb, but because she was beautiful.

A second attack on Sarah comes in Genesis 20:1–18, as the godly Abimelech is provoked to the temporary sin of seizing Sarah from Abraham. The context of this attack is Genesis 18:20, where God said that within a year Sarah would be pregnant by Abraham. This is what Satan was trying to prevent. God defeats Satan by visiting Abimelech, and immediately thereafter, Sarah does become pregnant. Although 21:3 says that Abraham named his son Isaac ("Laughter"), the name comes from Sarah's laughing in 18:12–15, so again it is the woman who names the seed.

Sarah's womb had been closed. It took a miracle from God to open her womb and two miracles from God to protect her as Abram/Abraham's wife. Clearly, God was the Father of this seed.

Isaac's wife Rebekah was also barren. When she became pregnant, after much time, she went to Yahweh to ask why her womb was so troubled. God answered with a prophecy concerning Esau and Jacob (25:21–23). Once again, the children are given by an act of God, and God himself speaks to the fate of the children, determining their lives as Father.

In Genesis 27, we find that Satan has provoked Isaac to favor sinful Esau over godly Jacob. Rebekah, the mother, knows which of the men is the true seed and acts to protect him. The mother of the seed acts to protect her child from Satan.

In Genesis 29:31–30:24, we read of the sons and daughter of Jacob. In each case, it is the mother who names the child. Moreover, the passage is organized so that the miraculous son (Joseph) is discussed last, after God miraculously opens the womb of his mother Rachel, though Joseph was actually about the same age as Judah.[113]

Joseph turns out to be the most faithful son, honored by his father—clearly the seed who threatens Satan. Satan tries to destroy him by killing him and, when that fails, sending him away to Egypt. God thwarts this plan by making Joseph successful in Egypt. Satan again attacks, seeking Joseph's life, and again Joseph is saved and merely imprisoned. Then God intervenes to elevate Joseph over Egypt, and Joseph saves his brethren as well. Clearly, Joseph, the miraculous seed of the woman, is also the son of God.

THE WAR AGAINST THE WOMAN AND HER SEED: EGYPT TO KINGDOM

In Exodus 1 we find that Satan turns the Pharaohs against the Hebrews and eventually seeks to kill all their sons. The daughters were to be kept alive, as women for the Egyptians, so that Satan could raise up his own seed through them. Satan was seeking to steal the bride and to prevent the seed from being born. Initially the command was simply that midwives were to kill boy babies. The midwives, however, acted as true mothers of the seed and deceived Pharaoh, preserving the male seed of the Hebrews. Like faithful Rebekah, they lied to protect the seed from the Satanic tyrant. So Pharaoh went further and ordered that all male children of the Hebrews were to be slaughtered.

In Exodus 2:1–3, however, we find that a certain mother acted to protect her seed. The entire story is about Moses' mother(s), not his father. Pharaoh's daughter became a surrogate seed-mother, protecting the child and giving him his name. Once again, Satan's attempt to wipe out the seed was thwarted, and eventually Pharaoh must have been forced to stop killing Hebrew babies. After all, there were lots of Hebrew men alive at the time of the exodus later on.

Thus far in the Bible history, every description of the birth of a child has focused attention on the activity of the mother, over against the human father, and in virtually every case the text has pointed to the active involvement of

---

113. Joseph was born at the end of the first seven years of Jacob's marriage to Leah and Rachel (Gen. 30:25 with 31:41), but it is virtually impossible to fit the births of all ten of his other brothers—let alone Dinah—into that seven-year time period.

God as Father. This continues to be pretty much the pattern throughout the rest of the Bible whenever the birth of children is described.

As we noted earlier, before the Flood Satan's campaign had two phases. First he tried to kill off the seed, and when that failed, he sought to seduce and corrupt the seed. Such a corruption would have the desired effect either of recruiting the seed to Satan's army or of provoking God to destroy the seed. Either way, Satan would win.

At the exodus, Satan employed this same two-phase approach. First he tried to intimidate the Hebrews, so that they would not leave Egypt, and when they left, he sought to kill them, first with Pharaoh's army and then with the Amalekites. When this approach failed, he sought to seduce them into apostasy at the Golden Calf incident and repeatedly throughout the forty years in the wilderness, but through the labors of Apostle Moses and his assistants, Satan was again defeated. We shall see exactly this same two-phase attack in the apostolic history recorded in Acts and Revelation.

As we continue our survey we come to Judges 4–5, where Deborah, the "Mother in Israel" (Judg. 5:7), raises up a generation of godly seed to defeat Sisera. In Judges 5:30, Deborah tells us that the enemy army hoped to take back Israelite girls as "wombs" (as it literally says). Satan was seeking to raise up his own wicked seed through the brides of the covenant.

In Judges 13 we find the story of the birth of Samson. Again it is the mother who is in focus, and again the woman is barren. Her name is not given, though that of her husband Manoah is. By doing this, the text calls attention to her as an archetypal mother. God appears to her repeatedly, but not to her husband. God opens her womb, and God is clearly the Father, spiritually, of her child. Samson grows up to be a mighty picture of the coming Messianic Seed, Jesus.

At the same time, God also visited Hannah and opened her barren womb (1 Sam. 1). Again the focus is on the mother, a barren woman. Again the miraculous seed was the child of God, given to the Tabernacle as Yahweh's son from his early years. Both of these men, Samson and Samuel, were Nazirites, holy warriors. In both stories we find that it is the mother who names the seed.

When God anointed David to be messianic king, Satan once again had an opportunity to kill one specific person and thereby prevent the birth of the Messiah. He provoked Saul on several occasions to try and kill David. Once David had wives and sons of his own, Satan attempted to take them for himself (1 Sam. 30). All of these attempts were thwarted.

The next Bible story that describes the birth of a seed-son is in 2 Samuel 12:24–25, the birth of Solomon. The account focuses on David rather than on his mother, but we are told that David dedicated his son to God, thereby affirming that God was his true Father (in accordance with the prophecy of 2 Sam. 7:14).

Satan now attempted to destroy or corrupt the messianic line as it came from David. The most important event in the history of that attempt came when wicked Queen Athaliah killed all the sons of the Davidic line (2 Kgs. 11:1). But God preserved Josiah in the Temple, thereby adopting him as His son. Once again, the seed of the woman is the Son of God.

THE WAR AGAINST THE WOMAN AND HER SEED: EXILE TO THE END

After the exile, Satan again tried the same two-phase approach we have already described. First he tried to wipe out all the seed-line, as recorded in the book of Esther. We note that it is a woman who intervenes to protect the seed nation.

Failing at this, Satan tried again to corrupt the seed nation by intermarriage, as we see in Ezra 9–10; Nehemiah 13:23–29; and Malachi 2. The faithful work of the pastors of the nation prevented this disaster.

When we come to Luke 1:7, we find that the mother of John the Forerunner was also barren and that God opened her womb. Her son, like Samson and Samuel, was a Nazirite. Here again, God is the Father of the miraculous seed of the woman.

All of this history reaches its climax with the virginal conception of Mary, of course. God is not only the spiritual Father of Jesus, but also the physical Father as well. The law of God required that Mary be put to death (Deut. 22:23–24), which Satan clearly hoped would happen, but Joseph justly decided merely to divorce Mary until God explained the situation to him.

After Jesus was born, Satan tried to kill him when Herod slew all the children of Bethlehem, but God delivered the Seed. Then Satan tried phase two again: seeking to seduce and corrupt Jesus at His temptations. Failing in this attempt, Satan returned to active persecution and succeeded in putting Jesus to death, foolishly failing to realize that the sacrificial death of the Seed would be the salvation of the world!

The story of Satan's war against the woman and her seed does not stop with the death of Jesus. History is not over at that point. True, Satan has definitely lost the first campaign in the war, but there is now the campaign to disciple all nations.

After Jesus, the Woman and the Seed are now one in the sense that the Church is Mother of the ongoing seed. In the book of Acts and in the Epistles, we see Satan working to seduce the woman and to destroy her seed. What is behind the scenes in those books is made explicit in Revelation.

First, according to Revelation 12:13, Satan tried to silence and kill off the early Jerusalem church. We read the events of this first phase of attack in Acts 3–8, where the Jews threatened the apostles, beat them, and finally had one of their assistants murdered. But this first phase of Satan's campaign failed when the Church was scattered from Jerusalem. It was no longer possible to kill them all easily.

So Satan moved again to his second phase. Failing as attacking Dragon, he moved as seducing Serpent, pouring out the waters of poisonous doctrine to corrupt the Woman (Rev. 12:14–16; cf. 8:10–11). These were the Judaizing doctrines. Paul and the other apostles and pastors warred against Satan, as we see in Acts and the Epistles. Indeed, on more than one occasion Satan also tried to kill Paul, commander of the anti-Judaizing forces in the Church. But the second phase of Satan's campaign also ended in defeat, and the true Church separated from the Judaizing heretics.

Then Satan returned to outright persecution and massacre, making war with the rest of the seed of the woman (Rev. 12:17) in the murders of Christians in Rome and Palestine in AD 64 and following. But just as Satan erred in putting Jesus to death, so he erred in putting the Church to death, because the Church ascended to heaven to sit on thrones with Jesus and experience a millennial resurrection on earth (Rev. 20).

This preliminary history, of the Apostolic Church, uncovers for us what we may expect throughout the millennial age until the final coming of Jesus at the end of history. At times Satan will attempt to kill off the Church, especially when believers are few in number in various cultures. When there are too many believers for such an attempt to be successful, Satan will try to seduce the woman/seed so that she becomes a mother for his own sons, so that the sons become members of his army. This is what happens when a part of the Church apostatizes, as when the North African Church switched to Islam, and as we see in the history of Orthodoxy, Romanism, and Liberal Protestantism.

In all of this, Satan's goal is to corrupt humanity so that we cannot grow up to be the Bride of the Son of God.

But he is doomed to fail. All he can do is hurt our feet, while we shall crush his head.

THE BRUISING OF THE HEAD

He will bruise your head, and you will bruise his heel (Gen. 3:15).

We come now to another great theme in the Scriptures: the crushing of the serpent's head and the bruising of the messiah's heel. I write "messiah" rather than "Messiah," because all of us in union with the Messiah (Christ) are also messiahs, and thus all of God's people have the foot-wound in this life. By the same token, all anti-Christs (anti-Messiahs) are afflicted with the head-wound. While it appears that the wicked are strong and march in ranks against us, the fact is that their head (Satan) has been bruised, and their own heads (minds) are twisted; thus, they must eventually fail. At the same time, it appears that God's people are disorganized and troubled, but from the perspective of eternity, our limp appears as a carefully orchestrated dance under our Head, and we shall eventually prevail.

Some of the more important aspects of the head-bruising theme are as follows:

First, in the Scriptures, which often teach by imagery and symbol, we often see that the heads of the enemies of God's people are literally crushed. This is a major theme in the book of Judges, for instance. Jael crushes Sisera's head with a tent peg (Judg. 5:24–27). A woman at Thebez drops an upper millstone on the head of Abimelech and crushes his skull (Judg. 9:53). Samson breaks the heads of the five Philistine kings and all their army commanders and chief priests as he pulls down their temple on them (Judg. 16:23–30). Also, destroying the top of a Temple is destroying its "head" (Gen. 11:4; 2 Chron. 3:15), as was his carrying off the gates of Gaza (Judg. 16:3; Ps. 24:7,9). Following on the judges, David as the greatest judge bruises the head of Goliath and then decapitates him (1 Sam. 17), taking the skull to Jerusalem to "the place of the skull," where Jesus was crucified. When we see the nail-bruised heel of Jesus lifted off the ground over Goliath's skull, we see a visible picture of the fulfillment of this primordial prophecy.

Second, the heads of a nation are its leader and his "three mighty men," that is, his army commanders and his priests (cf. Ps. 110:6: "He will shatter the head over a great land"). In Judges we see carefully noted that the heads of the enemy nations are put to death. Ehud kills Eglon (Judg. 3:15–25). Gideon kills the commanders Oreb and Zeeb, and the rulers Zebah and Zalmunna (Judg. 7:25; 8:21). Later on, Saul is condemned for failing to kill Agag, and Ahab is condemned for failing to kill Ben-Hadad (1 Sam. 15; 1 Kgs. 20).

Third, we recognize that the head is the seat of the intellect, and so the bruising of the head means the confusing of the intellect and the defeat of that intellect. At the Tower of Babel, God confused the heads of His enemies, and Jesus did the same to the Pharisees, Sadducees, and Herodians.

Fourth, under the Law God's people were free to take a Nazirite vow and thereby temporarily dedicate their heads to Him (Num. 6). Such Nazirites were usually holy warriors, "head-crushers extraordinaire." Such were Samson (Judg. 13), Samuel (1 Sam. 1:11; 15:33), and John (Luke 1:15; Mark 6), and such was the army raised by Deborah (Judg. 5:2). The great counterfeit Nazirite in the Bible is Absalom, and it is no accident that in his death, his head was wounded by his falsely dedicated hair (2 Sam. 14:26; 18:9).

Fifth, this leads us to the fact that hair is the glory of the head, for it grows out as a corona from the head. Men are not to wear such glory; only women are (1 Cor. 11). Only the Nazirite may grow his hair out, and then he is to cut it off and add it to the offering (Num. 6:18), thereby dedicating all the glory he has earned to God. Absalom's hair was his glory, and it was what killed him. Beyond this, the bruising of the enemy's head means the humiliation of his perverse glory. In a way, this flows directly from the sin of Adam, who sought glory from the Tree of Knowledge, but found only shame.

Sixth, the word "head" in Hebrew also refers to the source or fountain, the beginning. God created the world "at the head" (Gen. 1:1). The first parts of Israel's agricultural products were dedicated to Him as "head-fruits." The bruising of the heel of God's enemies means that they are cut off at the source.

Seventh, it is no accident that in the sacrificial system much attention is devoted to the bruising of the head. The animal takes our place and either has its head cut off after it has been killed (Lev. 1:8,12) or is killed by having its head wrung off (1:15). The crown of thorns on the head of our Savior fulfills this imagery, showing that He takes the head-wound that we deserve. As He was the Head, we are told that as He died, His people scattered—but only temporarily. As regards the wicked, they are scattered permanently as their heads are crushed. We see this latter phenomenon when the Moabites scatter after Ehud kills their head Eglon.

Finally, the only way to avoid having one's head crushed is to dedicate it (i.e., one's whole self) to God. The saints of Revelation 20 were "beheaded" in the sense that they were Nazirites, as all believers must be. Like John the Nazirite, who was literally beheaded, they offer their heads to God and are willing to lose them in His service.[114]

THE BRUISING OF THE HEEL

He will bruise your head, and you will bruise his heel (Gen. 3:15).

The bruising of the heel also has many dimensions and aspects. First, as with the crushing of the head, there is a significant instance of literal heel bruising in the Bible. Jacob was named "Heel" because he grabbed Esau's heel as he came from the womb. Esau would have experienced the heel-wound, but as a wicked man, he was replaced by godly Jacob. After wrestling with God and prevailing, Jacob was rewarded with a limp as a sign of his maturity. It is perhaps no accident that heel-wounded heroes are found in the ancient world and in traditional literature. One thinks of Achilles, who was invulnerable everywhere but his heel, or of the Fisher-King traditions.

Esau, the hunter, had always lived by his heels. While Jacob stayed at home and kept books, Esau roamed around as a prince with nothing better to do than sport for game. Esau may not have been mentally stupid, but his actions over the years show a confusion of the head that is revealing: He was bruised in the head and did not understand what is important and what is not.

The contrast between the limping Jacob on the one hand, and proud Esau with his ranks of four hundred men on the other, is the picture of the bruised heel and the bruised head. Jacob had always lived by his head, and he does so in Genesis 32–33, buying off Esau with a carefully prepared series of gifts. Now, limping, Jacob must live by his head more than ever, because he can no longer fight for himself.[115]

---

114. See Peter J. Leithart, *Revelation 12–22*, International Theological Commentary (London: Bloomsbury T&T Clark, 2018), 311–312.

115. My view of this episode has changed: "As I turns out ... all Esau seems to have intended was to welcome Jacob and provide him an escort (Gen. 33:12–15). Possibly Esau originally did

Second, the head is the most important, topmost part of the human person and thus is glorified with hair, or with a golden flower in the case of the high priest. The heel is the foundation. A heel wound virtually makes a man a cripple. A heel wound is no minor matter, but it takes someone with a head to know when and how to inflict it. The tribe of Dan was to be a community of wise judges, like the original serpent, and as such they would know exactly when and how to inflict the crippling heel wound (Gen. 49:16–17); Samson, the most brilliant of the judges, fulfilled this prophecy as he tripped up the Philistines by attacking the heels of their Temple. The wicked, being headless and thus confused, try to bruise our heels, but only partially succeed.

Third, in an interesting application of Genesis 3, Deuteronomy 33:24 says that God will use the creatures of the dust—the serpent and his insect companions—to inflict heel wounds on His people to teach them His lessons. They will be toppled and humbled. Jesus suffered this wound for us.

Fourth, the fact that the wound comes from a creature of the dust carries us into some wider meanings of the heel wound. The dust prosecutes God's judgment against humanity: "Cursed is the soil with reference to you" (Gen. 3:17). The sweaty toil imposed on man through the soil, as well as the thorns and thistles, are aspects of the heel wound. People wore sandals in the Bible for practical reasons, of course, but also to symbolize their avoidance of this curse. Clean animals must be shod, according to Leviticus 11. Foot washing takes on the meaning of removing the curse from one's feet. But the curse is only on the feet, not on the head. Also, the genitals are "feet" in the Bible (cf. Ruth 3:4, 7–9; 2 Kgs. 18:27; Isa. 36:12; Ezek. 16:25) and in Leviticus 15, the genitals are pictured as wounded and bleeding.

Fifth, in a race the heel is the back part, the hindmost part of a person. It can be used for horses' hoofs (Gen. 47:17; Judg. 5:22), the rear guard of a troop (Gen. 47:19), or even the exposed buttocks of a person (Jer. 13:22). Thus there is a contrast between the judgment on the source and head of the wicked, and on merely the tail of the righteous.

Finally, when our heel is struck, we fall down. Notice that when God appears to people in the Bible, they fall down. We can pray as we sit, lie in bed,

---

have bad intentions and then had a change of heart when he received all of Jacob's gifts (Gen. 32:13–21), but in fact the gifts don't seem to have been important to Esau. He was ready to give them back (Gen. 33:9–11" (*Primeval Saints: Studies in the Patriarchs of Genesis* [Moscow: Canon, 2001], 102). I argue that Esau, by this point, was a changed man.

walk around, etc., but when something serious happens, we tend to get down on the floor with our forehead on the ground. God strikes our heels in order to humble us before Him. The wicked do not bow the knee.

Now let us turn to a deeper aspect of the prophecy. The "head" is the ultimate source. By saying that the seed of the woman will bruise the head of the serpent, God is saying that the power behind the serpent, i.e., Satan, will be bruised.

Similarly, and more interestingly (since we all know that it is not the snake but Satan who is to be crushed), the word "heel" means "replacement." Thus, Jacob's name was not just "Heel" but "Replacement" (see Gen. 27:36). Thus, the phrase can be translated, "You will bruise his replacement." Who is the Replacement for the seed of the woman, if not Jesus? It is each replacement, each new "heel," who is bruised in the biblical narrative: Abel replaces Adam and is bruised. Isaac replaces Abraham and is bruised. Ultimately, Jesus replaces all the seed of the woman and is bruised. Then, as Jesus ascends to heaven, the Church replaces Jesus and is called to be bruised, to carry forth His suffering for the life of the world.

23

THE JUDGMENT ON THE WOMAN

GENESIS 3:16

*To the woman He said, "Multiplying, I shall multiply your pain and your
conception. In pain you will bring forth sons, and for your husband is
your urge and he will rule over you" (Gen. 3:16).*

WE need to note at the outset that while the serpent was cursed and the soil
will be cursed with respect to human life, neither the man nor the woman
is directly cursed. They will receive a curse if they identify with the serpent,
being cursed in union with him, and they will suffer a mediated form of curse
from the soil, but they are not directly cursed.

The curse, thus, is eschatological. God gives Adam and Eve a second
chance, as it were. If they repent and take Him up on His offer, then eventually
they will be free from the mediated curse from the soil. If they continue to
rebel, they will eventually be cursed in union with the serpent. In this we see

God's longsuffering toward us, for as long as we are in this life, it is not too late to repent. We also see God treating Adam and Eve as children, which they were, being only a few hours old. God spanks them; He does not damn them—yet!

We have seen that the child of the woman is her seed. She is compared to a tree, and her children are her fruit, which contains seed. The root of the words for pain here is *'atsab*, which is not the usual word for the pain of childbearing. This word is associated with grief, vexation, and sorrow. Several other words are used in the rest of the Bible for the pains of childbirth: *chebel* (pain), *chil* (writhing, anguish), *tsir* (writhing, pang), and *tsarah* (distress; the Hebrew word is the ultimate root of such English words as "sore" and "sorrow"). Umberto Cassuto suggests that the use of this word *'atsab* here is related to the word for tree, *'ets*.[116]

Cassuto points out that it was by the eating of the fruit of a tree that the woman sinned, and so a word resembling the word "tree" is employed in her judgment. More than that, I suggest, the woman is like a tree, casting seed. It is precisely her production of that seed that will now experience a "tree-like" pain.

Similarly, in verse 17, Adam is told that because the ground has been cursed with reference to him, he will experience *'atsab* pain as he works to produce edible seed from it. The soil that produced seed-bearing trees (*'ets*) will now produce seed-bearing pain (*'atsab*): thorns and thistles, Similarly, the woman, made of soil like the man, will produce her trees as pains: human thorns and thistles (like Cain).

Before moving further to a thematic exposition of these pains, I want to suggest a correction to the way this text is usually read. Generally speaking, the first phrase, "your pains and your conception," is read as a hendiadys, putting the two ideas together to form one statement: "Your pains in your conception." Then follows a second statement elaborating on the first: "In pain you will bring forth sons." And then follows a third statement: "And your urge will be toward your husband...."

Given the overwhelming predominance of chiastic ways of writing in the Bible, and in Genesis 1–4, I suggest a better way to read the sentences, to wit:

---

116. Umberto Cassuto, *A Commentary on the Book of Genesis, Part I: From Adam to Noah, Genesis I–VI*, trans. Israel Abrahams (Jerusalem: Magnes, 1961), 165.

> A. Multiplying, I shall multiply your pain,
>> B. and your conception:
>> B'. In pain you will bring forth children (sons),
> A'. and for your husband is your urge and he will rule over you.

Reading the sentence this way shows that part of the multiplying of pain is that the woman will have an urge to submit to a husband, even if he is a bad husband. We shall, of course, return to this aspect of the judgment later on. Reading this way also shows that the multiplication of conception does not mean the woman will have many more children than before, but that the process of bearing seed will be painful.

The original command was to be fruitful (again tree-imagery) and multiply. The same word and concept of multiplication recurs in the Abrahamic Covenant and down through the Bible as a blessing from God to His people. Such multiplication involves joyous conception and birth. Now the multiplying is accompanied by pain.

PAIN IN CONCEPTION AND CHILDBEARING

To the woman He said, "Multiplying, I shall multiply your pain and your conception. In pain you will bring forth sons, and for your husband is your urge and he will rule over you" (Gen. 3:16).

There are several dimensions to the pain accompanying conception and childbirth, from the woman's standpoint, but all of them have to do with death. Throughout the book of Genesis, and on into the rest of the biblical narrative, we see pain and even death associated with conception and childbearing. The wombs of Sarah, Rebekah, and Rachel were closed for many years, and it was only after years of pain and humiliation that they finally conceived. Compare also the story of Hannah in 1 Samuel 1. This is the pain of vexation, which as we have seen is part of the meaning of the word used.

Further, the fact that many women died in childbirth before the modern era is surely part of this judgment, as we see when Rachel dies giving birth to Benjamin. Also, many children are born dead or die soon after. This is the aspect of grief, which as we have seen is also linked with the word used.

We might also mention the physical pain a woman experiences on her wedding night, as well as the simple fact that many men, even as husbands, are fairly brutal in their "lovemaking." And we cannot forget the fact of rape. All these are pains of conception.

And we should understand that while the text says that the woman will experience pain as she brings forth sons, and this points specifically to the Messiah as Son, the Hebrew word can also embrace all children. Most aspects of the fulfillment of this prophetic judgment apply to the birth of daughters as well.

Beyond this, however, is the symbolic dimension. According to Leviticus 15, the very act of marital intercourse involves uncleanness, symbolic death, and according to Leviticus 12, so does the process of childbearing. Also, for several days out of each month, the woman experienced symbolic death while menstruating, and menstruation has to do exclusively with childbearing. These symbolic forms of death came only on the Israelites, not on the gentile God-fearers, because Israel was bearing the judgment of death as a nation of (suffering servant) priests on behalf of the rest of the nations. The suffering of the woman was alleviated somewhat among the nations because it was transferred to Israel. For the duration of the time of uncleanness, the woman was cut off from worship at the sanctuary, and this is the greatest of pains.

There are wider dimensions of this judgment as well. The history of God's people from the promise of the Seed of the Woman forward was one long labor, one long birth pang, to give birth to the Son and His people (Rev. 12:2). Jesus' suffering on the cross was His travail or birth pangs, issuing in His resurrection and the coming of the Kingdom (Acts 2:24). The whole creation groaned and travailed (same word as in Matt. 24:8) with her, until the formation of the Church was completed at the end of the Apostolic Age (Rom. 8:22).

In the same way, the Church suffers in union with Christ (Col. 2:24). The suffering of the Apostolic Church led to the victory over the Old Creation in AD 70 and the raising of the saints to sit on the angelic thrones in heaven (Rev. 20). The suffering of the present Church leads forward to the redemption of our bodies at the Last Day. All such suffering, then, is but birth pangs.

Some women die giving birth; others live. The Woman of the Old Creation would live in Christ, even if many of her last members would die in the Great Tribulation. Those members of the Woman who rejected Christ and who persecuted His bride would die in the birth pangs of the New Creation (1 Thess. 5:3).

Jesus said that the wars, famines, and earthquakes, which His people would endure along with the rest of the people (Acts 11:27–30), would only be the initial stages of labor for the Church. The Church would move into transition, heavy labor, when she began to be persecuted in earnest, as Jesus mentions in His next breath. The climax of the birth pangs would come with the martyrdom of the Apostolic Church in the Great Tribulation, and with the destruction of Jerusalem immediately thereafter.

The Book of Revelation, which concerns first of all the events of the Apostolic Age, shows us that Jesus is going to take His Church through similar situations throughout the course of history and that there will be a final childbirth tribulation at the end just before the Last Judgment (Rev. 20).

All of this suffering on the part of the Woman has to do with the bringing forth of the Seed in history: first of all, the Seed Jesus Christ, and then the Seed of the Church. Accordingly, the multiplication of vexation concerning conception and childbirth cannot be limited merely to the first nine months of a baby's life, but extends throughout life. How many mothers have suffered intensely because of the way their sons turn out. Eve must have suffered greatly when Cain murdered Abel. Such suffering is also part of the pains of conception and childbirth.

THE WOMAN'S URGE TOWARD HER HUSBAND

To the woman He said, "Multiplying, I shall multiply your pain and your conception. In pain you will bring forth sons, and for your husband is your urge and he will rule over you" (Gen. 3:16).

I want to use Rebekah as the premier example of the faithful Seed Mother who suffers because of her seeds, but before doing so, we need to turn to the second part of the judgment on the woman, which is that she will have an urge, often painful, toward her husband.

The leadership of the man, and his consequent dominance in marriage, is not part of the judgment that came upon humanity for Adam's sin. Genesis 2 has made it plain that the woman is the helper to the man, and ultimately she is the glory of the man. She lives longer than he does and completes his work. Men initiate things, while women complete things. Adam came first, but in the end humanity is a Bride. Jesus rules His Wife and does so perfectly, unlike Adam.

There is an ambiguity to the judgment pronounced here, and almost certainly the ambiguity is intended. First of all, the word "urge" is used in Genesis 4:7 in connection with sin's desire to dominate, which Cain must defeat if he is to live before God. Thus, it is rightly argued that the statement in Genesis 3:16 partly means that the woman will desire to dominate the man, but that in the end he will dominate her. This entire scenario, in which the woman rebels against her husband and he dominates her, is painful to all concerned.

Such rebellion perverts the proper function of womanhood, as we can see when we consider our rebellions against our Husband Jesus. This is a painful thing, involving the gnashing of teeth. And when such a woman is "put down" by her husband, that is also painful.

But the phrase can also be read, and again rightly, as meaning that the woman will have an urge to find a man to submit to. Few women escape this. In fact, for God to put such an urge in the heart of a woman can be His way of overcoming her sinful rebelliousness.

We see this urge in operation very often, as young women give up their virginity to please the boy they are attracted to. We see it also in the way a woman will so often cling to an abusive husband, defending and "enabling" him. Perhaps the most dramatic illustration of this phenomenon is the practice of a wife's being burned alive on her husband's funeral pyre, a custom in India that is still practiced on the sly. Accounts of such events plainly record that the women go to the fire quite willingly.

Such an urge can be transformed into something saving and wonderful, however, and we see this in the history of Rebekah, who though much vilified by commentators and preachers, is in fact one of the great Seed Mothers of the Bible. We shall consider her more in the following section.

For now, another positive aspect of this judgment is the fact that, however much trauma it may involve, the woman will in fact bear the promised Seed and she will find an urge to cleave to her true and holy Husband. Applying this promise to the Church, we see it come to pass in history, and we see it still today. Yes, all of us have the urge to rebel against our Husband Jesus from time to time, but the Spirit keeps alive within us the urge to submit to Him as well. And we have the promise that in the conflict between Jesus and His wayward Bride, He will win.

REBEKAH

Let us now consider this prophecy as it applies to Rebekah. Rebekah appears in Genesis 24 as a woman of great courtesy, hospitality, strength (watering ten thirsty camels by herself), and faith. She is, as Gordon Wenham points out in his commentary on Genesis, a new Abraham.[117] She immediately leaves her old land to move to the Promised Land to join the Seed Son as his bride.

It is clear in the text that she hopes to be the new Seed Mother and bring forth the Messiah, or at least contribute to His line. She suffers from being barren, and then when twins fight in her womb, she asks, "If this is so, then why do I live?" In other words, why is she alive if she is bringing forth not the holy Seed but two warring sons? What is her purpose? In time she will discover the purpose of her life, which is to rescue the Abrahamic Covenant from Isaac and Esau.

Unlike her husband Isaac, Rebekah accepts God's command that Jacob be treated as firstborn. Her suffering continues for 77 years, as her husband makes it clear that he will not obey God and that he prefers the sinful food associated with Esau. She must endure Isaac's repeating Adam's original sin, preferring the forbidden food, calling good evil and evil good. This is part of her pain of submission to her husband.

In the crisis (Gen. 27), God provides Rebekah with the information she needs to save the covenant for Jacob. By now Esau has been married to not just one but two wicked women, for 37 years. His own children are growing up, and they are as profane as he is, and though Esau's family vexes not only Rebekah but Isaac, Isaac determines to give the covenant to Esau anyway. Isaac intends to destroy the Abrahamic Covenant. So Rebekah steps in to save it.

Now, Rebekah knows that God's command will be fulfilled with or without Isaac. If Isaac blesses Esau, God will still find a way to give the covenant to Jacob. Rebekah's actions are thus not primarily designed to secure the covenant for him. Rebekah also knows that the covenant *should* pass through Isaac to Jacob, but as someone who has seen God work miracles in the past, she knows that it does not *have* to. Her God, the God of the Abrahamic Covenant, is, after all, the Almighty God.

---

117. Gordon J. Wenham, *Genesis 16–50*, Word Biblical Commentary (1987; reprint, Grand Rapids: Zondervan, 2015), 155.

Rebekah, however, has an urge toward her husband. She wants to save him, to see him repent and do the right thing. She knows that he feels guilty about what he is about to do, for Isaac plans to give the covenant to Esau in a private meeting, behind closed doors, secretly, in the dark—not publicly (contrast Gen. 49). Isaac's sneakiness tells Rebekah that his conscience is not clear about his plans.

So Rebekah devises a scheme to trap Isaac and bring him, she hopes, to repentance. She sends Jacob in to deceive him. Now, she knows full well that Isaac will eventually discover the ruse. Indeed, she's counting on it. In a few hours Esau will return with his meal for Isaac, and then Isaac will find out what has happened. The question is: What will Isaac do then?

Perhaps he will curse Jacob, and (try to) remove the covenant from him and give it to Esau. Rebekah states that she will take such a curse, if it should be given. She offers to die that the covenant might live, and in this, she becomes a second Isaac, offering her own death. Isaac had once been ready to die, but he is no longer ready to die to his lusts. Rebekah, the new Isaac, is ready to be cursed for the sake of the covenant. But she has reason to hope that Isaac will repent when he is caught out, and that is what happens. God blesses her endeavors.

Then Rebekah, acting as Abraham again, sends Jacob back to her homeland to get a good wife. This is what Isaac should have done, years ago, when Esau wanted to marry. But Isaac, having strayed from Abraham's ways, did not do it, and Esau married wicked wives. Rebekah asks, "If Jacob takes a wife from the daughters of Heth, from the daughters of this land, then what has my life been worth?" (Gen. 27:46). In other words, what is the point of my being the Mother of the Seed if the seed perverts his calling and destroys the covenant? So, she sends Jacob away.

And she never sees him again.

In the story of Rebekah, we see the Mother of the Seed suffering tree-pains. As a tree, she suffers as she sees her seed, Jacob, oppressed by father and brother for 77 years. She suffers as she loses him and sends him forth with only her prayers. And she suffers also the urge to submit to a wicked husband. Isaac was not always a wicked husband, and so her suffering was not as full as that of many women, but it was suffering nonetheless. She transforms her urge, however, when she allows herself to be led by the Spirit to bring Isaac to a point of crisis and repentance.

24

THE JUDGMENT ON THE MAN

GENESIS 3:17–20

And to Adam He said, "Because you hearkened to the voice of your wife,
and you ate from the tree, concerning which I commanded you, saying,
'Not shall you eat from it,' cursed is the ground..." (Gen. 3:17a).

YAHWEH'S judgment against Adam begins with a phrase that is generally overlooked as commentators move quickly to consider the actual judgments pronounced. Adam is judged for eating of the forbidden fruit, but also for listening to his wife in a way that involves obeying her. The Hebrew word for "listen" or "hearken" often includes the notion of obedience, as when we are told to "hearken" to God's Word.

There is something slightly odd in what God says here, because we are not told anything about Adam's listening to anything Eve said. Genesis 3:6 does not say that Eve said anything to Adam, or that she persuaded him to eat, or anything of the sort. It simply says that she shared the fruit with him and that he had been standing by all along. Nor does Adam say anything about any verbal communication from Eve in verse 12; all he says is that she gave him the fruit and he ate it.

Perhaps we are to understand that she talked with him when she gave him the fruit. Or perhaps we are to understand that her silent giving of the fruit to him is tantamount to her saying something to him and his obeying her voice.

The word for "voice" here is the same as the word for the "sound" of Yahweh coming to the Garden in verse 8. Yet in that situation, there was something heard, while nowhere in the narrative are we told that Adam "heard" anything, voice or sound, from Eve in connection with his sin.

We might be satisfied with the notion of a contrast between God's "sound/voice" and the unspoken communication from Eve. Adam chose to set aside what God had actually said to him out loud and chose to listen to the silent communication from his wife.

Yet, in the passage itself there is someone who speaks quite a bit, and that is the serpent. Since Adam was present throughout the temptation, it is clearly Satan's voice that he was hearkening to, not Eve's. Thus, it might make more sense for God to say either "Because you yielded to your wife's invitation" or "Because you hearkened to the voice of the serpent." What God actually said, however, seems to put the two together. But how? What does He mean us to understand?

I find nothing in my various commentaries on this matter. Perhaps it has been addressed at length somewhere, but I am not aware of it.

We might understand God as saying that it is always wrong to listen to your wife. That would be nonsense, because clearly there are many times when the wife is right and the husband wrong, or when the wife has greater wisdom, as in Judges 13. We might add that it is also not wrong to listen to animals, when they don't advise something wrong. Balaam needed to listen to his donkey. Thus, the sin lies in hearkening to our subordinates when they advocate something wrong and using them as an excuse for sinning.

I believe that the resolution of this apparent difficulty lies in a wider understanding of the judgment God proceeds to pronounce against Adam. To begin with, however, notice that Adam sinned in two ways: by listening to sinful advice that came from Satan through the serpent and (in a way) through his wife and by eating forbidden fruit. The judgment that comes to him concerns eating: Eating is mentioned five times in verses 17–19. That which Adam will eat comes from the soil. We should recall that what Adam ate came from his wife. Thus, the soil is parallel to the wife, for she, like Adam, is made of soil.

As we shall see, the soil is not cursed, and so neither is the wife. Rather, the soil is the (good) medium that prosecutes the curse to Adam, and thus so is the wife. As Eve silently offered fruit to Adam, so the soil silently offers food to him. As Eve's silent offering embodied a communication of rebellious language, so the soil's silent offering embodies a communication of curse language.

If we read the judgment in such a humaniform way, we can see immediately how relevant it is. Adam will eat of the fruit of the soil through painful toil, and it is through painful toil that men rear the children given them by their wives. The soil will produce thorns and thistles, and as we shall see, thorns and thistles are types of wicked children. Adam will return to the soil from which he came, but every man born in the world after Adam originated in the soil of a woman's womb, and thus a return to the soil is a kind of return to the womb. This last fact we can meditate upon in two ways. First, men return to a kind of second childhood in senility. Second, a return to the womb is a promise of resurrection, of a new birth, so that while the old body returns to dust, there is a new body that will be born from the new mother.

All of these themes are expanded and filled out in later passages of the Bible, but I submit that they start here, in a very compact form. By hearkening to his wife, Adam put himself into her, into union with her. Thus, while he did not come from her womb to start with, he will return to her womb in the end and be born again. In the largest sense, this is true when Adamic humanity comes into the womb of Mother Church and then is resurrected to a new life. Going back into the woman, who is relatively innocent but is still laboring under a difficulty, as we have seen, provides another dimension to her labor-pains as she brings forth the new seed, the replacement, the kingdom of God.

OVERVIEW: TOIL, EATING, AND DEATH

1. *"Cursed is the soil with reference to you.*
2. *In pain will you eat of her all the days of your life.*
3. *And thorn and thistle will she sprout for you.*
4. *And you will eat the plant of the field:*
5. *In the sweat of your nose will you eat bread;*

6. *Until you return to the soil;*

7. *Because from her were you taken.*

8. *Because dust you are,*

9. *And to dust will you return"* (Gen. 3:17b-19).

The judgment against Adam can be analyzed as follows: After the statement of the judgment in the first line, the second line lays out three topics: toil, eating, and death. These are taken up as follows:

A. toil (implied): thorn and thistle
  B. eating: the plant of the field
A'. toil: sweat of the nose
  B'. eating: bread
C. death: return to soil
  D. taken from soil
  D'. made of soil
C'. death: return to soil

As a review, the following is reprinted from chapter 21. The opening statement against the man (verse 17b) is parallel to the curse upon the serpent (verse 14), though the man is not cursed directly:

Serpent	Man
1. Cursed are you above all	Cursed is the ground with reference to you
2. Crawl on belly	In severe labor
3. Dust you will eat	You will eat of ground
4. All the days of your life	All the days of your life

The judgment on the man is then expanded (verses 18–19), following the same order and themes:

1. Ground produces thorns
2. Sweat of the nose
3. Eat food
4. End of life

The parallels between the serpent and the man serve to highlight something we have already clearly seen, that the man has chosen to identify with the serpent and to exchange being the son of God for being the son of Satan. Thus, the enmity between the serpent and the woman will often be expressed as enmity between man and woman, with men raping women throughout history and with women desiring to rule over men.

Moreover, having chosen to identify with the serpent, the man now experiences the same judgment as the serpent: to live with his nose to the ground, struggling for food, destined for death. Moreover, the reminder that man is made of dust, and the fact that the serpent eats dust, implies that man will be eaten by the devil in the end, instead of being taken (eaten) into God's heavenly fellowship. It is the new man, the second Adam, born painfully of the woman, who will provide an alternative to this dismal fate.

The judgment draws from Genesis 2:5–7. There we find that "no shrub of the field existed yet in the earth, and no plant of the field had yet sprouted," and these are referred to in lines 3 and 4. Then the man is made of dust and God breathes into his nostrils the breath of life, and these two matters are taken up in lines 5–9.

It is important, I believe, that the word "death" does not appear here in this judgment. God had told Adam that the penalty for eating the forbidden fruit would be death, and we can see that returning to the soil alludes to death, yet "death" is not used. The reason would seem to be that the punishment of death is going to be taken by the animal God kills to provide a skin for Adam. In that sense, Adam did indeed suffer death, via a substitute, on the day he sinned, just as God promised him he would.

Also, however, as we have seen, there is a strongly implied comparison of the soil with the woman in this passage. The word for soil is, as we have seen at length when we studied Genesis 2:7, feminine. We saw that the soil is the mother of plants and of humanity, while the father of the plants is the ground water, while the father of humanity is the breath of God. A return to the mother implies the possibility of a new birth.

Adam seems to understand things this way, because his immediate response is to name his wife *Eve*, the "mother of all living." Adam had listened wrongly to his wife and would return to Mother Earth, but the parallel between the two implies that the new mother, Eve, would bring him forth again in a new way, as the "seed of the woman." There would be a New Adam. And in that New Adam, humanity could be born anew on the other side of death and judgment.

Thus, there is judgment, and that judgment involves several kinds of death, but yet that judgment is not the fullness of death. It is a kind of death that implies a resurrection on the other side. Needless to say, this is a theme that the Word of God will revisit and amplify hundreds of times.

THE CURSE-PROSECUTING SOIL

"Cursed is the soil with reference to you" (Gen. 3:17b).

While we often hear of the "curse on the soil," this is not correct. The soil is not cursed. Quite the contrary: The soil is enlisted to the honor of prosecuting God's curse against sinful man. Nor does the soil prosecute a curse against anything other than humanity, and whatever suffering the animal realm may be said to undergo, it undergoes with reference to judging humanity. Plants and animals, made of soil, join in prosecuting the soil's curse against humanity.

The soil acts as both prosecuting attorney and executioner of mankind. It stands, in a way, with Satan, the Accuser, but not in any moral sense. As Satan brings charges against sinful humanity (Zech. 3), and as he is allowed to afflict sinful humanity (Job 1–2), so does the soil.

It is for this reason that, under the symbolic world of the Old Creation, men washed their feet before coming into God's presence. The soil on the feet acted to press charges against the sinner, and the sinner was advised to remove that prosecuting attorney before coming into the presence of the righteous judge of all the earth.

The word used for "curse" here, 'arar, basically means "to separate from" or "to banish." It means that something is separated from something else, in the sense of being opposed to it. Why would the soil be opposed to man? Because the soil is "righteous" and sides with God, and thus opposes man, who is now at enmity with God. The soil would no longer cooperate with man, and thus would bring judgment into his life. The soil, siding with God, will bring about that judgment. The soil, sticking to the man, will cry out to God for judgment against the man. The soil becomes God's appointed prosecutor of the curse.

Accordingly, dirt is something that a righteous man would want to wash off before coming into God's presence. There can be little doubt but that it was for this reason that men always wore shoes in the Old Covenant. There were other reasons, of course, but also this symbolic reason: Shoes kept their feet from contact with the curse-prosecuting soil. As we see in Leviticus 11, clean animals also wear "shoes." The only time a man did not wear shoes was on holy ground, for holy ground did not prosecute the curse (Exod. 3:5; Josh. 5:15). For this reason, the priests are not provided any shoes to wear while working in the holy ground of the Tabernacle and Temple (Exod. 28). Additionally, the curse on the soil explains the frequency of foot washing as we find it in the Old Covenant, right up to the crucifixion (Gen. 18:4; 19:2; 43:24; Judg. 19:21; Luke 7:44; John 13:3–15).

If a man deliberately went unshod, it was a sign that he was identifying himself with God's judgments and curse. Going barefoot was a sign of mourning (2 Sam. 15:30; 19:24; Ezek. 24:17, 23), of captivity (Job 12:17,19; Isa. 20:2; Mic. 1:8), or of abject poverty (Luke 15:22). Once the period of mourning or distress was over, he would wash his feet and return to wearing shoes.

The curse of death upon the dust played a role in the third Egyptian plague, when the dust became a living death of lice (Exod. 8:16–17). To throw dust on someone was to wish him dead, and to throw dust on your own head was a sign of mourning (Josh. 7:6; 2 Sam. 16:13; Job 2:12; Lam. 2:10; Acts 22:22–23; Rev. 18:19). To shake the dust off your feet or garments was to leave a curse on someone or some place (Matt. 10:14; Mark 6:11; Luke 9:5; 10:11; Acts 13:51). The enemies of God will "lick the dust," implying either that they are destroyed or put into mourning (i.e., they taste judgment: death; Ps. 72:9; Isa. 49:23).

It is only in connection with sinful man that soil is a curse-threat. A dramatic story that illustrates this principle is found in 2 Samuel 6:6–7. Nowhere did the Law say that the Ark of the Covenant might not come in contact with the soil, but the Law clearly stated that the Ark might not be touched by (sinful) human hands (Num. 4:15). Uzzah's presumptuous sin was that he assumed his own hands were cleaner than the dust into which the Ark was sliding, a point God took issue with! In fact "holy Tabernacle dust" was used in the Jealousy Inspection of Numbers 5 (verse 17). It was only when in contact with sinful human beings that soil became a threat. Thus, if the woman were guilty, the soil would bring a curse to her when she drank it.

Clearly, though, one would not bring curse-prosecuting soil into the presence of God. When the Israelite layman drew near to offer sacrifice in the forecourt of the Tabernacle and Temple, he unquestionably removed his shoes and washed his feet before entering. Also, in Deuteronomy 26:14, the faithful profess never to eat God's festive gifts in a state of mourning. Given the association of dust with death and mourning, we can be certain that they washed themselves, and particularly their feet, before participating in the feast.

The death of Christ removed the curse from the world, and thus from the soil. It is no longer improper to go barefoot at the beach or to wear shoes in church.

The soiled foot, thus, was a sign that a person is unworthy to come before God and act as priest for others. Recalling that "foot" is linked with the private parts in biblical language, removing the soil from the foot corresponds to circumcision.[118] Circumcision was the removal of the soil (recall that man is made of soil), which enabled a person to become a member of the nation of priests that stood before God on behalf of the nations. For the same reason, circumcision removes the "sandal" that covers the foot, and enables a person to move onto holy ground as a priest of God.

EATING IN PAIN

"In pain will you eat of her all the days of your life" (Gen. 3:17b).

The word for "pain" has already been encountered in verse 16, where the woman was told that God would multiply her "pain" in childbearing. As we saw in the previous chapter, the child of the woman is her seed. She is compared to a tree, and her children are her fruit, which contains seed. The root word for "pain" in verse 16 is *'atsab*, which is not the usual word for the pain of childbearing. Umberto Cassuto suggests that the use of this word *'atsab* here is related to the word for tree, *'ets*.[119]

Cassuto points out that it was by the eating of the fruit of a tree that the woman sinned, and so a word resembling the word "tree" is employed in her judgment. Similarly, in verse 17, Adam is told that because the ground has been cursed with reference to him, he will experience *'atsab* pain as he works to produce edible seed from it. The soil that produced seed-bearing trees (*'ets*) will now produce seed-bearing pain (*'atsab*): thorns and thistles. Similarly,

---

118. See Ruth 3:4, 7–9; Ezekiel 16:25; and 2 Kgs. 18:27 and Isaiah 36:12, where "urine" is "water of the feet" in the margin (*qere*) of the Hebrew Bible.

119. Cassuto, *Genesis*, 165.

the woman, made of soil like the man, will produce her trees as pains: human thorns and thistles (like Cain).

This word then is one more link between the soil and the woman. The woman experiences "tree-pain" in bearing children, and her husband will experience "tree-pain" as he "eats" of her fruit, as he rears her children, which often are thorns and thistles.

We need to understand this humaniform implication of the judgment, because taken literally it is not a true statement. Few of us experience pain as we eat food, and certainly we don't experience such pain every day, both of which are what the text literally says. Moreover, amplifying the text, as we must, by the ensuing statement that "by the sweat of the nose will you eat bread," is still not true for many people. In the pre-modern world, it was true that most people were engaged in agriculture and thus toiled for food. Even then, however, the wealthy did not toil, and their eating was in no way painful. In the industrialized world, needless to say, many people have never engaged in painful toil to produce the food they eat.

We might say that this judgment was true in a general way for humanity as a whole, and that the New Creation is gradually alleviating this judgment so that fewer and fewer people toil for food. That's true enough, but it does not go far enough.

And we may say that all people toil at something and that the fruits of their toil are exchanged by barter or money for the food they eat. That's also true enough, but there is more.

The "more" is that eating is a regular symbol in the Bible for covenantal relationships with other people. We "eat" each other, and this is seen especially in the Lord's Supper, where the bread represents the Church as a whole (1 Cor. 10:16–17). Such mutual "eating" is involved in the mutual kiss. In particular, "eating" is used in the Bible as a metaphor for marital union, as in the Song of Solomon, and in the notion of a "marriage supper."[120]

"In pain will you eat of the soil" thus carries the implication "in pain will you experience marriage." Part of that pain is the thorns and thistles that will come forth, but part of it is just the difficulty of marriage. All marriages are difficult, but it was not so in the beginning. By God's design, man and woman should have gotten along perfectly in marriage, each joyously complementing the other. We don't experience such marriages in this fallen world. By God's

---

120. For a full discussion of this, see my paper, "The Meaning of Eating in the Bible."

grace our marriages are not as unpleasant as they might be, but no marriage is bliss all the time.

The woman experiences pain in childbearing, and the man experiences pain in marriage. His "helper fitted to him" is never everything he thinks she should be, and of course that is partly because his expectations are warped. And of course, since the woman came from the man originally, and all human beings are fallen in Adam, wives also experience pain in marriage as well, since no husband except Jesus is perfect.

More broadly, since all human beings are made of soil, all human interaction is equivalent to "eating of the soil," and thus all human interaction is sometimes painful. Whether we marry or not, we will have painful relationships with other human beings.

Only by taking into account the humaniform implications of this judgment can we do full justice to the phrase "all the days of your life." Even if we live in the lap of luxury all our days and never toil for food in any sense, yet every human being will experience pain when he "eats" of the "soil" of other human beings, and that pain will be with him throughout his entire life. Only death will make possible a new birth to a painless and eternal life.

SPROUTING THORNS

"And thorn and thistle will she sprout for you" (Gen. 3:18a).

Genesis 2:5 states that before humanity was created, no "shrub of the field" existed and the "plants of the field" had not yet budded. We saw when we studied that sentence that God suspended these events until after mankind had fallen into sin. As a result of sin, the shrubs would grow up as thorns and thistles, while the grain plants would bud and sprout their food in a way that would require labor to harvest. We come now to God's delineation of this new state of affairs. The grain plants and the sweat of the nose will occupy us later on. Here we begin to look at thorns and thistles.

God's garden consists of trees, while man's fallen anti-garden consists of thorns. God's good trees are described in Psalm 1 and in many other passages, such as Judges 9, which use the olive, fig, and vine as symbols of the wise and godly. Here we are concerned with other plants, like the bramble of Judges 9.

The word "sprout" is the same as is found in Genesis 2:5. Back in chapter 3, I interpreted the sprouting of the plants of the field as referring to their putting forth buds and grain. Here, as in virtually all other passages of the Bible, it is sprouting from the soil that is in view.

Before proceeding farther, it is necessary for me to defend my understanding of Genesis 2:5. I interpreted the "plant of the field" as grain plants, and this is because quite clearly that is what they are in Genesis 3:18b: "you will eat the plants of the field," which is amplified by the following phrase, "by the sweat of your nose will you eat bread." Since thorns and thistles are not food, they are not the source of the bread of 3:19a.

The thorns and thistles are part of the reason for the toil. They are the tares among the wheat. Planting, harvesting, winnowing, and grinding grain involves labor and sweat by itself, but that toil is only increased by the presence of tares, of thorns and thistles, among the grain. Thus, it is clear that two kinds of plants are in view in 3:18–19 and that they are the same plants as in 2:5.

Some expositors, among them Cassuto, argue that no grain plants existed in the earth until after the fall of man.[121] This is based on taking the two phrases in 2:5 as strictly parallel: no shrubs existed and no grains had sprouted from the earth. The problem with this reading is that Genesis 1:11–12 rather clearly means that grain plants did exist already, from the third day of creation week forward. The same word for "plant" is used, though the plants are not said to be "of the field."

Cassuto argues that the Day 3 plants were trees and grains, but not "of the field" in the sense that they did not exist in fields cultivated by human beings.[122] The problem with this interpretation is that the shrubs are also said to be "of the field," and yet such "fields" are not those cultivated by mankind.[123]

No, rather the contrast is between the Garden, where the trees are, and the field, where the other plants are. The notion of man-cultivated fields is not at the root of the distinction. Instead, we have God's grove of trees and then the rest of the world, which at this time of history is the "field." It is not man's orchard and field that are in view here, but God's.

Thus, we have a problem: If the grain plants were made on Day 3 but also did not exist until after Adam was created and fell into sin, there is a

---

121. Cassuto, *Genesis*, 102.

122. Cassuto, *Genesis*, 102–103.

123. Moreover, Cassuto thinks that Genesis 1 and 2 come from two different traditions and are not a completely unified presentation, except as modified by a "final redactor" (*Genesis*, 71ff.). Naturally, Christians cannot use such an approach.

clear contradiction in the text. That contradiction is easily removed once we understand that the grain plants did exist, but had not yet sprouted grains. Thus, in 2:5 it is the grains themselves that had not yet sprouted, while in 3:18 it is the soil that sprouts thorns and thistles.

The word "sprout," we may add in conclusion, is not a technical term that *must* always mean the growth of a plant from the earth. It is used of hair as well (Lev. 13:37; Judg. 16:22; 2 Sam. 10:5; Ezek. 16:7). Possibly it means the budding of grown plants in Isaiah 55:10.

In conclusion, since the grain plants already existed in the earth at the time of Genesis 2:5, the sprouting of those plants must refer not to their coming forth from the soil but to their putting forth their fruit.

THORNS AND THISTLES

"And thorn and thistle will she sprout for you" (Gen. 3:18a).

The only other time "thistle" appears in the Bible is in the phrase "thorn and thistle will grow on their altars" in Hosea 10:8. Since altars were made of earth (or stones of the earth), this speaks of a curse moving through the wicked altars to the people who worship at them.

The word "thorn" appears more often in the Bible. It means in Hebrew just what it means in English. Of particular interest is 2 Samuel 23:6, "But the worthless, every one of them will be thrust away like thorns." Such wicked people stand in contrast to the righteous, who are "tender grass" (verse 4). The wicked are also compared to thorns in Psalm 118:12; Isaiah 33:12; Jeremiah 4:3; and Ezek. 28:4.

Another word for "thorn" is used in Psalm 58:9, and it is the same word translated "bramble" in Judges 9:14–15. The bramble is a thorny plant, and in Judges 9 refers to wicked rulers. The bramble, like the thorn, catches fire and destroys all who join themselves to him.

A humaniform understanding of the thorn helps explain an interesting problem found in Exodus 22:6: "If a fire breaks out and spreads to thorns, so that the stacked grain or the standing grain or the field is consumed, he who started the fire shall surely make compensation." We may ask, "What if the fire breaks out and spreads through something other than thorns? What if it just jumps a fence of stones?" Clearly, the same kind of restitution would be in order. But that raises the question of why Yahweh would phrase His law in such a particular way.

I submit that just as God's presence is seen and felt through His being a "consuming fire," so the presence of any human being, the image of God, is seen and felt through "fire." In particular, gossip is linked to fire breaking out in James 3:6. Accordingly, a humaniform application of Exodus 22:6 would mean that if a person spreads the fires of evil rumors and gossip, with the result that another person's livelihood is ruined, he owes compensation for the results of his fire. Such gossip and rumor spreads from the man or woman who originates them, through the "thorns" of society, and destroys another person.

Returning to the immediate context of Genesis 3, we need to understand that the thorns and thistles are people who grow out of the soil of the woman, who is also the mother of the seed. She will have two kinds of children: trees and thorns. Genesis 4 will show us an example of each: Abel and Cain.

Finally, we would be remiss not to mention Jesus' crown of thorns. In terms of biblical imagery, this crown is not just a source of physical pain but also a symbol of humanity. All of wicked humanity is a crown of thorns, bruising the head of Jesus. The crown of thorns is a symbol of our sins placed upon Him. We can rejoice to see that our Savior is now crowned in a rainbow (Rev. 10:1).

BREAD AND SWEAT

"And you will eat the plant of the field:
In the sweat of your nose will you eat bread" (Gen. 3:18b–19a).

Several matters call for our attention here. To begin with, there is an implied contrast between the plant of the field and the trees of the Garden of Eden. Adam will be cast from the Garden, and his primary food in the future will be the food that grows outside of it.

The "plant of the field," "bread," would be man's primary food. In the Garden the primary food, the first food, was fruit. That is now changed. We pray for "daily bread," not for "daily fruit," and indeed the Hebrew word for "bread" often just means "food" in general.

It's clear enough that this is what Adam faced. If he planted an orchard, it would be several years before he would get any food from it. He would have to start with grain plants, with bread. Thus, the order is bread, and then wine, the stuff of fruits. We have explored this already in earlier chapters.

Such food will cost him painful time and labor. To be sure, a sinless humanity would have planted orchards and gardens again, and such plantings and cultivations would not have been labor free. It might not have been easy, for humanity would have learned more about the world from the effort of planting and harvesting. But the effort would have been joyous, like the effort of dancing. Now, however, such labor for food will be mixed not with joy but with fear, fear that the crops might not be fruitful, fear of weather, fear of locusts.

Anthropologist Arthur C. Custance shows that bodily sweat arises from heat, from emotion, and from mental effort, and that sweat appears in different parts of the body and with varying odor according to these three conditions. By itself, sweat is a perfectly natural aspect of human life, apart from the fall. A primary cause of excessive sweating, however, is fear. Custance points out that the forehead, unlike other parts of the body, sweats in response to all three stimuli, so that there is a concentration of the sweat function in the brow. Of course, it is sweat from the brow that drips from the nose.[124]

While most translations read "sweat of the brow," in fact the Hebrew reads "sweat of the nose," and there is no doubt what is meant. "Nose" in Hebrew never means "forehead." Back in chapter 4, we found that the nose is the center of the face in the Bible and, as such, is one way of centering the whole human person. God breathed life into Adam through his nose, of course. It is not surprising, then, that when God passes judgment on man, that judgment is tied to the center of man's life, at his nose. The nose that had breathed in God's very breath in Genesis 2:7 would now drip with sweat because of man's sin.

Since the water of this sweat flows down from the forehead to the nose, there is a hint of baptismal grace in this phenomenon. It is this baptism of the nose, of the defiled center of the face, that makes possible our daily bread as a continuing gift from God. The "baptism" of the nose leads to the "supper" of the bread, just as the initial inbreathing of the Spirit's life through the nose lead to the initial food of the Garden.

---

124. Arthur C. Custance, "The Meaning of Sweat as Part of the Curse" (1962), reprinted in *The Flood: Local or Global?*, The Doorway Papers 9 (Grand Rapids: Zondervan, 1979). Online: https://custance.org/Library/Volume9/Part_V/Introduction.html.

Genesis 3:19a points forward to Jesus in a very particular way. It was through the bloody sweat of Jesus, from His nose, that bread comes to us in the Lord's Supper. Through His sweat, we eat bread, including our daily bread. Yet there is also a difference, since blood does not come baptismally down from the brow, but from the breaking of the vessels of the body within. Thus, while the watery sweat on the nose speaks positively of new life, the blood from Jesus' nose anticipates the crushing of His flesh (not His bones) in His death.

Bread is good, and so are the plants of the field that provide it. Continuing our humaniform application of this passage, the reference here is to the good children that come forth from the soil of the woman. We will enjoy them, but it will cost us pain and labor to bring them up. Child rearing is difficult. It is hard, like the winnowing and grinding of wheat to make bread. Only afterwards is it pleasant, when our children grow up to be righteous and godly.

We have seen that the woman bears "pain" in childbearing and that this can be understood to include child rearing as well. The man, we have seen, will experience "pain" in his marriage, and this means that the woman will as well. Now we can add that the man experiences "pain" in child rearing. The actual bearing of the child is painful to the woman, but afterwards she has the joys of holding and nursing a baby. Later on, the father must take over and do the hard and painful work of bringing his son or daughter to maturity. Only when the child is grown and becomes (we hope and pray) a "plant of the field" instead of a "thorn or thistle" is there any real and lasting pleasure for the father.

DUST TO DUST

"Until you return to the soil;
Because from her were you taken.
Because dust you are,
And to dust will you return."
And the man called the name of his wife Eve,
Because she was the mother of all living (Gen. 3:19–20).

This prediction and judgment is clear enough as it stands: The sin of man means that he will return to the dust. Obviously, though this is said to Adam, it includes Eve and all women as well, for Adam is the head of the whole human race.

In a particular way, however, this judgment applies to Adam and to him alone, for he alone of all human beings who have ever walked this earth was taken directly from the dust of the earth. It is only because we are in union with Adam that we also return to the dust. Eve was taken from Adam's side, and thus she must return to dust with him. All of us are descended from him and are under his judgment with him, and thus we must return to dust with him also. Jesus, however, had God as His Father, and not Adam, and thus did not return to dust, for He was not united to Adam essentially. He took upon Himself Adam's judgment, but only for three hours on the cross.

It is the humaniform implications of this statement that call for our more extended attention. Adam came forth from Mother Earth, but God has made it quite clear already that there is a new mother, a second mother, who is Adam's wife. The man and his woman were told to "be fruitful and multiply." Also, the woman was told that she would have a seed who would crush the serpent's head. From this, Adam can see that there is another mother besides the dust that gives him birth originally.

I suggest that Adam's response to God's judgment shows that he hopes in a new mother. The name Eve means "Life." But in what sense? If we take it that she is now called Eve because she will have children, there is nothing new in that. Why would Adam give her that name at this particular point in the narrative? Why not call her Eve from the start?

The clue is that she "was" the mother of all "living." The word "living" is very general and seems not to have any particular reference. Clearly Eve "was" not the mother of all living things. The reference has to be to human beings. But she is not yet the mother of anyone. The Hebrew does not say that she "would be" the mother of all living, but that she already "was" the mother of all living. Exegetes have puzzled over this and have tried to find evidence that the perfect tense can have some kind of future meaning, but without any convincing success. There must be some sense in which Eve was *already* the mother of all "living."

There is a way in which Eve already "was" the mother of all "true" life and that is that she has been told that from her will come the Messiah, who will reverse death and provide life. This is already true. Eve already is the mother of "living" in that sense, the sense of a new life. Understood in such a way, Eve becomes the mother of "all living" in the sense of true life, not in the sense of mere reproduction of children.

I submit that Adam's naming of his wife "Life" is an affirmation of his faith in everything that God has said. Through the woman would come a Savior who would destroy the death-bringer through His own suffering. This is the life that Adam is speaking of. It is a "living" on the other side of death and dust.

Adam accepts that he must die and return to dust, but he also puts his hope in a new life. Returning to Mother Earth will not be the last word, because there is a new mother, the mother of the seed. Humanity can transfer into that new mother, which ultimately is the Church, and be born again, can live again, because that mother is the mother of all living.

Such an understanding not only makes sense of this statement in its preceding context, but also illumines what follows. After Adam's profession of faith in God's promises, God covers him and Eve in a sacrificial skin before sending them out of the Garden—something that must be done for their own protection: Had they remained in the holy environment of the Garden, they would have been destroyed.

Thus, the parallel between the soil and woman comes to full play here. All human beings will return to dust, their original mother, but they can also "return" to a new mother. The flesh will perish, but the spirit will be saved and eventually a new flesh be given as well.

At this point it is important to notice to whom the promise is given. It is to the woman, not directly to Adam. The woman will be saved from death by her seed, the Messiah. Anyone who wants to be saved, thus, must come into union with the mother. And that includes Adam as well. Jesus dies for His mother/bride, the Church (understood in the widest sense), and those who are to find new life must be in that mother/bride, for she is the mother of all living.

Adam confesses that this is true. He does not claim to be the father of all living. He has brought death to humanity and cannot bring life. Eve, being deceived and thus not the death-bringer, is the one who will bring life. God had not said that the seed of the man would bring salvation, and Adam does not try to claim that any such thing will happen. He accepts God's Word. As death came through Adam, so salvation will come through Eve. Of course, this will not be because of her own work, but because of the work of her Seed. But that seed is the seed of the *woman*, not the seed of the *man*.

Thus, Adam confesses his faith in God's saving plan, God's plan for new life. We can expect to meet Adam in heaven when we die.

ADAM'S JUDGMENTS AND EVE'S

We need now to return to some comments we made at the beginning of this chapter. We saw that God began His judgments against Adam by saying that they were befalling him because he hearkened to the voice of his wife. Adam had put himself into union with Eve, and what this means is that the judgments that befall Adam are extensions of the judgments that befall Eve.

This is most gracious on God's part. We have seen that Adam was quite self-conscious in his rebellion against God, while Eve was deceived. God might have counted Adam as fully rebellious and damned him on the spot. Instead, God allows Adam to consider himself as united to Eve in her deception. United to Eve, Adam will escape the full brunt of God's righteous judgment. Also, as we have seen, united to Eve Adam will have the hope of a future life to come, through the Messianic Seed.

What we must do now is show how the judgments that came against Eve are applied to Adam. The judgments on Adam are not something different from the judgments on Eve, but are extensions of them.

> Cursed is the soil with reference to you.
> In pain will you eat of her all the days of your life.
> And thorn and thistle will she sprout for you.

Transferring this judgment back to Eve, it is easy to understand what it means. The woman's body is made of soil, just as the man's is. Her body will act against her and cause her pain. In particular, that pain will be associated with childbearing, so that she brings forth thorn and thistle. Thus, God had said to Eve: "Multiplying, I shall multiply your pain and your conception. In pain will you bring forth sons" (3:16).

> And you will eat the plant of the field:
> In the sweat of your nose will you eat bread.

To understand this, we need to remember the enmity put between the serpent and the woman. The serpent will eat dust. The woman, by contrast, must have other food, for she is the serpent's enemy. Her food will be bread, but it will be gained through pain and difficulty.

> Until you return to the soil;
> Because from her were you taken.
> Because dust you are,
> And to dust will you return.

As we have seen, the "pain" of conception is linked often with the death of the woman. That is the fullest extent of the "pain." Yet the pain is also linked with bringing forth the Messianic seed, and there lies the hope on the other side of the pain, on the other side of death. Adam will also return to death, but in terms of the parallels, he can see that his death is linked with a new life.

Such a new life cannot come from the dust, however, since the serpent eats the dust. Those who return only to the dust are doomed to be incorporated into Satan and will experience his judgment with him in the eternal fires of hell. To escape being eaten by Satan, we must be raised from the dust. We must be repositioned into Eve, the mother of all living, the new mother, so that we can be saved by her Seed.

This is the confident hope that Adam expresses when he calls Eve the mother of all living. The original mother of all living things was the earth, but all her offspring will return to dust and be eaten by the serpent. For Adam to be saved, he must have a new mother, so that while his body returns to dust, yet before the serpent has a chance to eat him fully, he will be raised in union with the new life-mother.

Now in the previous section I made the point that Eve is not the mother of all "living" in the sense that mother earth was. Possibly this is not enough to say, for the entire cosmos is repositioned in union with Jesus and thus in union with mother Church as well. Living things, in the Bible, include animals as well as human beings, though not plants. Animals as well as human beings were preserved on the ark of Noah and came into the new world. Thus, in the fullest sense, Eve becomes the mother of a new world, of a new cosmos, for she is the mother of the Messiah in whom that cosmos is preserved and renewed.

25

THE STRUCTURE OF GENESIS 3 REVISITED

AS I have progressed slowly through Genesis 2 and 3, I find that from time to time I must go back and adjust what I have written previously. It is becoming apparent to me that there are important deep-connections between the various paragraphs in these chapters, and only by comparing them can we see what these are.

Thus, I need to make an adjustment in what I originally wrote regarding 2:25–3:7a, because doing so will bring that paragraph strikingly into line with the two paragraphs that follow and with the structure of Genesis 2, something I was unable to detect until now.

All three paragraphs in Genesis 3 begin and end with the theme of nakedness (2:25 + 3:7a; 3:7b + 3:10b; 3:11 + 3:21). Each paragraph is clearly a chiasm. The fact that they each begin and end the same way, and that they have the same structure, suggests that they are parallel to each other throughout in some profound and interesting ways. I think that this is indeed so and want to begin discussing it here.

Originally I divided 2:25–3:7b according to the various actors and speakers as follows:

A. Naked and not ashamed (2:25).

    B. Serpent arrives (3:1a).

        C. Serpent speaks; Adam and Eve listen (3:1b).

            D. Woman speaks instead of Adam (3:2–3).

        C'. Serpent teaches falsely (3:4–5).

    B'. Adam and Eve accept serpent's words (3:6).

A'. Naked and ashamed (3:7a).

I now think that I did not pay close enough attention to the actual content of the various statements. If we do, we find parallels with the third paragraph in Genesis 3 (verses 11–21). That paragraph has the following form:

A. God asks how they knew they were naked (3:11a).

    B. The woman accused and interrogated (3:11b–13).

        C. The serpent and dust; "Cursed" (3:14).

            D. The woman's seed; "I am putting" (3:15).

                [E. Serpent and woman: Who will rule? (15a).]

                    [F. Serpent and child: Child will crush. Child will suffer (15b).]

                    [F'. Woman and child: Child will be born. Woman will suffer (16a).]

                [E'. Husband and woman: Who will rule? (16b).]

            D'. The woman's seed: "I am increasing" (3:16).

        C'. The man and dust; "Cursed" (3:17–19).

    B'. The woman honored (3:20).

A'. God covers their nakedness (3:21).

The second paragraph (verses 7b–10) can be matched with verses 22–24, as Yahweh God comes to the Garden for sabbath interaction with man, and then Yahweh God expels Adam and Eve from the Garden in sabbath judgment. Thus, these two paragraphs form bookends to the chiasm of verses 11–21.

Notice that in this third paragraph (verses 11–21), the second section is an interrogation of the woman, while the penultimate section is a reconciliation between the man and the woman. If we bring this structure back to the first paragraph, we can revise that chiasm to reflect, in the second position, the serpent's interrogation of the woman and, in the penultimate position, a form of false union between the man and the woman:

A. Now the two of them were naked, the man and
his woman, and they did not sense shame (2:25).

   B. And the serpent: He was crafty, more than all the beasts of the field
   that Yahweh God made. And he said to the woman, "Indeed, did
   God really say, 'Not shall you eat from any tree of the garden'?" (3:1).

      C. And the woman said to the serpent, "From the fruit of the trees of
      the garden we may eat. And from the fruit of the tree that is in the
      center of the garden, God said, 'Not shall you eat from it, and not
      shall you touch it, or you will die'" (3:2–3).

         D. And the serpent said to the woman, "Not dying you shall die. For
         God is knowing that in the day of your eating from it your eyes will be
         opened and you will be like God, knowing good and evil" (3:4–5).

      C'. And the woman saw that good was the tree for food, and that
      pleasant was it to the eyes, and desirable was the tree for gaining
      wisdom, and she took from its fruit, and she ate (3:6a).

   B'. And she gave also to her husband with her, and he ate (3:6b).

A'. And the eyes of both of them were opened,
and they knew that they were naked (3:7a).

This revision brings the paragraph startlingly into line with the seven
paragraphs of Genesis 2, which in turn reflect the seven days of Genesis 1.

SEVEN DAYS AND THE FALL (GEN. 2:25–3:7A)

We have been considering how the narrative of the fall of man follows the
sequences of Genesis 1 and 2. In previous chapters, I have shown how Genesis
1 and 2 follow each other thematically. I am making a slight change at this
point. Both ways of showing parallels are correct, but this "new" way of doing
it takes into account the fact that the work of the fifth is not said to be good
until the first work of the sixth day has been completed, so that all animals
are grouped together. The change also has the effect of putting the threat of
death in the fourth position, which is where the theme of death occurs in the
later sections.

Original

Day 4	2:15 enthronement
Day 5	2:16–17 blessings and curses
Day 6	2:18–24 helpers and community

New

    Day 4   2:15–17 enthronement and death

    Day 5–6a 2:18–20 animals

    Day 6b   2:21–24 community

We cannot be surprised that there is more than one "correct" way of showing the parallels, because (a) though there are seven days, there are more than seven actions in Genesis 1, since the third and sixth days have two actions on them; (b) though the actions of Yahweh God in Genesis 2 can easily be seen as linking with the seven days as a set of seven, there are in fact more than seven actions of Yahweh God in Genesis 2, which introduces flexibility; and (c) these early and thus highly compact beginnings of God's Word-revelation naturally encompass in seed form many motifs that are later expanded in more depth and detail.

Day 1: God makes light.

    2:4–7. The empty, formless earth is given a light, humanity.

    2:25. The nakedness of man, the earthly light, is not hidden by any garment, by any shame.

Day 2: God makes the firmament chamber between heaven and earth.

    2:8. God makes the Garden-sanctuary and puts the man into it.

    3:1. The serpent enters the Garden and asks about it.

Day 3: God makes land, and trees and grain.

    2:9–14. The food of the trees is emphasized, and the center of the Garden, and the rivers that flow out carrying the influence of this situation to the world.

    3:2–3. Eve speaks twice of the food of the trees, and of one of the central trees. The parallel reminds us, implicitly, that whatever happens at the center of the Garden will flow out to the whole world. Thus, we are given a picture of the history-determining position of Adam and Eve.

Day 4: God establishes heavenly lights to rule.

    2:15–17. Adam established as ruler, placed there by God and given the condition of his ruling and the threat of death.

    3:4–5. Satan directly attacks God's over-lordship and tells Adam and Eve that a higher position of rule can be theirs. Satan's statements quote and pervert 2:16–17.

Day 5–6a: God creates animals, commanding and blessing them, and pronouncing things good only after the creation of land animals on Day 6b.

2:18–20. The animals are *not* good as helpers for man.

3:6a. The woman disobeys the command, failing as man's helper.

Day 6b: God creates humanity, blessing them with (a) fruitfulness and (b) food from the soil.

2:21–24. God establishes community between man and woman.

3:6b. The woman gives the fruit to the man, a sign of community, but a false community.

Day 7: God enters His rest.

2:25–3:7a. Adam and Eve fail to enter God's rest and make clothes for themselves.

3:7a. Adam and Eve cover their light.

What these parallels do for us, first of all, is expose the fact that not only does the generation of man's first home follow the same shape or form as the generation of the cosmos, but that the fall of humanity follows the same shape or form. The image of God copies God's activities, but in this case perverts them. As we shall see, the next paragraph, God's coming to the Garden, follows the same form.

SEVEN DAYS AND GOD'S COMING TO THE GARDEN (GEN. 3:7B–10)

We have seen that the seven days of creation, the narrative of the Garden of Eden, and the narrative of the fall all have the same basic shape. These parallels also set up the form or shape of the two paragraphs that follow, God's initial interrogation of Adam, and God's judgments.

The second paragraph of Genesis 3, which is the fourth iteration of this shape, looks like this:

A. ³:⁷ᵇ And they sewed fig leaves and made for themselves girdings.

  B. ⁸ᵃ And they heard the *sound/voice* of Yahweh God
    walking about in the *garden* as the Spirit of the day.

    C. ⁸ᵇ And they *hid*, the man and his woman, from the face
      of Yahweh God among the garden's trees.

      D. ⁹ᵃ And Yahweh God called to the man.

C'. ^{9b} And He said to him *"Where* are you?"

B'. ^{10a} And he said "Your *sound/voice* I heard in the *garden,*

A'. ^{10b} "And I was afraid because I was naked and I hid."

Let us now correlate this sequence with what we have already observed.

Day 1: Light

2:4–7.	Man as light.
2:25.	Man's light not hidden.
3:7b.	Man's light hidden by a self-made covering.

Day 2: Firmament

2:8.	Garden.
3:1.	Serpent enters Garden.
3:8a.	Yahweh enters Garden.

Day 3: Land and Trees

2:9–14.	Tree, food, and outflow.
3:2–3.	Eve speaks of trees and food.
3:8b.	Hiding among trees; retreat instead of outflow.

Day 4: Firmament as Silent Rulers

2:15–17.	Adam as speaking ruler; threat of death.
3:4–5.	Serpent as speaking counterfeit ruler; rejection of death threat.
3:9a.	Yahweh speaks as Ruler; beginning of implementation of death threat.

Day 5: Commands to Creatures

2:18–20.	Creatures as inadequate helpers.
3:6a.	Woman disobeys command; inadequate as helper. (She should have obeyed God and ignored Adam's silent encouragement to sin.)
3:9b.	Yahweh interrogates. Interrogation as the "reverse" of command.

Day 6: Humanity and Community

2:21–24.	Community.
3:6b.	False community created around false sacrament.
3:10a.	Community with God, as He draws near after having left Adam and Eve alone ("I heard You drawing near").

Day 7: Sabbath Judgment

2:25–3:7a.	Sabbath sin.
3:7a.	Covering nakedness.
3:10b.	Hiding because naked.

In the next section, we shall apply this same shape to the fifth section, the judgments God pronounced.

Seven Days and God's Judgments (Gen. 3:11–21)

The fifth iteration of the sequence we have been considering is in 3:11–21. Here we find God's judgments moving through the same sevenfold sequence, building on all that has gone before and providing us with some interesting insights.

1   Day 1: Light
2   2:4–7. Man as light.
3   2:25. Man's light not hidden.
4   3:7b. Man's light hidden by a self-made covering.

5   [11a] And He said, "Who told you that naked you are?"

The parallels between Genesis 1 and Genesis 2 establish that man is the light of the world. The naked man is a light, which was to be glorified eventually with glorious garments, as God's light refracted through His "garment" becomes a rainbow around Him.

The beginning of each iteration of the heptamerous sequence concerns that light. Man had hidden his initial light in 3:7b with garments of leaves. Now the God who initially said "Let there be light" asks "What have you done with your light?"

1   Day 2: Firmament
2   2:8. Garden.
3   3:1. Serpent enters Garden.
4   3:8a. Yahweh enters Garden.

5   [11b] "From the tree that I commanded you not to eat from it, did you eat?"

The Tree of the Knowledge of Good and Evil is the "firmament" or barrier that man was not to cross until God was ready. The Serpent, or Lucifer, was positioned as a "star," specifically the "son of the morning" or "morning star" (Venus), the first star that arises in the morning, at the beginning of the day, at the beginning of history. He was over humanity, tasked with teaching them God's ways. Asking the "Socratic question" was itself good, for he was making Adam and Eve think about God's barrier-command. His sin came when he encouraged mankind to try and break through the firmament and ascend to the throne of God. Thus, for the serpent to enter the Garden can be correlated as a manifestation of the firmament-theme. Similarly, for Yahweh to enter the Garden also correlates with the firmament, because He set it up and maintains it.

Yahweh's question is about this firmament tree: Did you eat of it? Did you try to cross the boundary I set up?

1   Day 3: Land and Trees
2   2:9–14. Tree, food, and outflow.
3   3:2–3. Eve speaks of trees and food.
4   3:8b. Hiding among trees; retreat instead of outflow.

5   ¹² And the man said,
    "The woman whom You gave with me,
    she it was who gave me of the tree, and I ate."

Verse 12 concerns the eating of the fruit of the trees of the Garden. Eve had seen that all the fruit was good, and now Adam blames her for his eating. As Adam and Eve hid among the trees in 3:8b, so now Adam tries to hide behind Eve.

It might seem that verse 13 should also be put here, as Eve also confesses to eating and blames the serpent for misleading her. But because of the chiasm of the passage, verse 13 belongs with the next section, which concerns the woman's relationship with the serpent.

1   Day 4: Firmament as Silent Rulers
2   2:15–17. Adam as speaking ruler; threat of death.
3   3:4–5. Serpent as speaking counterfeit ruler; rejection of death threat.
4   3:9a. Yahweh speaks as Ruler; beginning of implementation of death threat.

5   Chiasm:

    A. ¹³ And Yahweh God said to the woman,
        "What is this that you have done?"
    And the woman said,
        "The serpent deceived me,
        and I ate."
    ¹⁴ And Yahweh God said to the serpent,
        "Because you have done this,
        Cursed (banned) are you

    from all cattle
    and from all beasts of the field;

  B. Upon your belly you shall go.
    And dust you shall eat all the days of your life."

    C. [15] "And enmity will I put between you and the woman,
        And between your seed and her seed.
        He will bruise your head,
        And you will bruise his heel."

  B'. [16] To the woman He said,
    "Multiplying, I shall multiply your pain and your conception.
    In pain you will bring forth sons,

 A'. And for your husband is your urge
  And he will rule over you."

This is the center of the passage, and it concerns both who will rule and the theme of the death-threat. There is a chiasm in this section, which places the promise of the Messiah at the center, and thus at the center of the entire judgment section:

  A. Serpent over the woman and then demoted from rule (13–14a).

    B. Serpent cursed in his belly (14b); what he eats, takes into himself.

      C. The Messiah (15).

    B'. Woman judged in her belly, in childbearing (16a); when she bears, gives out of herself.

  A'. Man established as ruler of woman (16b).

Lucifer, man's original teacher, was positioned as a star (the morning star, at the beginning of history) over humanity. The woman rightly points to the serpent as tricking her (2 Cor. 11:3; 1 Tim. 2:14). The death threat is now visited upon him, and he is demoted to the lowest place, beneath all other animals. Dust being associated with death, for Lucifer to eat dust means he will eat death. Since man is made of dust, Lucifer's death will come when he "eats" man, particularly when he tries to "eat" the Messiah. The death of Jesus will become the death of Satan.

Verses 15–16 are chiastic and carry forth the themes of rule and death:

A. Serpent and woman: Who will rule? (15a).

   B. Serpent and child: Child will crush. Child will suffer (15b).

   B'. Woman and child: Child will be born. Woman will suffer (16a).

A'. Husband and woman: Who will rule? (16b).

The serpent has sought to usurp Adam's place in the "firmament" over the Garden, but God will restore the husband over the wife. Moreover, the son of the woman will come and rule the serpent, destroying him.

1	Day 5–6a: Living Creatures and Commands
2	2:18–20. Creatures as inadequate helpers.
3	3:6a. Woman disobeys command; inadequate as helper. (She should have obeyed God and ignored Adam's silent encouragement to sin.)
4	3:9b. Yahweh interrogates. Interrogation as the "reverse" of command.

5   ¹⁷ And to Adam He said,

"Because you hearkened to the voice of your wife,

And you ate from the tree,

concerning which I commanded you, saying,

'Not shall you eat from it';

Cursed is the soil with reference to you.

In pain will you eat of her all the days of your life.

¹⁸ And thorn and thistle will she sprout for you.

And you will eat the plant of the field:

¹⁹ In the sweat of your nose will you eat bread;

Until you return to the soil;

Because from her were you taken.

Because dust you are,

And to dust will you return."

The earth brought forth the living creatures who were to be Adam's secondary helpers. Now the earth will bring forth thorns and thistles to make his work harder. The swarms of creatures on Day 5 and 6a are now matched with a swarm of weeds and thorns. Adam had perverted his wifely helper, and by extension had perverted all his helpers, and now they will "help" him by driving him to despair or to prayer.

The soil was Adam's mother, for he is the generation of the heavens and the earth, of the Spirit's breath and the dry dust. The soil is parallel to Eve. At Adam's silent instigation, Eve ate of the death-dealing fruit in the third iteration (3:6a). Thereby, Adam poisoned Eve, and by implication poisoned the earth, for Eve is the future mother, replacing the dry soil for all future generations of mankind. Having poisoned the earth, Adam now finds that the soil deals death to him. The judgment is entirely appropriate.

Notice also that in 3:6a, the woman gave beautiful and tasty fruit to the man. Now the man will receive thorns and thistles. The death-bearing thorns and thistles come "because" the man ate of the death-fruit given him by the woman. The original mother of man now gives inadequate food, but the woman, the new mother, will bring forth a much better Seed, the Messiah. Man is thus forced to stop looking back to the original mother, "mother nature," for seed, and to look to the new mother and to the Seed of the woman. When Adam calls the woman Eve, the "mother of all living," he shows that he has shifted his faith in this new God-promised direction.

The judgment against the man here in this fifth section picks up from the judgments against the serpent in the fourth section. This is because the man cooperated with the serpent as a silent partner. The opening statement against the man (verse 17b) is parallel to the curse upon the serpent (verse 14), though the man is not cursed directly:

1. Cursed are you above all	Cursed is the ground with reference to you
2. Crawl on belly	In severe labor
3. Dust you will eat	You will eat of ground
4. All the days of your life	All the days of your life

The judgment on the man is then expanded (verses 18–19), following the same order and themes:

1. Ground produces thorns

2. Sweat of the nose

3. Eat food

4. End of life.

1	Day 6b: Humanity and Community
2	2:21–24. Community.
3	3:6b. False community created around false sacrament.
4	3:10a. Community with God, as He draws near after having left Adam and Eve alone ("I heard You drawing near").
5	[20] And the man called the name of his wife Eve, Because she was the mother of all living.

We have seen that Adam's calling his wife "Life" is a confession that he accepts God's promise of the future Messiah who will come from his wife. God has promised to bring life out of death, a savior out of the poisoned soil of Eve, and Adam accepts this. Chiastically, Adam's acceptance of Eve reverses his rejection of her, his attempt to blame her for his own sin. It restores true community.

Community is the large theme of the sixth day. God said, "Let *Us* make man," and He made them male and female. Human marital community, and the larger community of man downwards to the beasts and upwards toward God, is also thematic in 2:18–24. That community is counterfeited and poisoned when Adam receives the fruit from Eve in 3:6b and begins to be restored as Adam sees Yahweh draw near to them in 3:10a.

What is of interest is the parallel between the fruit given to Adam by Eve and the Life-Son who will be given to humanity through Eve. Something new and better is going to come from Eve, from her hands. With the whole of the Bible before us, we can see the parallels quite clearly:

Adam silently provokes Eve to eat the fruit, and she does.
The Spirit of God places Jesus into the womb of Mary.

Having eaten the fruit into herself, Eve offers it to Adam.
Mary gives birth, and hands Jesus over to the world, through the cross.

Adam eats the fruit of death.
We eat the Bread of Life, Jesus.

It is not just Mary as an individual that is in view here, of course, but Mary as the culmination of the entire Bride of the Old Creation, as the culmination of the promise to Eve, as the last Eve. The savior comes from Eve, and from Sarah, and from Rebekah, and from Leah, and from Ruth, etc., down to Mary. Jesus is the new fruit offered to all. He hung upon the tree, replacing what Adam and Eve stole, and now we eat of Him in the Lord's Supper, which signifies our fellowship with Him at all times and in all ways.

It is the Supper that restores community. The meal Adam and Eve ate at the Tree of Knowledge destroyed their community, even though it had the outward marks of community. The meal we share with Jesus restores all true community in the bond of the Spirit.

1   Day 7: Sabbath Judgment

2   2:25–3:7a. Sabbath sin.

3   3:7a. Covering nakedness.

4   3:10b. Hiding because naked.

5   [21] And Yahweh God made for Adam and for his woman tunics of a skin,
     And He clothed them.
     [22] And Yahweh God said,
          "Behold, the man has become like one of Us,
          knowing good and evil.
          And now lest he send out his hand
          and take also from the tree of life
          and eat and live forever…."
     [23] And Yahweh God sent him out from the Garden of Eden
          to work the ground from which he was taken.

God killed an animal and from it provided tunics for Adam and Eve. ("Skin" is singular, which at least implies only one animal for both tunics.) God had said that in the day they ate of the forbidden fruit they would die, and now a substitute dies in their place.

The word "tunic" (*kethoneth*) indicates a garment of privilege. It is used eight more times in Genesis—in Genesis 37:3 for the tunic Jacob made for Joseph as a sign of his authority, and then seven more times in 37:23–33 in the story of the brothers' attack upon Joseph. The sevenfold use of the term in this passage indicates that it was the garment as a sign of authority that was a large part of what provoked the brothers.

The same kind of garment was worn by the daughters of King David (2 Sam. 13:18,19). It was also worn by Hushai the Archite, who tore it (2 Sam. 15:32). Hushai is called "David's Friend," a title indicating that he was David's chief counselor. Compare Abraham as God's Friend, and Jesus' statement that we are no longer His servants but His friends because He has told us everything (Jas. 2:23; John 15:15; Gen. 18:17ff.; 1 Kgs. 4:5). When Hushai tears his garment, it is a sign that the royal house and the kingdom have been torn.

Tunics were included in the garments of the priests of Israel (Exod. 28:4, 39, 40; 29:5, 8; 39:27; 40:14; Lev. 8:7, 13; 10:5; 16:4). These tunics were made of pure linen, which is vegetable fiber, in contrast to the tunics of animal skins placed upon Adam and Eve. The pure linen garments are said to be "holy," and the multicolored sash that bound it, with the other outer garments, are said to be "for glory and beauty." Since the colored yarns were made of wool, from animals, it is possible that we should see this as God covering Adam and Eve in garments of rudimentary glory.[125]

Leviticus 16 delineates the ritual of the Day of Covering (which is the accurate translation, not "Day of Atonement"). On this day, the Cover (not "Mercy Seat") of the Ark of the Covenant was covered by blood sprinkled on it. That Cover represented the firmament between heaven and earth,[126] and blood put upon it meant that God viewed the world through the blood of a propitiatory offering. The world of God's people, Jew and Gentile (16:29–31), was covered by this blood, under the protection of this blood, which averted His wrath. The High Priest wore only special linen garments while doing this ritual. At the end of the ritual, the High Priest would put back on his garments of glory and beauty, and thus he was re-covered as God's High Priest. In other words, the High Priest was restored to a position of glory and rule on the basis of the shed blood of the animal sacrifices, and this was signified by his being re-covered with garments made of both vegetable and animal fibers.

In short, on the Day of Coverings, the High Priest (representing all God's people) replayed the events of Genesis 3. First he was covered in linen—vegetable. Then animals were killed. Then he was covered in glorious linen plus wool—animal skins. His glory garments also included a third element, minerals (gold and gemstones).

With all this information in mind, we can see that God was honoring Adam and Eve as royalty, with a kind of glory, when He gave them tunics. They had made aprons to cover their shame, but God does something much more than give them better aprons. He gives them glory.

We might see all this as somehow ironic or sarcastic on God's part: "Well, you've made yourselves kings by seizing the forbidden fruit before you were ready for it, so now I'll dress you with royal garments." But we have seen that

---

125. The glory garments of the High Priest also included gold and gemstones. He was clothed in vegetable, animal, and mineral materials. He was clothed in the whole world. On the nature of colored yarn as wool, see Jacob Milgrom, "Of Hems and Tassels," *Biblical Archaeology Review* 9:3 (May/June, 1983), 61–65.

126. The Ark consisted of two separate items: the Ark or chest proper, and the Cover with cherubim attached to it over it. The Cover represents the firmament, with humanity-Ark below and the angelic heaven above. God's people, the Ark, are to have the Law inside themselves as the tablets of the Law were inside the Ark. The Cover is analogous to the Sea of Glass, on which stand the angels and over which God presides on His throne, as His glory also hovered over the angels on the Ark.

Adam has repented and has accepted God's word by calling Eve the mother of all future life. It is true that there is no going back. Adam and Eve cannot return to being babies in the Garden. They have indeed made themselves kings prematurely. But when they repent God promises to enable them to grow into being true kings in spite of their sin. By the blood, they are covered. And by the blood, the covering they receive is a sign of privilege and glory.

The giving of the tunic means that Adam and Eve are allowed to begin again as priests, to have the first form of clothing given them, so that they can grow up into the more glorious outer garments. Moreover, as with Joseph, Hushai, the priests, and the Davidic princesses, the tunic is a sign of princely rule under a father. It is a sign of authority, but authority that is in submission to higher authority.

And as a sign of royal authority, the tunic is associated with the sabbath. It is a sign of being at rest with God, joining in His rest, though not yet fully ascended to sit at His right hand in garments of glory.

It should be noted also that the seamless garment stripped from Jesus at His crucifixion was a tunic, the Greek word being equivalent to the Hebrew (John 19:23–24). The temporary royal covering provided for Adam by God is now removed from Jesus, so that He is naked like Adam in the Garden. Passing through the death of the Tree of Knowledge (i.e., the cross), Jesus is raised in the fullness of what glorious garments meant: a glorified body.

Finally, the fact that these tunics were made of skins points not only to animal sacrifice, implicitly, but more explicitly means that Adam and Eve are restored to dominion over the animal world. The animal world is once again the glory around them, as the angels are the glory around God.

This seventh day (Sabbath) section of the judgments includes not only verse 21, but also verses 22–24, which we will discuss in the next chapter. As God is enthroned in sabbath rest, as king, so Adam and Eve are clothed in royal tunics (verse 21); but unlike God, they are not enthroned in a palace but are sent and then driven from it (verses 22–24).

26

EXILE FROM THE GARDEN

GENESIS 3:22–23

And Yahweh God said, "Behold, the man has become like one of Us, knowing good and evil. And now lest he send out his hand and take also from the tree of life and eat and live forever...." And Yahweh God sent him out from the Garden of Eden to work the ground from which he was taken (Gen. 3:22–23).

THE serpent had said that when Adam and Eve ate the forbidden fruit, they would become like God. God confirms that this is so. This is not sarcasm or irony, as some have suggested. Nor does God mean Adam has become like one of the angels, including the angels in "us," as some have also suggested.

Let me remind the reader that the prohibition on the forbidden fruit was temporary, and so both Satan's promise and God's confirmation are true. "Knowledge of good and evil" does not mean awareness of bad and good, but rather the kingly right to pronounce judgments as a "god." The word "god" (*'ĕlohim*) is used for human judges. Adam was supposed to wait until he was old enough and mature enough to be promoted, but he promoted himself.

God confirms Adam's self-promotion. God never runs history backwards, undoing what man has done. Rather, God moves history forward and transforms human evil into good, ultimately by sending His Son to die on the cross for our sins. We have seen that Eve as the new mother of all New Life, and the promise of the Messiah, point toward to God's great action in the future.

Thus, God allows that Adam has now become a king of sorts. Adam must now act in terms of this responsibility that he has seized. He cannot undo what he has done, and God will not undo it. Adam has prematurely taken upon himself this weighty task, and now he must grow into it by grace.

What is this task? It is clear from verse 23: It is to work the soil of the world outside the Garden. The Garden was Adam's nursery, where he would grow up until he was ready for the greater task of working and guarding the whole world. Now he must go out and do just that, even though he is not mature enough to do it. He will have to grow into this new and heavy responsibility.

Recall that Adam was made of soil outside the Garden and was then put into it. Adam was shown the world he would eventually rule and then was put into a nursery so he could grow up. In the nursery he would have simple tasks that would fit him for the more complex tasks he would face when he went back into the world.

Thus, the order was supposed to be:

1. A brief life in the world.
2. Life in the nursery-Garden, granted by the Tree of Life.
3. Return to the world, granted by the Tree of Knowledge.

God sends Adam out for another reason: Lest Adam send out (same word) his hand and take from the Tree of Life. God says that eating this tree would give everlasting life to Adam. Of course, Adam was originally supposed to eat of this tree, which would have nourished him as he grew up in the Garden. Indeed, it was his ticket to stay in the Garden. But now that Adam has fallen, this sacramental Tree would have the effect of confirming him in his sin. It would mean that Adam could never be saved, and God acts to prevent this.

The Tree of Life, which was supposed to be Adam's first sacramental tree, now becomes an eschatological tree (Rev. 22:2, 14). It is given only after

Jesus has finished His work. (Notice that the New Jerusalem is a picture of the Church, and people are invited to convert and enter it.)

Adam was supposed to be confirmed in eternal life at the Tree of Life and then grow up until he was ready for kingship at the Tree of Knowledge. He would not have needed to go back to the Tree of Life, for he would already have its gift.

Instead, Adam went to the Tree of Knowledge and got its gift first. Now he is a king, but a fallen king. Jesus comes as that fallen king, taking the fall upon Himself as a king, proclaimed king on Palm Sunday, crowned as king by the Romans, crucified with the title of king above His head. Jesus served first as a priest, not as a king, humbly waiting until He was ready for the Tree of Knowledge. That Tree was the cross, where Jesus was proclaimed King. By His death for us, Jesus restores us to true kingship, and now we can be allowed to eat of the Tree of Life and live forever.

The new Tree of Life is our ticket back into the Garden. But because Jesus has come as King, the Garden is now transformed into the glorious city of New Jerusalem. We come into a new kingly Garden ruled by a New kingly Adam. Now we can be sent forth into the world to disciple all nations, for in Jesus we have the gifts of both Trees.

DRIVEN OUT

And He drove out the man. And He placed at the east of the Garden of Eden the cherubim... (Gen. 3:24).

Yahweh God "sent" the man forth from the Garden of Eden into the world from which he had originally come. As we have seen, this had been Adam's destiny all along, but Adam rebelliously and prematurely ended his "elementary school" training in the "kinder-garten" (child's garden) and thus was sent into the wider world much earlier than he should have been.

It was not Adam as an individual only who was sent out and driven out. It was "the man," Adam as the concentration-point of humanity, Adam as mankind. Eve, being originally part of Adam, and thus part of original humanity, was also sent and driven out.

Now the text adds that God "drove" the man out. We can see this parallel between sending and driving in Exodus 6:1:

With a strong hand he [Pharaoh] will send them [Israelites],
and with a strong hand he will drive them from his land.

And Exodus 11:1:

After that [the last plague] he [Pharaoh] will send you [pl.] from here;
and in his sending, driving he will drive you [pl.] completely from here.

One thing that is clear from the addition of "drive" is that mankind would not be allowed back into the Garden. If he had merely been sent out, he might have returned for occasional visits. But no, God will not allow him back in, except through the sword and fire of the cherubim (which we shall investigate in the next section).

Less clear, but implied I think, is that "sending" is verbal while "driving" is physical. I imagine Adam did not want to leave the Garden. Now that he had repented, he wanted a second chance. He wanted to start over. But God did not let him start over. Adam would have to continue his life outside the Garden and learn mature wisdom "on the job" the hard way, instead of learning it the easy way in the nursery of the Garden.

Verse 23 focused on the man and his new estate in the land. Verse 24 focuses on the Garden, which now has no man to guard it. But it is not left without guardians, for the cherubim take up the task mankind has neglected. Men will not replace the cherubim, and return to guarding the Garden, until the coming of a new creation.

CHERUBIM AND A FLAMING SWORD

And He placed at the east of the Garden of Eden the cherubim, and the flaming sword turning every which way, to guard the way to the Tree of Life (Gen. 3:24).

The Hebrew word *kerub* (plural, *kerubim*) is not evidently related to any other Hebrew word. The Akkadian word *karibu, keribu* refers to an intercessor, with the verbal form meaning to bless, praise, or adore. This seems to be the same word. In the Bible, the cherubim hold up the throne of God and worship him. As we shall see, one has to pass through, or by, the cherubim to approach God, and thus they are intermediaries or intercessors.

They clearly are a species of angel, second in rank to Lucifer himself, but above the archangels and angels. And they seem to be the same as the seraphim of Isaiah 6, a correlation that emerges from two considerations. First, the seraphim occupy the same position as cherubim elsewhere in the Bible. Second, the cherubim evidently can take on more than one form, with either two or four wings and faces; thus, six-winged cherubim are also a possibility.[127] In Isaiah 6 they are called "seraphim" because of their flaming fiery appearance (*saraph*, "burn"), and the association of the cherubim of Gen. 3:24 with the flaming sword provides another link between the two terms.

Cherubim—how many we don't know, but probably two—were placed at the east of the Garden of Eden, and since the Garden was on the east side of the Land of Eden, they blocked access to both locations. Since Eden was high ground (rivers flow downhill from Eden) and the Garden was lower than the Land of Eden (the river flowed into it, and then down to the rest of the world), the Garden and the Land of Eden were above the cherubim. In this way they can be seen as not only guarding but upholding the throne(s) of God.

This spatial arrangement is amplified in the Tabernacle, which is a world-model. We can start with the Ark and Cover ("Mercy Seat" is a mistranslation). The Ark is a gold-covered wooden chest, and laid on its top is a slab of gold with two cherubim growing out of it. Above the outstretched wings of the cherubim is the glory-presence of Yahweh. This configuration represents earth, firmament, and throne-heaven. Humanity is represented by the Ark beneath, which includes the tablets of the Law "written on the heart," as well as Aaron's rod and the pot of manna. The Cover is the firmament boundary between humanity and God, which must have blood put upon it in order for God and man to be reconciled (Lev. 16). The blood is shed, figuratively, by the sword of the cherubim: Some Man must die under the judgment of the angels, the new guardians of the Old Creation, in order for His blood to dissolve the Cover-barrier between God and man.

This simple configuration is replicated in the Tabernacle as a whole, which has three environments: the Throne Room or Holy of Holies, the Firmament Heavens or Holy Place (with the sevenfold lampstand for sun, moon, and stars), and the Courtyard. The Tabernacle has not only this vertical symbolism, but a stair-step symbolism as well, as each location is symbolically

---

127. Two wings and perhaps two faces in Tabernacle and Temple; four wings and four faces in Ezekiel 1 and 10 and Revelation 4.

a step above the preceding one. The journey through the Tabernacle is, thus, a journey simultaneously up to heaven and back up the mountain to the Garden—and beyond heaven to a new earth, beyond the Garden to the Land of Eden.[128]

A cherubim-embroidered veil guards the way to the Throne Room, and cherubim-embroidered tapestries surround both the Throne Room and the Holy Place. Only a blue veil is at the doorway of the Holy Place, because the human priests were given limited access under the Law, and human guards replaced the cherubim at the doorway into the Holy Place.

The doorways into the three zones of the Tabernacle were on the east side only, again pointing back to the Edenic configuration.

Ezekiel sees the Tabernacle in its later form, Solomon's Temple, in a vertical configuration, as a cherubic chariot. Inside an altar formed by the wings of the cherubim, he sees fire flashing back and forth like lightning. Though a different Hebrew word is used, we should not miss the connection to the flaming sword that turns every which way. Above this altar is a blue crystal barrier, which is also a throne, and a human figure divided in half, a manifestation of the Tabernacle proper and its two halves.[129]

Under the Law, unblemished animals but not men could make the journey back to the Garden of Eden. This is seen most clearly in the Ascension Offering of Leviticus 1 (mistranslated "Burnt Offering"). The worshipper leans on the animal, who then carries him, so to speak, in an ascension up to God. The animal undergoes the knife and then is placed into the fire. Then, purged of dross (the ashes), the animal is converted into smoke and ascends to God.

As can be seen, the animal on its journey back to Eden must pass under the knife of the cherubim (wielded by the worshipper) and must undergo the purging fire as well (provided by the assisting priest). We can clearly see the application of this movement to Jesus' crucifixion, and to ourselves. We must die in our baptism and be purged throughout our lives before we will be ready to enter the Palace-Garden of heaven, and then the New Earth. But for us, it is no longer cherubim who wield the sword and fire, but the New Adam, Jesus Christ. It is He who kills us in our baptism and who sends the fire to purge us

---

128. For a full discussion, see my *Studies in Exodus* lectures.

129. For more details, see my essay, "Chariot of Fire: The Ordination of Ezekiel," Biblical Horizons Occasional Paper 13 (April 1991).

and fit us for His palace. He is now the leader in worship and the intermediary between us and God.

27

THE SONS OF ADAM AND EVE

GENESIS 4:1–2

WE saw that Genesis 2–3 as a whole tracks the seven days of creation, and now we shall see that Genesis 4 does the same. Thus:

Day 1 2:4–7, the earth formless and unlighted, then the human light made.
4:1–2, "generations" of Adam and Eve, out of their "earth."

Day 2 2:8, the Garden as firmament between Eden and the world.
4:3–5a, fruits of the world (parallel garden) brought to the gate of the Garden.

Day 3 2:9–14, trees of life and judgment out of earth; division of earth and water.
4:5b-8, murder and two judgments; division of people.

Day 4 2:15, Adam placed into Garden as light.
4:9–14, Cain expelled from land/garden area.

Day 5 2:16–17, blessing and judgment, especially death.
4:15, Cain protected from death.

Day 6 2:18–24, humanity; woman brought to man.
　　　4:16–24, new evil humanity: marriage and descendants.

Day 7 2:25–3:24, sabbath sin and judgment.
　　　4:25–26, worship restored.

This outline may be adjusted somewhat as we proceed, but the general point is clear.

The following are key words:

Elohim — 35 times (5 x 7) in Gen. 1:1–2:3
Yahweh Elohim — 20 times in Gen. 2:4–3:24
Yahweh — 10 times in Genesis 4
Abel — 7 times in Genesis 4
Cain — 15 times in Genesis 4, but directly 14 times (subtracting 4:24)

The name for God changes twice. We may say that Elohim is the name given in these passages for God as creator and shaper of the whole world and universe. Yahweh Elohim is the name given for God as ruler of the sanctuary-garden. Yahweh is the name given for God as actor in the wider world outside the Garden.

We may also say that Yahweh is the covenant name for God, the God who makes covenant with human beings. He is called Yahweh God in Genesis 2–3 to stress that Yahweh is also the Creator. Once that point is made, He is called Yahweh thereafter. Yet this point could be established by calling Him Yahweh God only once, in 2:4, so the twenty-fold use of the term in the Garden story provides a close association with the Garden-sanctuary. The name "Yahweh God" recurs next in 9:26 and then in chapter 15, both of which concern priestly people and sanctuary concerns. Thus, it seems that, at least as the Bible starts out, Yahweh God has this sanctuary association. The name Yahweh by itself, thus, would seem to be a pointer "in the land" back to the sanctuary.

The fact that "Cain" appears 14 times and "Abel" only 7 times in Genesis 4 would seem to indicate not only that Cain is the main character, but specifically (given the precise numbers) that he is doubly preeminent over Abel. He is firstborn, and by implication has the double-portion, and he corrupts that portion.

THE CONTINUATION OF THE GENERATIONS OF HEAVEN AND EARTH

And the man ('adam) knew Eve, his woman. And she conceived, and she bore Cain (Qayin). And she said, "I have acquired (qanithi) a man ('ish) with Yahweh." And she continued to bear his brother Abel (Hebel) (Gen. 4:1–2a).

As we saw back in Gen. 2:4–7, Gen. 2:4–4:26 is the generations or offspring of the heavens and the earth. We saw that plants are the offspring of father-water and mother-ground, but that human beings are the offspring of father-breath (spirit) and mother-ground. The man who was born of the womb of earth by God the Father is called *'adam*, and this first man is named Adam.[130]

It is important to see that we don't come to the "generations of Adam" until we get to the next section, beginning in 5:1. It is true that all human beings are the generations or offspring of Adam, but first they are all the offspring of God and the ground, of heaven and earth. Thus, in describing the first children of Adam, and their initial descendants, we continue to consider them as offspring of heaven and earth.

The word *'adam* connotes the idea of man as the offspring of God, as God's appointed agent in the world. The word *'ish* connotes man as man and as husband. Gen. 4:1 does not say, as we might expect it to, that the *'ish* knew Eve, his *'ishshah*, but that the *'adam* knew her. Here Adam is acting not merely as husband, but as God's appointed agent to continue to produce God's adamic agents in the world. He is continuing God's fatherly work.

The use of *'adam* at the head of this story also acts to alert us to another important matter. The original Adam was put into the Garden to guard and beautify it. He was God's priest, His palace-servant (which is what "priest" means). The sons of this Adam must also function as adams. They too must be priests, though they guard not a garden but a land. Like the first Adam, they must render worship and submission to Yahweh. Like the first Adam, they must guard not only property but one another: As Adam was to guard Eve, so the older brother must guard the younger.

Leviticus 1 begins by speaking of an "adam" who draws near to God to bring an animal near as his representative. This is what a true adam does. In

---

130. Compare Luke 3:38, Adam as the first son of God.

the Garden, when God arrives, the original Adam and Eve fled from Him. They did not come near. In Genesis 4, we shall see the next two adams draw near, but only one draws near with an animal representative. In time, we shall see the wicked adam again flee from God, not physically but morally, when Cain refuses to answer God's question about Abel. Because the original Adam did not draw near to God but fled from him, he was moved farther away from God, moved outside the Garden. We shall see Cain also moved yet farther away, into a land of wandering.

Moving farther and farther away from God means moving away from a "middle" position between heaven and earth. Instead of moving up towards God, humanity is moving down towards the ground, until in death he returns to the soil, which is the final end of this movement (Gen. 3:19). Not until Jesus is resurrected and glorified does humanity move in the opposite direction, so that the "second man" becomes fully heavenly (1 Cor. 15:47–49).[131]

Eve's statement that she has brought forth an 'ish with Yahweh also points to God's continuing work in bringing human beings into the world. Adam could "know" his wife all he wanted, but unless God acts, there will be no image-of-God brought forth into the world. God continues to be active in sending His breath to the soil of humanity to make new human beings.

There is another hint in Eve's statement. As we wrote above, the word 'ish often connotes "husband." God had told Adam and Eve that the seed of the woman would be a new Adam, a savior. Accordingly, this son of Eve would be a replacement for her fallen husband. Eve naturally would think that her first son would be this person. It is interesting to consider that when Moses' wife Zipporah circumcised her son, she called him a "bloody bridegroom" because of the circumcision (Exod. 4:20).[132] Here is the same thought that the son will act in significant (non-sexual) ways as a husband for the mother, whose husband has fallen. We see this also in that the Church is considered both the mother of the Messiah and His bride (as in Rev. 12, 21).

Eve, of course, is doomed to be disappointed in the performance of her son. He is not going to be the messianic husband she hopes for. Quite

---

131. Though Adam was the offspring of God's Spirit and the ground, he was not a God-man in the sense that Jesus is, for Jesus is the incarnation of the second Person of God Himself.

132. James B. Jordan, "Proleptic Passover: Exodus 4:22–26," in *The Law of the Covenant: An Exposition of Exodus 21–23* (Tyler, TX: Institute for Christian Economics, 1984), 243–260.

the opposite. Cain is the anti-messiah, who murders rather than guards the younger "sheep" of God's household.

CAIN AND ABEL

And the man ('adam) knew Eve, his woman. And she conceived, and she bore Cain (Qayin). And she said, "I have acquired (qanithi) a man ('ish) with Yahweh." And she continued to bear his brother Abel (Hebel). And Abel became one tending flock; and Cain became one serving ground ('adamah) (Gen. 4:1–2).

The first son of Adam and Eve was named Cain. The name *Qayin* means "smith, metal-worker," and recurs in the name Tubal-Qayin, the father of the forge, in 4:22. There is also a pun on his name, since Eve associates the name with something acquired (*qanithi*). Metal is hard ground, and so Cain, as one who serves the ground, is also one who forges metal. Digging up the ground so as to plant crops is close to digging up the ground to find ore to forge into metal.

"Cain," thus, is a name that connotes strength. Adam was set to serve the ground (2:15, "to serve and guard" the Garden). As we saw last time, Cain is the new Adam, the first from Adam, the continuation of the generations of the heavens and the earth. Eve names her son "Cain" to say that he is the new Adam, who will with strength carry on Adam's work, and perhaps be the promised redeemer.

The name "Abel" implies exactly the opposite. *Hebel* means "vapor," and is the word often mistranslated "vanity" in Ecclesiastes. We are not told that Eve or Adam gave their second son this name, and it may be that this was not actually his name in life. It may be that the author of Genesis gives him this name for symbolic reasons. Other passages of the Bible clearly change the names of their subjects. Saul's son Ishbaal ("Man of the Lord") is called Ishbosheth ("Man of Shame") in some passages. The name of the wicked Gaal of Judges 9 means "Loathsome," doubtless not what his mother or his people called him. Ecclesiastes tells us that man's short life is but a vapor, and perhaps the author of Genesis uses this name for this man because of his short life.

But possibly he really was called *Hebel*. As we have seen, Genesis 4 once again tracks the sequence of Genesis 1 and of Genesis 2. "In the beginning,

God created the heavens and the earth." Now Adam has two sons: one earthy and one heavenly (vaporous). If Adam and Eve did call their second son Abel, they were not thinking of a short and evanescent life, but of a new heaven to go with their new earth.

Plants and animals: When we go back to Genesis 2, we find that Adam watched God plant the Garden, and then he was put into it to serve the plants of it. After that, God brought animals to Adam to name, so that he became one who tends or shepherds animals. That was the order: first plants, then animals.

The sequence of redemption and restoration reverses this order. First we must bring bloody sacrifices, and then place plants on top of the animals as a Tribute Offering (Lev. 1–2). First come the bloody animal sacraments of the Old Covenant, climaxing in the bloody human sacrifice of Jesus, and then the bread and wine sacraments of the New. In an important sense, plants are more fundamental than animals, since animals eat plants. The greater and more fundamental redemption of the New Creation is signified by a restoration of man to the duty of cultivating plants, of cultivating the ground out of which plants grow.

Bloody animal sacrifice is the way back into the Garden, where the plants are. We can see this in the Tabernacle, for in the Tabernacle was a stylized almond tree (lampstand) and such vegetable products as incense, bread, and beer, but no animals and no symbols of animals. The animals were killed outside, at the doorway of the Tabernacle.

Now, if Cain is going to be the leader who saves humanity and brings us back into the Garden, we should expect him to be the one who tends flocks of animals. But that is not the case. Rather, Cain is like Adam, a manager of plants. It is the second born, Abel, who tends flocks. As we shall see, if Cain is to bring an acceptable sacrifice to God, he will have to obtain an animal from Abel. All of this fits with the theme that it is a second Adam, a younger son, who must redeem the first Adam, the older son. Since Cain is the new Adam, associated with plants, it must be Abel, the younger son associated with animals, who represents the redeemer.

28

THE OFFERINGS OF CAIN AND ABEL

GENESIS 4:3–5A

And it was the cutting off of days.

And Cain brought from the fruit of the ground tribute to Yahweh.

*And Abel, he also brought from the firstlings of his flock and from their
   fat.*

And Yahweh took notice of Abel and of his tribute.

And of Cain and of his tribute He did not take notice (Gen. 4:3–4a).

WITH the offerings of Cain and Abel we move to the second section of the
narrative. The men "brought" their offerings, and in context, this has to mean
that they brought them near to God. God's presence was located with the
flaming sword—the fire of His presence—at the east side of the Garden of
Eden. Since this was high ground, we can assume that Cain and Abel ascended
a slope to come near to this place. This was a place between God's realm
("heaven") and the rest of the earth, and thus was symbolically equivalent to

the Garden between the higher Land of Eden and the rest of the earth, and equivalent to the firmament between heaven and earth.

This paragraph and the preceding one both contain a chiastic structure that calls attention to the contrast between the two men. In both cases, the order is Cain – Abel – Abel – Cain:

> A. And the man ('adam) knew Eve, his woman.
>> B. And she conceived, and she bore Cain … with Yahweh.
>>> C. And she continued to bear his brother Abel.
>>> C'. And Abel became one tending flock;
>> B'. and Cain became one serving ground (4:1–2).
> A. And it was the cutting off of days.
>> B. And Cain brought from the fruit of the ground tribute to Yahweh.
>>> C. And Abel, he also brought from the firstlings of his flock and from their fat.
>>> C' And Yahweh took notice of Abel and of his tribute.
>> B' And of Cain and of his tribute He did not take notice (4:3–5a).

These two paragraphs are formally quite similar in other ways as well. Both begin with an introductory sentence. Both B lines add a statement about Yahweh that is not repeated in the C lines: "I have acquired a man with Yahweh" and "tribute to Yahweh." But the second paragraph ends dramatically with a reversal, signified by the inverse parallelism:

> Yahweh took notice,
> of Abel and of his tribute;
> And of Cain and of his tribute
> He did not take notice (4:b–5a).

Yahweh "took notice" of Abel and his tribute and not of Cain and his. The verb here means to see and take action, generally approving action. We may ask how it was manifest that Yahweh took notice of Abel and not of Cain. It has been suggested by some that the fire of the flaming sword came forth and consumed Abel's tribute, but not Cain's. This makes a good deal of sense as a possibility, since the tributes were "brought" to some location near to God's presence, and since fire coming forth from God is how He expressed His approval of offerings in Leviticus 9:24; 1 Kings 18:38; 2 Chronicles 7:1; and Acts 2.

Each son brought tribute appropriate to his labor, his works. But works are not the way to be restored to God. Considered as works, these gifts were bribes and were unacceptable. What God requires is not our works but our selves. We must bring an offering appropriate to our selves, appropriate to who we are, not what we have accomplished. And because we are sinners, we must bring to God a sign that we deserve to die.

The men knew what this meant, because God had killed an animal when He spared Adam and Eve from immediate and final death. They also knew that a beast had misled Adam and Eve, so that a beast must be killed, and this will become important later on when God tells Cain to kill the beast that crouches at his door.

God evaluated both the men and their tribute. It is important not only that we be right with God, but also that we approach Him the right way. Our faith is seen in our worship.

Cain did not bring the first fruits or the best of his produce, but Abel brought the firstlings (best) of the flock and the fat (best) of the firstlings. The "fat" might mean the best animals, but more likely it means the fatty part of the animals, which in the Levitical system later on was reserved for God. If it means the latter, then it is at least implied that Abel ate the rest of the offerings in a communion meal with God, as a kind of Peace Sacrifice (compare Lev. 3).

Both offerings are called tribute. In Leviticus 2 and related passages, we see that the Tribute Offering is also shared as a meal enjoyed by the priest with God.

The Tribute Offering in Leviticus consists only of grain, and bloody offerings are not called tribute. In a larger sense, of course, all offerings are tribute brought to God. But what kind of tribute does God want? It is clear that He does not want a mere gift or a bribe. Giving gifts and bribes to the gods is the essence of paganism and is what Cain did. True tribute is to offer ourselves to God, as those who deserve to die but who have been accepted by God on the basis of a substitute. In the Levitical system, the Tribute grain was always offered after and on top of the bloody animal substitute.

Whether Abel sat down and shared a meal with God on this occasion or not, it is clear that he was accepted by God. He was in fellowship with God. And Cain was not. Cain was estranged from God.

When we remember that God has just cursed the ground "with reference to you," we can see another dimension of Cain's folly. Cain practically asks to be cursed, waving the curse before God's face by bringing "from the fruit of the ground tribute to Yahweh." I don't think Cain was daring God to curse him, but his action signified it, and perhaps that is what he was doing. It certainly was the eventual result.

In Leviticus 2, the Tribute is said to be a "memorial" to remind God of what He has promised and done in the past and to remind Him of us who stand before Him. Abel's memorial-tribute reminded God of His promise to kill someone else so that Abel might live. Cain's memorial-tribute reminded God of the curse.

Memorial-tribute brought before God causes an inspection of jealousy. In Numbers 5, the woman suspect of adultery is to bring tribute grain as a memorial before God, so that God will act either to curse or to vindicate her. The same thing happens in the memorial of the Lord's Supper (1 Cor. 11:27–31). The fact that the offerings of Cain and Abel were "tribute" means that they were calling on God to come and inspect them, and to judge them.

Another dimension of this story is that if Cain had wanted to bring a proper tribute, he would have had to obtain an animal from Abel. He would have had to go through Abel to get to God, in a sense. He would have had to see Abel as some kind of intermediary to bring him to God. Several lines of evidence confirm that Cain should have understood this and acted in terms of it.

First, we have seen that Cain is the "earthy" brother and Abel (Vapor) the "heavenly" brother. Thus, the very names of these men, as found in the text, imply Abel's position as mediator between God and Cain.

Second, Cain is the new Adam, the offspring of Adam. As firstborn, he is a new Adam, and since Adam is fallen, he is like Adam in that respect as well. Throughout Genesis, it is the younger son who replaces the firstborn and saves the firstborn. The messianic promise in Genesis 3 implied this, for it tells us that a later Adam must come to restore the first Adam. Since Cain could understand that he stood in the place of the first Adam, as his direct heir so to speak, he could figure out that Abel might stand in the place of the new Adam, the savior.

Third, as we saw earlier, our relationship with the ground and with plants is in a sense more fundamental than our relationship with animals. God's goal is to restore us to a right relationship with the ground, so that Adam is redeemed. But this can happen only by redemption, accomplished by the shedding of blood, signified by the death of an animal. We may say, then, that animals are the way back to plants, as redemption is the way back to creation. And from this we can see that Abel's work with animals is the way back to Cain's work with plants.

All three of these lines of reasoning were available to Cain. He had all the information necessary to figure this out, and he had plenty of time to think about it and to ask his parents about it.

29

CAIN MURDERS ABEL

GENESIS 4:5B-8

And it was hot to Cain, very much.
And his face fell (Gen. 4:5b).

WE begin with Cain's reaction to Yahweh's rejection of him and of his offering. Literally, the Hebrew says that it became hot to him. This is usually understood to mean that he burned with anger, since in most cases that is what the verb implies in context. In a few places, however, a sullen depression is implied, as in 1 Samuel 18:8 (Saul depressed over the praises accorded to David), and Jonah 4:1, 4, and 9 (Jonah depressed and ready to die because God spared Nineveh).

There is no real need to choose here. Cain was embarrassed and humiliated, and his face was "hot" for that reason. This turned to the heat of anger, and anger leads to depression and a sullen spirit. The light went out of Cain's face, and he went around looking down and scowling.

There may well be more, however, in that the precise word chosen does mean "become hot." The offerings brought to Yahweh were burned before Him. Since his offerings were rejected, Cain himself experienced heat. And Cain will pass that heat on, so to speak, when he murders Abel as the first "human sacrifice."

And Yahweh said to Cain,
"Why is it hot to you?
And why has your face fallen? (verse 6)

Yahweh invites Cain to think about his situation. Why is he feeling this way? God comes as a parent to a child, trying to get the child to understand himself, and to do right.

Is it not so that if you do right, a lifting up of...?
And [that] *if you do not do right: at the door sin is a croucher,*
and for you is his desire,
and you must master him?" (verse 7)

The first phrase of verse 7 is problematic, because in Hebrew the word translated "lifting up" is in the construct state, which means there should be a noun after it saying what is going to be lifted up. But there is no such noun. It is possible for the word to stand by itself, but this is rare.

There have been several proposals for the missing noun, but two are important. One is that Cain's face will be lifted up and no longer be downcast. The other is that Cain will be lifted up and restored to his position as firstborn and leader, which by implication he has lost when God accepted Abel and rejected him. The problem with both of these interesting proposals is that since the noun is missing, we cannot determine which it might be.

I propose that the noun is deliberately missing, so that we are supposed to meditate on the ways Cain would be lifted up. God is saying both that Cain's face will be lifted up and that he will be restored to preeminence as firstborn. He will be lifted up in all the ways that are relevant to his situation. The noun is omitted because it is a general raising up that is in view.

Yahweh now speaks about sin crouching at the door, which can be translated as we have done: Sin is a croucher at the door. This may be a new statement, giving information to Cain that he did not already possess. But it is better to read it as the second half of God' s question: "Is it not the case that...?" As we shall see, Cain knows what God is talking about, and God is asking him to remember it.

Yahweh begins by telling Cain that if he does not do right, then he will sink lower than he already is. Sin is crouching down and will drag him down to the same position. The word for "sin" here is very common, but it is only one of several words used for sinfulness. The word means to miss the mark, or to go astray. I think that in context "going astray" is the main idea. There is a wrong pathway that is available to Cain, entered by a door. The personification of that wrong pathway is waiting at the door to lead Cain astray. This is in fact what literally happens, since after murdering Abel, Cain is driven out into a land of wandering.

The word for "sin" is feminine, but immediately masculine verb forms are used for what she/he will do: "Going astray (f.) is a croucher (m.). For you is his desire, and you must master him." The shift in gender puzzles some commentators, though occasionally this kind of shift in gender happens in Hebrew. But it should not be such a puzzle, because the original serpent is in view: the One Who Leads Astray. Indeed, in Akkadian, the word translated "croucher" here is used for demons who attack people at doorways.[133] We should not think of some general demon here, of course, but in context we should indeed think of Satan and the serpent.

The Garden of Eden was the large doorway into the higher-ground Land of Eden. There the serpent had crouched to lead Adam and Eve astray. Now the same croucher lies in wait for Cain. Adam had put himself under an animal's authority, but at least that animal stood upright. Now the serpent has been cursed to crawl on his belly. He crouches low, and if Cain submits to him, he will sink lower than Adam sank.

Commentators have pointed out that the language of desire and mastery here is also found in Gen. 3:16, where God says that the woman's desire will be for her husband and that he will master or rule her. We saw that this is most likely a positive statement, restoring Adam to leadership over Eve and restoring Eve to love for Adam. But using this language here points us back to Satan's desire for Adam and Eve, and Adam's failure to master the situation. Remember that Adam was standing by during Eve's conversation with the serpent and passively failed to intervene to protect her and to master the situation in the Garden he was supposed to govern.

---

133. Cf. Hamilton, *Genesis 1–17*, 227.

Cain knows this history. God is reminding him of it. "Is it not the case, Cain, that the One Who Leads Astray is crouching at the door into a place of wandering, of exile, just as he crouched in the Garden to lead your parents into exile? He wants you, but you must not be like Adam. You must master him."

The Cutting Off of Days

When did Cain kill Abel? Obviously we cannot be sure, but there are two relevant considerations. First, it was most likely shortly before AM 130, because Seth was born soon after (Gen. 4:25; 5:3). Second, it is reasonable to assume that Cain already had a wife (a sister), because if he had been driven out before marrying it would have been difficult for him to obtain one from Adam and Eve afterwards.

What time of year? Gen. 4:3 states that the two men offered sacrifice "at the end of days." This expression can simply mean "after many days," but since it is literally "at the cutting off (*qets*) of days," in the present context it almost certainly designates harvest and thus means in the autumn, the same time as the Day of Atonement and the Feast of Ingathering in later Israel's calendar. It was Cain, apparently, who was in a position to determine this change of time: He was the farmer as well as the firstborn son of the house. Abel followed his lead and also brought a sacrifice.

The term *qets* is interesting. It always indicates the cut off point of some set period of time. It is related phonetically to the words *qatsir* (harvest) and *qatsar* (to reap, cut down).[134] The harvest entails cutting down the fruit of the ground and is the cutting off point for the agricultural or national year. This time is also spoken of as the "going forth of the year" in Exodus 23:16.

Because this is a debated point, I want to demonstrate my position more fully. Does "the cutting off of days" simply mean "after a time" or does it mean "at the end of the year"? What we notice is that the term *qets*, when used with a specific length of time, means the definite end of that definite period of time:

---

134. Hebrew lexicons ascribe *qets* and *qatsir* to two different roots, but this is speculative and depends on an evolutionary view of the development of language. The ear readily connects the two, and the connection in meaning is also clear.

Genesis 8:6 – at the cutting off of 40 days.

Numbers 13:25 – at the cutting off of 40 days.

Deuteronomy 9:11 – at the cutting off of 40 days.

Judges 11:39 – at the cutting off of 2 months.

Isaiah 23:15, 17 – at the cutting off of 70 years.

Jeremiah 42:7 – at the cutting off of 10 days.

Ezekiel 29:13 – at the cutting off of 40 years.

Some passages clearly indicate the cutting off as the time of harvest, the actual end of the solar or national year:

Deuteronomy 15:1 – at the cutting off of every 7 years.

Deuteronomy 31:10 – at the cutting off of every 7 years.

Jeremiah 34:14 – at the cutting off of 7 years.

Other passages hint that the cutting off of the years spoken of was in the autumn:

2 Samuel 14:26 – at the cutting off of every year. Absalom cut his hair at the end of every year. Since Absalom was a royal prince and the regal year began and ended in autumn, this is probably the autumn.

2 Samuel 15:7 – at the cutting off of 40 years. Absalom begins his revolt at this time, right at the end of the fortieth year of David's reign. David dies during the following year, and Solomon comes to the throne, so the next year is the first of Solomon's.

1 Kings 2:39 – at the cutting off of 3 years. Shimei, Solomon's last enemy, is killed. Now the Temple can be built, in the fourth year (1 Kgs. 6:1). Thus, this event most likely closed out Solomon's first three years.

2 Chronicles 8:1 – at the cutting off of 20 years. This was in the autumn, as can be seen from 2 Kings 8:2.

2 Chronicles 21:19 – at the cutting off of 2 years. Since the reigns of the kings were dated by solar years, beginning in autumn, the death of Jehoram may well have been right at the end of his last year.

One passage uses the term "cutting off of years" to refer to the lunar year, beginning in the Spring.

Exodus 12:41 – at the cutting off of the 430 years. This event was on the fifteenth day of the first month, the seventh month of the solar year.

Let us now examine the remaining instances of this phrase:

Gen. 16:3 – at the cutting off of 10 years. Ishmael was conceived, and he was born the same year (the eleventh year). At the time of his birth, Abram was 86. There is nothing to indicate whether the phrase here refers to the spring or to the fall, but since later on the phrase "time of reviving" refers to the spring, it is reasonable to assume that the phrase "cutting off of years" here refers to the fall.

Gen. 41:1 – at the cutting off of 2 full years. This was two full years after Pharaoh dealt with his baker and cupbearer. His visions concerned harvests and might thus have come at the end of the year or in the spring. This is, however, the end of a definite period of time.

1 Kings 17:7 – at the cutting off of days. Elijah's brook dried up. This might indicate the turn of the year, after a summer of heat, but it might not. Unlike Gen. 4:3, where precisely the same phrase is used, there is no indication of a harvest.

2 Chronicles 18:2 – at the cutting off of years. Jehoshaphat visited Ahab, who put on a feast for him. Giving the royal context and that the kings measured their rules by the solar year, this phrase hints that it was at the turn of the year, in autumn.

Nehemiah 13:6 – at the cutting off of days. After his time of service at court, Nehemiah asked to return to Jerusalem. There is no hint that this phrase indicates a set time of the year, but simply that after a time Nehemiah asked to return. Here again, however, the phrase does indicate the end of a definite period of time.

What we have seen is that "at the cutting off of days/years" indicates the end of a definite period of time, usually explicitly defined in the text. We have also seen that it very often refers to the turn of the solar/national year in autumn, especially when associated with harvests. We are on very good ground, therefore, in seeing it referring to the end of the solar year in Gen. 4:3, especially since harvest is in view.

The Day of Atonement and the Feast of Ingathering came in the seventh (sabbath) month, at the end of all harvests. Extrapolating backwards from information given at Sinai, and remembering that Moses put Genesis in its final form, we may readily imagine that Cain and Abel brought their sacrifices in the seventh month. According to Exodus 23:16; 34:22; and Leviticus 25:8–10, the year ended in the seventh month. Thus the first month of the solar year was the seventh month of the lunar year, for the cycle of lunar months began in the spring with the first month (Exod. 12:2).[135]

Thus, it seems most likely that Cain and Abel offered their sacrifices at the end of the sixth or at the beginning of the seventh month, at the end of the solar year.

If this is the "cutting off of days," then the beginning of days would be in autumn, in the seventh month. Thus, we can suppose that the creation of the world, recorded in Genesis 1, took place in autumn.

At the same time, however, the Bible always presents humanity as moving from priestly service to kingly reign, thus from the first to the seventh months. It makes sense for the regnal, solar year to begin after the priestly, lunar months begin. Since Adam and Eve were placed in the Garden of Eden to serve, not in the Land of Eden to rule, it makes sense that time for them began with the lunar months in the spring, moving forward toward the solar year of the fall. Thus, there would be a six-month Year before the beginning of Year 1 in the fall.

Interestingly, the Tabernacle, the first and priestly cosmic-replica built by Israel, was completed and entered in the first month, the beginning of the ecclesiastical year (Exod. 40). By way of contrast, the Temple, the second and royal cosmic-replica, was completed and entered in the fall, the beginning of the civil year (1 Kgs. 6:38; 8:2; 2 Chron. 7:1–3).

From all this, I assume that the creation took place at the vernal equinox/new moon, not in the fall. Year 1 began in the seventh month after creation.

THE MURDER OF ABEL

And Cain said to Abel his brother....
And it was while they were in the field,
and [that] Cain stood up to Abel his brother,
and he slew him (Gen. 4:8).

---

135. The Bible speaks of the day as beginning at evening, as in Genesis 1, "there was evening and morning, one day." Similarly the year begins around the autumnal equinox, as the year darkens.

311

We come now to the murder of Abel by Cain. The verse begins with a problem. It cannot be translated, "And Cain spoke to Abel," because the particular verb for "say" is never used that way. Some ancient translations fill in what Cain said: "Let us go to the field," but this is not found in any Hebrew text we have, so we must discard it. Some commentators have sought to find other possibilities for the verb by looking at other ancient Semitic languages, such as "Cain despised Abel," or "Cain was watching for Abel," or "Cain made an appointment with Abel." Again, though, there is no backing in Hebrew for such alternatives, and "said" is the common verb used throughout this passage and the Hebrew Scriptures for something about to be said.

Thus, we need to leave the text as it is. Cain said something to Abel, but we are not told precisely what it was. Yahweh had said something to Cain (verse 7), as Cain's true father (verse 1). Now Cain says something to Abel, as Abel's older brother. It does not matter what was said. What matters is that Cain is still firstborn, and Abel is still submissive to Cain. Cain speaks, and Abel listens.

The phrase "his brother" brings this out. Cain said something to Abel, his (younger) brother. Cain is the leader. He has failed once, and now he will fail again to be a true older brother. Having failed to give proper leadership in worship, he now turns to murder his younger brother. He violates both aspects of what it means to be firstborn, both aspects of what it means to be an image of the Divine Older Brother, the Son of God.

We now move to the field. The Field is the second environment, after the Garden and before the World, which is the environment in which the Sethites will sin by marrying the daughters of Cain. Later in the Bible, the Field will be the Land, the Garden the Sanctuary, and the World will be the gentile World. As the Garden is the priestly environment of worship, so the Land/field is the kingly environment of culture.

Cain "stood up to" Abel. Standing up is often the word for a king's assuming office later in the Bible, as in Daniel 11, where one king after another stands up until finally Michael (Jesus) comes. Thus, we cannot fall far from the mark by saying that Cain stands up to exercise his kingly firstborn office to, or toward, Abel.

And then he slays him. The verb here is used in 2 Samuel 4:11–12 for the act of David in executing the murderers of Ishbosheth, and more importantly in Gen. 9:6 for both murder and judicial execution. Cain completely corrupts and reverses his office. Instead of being a brother's keeper, he becomes a brother's killer. Later on, Esau purposes to slay Jacob (Gen. 27:42).

The death of Abel is not only the first murder in the history, nor is it only the first time a "king" has slain a faithful "subject." It is also the first human sacrifice in history. While the verb "slay" is not ever used for animal sacrifice, the context here brings out the parallel, which is pregnant. Cain has failed to kill an animal, and now he kills a human instead. Yahweh had encouraged him to kill the beast, and Cain obeys God, so to speak, by making Abel the beast that he kills.

Sin and Satan were Cain's true enemies, but that is not how he viewed it. In his warped mind, Abel was the enemy. Abel had gotten him in trouble with God. Abel was the thorn in his side, and Abel had to die so that Cain could feel good. And Cain did feel good. As we shall see, the death of this human sacrifice made him feel liberated, brought him into a false sabbath, and enabled him to go out and build a city.

Thus, Cain *imputed* his own sinfulness to Abel. Abel became the beast that crouches at the door, because beastishness was put upon him. "He who knew no sin was made sin" by Cain and died for Cain's sin. Every murder in history has been the same. Instead of fighting his own anger and trusting God and accepting the substitute of an animal (of Jesus Christ), the murderer takes it out on a weaker fellow man, a weaker, "younger," brother.

Cain built his city on the blood of his younger brother. Every humanistic civilization is built on the blood of weaker brothers. Rome was built on the spot where Romulus slew Remus, and this myth (whether historically true or not) gives expression to this fact. We can think of the millions killed as the "foundation" of the Nazi and Soviet states, but we should also think of the sometimes-murdered American Indians and often-oppressed African Americans whose blood lies at the foundation of American civilization. The only true and lasting City is built on the blood of the Second Adam, the final Younger Brother, Jesus Christ.

30

THE EXPULSION OF CAIN

GENESIS 4:9–15

THE BROTHER'S GUARDIAN AND THE DIVINE RIGHT OF KINGS

And Yahweh said to Cain, "Where is Abel, your brother?"
And he said, "I do not know.
Am I myself my brother's guardian?" (Gen. 4:9)

THE word "brother," referring to Abel, appears seven times in this passage (verses 2, 8 [2x], 9 [2x], 10, 11). Abel is identified at his birth as the "brother" of Cain in verse 2. It is clear that "brother" here connotes "younger brother" and not just a brother in general.

It is not infrequently remarked by anti-socialistic commentators (and I am certainly anti-socialist!) that Cain is here being sarcastic. Supposedly Cain said, "Am I my brother's keeper?" as if Cain were supposed to keep

Abel in a cage or something, providing for him as if he were some helpless or supposedly helpless person living on Cain's welfare. We are not supposed to "keep" each other, it is said, but to be "brotherly" to each other. That is quite correct, but it is not what Cain's question is about in this context.

No, the language here is pregnant with meaning. First of all, the word is not "keep" in the modern sense, but "guard." Adam was told to "guard" the Garden of Eden (2:15). His wife was in the Garden, and so he was supposed to guard her from harm. As we have seen, he did the reverse: Adam helped set Eve up to eat of the forbidden fruit by remaining silent while she was being tempted. Adam acted to "kill" Eve, for God had threatened death to anyone eating of the forbidden fruit. This is the opposite of guarding.

Second, Cain uses the long form of the first person pronoun, and in Hebrew the pronoun is not used at all except for stress. He is asking, "It is *my* job to be my brother's guardian?"

In context, the answer is clearly "yes." Cain as older brother was indeed supposed to be the guardian of the younger brothers. He was the leader. He was supposed to set the example. And yes, he was supposed to watch out for the welfare of his younger siblings. We see this later on when even flawed Reuben seeks to save the life of Joseph (Gen. 37; cf. 42:37).

We have remarked that the Garden is the area of "priestly" activity and that Adam failed to guard the bride in the sanctuary, but instead "killed" her. Now we have moved to the Land, which is the area of "kingly" activity, where brothers live with brothers. Cain now fails to guard his brother, but instead kills him.

God's question is basically the same in both cases. He asks Adam "where" he is, and He asks Cain "where" his brother is. Both "where" questions uncover "killings." Adam follows immediately by seeking to avoid blame by blaming Eve, and also blaming God for giving him Eve (3:12). Cain's response is similar: He seeks to avoid blame by saying that he does not know where Abel is, and why should he? And he later accuses God of unfairness (4:13).

Perhaps most importantly, Cain renounces his firstborn status. He claims that, as for him, he himself is not the guardian of his younger brother. This statement is only the seal on his action. By failing to guard his younger brother, Cain has defaulted on what it means to be leader, "king," of the society. In Genesis, firstborn sons are always set aside for younger ones, and this has to do with the theme that the first Adam has failed and a younger, new Adam is needed. But sometimes the default of the firstborn is not merely a matter of God's decree, but of failure to perform the office—indeed, not just failure to perform, but reversing what the office of firstborn kingly guardian means by murdering or seeking to murder the younger brother. Think of Esau's determination to kill Jacob, and of Joseph's older brothers' determination to kill him.

There is no "divine right of kings" in the Bible. The king who refuses to guard his people and who murders them instead is a king who should be replaced. Jehu killed the line of Ahab for this reason, that they had failed to guard the people but had brought death upon them instead. Cromwell had Charles I of England put to death precisely because he had brought unnecessary death upon the people he was sworn to guard.

Those kings who were anointed "messiahs" were in a different category. David refused to kill Saul, though he deserved it, because he was Yahweh's anointed. David himself stood in danger of losing the crown after murdering Uriah, but God spared him; again, he was Yahweh's anointed. The myth of the "divine right of kings" was grounded in the notion that the kings in Christendom were also "anointed," and many (like the kings of England) claimed descent from David (feeding the "British Israelite" mythology). But in the New Covenant, only Jesus has divine right. Only He is the anointed "Messiah" of the Lord. Earthly kings and rulers who oppress and murder their people have no right to stay in office, and the best Christian theology has always affirmed a right of resistance against such rulers, though only if led by "lesser magistrates" who are themselves rulers and whose attempts to guard their people have been undermined by the greater rulers over them.

BLOOD AND EXILE

And He said, "What did you do?
The blood of your brother is crying to Me from the soil.
And now [at this time] you yourself are cursed from the soil,
Which opened her mouth to receive the blood of your brother from your hand.
When you serve [work] the soil, she will not continue [add]
to yield her strength to you.
Agitated and wandering [homeless] will you be in the earth" (Gen. 4:11–12).

Later passages of the Bible teach us that human blood shed by humans cries out for vengeance. In the special land of Israel, the nearest of kin is appointed by the Land to act as avenger. More generally, the civil magistrate is to act as avenger of blood. (Exod. 21:13; Num. 35; Deut. 19, 21; Gen. 9:5–6; Rom. 13:4.) At this time in history, there is no nearest of kin (brother) and as yet no civil magistrate (Gen. 9:5–6), so Cain is not put to death for his murder.

What Genesis 4 focuses on is that the shedding of innocent blood causes exile from the land, a theme picked up in the prophets before the exile of Judah into Babylon (cf. especially Ezek. 22). 2 Kings 24:4 makes it clear that such bloodshed must be paid for eventually, even if God temporarily spares the guilty. Accordingly, Jesus told the apostate Jews that God would bring upon them the judgment for all the innocent blood shed upon the earth from Abel forward (Matt. 23:35), and when the Christians are massacred in Revelation 14, their blood covers the land and calls down the bowls of wrath upon Babylon-Jewry in Revelation 16.

Looking at the specifics of Genesis 4, we find that the soil (*'adamah*) from which man (*'adam*) was made will be the agent to bring about a curse directly upon the murderer. In Genesis 3:17 the soil was said to mediate a curse toward mankind in general, so that the soil would only with difficulty yield her produce: "Cursed is the soil with reference to you." Now that curse is greatly intensified: "Cursed are *you* from the soil." The "you" is intensive. The soil would work with Adam, though grudgingly. The soil will reject Cain altogether. Cain will be exiled from the soil.

Cain had been a tiller of the soil and had brought of the fruits of the soil to Yahweh (4:2–3). Now the soil will no longer produce for him as she had formerly done. Cain will continue to dwell on the earth, the more general term for this creation, but he will have no settled place. The two words I have translated "agitated and wandering" are virtual synonyms, but the first one seems to indicate more of an internal state and the second more of an external condition. It is usually taken to mean that Cain's internal restlessness will find external expression in his inability to settle down.

In fact, though, Cain did settle down when he built the first city, Enoch (4:17). From this we see that the curse is not precisely to wander to and fro, but rather is a curse of homelessness. Both pilgrims and explorers move from place to place, and God sent Israel out into the nations after the exile as His agents. True pilgrims have a home, even if it is only in heaven. Cain had no home any longer and had to try to make one for himself.

This move from land to city is, in fact, an eschatology, though in this case a false one. Later on, God separated the Levites from the Land into cities, but this was a blessing (Num. 18) and anticipated the coming of the New Creation, which is New Jerusalem, not new Land. As Paul writes, the first man is of the earth (land), but the last man was of heaven (city) (1 Cor. 15).

Thus, contrary to some thinkers, there is nothing bad about city as opposed to land. Modern "agrarianism" is a pagan rejection of the New Creation, a kind of "Judaizing" insistence on the land in preference to the Garden City. It is not an accident that the Pauline Epistles and the letters to the seven churches in Revelation 2–3 are addressed in terms of cities.

Rather, the issue is this: Do we graduate from Homeland to Home City, or are we exiled from Homeland to anti-city? Another issue is this: Who gave the old Homeland and who builds the City? Is it built by Cain in a vain attempt to make a new home for himself, or is it the New Jerusalem that proceeds out of heaven, built by Jesus for His bride?

Cain's situation was this: He had been cut off from the Old God-given Homeland, the soil, but he did not want to wait for the New God-given City. He was not like Abraham, who was also cut off from the soil, but who looked and waited for the City (Heb. 11:8–10). No, Cain chose to make his own future, to build his own city.

But his city did not last. It was washed away in the Flood.

THE STRUCTURE OF GENESIS 4 REVISITED

Back in chapter 27, I argued that Genesis 4 follows the same sevenfold flow of events as Genesis 1 and Genesis 2–3. Now that I have spent more time with the passage, I should like to revisit that original outline and make some adjustments.

I now think that Genesis 4 moves through this sequence twice, once culminating in a sabbath-judgment of Cain, and then again culminating in the institution of worship in the days of Enosh.

Day 1 // 2:4–7 // 4:1 - insemination of Eve with the "spirit" of Adam, and the birth of Cain.

Day 2 // 2:8 // 4:2a - birth of Abel: mediatorial firmament set up.

Day 3 // 2:9–14 // 4:2b - distinction of flocks and fruit of the ground.

Day 4 // 2:15 // 4:3–5 - time of worship.

Day 5 // 2:16–17 *//* 14:6–7 - judgment threatened to Cain.

Day 6 // 2:18–24 *//* 4:8 - murder of Abel.

Day 7 // 2:25ff. *//* 4:9–16 - sabbath judgment on Cain.

On Day 1, God created light, light that came from the hovering Spirit. In Gen. 2:4–7, we find that the earth is still to some extent formless and covered with water, and then that God sends His Spirit into dust to make man, a form of light in the world. Adam would be placed into the Garden, a firmament area between the higher ground of Eden and the rest of the world. I originally tied Gen. 4:1–2a, the births of Cain and Abel, with the creation of Adam, but I think this needs revision. Cain (*Qayin*) means "smith" and relates to the firmness of the earth, while Abel (*Hebel*) means "vapor" or "mist" and relates to the heaven—but to which heaven? It is clear from what follows that Abel links with the firmament made on Day 2.

So let us look back at Gen. 4:1. Adam knew his wife, and this links with God's sending His Spirit into dust to make Adam. The "adam" that Adam makes with Eve is Cain, and Eve's statement that she has acquired a man with Yahweh brings this first event to a close. Cain is the new Adam. He should be the new Light. Gen. 4:2 begins, "And she added," indicating a new event. Here we have the birth of Abel.

On Day 2, God made a firmament between heaven and earth, a place of mediation between the two for the duration of history. In Gen. 2:8, God planted the Garden, which as noted was between Eden and the world. Here again, this is the environment of mediation between a higher and lower area and is the place of worship, the original sanctuary.

Originally I linked this with Gen. 4:2b–4a, as Cain and Abel brought the fruits of the world (parallel to the Garden) to the gate of the Garden. I want to revise this now. I think that only verse 2a corresponds to the place—in this case, person—of mediation, Abel. And what will go with him is the place of mediation, the new firmament. Cain, with his fruits of the soil, is under that firmament and will need to go through Abel's flocks to come to God.

Notice that on Day 2, God set up the firmament, and on the first part of Day 3, God divided land and sea. Only then did He say that it was good. He did not pronounce the firmament good until the land was also separated from the sea. Now notice the order of presentation in Gen. 4:2b: Abel was an overseer of flocks (firmament parallel) and Cain was a servant (worker) of the soil (earth parallel). We have moved down in time again: The men are now grown. This statement is followed by the statement "And it was in the cutting off of days," which begins a new section.

The link between Day 2 and Day 3a is important. The distinction between firmament and waters under the firmament is parallel to the distinction between raised-up land and seas below the land. Later on, when this configuration is given symbolic form, there is an Altar of Incense in the firmament Holy Place and an Altar of Earth in the Courtyard. Abel's flocks are altar animals, and the distinction between Abel's flocks and Cain's plants corresponds to the separation of land and sea. Indeed, the order of presentation in 4:2b (Abel's flocks and Cain's plants) matches the order in 1:10 (land and sea). The symbolism has shifted, in that the land plants are associated with the altar-land in Genesis 1 and with Cain's "sea" in Genesis 4, but the meaning is the same: The "sea" must go through the "land" to move toward heaven. This is also parallel to Gen. 2:9–14, the trees of Eden and the outlying watered worldly areas.

We have seen that not only does Abel have a heavenly name ("Vapor"), but that animal death is the only way fallen man can have mediation with God (a fact emerging from Genesis 3). Thus, Abel's flocks are the place of mediation between God and fallen humanity, a fact Cain refused to recognize.

On Day 4, God set up the lights in the firmament as rulers and luminaries and determiners of days, years, and festivals. In Gen. 2:15, God placed Adam into the Garden to work and guard it. The Garden was the sanctuary, the place of worship. What we find in Gen. 4:3 relates to Day 4, for the "cutting off of days" is something indicated by the firmament luminaries—as we have seen, probably the autumnal equinox. The time of worship in Gen. 4:3–5, thus, links with Day 4.

On Day 5 God pronounced His first blessing, on the fishes and fowls. In Gen. 2:16–17, God pronounced His first threat, the threat of death for disobedience. Here in Gen. 4:6–7, God comes to Cain (the fifth event in the narrative) and warns him, promising blessing for obedience and curse for disobedience.

On Day 6 God made mankind, and in 2:18–24 God made Eve for Adam. What follows is that Adam "kills" Eve by silently inviting her to eat of the Tree of Death. The sixth event in Genesis 4, in verse 8, is Cain's murder of Abel.

We come finally to Day 7, the sabbath. Gen. 2:25–3:24 delineate the sad events of that first sabbath and culminate in God's judgment upon Adam. Here we find, as the seventh event, God's coming to Cain to pass judgment upon him, in Gen. 4:9–15. The shape of this judgment matches the shape of the judgments in Gen. 3:11–24, to wit:

3:11 God asks Adam what he has done.
4:9a And Yahweh said to Cain, "Where is Abel, your brother?"

3:12 Adam seeks to pass the blame to Eve.
4:9b And he said, "I do not know. Am I myself my brother's guardian?"

3:13–19 God passes judgments on serpent, Eve, and Adam.
4:10–12 God passes judgments on Cain.

3:20 Adam accepts God's judgments.
4:13–14 Cain rejects God's judgments.

3:21 God makes clothing for Adam and Eve.
4:15 God puts a mark on Cain.

3:22–24 God drives out Adam and Eve.
4:16 Cain leaves God's presence.

What I think emerges from this revised outline makes even clearer that Abel was the first mediator and foreshadowing type of Jesus Christ. It is now clear from the order of presentation in Genesis 4 that Abel's birth makes him a "firmament" between heaven and earth, and his name, "Vapor," is related to that positioning. Abel's flocks, being animals appropriate for mediatorial slaughter, are an altar-aspect of that firmament. Cain's refusal to go through Abel's flocks to reach God is a rejection of that mediatorial firmament and altar.

There is another "hidden connection." Cain's murder of Abel in 4:8, the sixth event of Genesis 4, parallels the formation of Eve in Gen. 2:18–24. Adam was to guard Eve as Cain was to guard Abel. Both are "weaker vessels." Now, Adam has pronounced that Eve is the "mother of all living," agreeing with God that new life and a new saving covenant will come through her. Hence, an assault on Eve is an assault on all possibility of new life in a new covenant. The assault by Cain upon Abel is parallel to this. Abel, as mediator is the way of life, and by attacking Abel, Cain can find only death. He has rejected the new life offered by God through sacrifice, through Abel.

THE KING OF THE EARTH

In the previous section, we saw that Abel was the mediator between heaven and earth. We might have expected Adam and Eve's first son, Cain, to be that person. But there is a reason why he was not. In this section we explore that dimension of the narrative.

On Day 1, God created light. In Gen. 2:4–7, God sent His Spirit into dust to make Adam, the human light of the world. Adam was to serve as a priest in the Garden and graduate to being a king in the Land (the outer world). When Adam seized kingly responsibilities, he was expelled into the outer world. Adam is now a fallen priest who has made himself a king and has been confirmed in that new estate by God.

In the beginning God created the heavens and the earth. It was the earth that was dark, and light was placed into the earth. Adam's first son, Cain, corresponds to that light. His name, "Smith," makes him earthy. Then on Day 2, God made a firmament out of the earthly water to be between heaven and earth. Abel is that firmament, as we have seen.

We can now begin to see why Adam's first son was a king, while his second was a priest. Adam is the image of God, even though fallen, and so he acts as God acted. First Adam makes light, a new "adam," and then he makes a firmament. Light rules, in that when God evaluated what He had made in Genesis 1, He "saw" what He had made and called it good.[136] Cain is now the new light. He is the firstborn, and the ruler of the brothers.

Adam is also a tunic-vested king, now, in the outer world. His first son, the earthy "smith," is an earthly king. Since Adam was expelled from the Garden and is exiled from this place near to heaven, his son Cain, emerging from him, cannot be a heavenly light. He must be an earthly "light." He is a king-light in that he is firstborn, but in order to come near to heaven, he must go through the priestly mediator, Abel.

To use more familiar language, Cain corresponds to the State and Abel to the Church. The Church is the avenue to heaven, and rulers of the State must go through the Church to get to heaven, as Cain had to go through Abel. At the same time, the State must protect the Church, as Cain was to protect Abel, his younger brother.

---

136. Cf. Matthew 5:14–16; 6:22: "The lamp of the body is the eye."

Cain's murder of Abel, and then his building a new city, is a prototype of fallen human history. The rulers of the State must murder, or somehow suborn, the officers of the Church if they are going to set up their own cities. By saying that the scribes and Pharisees would be held responsible for the murders of Abel and Zechariah (Matt. 23:35), Jesus said that they would be counted as Cain and as King Joash, who had Zechariah the priest murdered (2 Chron. 24: 17–22). Jesus might also have mentioned Saul's murder of the priests at Nob (1 Sam. 22) and other incidents as well. It was the State, in the triple form of Sanhedrin, Herod, and Pilate, who murdered Jesus.

Thus, Cain's murder of Abel was not only the first murder in human history. By paying careful and close attention to the text, we have seen that it was the first human sacrifice. It was the first act of oppression by a stronger (firstborn) against a weaker younger brother member of society (compare Rom. 14 and 1 Cor. 8). It was also an assault on the heavenly mediator and an attack upon the earliest form of the Church.

Jesus said that the rulers of the gentiles lord it over them, while His followers must be servants of all (Mark 10:42–44). Cain showed himself to be a true "king of the earth." Had he had a humble servant's heart, he would have gone through Abel's flocks to God. Instead, he wanted God on his own terms. Failing this, he went out to make himself a god over his own city.

CAIN'S COMPLAINT

And Cain said to Yahweh, "Greater is my liability than is bearable.
Behold, You drive me today from being upon the face of the soil,
And from Your face I shall be hidden,
And I shall be agitated and homeless in the earth;
And it will be that anyone finding me will kill me" (Gen. 4:13–14).

CAIN'S initial statement is that his liability (i.e., his deserving-ness of punishment) is too great for him to bear. This is, of course, not true. David was forgiven for the murder of a subordinate, a "younger brother," a loyal Ark-honoring member of God's host. Cain would still have been punished, but he might have been forgiven. Abel's flocks were still in existence. But Cain refuses God's way of mediation and redemption.

We need to see this as another instance of the wicked blaming the righteous for the evil that befalls them for their own sins.[137] Pharaoh in Genesis 12 and Abimelech in Genesis 20 and 26 seek to blame Abram and Isaac respectively for the consequences of their own tyrannical actions. Later, Ahab blames Elijah for troubling Israel. Here Cain blames God, as had his father Adam ("The woman You gave me...").

We might read Cain's statement as a confession that Yahweh's judgments are righteous and are only what he deserves. If the rest of the story indicated anything positive about Cain, we might entertain that possibility. After all, when Adam named his wife Eve, this was a confession of his acceptance of God's judgments, as we saw. God proceeded to cover Adam, and we hear Eve praise Yahweh in Gen. 4:1. In Gen. 4:16 we read that Cain went out from the face of Yahweh, but while this parallels Adam's departure from the Garden and by itself does not indicate anything about Cain either way, if Cain had truly accepted the punishment of homelessness, he would not have built his city but would have waited for God to restore him.

Cain does not ask for forgiveness; he only complains. He does not repent; he only regrets. God has punished him, and it is too much for him. God has driven him away, and by implication this is too much.

There is a parallel in verse 13 between the face of the soil and the face of Yahweh. Originally, because of Adam's sin, the soil had mediated a curse to humanity, but since the curse was mediated, it was mitigated. Now both soil and Yahweh turn their faces away from Cain. And Cain does not seek God's face.

Cain will be homeless, a wanderer on the earth. He fears that some later son of Adam will find him and kill him. Cain has now become suspicious. He thinks other men will behave like him. They also will be man-killers. They will usurp God's right of capital punishment, even though it has not been given to men yet (Gen. 9:5–6). God proceeds to give Cain a test:

And Yahweh said to him, "Not so.
Anyone killing Cain will suffer sevenfold vengeance."
And He put on Cain a mark, that anyone finding him not kill him (Gen. 4:15).

---

137. I have explored this theme in Genesis in my book *Primeval Saints*.

God gives Cain some kind of mark on his body, though we have no idea what it was or how it functioned. But it is an invitation to trust God's protection. Will Cain trust God?

No. Cain goes out and builds a walled city to form a protection for himself.

Cain's "Clothing"

And Yahweh said to him, "Not so.
Anyone killing Cain will suffer sevenfold vengeance."
And He put on Cain a mark, that anyone finding him not kill him (Gen. 4:15).

The "sabbath" judgments on Cain parallel the sabbath judgments on Adam and Eve in Genesis 3:

> *3:11* God asks Adam what he has done.
> *4:9a* And Yahweh said to Cain, "Where is Abel, your brother?"

> *3:12* Adam seeks to pass the blame to Eve.
> *4:9b* And he said, "I do not know. Am I myself my brother's guardian?"

> *3:13–19* God passes judgments on serpent, Eve, and Adam.
> *4:10–12* God passes judgments on Cain.

> *3:20* Adam accepts God's judgments.
> *4:13–14* Cain rejects God's judgments.

> *3:21* God makes clothing for Adam and Eve.
> *4:15* God puts a mark on Cain.

> *3:22–24* God drives out Adam and Eve.
> *4:16* Cain leaves God's presence.

God put royal "tunics" on Adam and Eve, made from a slaughtered animal. Adam had seized kingly prerogatives, and God had confirmed them. Adam would be sent into the outer kingly world, but clothed in garments provided by God as Priest, via blood sacrifice. This is how a true king dresses. Adam wore these garments and renewed them through animal sacrifices.

Cain, the new king, has rejected these garments. He has rejected Abel's flocks. He now stands naked and exposed to judgment. God's putting a mark on Cain corresponds to His giving clothing to Adam and Eve, but this time there is no animal sacrifice. Cain has rejected the way of sacrifice.

So what is this mark? We do not know what it looked like or how it functioned, but it must have been placed on his skin. Skin is a form of clothing. Stripping the sacrificial animal of its skin in Leviticus 1:6 is removing its clothing. The verb for "strip" means to remove clothing (see Lev. 6:11 and especially 16:23). By putting this mark on Cain, God is adding to his original skin-clothing.

I believe we should see this mark as some kind of "common grace" protection for Cain. Common grace is God's self-restraint of judgment upon guilty humanity. It is temporary. Jesus said that Cain would eventually be punished for murdering Abel (Matt. 23:35). That punishment has been postponed, but it will come at the end of history. A form of that punishment came, as Jesus said, with the destruction of Israel in AD 70.

Common grace comes from God. It is the patience and forbearance of God, designed to lead to repentance (Rom. 2:4). It is a grace shown in different ways to all sinners. God showed this grace to Cain. Did Cain repent and accept God's judgment and protection? No, Cain went out and built his own walled city for protection.

God's mark on Cain was to prevent his being murdered. While there was as yet no State or civil order in the earth, this mark relates to the restraint on anarchy and lawlessness provided by civil order. Civil government, even evil government, provides some restraint on anarchy and lawlessness. This is true in Christian lands, where the magistrate may be said to wear the blood-soaked royal tunics provided by the priestly work of the Church, and also outside of Christian lands, where such tunics have been Cainly rejected.

The mark of common grace restraint comes from God, and thus it is part of the duty of the Church as God's agent to provide this mark. Even if magistrates are wicked, the Church can restrain them by warning them prophetically. We see this in the book of Kings, where some wicked kings were restrained by their fear of what the prophets said. When the Church apostatizes and fails to provide the mark to wicked men by prophesying to them, then common grace diminishes and eventually disappears. The nation becomes so full of wickedness, anarchy, and lawlessness that God brings full cultural obliteration. Before the Flood, the priestly line of Seth intermarried with the daughters of Cain, until eventually only Noah was left. The world became so wicked, so deaf to Noah, that God destroyed it.

Sevenfold Vengeance

Why will Cain be avenged sevenfold? One would think that one murder would bear the same punishment as another. Cain's act was horrible, as we have seen, not only as a murder of a weaker person, but also as an assault on God's mediator. Here God says that murdering Cain will be even worse. Why?

The answer is that Cain is God's to deal with, and anyone who murders him will be usurping God's prerogative. It is not until Genesis 9, after the Flood, that God grants to civil magistrates the right and duty to exercise capital punishment. Before that time—and after that time, apart from God's specific grant of authority—anyone who takes vengeance into his own hands is directly defying God.

How many of us dream of vengeance! If the magistrate, or some other authority, will not see the light and give us vengeance, we dream of taking it ourselves. We seek in oblique ways to get even. This is a serious matter. God has decided to be patient and exercise common grace, as we have seen. We must do the same. We must beware the mark of Cain, and not take our own vengeance.

Otherwise, God will wreak sevenfold vengeance on us.

31

THE CITY OF CAIN

GENESIS 4:16–24

And Cain went out from the face of Yahweh.
And he settled in a homeless land, east of Eden (Gen. 4:16).

SINCE verse 16 is parallel to Gen. 3:23–24, it may be noteworthy that God first sent and then drove Adam and Eve out of the Garden, while Cain went away on his own. Clearly God had sent Cain out, but it appears that Adam did not want to go and had to be driven out. Cain seems willing to go. He is not interesting in trying to remain near Yahweh.

The word "homeless" in verse 16 is a form of the same word as "homeless" in verses 12 and 14. This is not the name of some specific location. The Hebrew does not read "*the* land of Nod (Homelessness)," but "a land." If some specific named land were in view, we might supply the "the" in English anyway, taking it as implied in the Hebrew. Here, however, there is no reason to think of any "land of Nod." Rather, Cain went into a homeless land located east of Eden.

This has meant to some expositors that Cain wandered from place to place. If he had accepted God's judgment and sought Yahweh, that is what he might have done. The next statement, however, is that Cain built himself a city. He made himself a home in the homeless land. He did not wander.

The fact that Cain entered a homeless land indicates that he left a homeland. We see in this an important distinction in sacred geography that will become important later on. Genesis 2 presents us with the high Land of Eden, with its Garden on its east side. Immediately to the east of this is the homeland where Adam and Eve and Cain and Abel lived. We may see this as next to the slope leading up to the Edenic plateau. Farther away is the homeless area into which Cain moved.

This fivefold geography is replicated in various ways in later parts of the Bible. The Holy of Holies corresponds to the highest Land of Eden. The Holy Place is a replica of the firmament heavens and thus also of the Garden of Eden. The Courtyard with its Altar corresponds to the slope leading up to the Garden. Around it is the camp of Israel in the wilderness, and the Promised Land after Israel enters it. It links with the Homeland where Adam and Eve dwelt. Farther away are the gentile lands, the river-watered lands of Genesis 2, the gentile Sea.

Cain has become the first "gentile," but he is not a God-fearer. He does not seek Yahweh. He makes no trips to the slope of Eden to offer tribute along with Adam, Seth, and Enosh. He never repents. He goes away, and he stays away.

SYMBOLIC SPACE

We modern evangelicals are sometimes reluctant to face the clear up-and-down imagery of the Bible. We know that the earth is a sphere and that "up" can be in any direction. We are told that ancient peoples thought that the earth was flat, with heaven above and an abyss of the dead below, and that the Bible is written with this "primitive worldview" in mind.

There is no reason to be embarrassed by this matter, however. The fact is that many ancient peoples knew full well that the earth is round, but still spoke about heaven above, earth beneath, and an abyss below the earth. For those peoples, such language was clearly understood in a symbolic fashion. The same is true for the Bible.

Now, "symbolic" does not mean "unreal." In some real sense, heaven *is* above the earth and hell *is* below it. This does not mean that heaven is a large sphere beyond the stars, while the abyss is physically located inside the earth. Precisely what it does mean in a physical sense is hard, perhaps impossible, to say. But it is true for us psychologically, as when we think of rulers and bosses as "over" us. And it is also true in the sense that God appears above people when He appears to them in the Bible—up on Mount Sinai, for instance.

What we are calling symbolic space clearly appears in Genesis 2–4. The Land of Eden was on high ground, with a river flowing down into the Garden of Eden and from there out into the wider world. There was thus a slope leading up to the Garden, and this slope or "courtyard of the sanctuary" was where Cain and Abel "brought" their tribute. It is symbolized by the altar, a symbolic mountain, in the Tabernacle courtyard. Lower down was the "field" where Abel and Cain labored and where Cain slew Abel, the same area as the Land of Canaan "below" the Tabernacle and its courtyard. Below this field was the sea, "sea-level," which later in the Bible represents the lands around Canaan, the gentile lands. It is this area into which Cain went when he left the "homeland" of the field near the Garden slope.[138]

Up-and-down imagery is also found in the narrative of Cain and Abel in another way. Cain's countenance "fell" (4:5) and at his feet was a "croucher" waiting to devour him (verse 7). If he repented—if he trod the croucher underfoot—he would be "lifted up" (verse 7) The croucher (Satan) wants to lure Cain downwards, away from the slope and the homeland, into a lower "homeless land" (verse 16). God offers to lift Cain—not only his countenance but his whole person—up into His fellowship.

Cain had been brought low, but instead of humbly seeking God the right way, he "stood up" against Abel and killed him, sending him and his blood down to the ground (verses 8, 10). Cain rises up in a rebellious way, putting himself spatially between God and Abel as judge, instead of remaining below Abel and going through him (that is, through his flocks) to God.

Humanity is called to live in the "middle" area, between heaven and hell, between above and below. Adam was to abide in the Garden between Eden above and the world below, until God was ready to elevate him. When he tried to seize the Land of Eden—which is what trying to become like God meant,

---

138. For another passage that trades very heavily on significant up-and-down imagery, see 2 Kings 1–2.

in part—Adam was driven further down into the outer world. Had Adam remained faithful, he would have been given both Eden and world.

In the same way, Cain was to abide in the Field and let Abel conduct him up the Slope (just as the Israelites later on were to abide in the Land and let the priests conduct their sacrifices up the "slope" of the altar in the courtyard). When Cain "stood up" against Abel, he was trying to force his way into Abel's role, just as when King Uzziah's heart was "lifted up," and he forced his way into the Tabernacle against the protests of the High Priest. Uzziah was struck with "leprosy" and had to "live apart" for the rest of his life (2 Chron. 26:16–21). In the same way, just as Adam was exiled downstream, so Cain was exiled further away.

God wanted to lift Cain up, when God was ready. Cain decided to stand up on his own and was driven out and down, down to live with the "croucher." Those who seek to usurp higher places before God is ready to "lift them up" are eventually driven lower.

Here we see once again that there is no "covenant of meritorious works" in the Bible. Adam was not supposed to "earn" his way into the high Land of Eden by accumulating "merits" through good works. He was supposed to abide patiently in the Garden and wait for God to lift him up. Similarly, Cain was supposed to abide patiently in the Field and wait for God to lift him up. Heaven, Eden, the New Creation—these are not things we or anyone else earns. They are gifts that God gives when He is ready and when we are ready for them.

Jesus did not "earn" heaven for Himself or for us. Rather, He remained patiently faithful and obedient, and even suffered, until God was ready to raise Him up. We go to heaven, and into the New Creation, not because Jesus earned anything by meriting it for us, but because we are given the benefit of His patient and faithful abiding.

THE GENERATIONS OF CAIN

Gen. 4:17–24 follows again the sevenfold pattern established in Genesis 1 and 2–3 and 4:1–16. This is apparent from its beginning and end, but the middle is arguably less clear. Here is my first attempt, which I may modify after studying the passage fully as we go along.

Day 1 // 2:4–7 - light // the human light.

(4:1 - And the man knew Eve, his woman, and she conceived, and she bore Cain.)

4:17a - And Cain knew his woman, and she conceived, and she bore Enoch.

Day 2 // 2:8 - Firmament // Garden.

4:17b - And he became a city-builder, and he called the name of the city after the name of his son: Enoch.

Day 3 // 2:9–14 - land and sea and plants // rivers.

4:18 - the generations (rivers) that flow from Enoch, the new person/garden.

Day 4 // 2:15 - ruling luminaries in firmament // Adam enters Garden to rule it.

4:19 - Lamech (sun) and his wives (moons, stars). Lamech as god, father of human culture, who usurps God's right to put men to death.

Days 5–6 seem to be collapsed together, as the family of the new humanity made by the god Lamech. But perhaps they can be broken out as follows:

Day 5 // 2:16–17 - commands to swarms of fishes and birds // command to Adam.

4:20–21 - Adah's two sons: Jabal's flocks and herds, which move from place to place as Jabal is "father of those who dwell in tents," corresponding to swarms of fishes; and Jubal's music corresponding to birds.

Day 6 // 2:18–24 - creation of mankind, told to multiply / / creation of woman.

4:8 - Cain murders Abel.

4:22 - Zillah's two children: Tubal-Cain's forge that makes helpful implements parallel to land animals that are secondary helpers for men, and Naamah parallel to the creation of Eve. Unlike Cain and Abel, these brothers with different vocations don't kill each other.

Day 7 // 2:25ff - sabbath // sabbath judgment.

4:9–16 - sabbath judgment on Cain: Only God can put a man to death.

4:23–24 - Lamech usurps God's place and passes his own judgment, putting a man to death.

(*Day 8* - a new beginning.)

4:25–26 - birth of Seth and beginning of the use of the name "Yahweh" in prayer.

Looking at significant terms and other literary aspects, it may be noted that "Cain" brackets the passage, appearing only at the beginning and end. Also, there are a number of pairs in the passage, leading to Lamech's "Sword Song" at the end:

Enoch as son and city

Two wives for Lamech

Two children from each wife

The three double-parallel lines of Lamech's song/poem (verses 23–24)

It may be significant that Lamech, the false god, appears four times, and the name of the true God, *'el*, also appears four times (twice each in the names Mehuja-el and Methusha-el.) If, as may be, "Methu-sha-el" means something like "El is dead" or "Death to El," then Methushael as the father of the false god Lamech fits with this theme. We shall explore this later on, of course.

PRIEST-KINGS

And Cain knew his wife,

And she conceived,

And she bore Enoch.

And he was building a city,

And he called the name of the city after the name of his son: Enoch (Gen. 4:17).

Before we begin, we must establish who built the first city. Some commentators note that the "he" of the second part of the verse should logically refer back to what immediately precedes it, Enoch. In that case Enoch built the city. Why then is the city named Enoch "after the name of his son"? Does this mean Enoch named his own son Enoch Jr.? No, this cannot be, because Enoch's son was Irad. Hence, these commentators assume a textual corruption, and that the name of the city should be Irad. Irad does seem related to the Hebrew word for "city," but that does not mean the city was named Irad.

This interpretation lies too thin upon the ground. Given what the verse as a whole says, the reader immediately realizes that the "he" who built the city is Cain, as the majority of all readers have always done. The present participle, indicating continuous activity, of "he was building a city" seems to indicate that Enoch was born while the city was being built. The sense might be "And she bore Enoch, *while* he was building a city."

These two statements correspond to Days 1 and 2 of creation week, as humanified by Gen. 2:4–7 (Adam as human light) and 2:8 (Garden between high ground of Eden and the rest of the world). The Garden of Eden was a sanctuary, and thus so is the city of Enoch. It is not merely a political institution but a religious one, a counterfeit of God's original place of worship. It is a place not of kings but of priest-kings who create and maintain their own religion against true religion.

Enoch (Hebrew, *Chanokh*) means "Dedicated" and implies a kind of priesthood. The same name is found in Genesis 5 for the godly Enoch. Cain was the first "priest-king"—as we have seen, he was a "king" to start with, and he murdered the "priestly" Abel and usurped his position also—and thus so are his descendants. He establishes his son as dedicated priest in his dedicated holy city.

First Cain and then Enoch were priest-kings over the civilization that began with the city Enoch. A separation of "church and state" is clear in the Sinaitic Law and is maintained in the New Covenant in Romans 13. Before Sinai, however, God had not instituted this separation. We find godly priest-kings like Melchizedek and Jethro, and in a corresponding way, Abraham, Isaac, and Jacob. Jesus, of course, is priest-king over the Final City.

Hence it was not necessarily wrong in the abstract for Enoch to be a priest-king. Rather, what was wrong was that he did not subordinate himself to God, the ultimate Priest-King. Cain and his line followed out Satan's original advice: Make yourselves gods.

It is certainly of interest to consider that we may have the city-name Enoch still with us in English. Arthur Custance argues that Enoch was the original city and as a result just became the word for "city" in the pre-Flood language and continued to mean "city" afterwards through various transformations, until we have it today in "burg." *Chanokh* (Enoch) becomes Unuk and then Uruk. From there it becomes Wark, and finally Perg or Purg. These transformations are quite common in languages, such as "n" to a rolled "r" and the "w" sound to "p" or "b." (Say these consonants out loud, and you'll see that your mouth is in the same shape for those that transform.) Purg has come down in "Indo-European" languages as Burgh or Borough.[139]

---

139. Arthur C. Custance, "The Genealogies of the Bible: A Neglected Subject," chapter 1, "The Old Testament," in *Hidden Things of God's Revelation*, The Doorway Papers 7 (Grand Rapids: Zondervan, 1977), 5–6, online: https://custance.org/Library/Volume7/Part_V/Chapter1.html.

Characteristics of the Wicked City

What can we say about Cain's wicked sanctuary-city of Enoch? First that it was built with a brother's blood as its cornerstone. The Church is also built in this way, for Jesus was the younger brother of the whole Adamic race, slain by that company of older brothers because they hated Him. His death is the foundation of the Church.

Human sacrifice has always been at the foundation of the cities of men. We see it in the possibly legendary story of the founding of Rome, which came into being when Romulus plowed a circle in the earth and proclaimed himself king and god over it and then slew his brother Remus the instant Remus put a foot into it without permission. We see it in 1 Kings 16:34, when Hiel rebuilt Jericho on the blood of his first-born son. We see it in the bones of infants slain as "threshold sacrifices" at the entrances of ancient buildings and cities. And we see it, in a type, in the animal sacrifices that Israel was to offer at the "doorway" of the Tabernacle and Temple, sacrifices of a "*son* of the herd," which represented their sons and pointed back to Isaac and forward to Jesus. In another way we see it in the bloody wars that have attended the foundation of virtually every human culture since the dawn of time.

Second, we can say that Cain's city was rapidly founded and grew in strength rapidly, precisely because this sacrifice had been made. The writings of René Girard have explored at length the cultural peace and power that comes after an incident of scapegoating and sacrificial murder.[140] In a time of social chaos, someone is found to blame and is killed; then social peace ensues as a result of the psychic relief that such a murder provides, though only temporarily. Cain was downcast and upset, and he placed the blame for this on Abel. After killing Abel, Cain felt good. He felt the burden lift from his soul. He entered into a false sabbath, out of which he found energy and strength, the energy to build a city.

If Cain had repented, the burden would have come back, though with God's help he would have learned to deal with it and eventually overcome it. Such a long-term solution Cain rejected. Believing cultures and civilizations grow much more slowly precisely because believers wrestle with sin and

---

140. See, in particular, René Girard, *The Scapegoat*, trans. Yvonne Freccero (Baltimore: Johns Hopkins, 1986).

personal doubt. Believers are more careful. The wicked do not hesitate to conquer and enslave. They have no self-doubts to hold them back.

Culturally, the wicked get there first. Cain's cultural power was based on the release of sabbath energy and reinforced by tyranny. We cannot be surprised to learn that the fathers of agriculture, music, and metallurgy came from Cain's line. I call this the "Enoch Factor," that the wicked build their civilizations first and rapidly. But the City of Man cannot last. It must be renewed by more killing and eventually either self-destructs or is destroyed by another city of man. The "Jerusalem Factor" means that the righteous build more slowly, but more permanently. The final City is the City of God. And as time goes along, we find more and more that it is Christians who are the pioneers of cultural development, as the Jerusalem Factor replaces the Enoch Factor.[141]

Third, we can ask the question: Who was in this city? From Gen. 5:3 and 4:25, it seems clear that Seth was born to Adam shortly after Cain murdered Abel. Seth was born 130 years after the creation. Surely Adam and Eve had had other sons and daughters by this time. This must be true, for one of the women went with Cain as his wife. And it takes little imagination to realize that Cain and Abel were likely already married. By this time in history there was a company of sons and daughters and grandchildren of Adam, possibly hundreds of adult people, and some of them likely followed Cain while others remained faithful to Adam and Eve. Indeed, since it was necessary for Seth to be born to replace Abel, it may even be that all the sons of Adam followed Cain, with possibly only a few daughters remaining behind.

If Cain had already had sons by this time, evidently he felt that only a son born in his new land, in connection with the building of his city, would count as his full heir and inherit the kingship over the city.

THE DEVELOPMENT OF THE SECULAR CITY

And was born to Enoch, Irad.
And Irad begat Mehujael.
And Mehijael begat Methushael.
And Methushael begat Lamech (Gen. 4:18).

---

141. For a fuller treatment of the "Enoch Factor," see James B. Jordan, "The Case Against Western Civilization, Part 2: The Enoch Factor," *Open Book* 37 (December 1997).

Modern commentators confess that these names are not easy to decipher, though clearly they are important, as names always are in the Bible. They usually suggest that the names come from languages other than Hebrew, and look at Arabic and other languages for clues. I think this is an error. Whatever language these men may have spoken and whatever their names may have sounded like originally, this is a text written in Hebrew for Hebrew readers. We should assume that the meanings of the names would have been intelligible to Hebrew hearers. Even if the meanings were not immediately obvious to Hebrew hearers and readers, as they meditated upon them they would understand them.

The second assumption is that these names have essentially positive meanings, like "priest of God" and the like. Again, I don't think so. The Bible clearly changes the names of wicked people sometimes in order to point to their character. Gaal in Judges 9 means "loathsome," but we can be sure his mother did not name him that, and that people did not call him that (to his face at least) during his life. The writer of Judges has given him this name. Similarly, Saul's son Ish-baal (Man of the [divine] Lord-husband) is changed to Ishbosheth (Man of Shame) to reflect the judgment on Saul's house.

Looking strictly at Hebrew possibilities, the names in Genesis 4 indicate, I believe, a progression of evil.

Irad (*'irad*) may mean "wild ass," but also seems to come from the word for city (*'ir*, as in verse 17) and perhaps means "city-dweller." In that case, the Hebrew listener to the text might hear something like "The Man who Dwells in a City like a Wild Ass" or even "Man of the Untamed (by God) City."

Mehujael (*Mechu-ya-'el*), whose name is written Mehijael (*Mechiiya'el*) when it appears the second time in verse 18, might be heard as "He Who Strikes Out Against Ya(hweh) El(ohim)" or "He Who Blots Out Ya(hweh) El(ohim)." Note the similarity of the first syllable with m*acha'* (strike), *machach* (strike), and *machah* (wipe out). We know from verse 26 that in the third generation from Adam through Seth, men began to pray by the name Yahweh. Since this name was in circulation among the godly Sethites, the anti-God Cainites are pictured as opposed to both Elohim (God the creator) and Yahweh (God the covenant-keeper), either lashing out against Him or seeking to blot out His name (or both).

Methushael (*Methu-sha-'el*) might be heard as "He Who Kills the Peace of God." It is related to the godly name Methuselah (*Methu-shalach*), which may mean "His Death is Peaceful" or perhaps "His Death is a Putting Forth (of God's Hand)." The root seems to be *shalah*. If Mehujael struck out against God, Methushael seems to be one who kills the people of God, who live in peace and quietness.

The name Lamech (*Lamekh*) is difficult. I suggest that just as Rebekah is a play on *barak* (blessing) by reversing the first two letters, so *Lamekh* is a play on *melekh* (king). It is also the name of Noah's father, and the two men are opposites, as by implication are their sons: The godly Lamech looks to God for comfort and vengeance upon the wicked; the wicked Lamech takes his own vengeance as a murderer.

Reading 4:18 as a Hebrew might have heard it, then, we hear: "And to the Dedicated One was born the Rebellious-City-Dweller. And the Rebellious-City-Dweller begat the One Who Strikes Out Against Yahweh-Elohim. And the One Who Strikes Out Against Yahweh-Elohim begat the One Who Kills the Peace of Elohim. And the One Who Kills the Peace of Elohim begat the King."

In this way we can see that Cain's initial kingly rebellion against God becomes worse and worse over the generations and reaches a climax in the seventh generation, with the coming of Lamech, the evil god-king *par excellence*. Cain started with defiance and rebellion against God. His descendants sought to wipe Him out and conquer His people. The development of the secular city reached its climax with the coming of Lamech, who made himself a god and ruled the world.

THE ALTERNATIVE TO THE SECULAR CITY

We should match the names in Genesis 4 with their godly contemporaries in Genesis 5. Since Seth was born when Adam was 130 years old (5:3), evidently soon after the murder of Abel and the departure of Cain (4:25), Seth would be a contemporary of Enoch. From this it follows:

Cainite Line	*Sethite Line*
Enoch	Seth
Irad	Enosh
Mehujael	Kenan
Methushael	Mahalelel
Lamech	Jared
sons of Lamech	Enoch
	Methuselah
	Lamech
	Noah

The comparisons are instructive. Seth means "Foundation," and thus is similar to Enoch in meaning. Adam begets a new foundation at the time Cain is setting up his own new foundation, his new dedicated garden and son.

Enosh means "Humble Man." Irad has to do with the Rebellious City. The names are largely opposites.

Kenan (*Qeynan*) is usually understood as a variant of Cain (*Qayin*). I don't think so. I think it comes from *qun*, "chant a lamentation" (e.g., 2 Sam. 1:17; 3:33; 2 Chron. 35:25; Ezek. 32:16). If Mehujael is speaking out against God, Kenan is lamenting his doing so. If Mehujael is striking out against God and His people, Kenan is singing lamentations about the slain.

Mahalelel means "Praise of God." This is the opposite of Methushael, "One Who Kills the Peace of God." It also provides a counterpoint to his father Kenan the Lamenter.

Jared (*Yared*) evidently comes from *yarad*, meaning "to go down, descend," the root of the name "Jordan" as the Jordan river is the low point of the land. I suggest that Lamech's father and grandfather have made war on the line of Seth and have conquered them by this time, so that Lamech is king of the world. God's people have been brought low, hence the name Jared, perhaps meaning "One Brought Low." It would also indicate that Jared was humble under the God who had sovereignly brought all this to pass.

Enoch means "Dedicated" (to God), and such he surely was. We know from Jude 14–15 that Enoch prophesied against the ungodly of his day. Jude writes about wicked Christians, apostates, and thus that is what Enoch was speaking against. His words were directed against the Sethites (sons of God) who were beginning to intermarry with the Cainite (daughters of men).

We can see readily why this apostasy began at this time. First, clearly the Cainites had developed a mighty civilization. Enoch lived during the time of the three brilliant sons of Lamech. They were the experts in animal husbandry, music, and metal-working. Such a high culture draws the desire of those in simpler cultures to imitate it.

Also, second, we have seen it strongly implied that by this time Lamech had conquered the world. Hence, the Sethites were living as inferiors (brought low, Jared) in this wicked high culture.

Third, the women of the citified Cainite line by this time were "fair," not hardened and wrinkled by labor under the sun. The temptation to imitate this culture and to try to join up with it and marry its prettier women was evidently too strong for the Sethites as a whole. Enoch, however, remained dedicated to God.

God protected His faithful remnant, it seems. Methuselah lived longer than anyone else in the Bible and his name may mean, "His Death Is Peaceful." Or it may mean, "His Death Is a Putting Forth," prophesying God's putting forth His Hand against humanity in the Flood. He died just before the Flood.

Lamech's name, as we have seen, is a play on the word for king. Here is a godly kingly figure. He may not have ruled the land; it seems the Cainites did so. But he shows what a true king is like, for he submits himself to God's Kingship and waits for Him to act.

Noah means "Rest," and rest from all these horrors and sins came with the Flood.

THE FAMILY OF LAMECH

And Lamech took to himself two wives.

The name of the first: Adah.

And the name of the second: Zillah.

And Adah bore Jabal.

He was father of those who dwell in tents and have livestock.

And the name of his brother was Jubal.

He was father of all who play lyre and pipe.

And Zillah, she also:

She bore Tubal-Cain, forger of every tooling of bronze and iron,

And the sister of Tubal-Cain: Na'amah (Gen. 4:19–22).

While the sons of God who married the daughters of men in Genesis 6 are clearly the Sethites marrying Cainites, because their women were fair, it is also true that "sons of God" can refer to kings. Lamech, it seems, making himself a god, was drawn to pretty women, "because they were fair." We don't know if his wives were Sethites, but we know they were attractive. Adah (*'Adah*) means "ornament, pretty." Zillah (*Tsillah*) can mean "shady" or more likely "pretty voiced" (from the word for "tinkle").

Gen. 2:24 had said that a man was to stick to his wife. He cannot take a second wife if he is sticking to his first. Biblically speaking, polygamy and bigamy are always sinful, though if you take a second wife, you cannot put her away. Similarly, if you wickedly chop off your arm, you can repent, but you won't get your arm back.

Kings like to have many wives. They are powerful and can afford it. But it's always sinful and disastrous, as the histories of David and of Solomon show.

The children of Lamech are arranged in two pairs:

From Adah:
  Jabal, herdmaster
  Jubal, songmaster
From Zillah:
  Tubal-cain, forgemaster
  Na'amah, "sweet singer"

In both cases, the younger is associated with music. Na'amah's name as "Sweet Singer" helps resolve the meaning of her mother's name: not "Shade" but "Pretty Voice." Na'amah was doubtless "fair" and probably a good example of the kind of woman that the Sethite "sons of God" sought after.

The three sons' names all come from the same Hebrew word, *yabal*, meaning "to bring, carry, lead," or more fully "to cause to transport an object from one place to another." It is behind one of the words for "stream." These men are the streams or fountain-heads of their respective callings. Other men, "downstream" from them, learned from them.

Jabal (*Yabal*) was "father of those who dwell in tents and have livestock" (verse 20). His name means that he moved his animals from place to place, living in tents. In Phoenician, a near language to Hebrew, *yobel* means "ram," and so there is a possible pun here.

Jubal (*Yubel*) was "father of all those who play lyre and pipe." The sound that streams from these musical instruments is picked up in the word *yobel*, which means "ram's horn" as a musical instrument. The word *yubal* (with a short "a") appears in Jeremiah 17:4, where it means "babbling brook, stream."

Tubal also comes from this same root word. The word *tebel* means "world," and so we might have "World of the Smith" for Tubal-Qayin. (Cain, *Qayin*, is the same as the Cain who was son of Adam). I think it more likely means "The One Who Streams Forth Metal as a Smith." Tubal-Cain knew how to liquefy and smelt metal and how to beat it out into shapes.

With these sons, Lamech made himself a new Adam. Adam's two sons are duplicated here: Abel's flocks with Jabal's livestock, with Jubal's music attending; and Cain as smith with Tubal-Cain as smith, with Na'amah's music attending. Lamech's father and grandfather had sought to wipe out God and make themselves gods. Lamech, as their son, is a god himself but also a new Adam, child of these gods. Adam's sons were to issue forth into the world. Now Lamech's sons are "streams" that issue into the world through cultural dominance.

LAMECH'S SONG

And Lamech said to his wives:
"Adah and Zillah, hear my voice;
You wives of Lamech, hearken to my saying:
For a man have I slain for wounding me;
And a youth for striking me.
For sevenfold is Cain avenged.
And Lamech seventy and seven! (Gen. 4:23–24).

First, whom did Lamech kill? The word "youth" is *yeled*, which comes from *yalad*, meaning "beget." The noun can be used for young men and small children in general, but often means one's own child. Given the theology that we shall investigate below, we can be pretty sure that Lamech slew one of his own sons and not someone else's child. The attack of a son upon a father's rule anticipates the behavior of Ham toward Noah later on.

We can guess which son Lamech slew, for "Tubal-Cain," minus the "tu," sounds just like Vulcan, the god of the forge and thus of volcanoes in the Latin language.[142] The Greco-Roman myths about Vulcan (Hephaestus in Greek) tell us that at his birth his parents Jupiter (Zeus) and Juno (Hera) cast him down from Olympus because he was ugly and that he was lamed permanently when he hit the ground after several days. Myths also say that later on Vulcan split open Jupiter's head with a hammer and released Athena, who was born from the high god's head. Both of these stories look like corrupted versions of an attack by Tubal-Cain upon Lamech and Lamech's killing him for it.

There are allusions back to Genesis 2 in Gen. 4:16–24. We have a new wicked god, Cain, who plants a new wicked garden, the city of Enoch, for his

---

142. Cf. Custance, "Genealogies," 7–8.

new wicked Adamic son, also named Enoch. We also have a river flowing in this new wicked garden, consisting of the line of Cain's descendants. Then, as in Genesis 2, Lamech finds a wife—in fact, two of them—in the garden-city of Enoch. Lamech's own children become four rivers that flow out of Enoch into the world of cultural pursuits. Then, analogous to Genesis 3, we come to a judgment scene, when Lamech kills one of his sons, just as God has promised death to His son, Adam, if he rebelled and seized the forbidden fruit. Adam had struck out against God, and Lamech's son had struck out against him.

In all of this we see that human beings continue to be the images of God. They act like God, for better or for worse. They either image God properly, as sons under their Father, or wickedly, usurping the place of God.

Lamech goes beyond God in his actions. God had said that Cain would be avenged sevenfold. By taking a 77-fold vengeance Lamech tries to make himself bigger than God. Moreover, God did not kill Adam, though He put him under a kind of death consisting of exile. Neither did God kill Cain, but also exiled him. Lamech goes much farther. We are reminded of the book of Esther, in which the decent king Ahasuerus only exiles his rebellious wife, but wicked Haman seeks to put rebellious Mordecai, and all his people, to death.

HISTORY FORESHADOWED

There is another aspect of Gen. 4:16–24 that is important for us to consider. Biblical history moves from priest to king, from the Sinaitic Covenant, which focuses on priests, to the Kingdom Covenant, which of course focuses on kings. When the king arrives, song arrives. Saul was swept up in a company of musician prophets (1 Sam. 10:5–9), but failed to organize this band into a structured company of prophetic Levites to praise God. This is what David did, and 1 Chronicles devotes a lot of attention to it.[143]

A typical foreshadowing of this biblical history is found in Gen. 4:16–24. We begin with Cain, who murdered the priestly Abel and thereby usurped his place. The line of Cain down to Lamech we can associate with the period of the Judges, after Sinai, so that Cain's conquering sons are like anti-Joshuas and anti-Judges. Then we come to the king, Lamech, whose name we have seen is

---

143. See Peter J. Leithart, *From Silence to Song: The Davidic Liturgical Reformation* (Moscow, ID: Canon, 2003).

a play on the word for king, *melech*. Like David later on, Lamech is a singer and a composer of songs.

David, however, composed songs in the praise of the True King, Yahweh. Lamech composes songs in the praise of himself. We see in this comparison, again, that Lamech is usurping the place of God.

Now, of course, Gen. 4:23 does not say that Lamech sang this poem, and maybe he did not. At the same time, it has the same basic two-line form as all the songs and psalms of the Bible. Moreover, in the preceding two verses we have just read about Jubal as the maker of musical instruments and seen the name Na'amah, which means "sweet singer." We are in a context of music and song.

Another point of interest is that the first double-line of Lamech's poem is addressed to his wives:

Adah and Zillah, hear my voice;
You wives of Lamech, hearken to my saying

We should correlate this with the psalms of David also. David wrote songs for Yahweh's bride, Israel, to hear and to sing—especially to hear, because they were sung primarily by the Levitical musicians and heard by the rest of Israel. David's songs were *for* Yahweh's bride, just as Lamech's song was for his wives.

Beyond this, the four children of Lamech link closely again with the worship that David, the true king, set up. Like Jabal, David was a shepherd. Like Jubal, David designed musical instruments. Like Tubal-Cain, David gathered the bronze and iron and other things to build the Temple. Like Na'amah, David was the "sweet-singing psalmist" of Israel (2 Sam. 23:1, where the same word *na'am* is used of David's singing).

If David corresponds to Lamech's sons, then the person who corresponds to Lamech himself is Saul. Like Lamech, who killed a son, Saul sought repeatedly to kill his adopted son David. We don't have recorded any wicked songs from Saul, but remember that Saul was swept up into the company of musician prophets and so is associated with poetry and song.

Lamech was the seventh from Adam. David was the eighth son of Jesse. Should we put these facts together and see Saul as a king of seventh also, followed by an eighth who begins a new week, a new and circumcised (on the eighth day) kingdom?

And is it possible that the reason Tubal-Cain, an eighth from Adam, rose up against Lamech was that he had been converted? It is true that David did not strike at Saul (but see below), but Tubal-Cain may not have been so wise, growing up in a violent household and culture. We cannot know until we get to heaven, but it is interesting to speculate.

David did strike at Saul on one occasion, though he repented of it (1 Sam. 24). On another occasion, David made a symbolic strike at Saul's head, in order to show him that only David was good enough to be Saul's protector (1 Sam. 26). We have seen that Greco-Roman myths associate Tubal-Cain with an attack on the head of his father. Here again, the parallels are suggestive, but we cannot know anything at all and can only speculate. But I guess it would not surprise me to find Tubal-Cain in heaven!

32

A New Beginning

Genesis 4:25–26

And Adam knew his wife again.
And she bore a son.
And she called his name Seth (sheth),
"For God has appointed (shath) *to me another seed in the place of Abel,"*
For Cain killed him (Gen. 4:25).

WE come to an eighth "day" after the sets of seven "days" we have been examining for so long in these studies. It is a new beginning, the beginning of another set of seven, as we shall see later on. We can distinguish four aspects of this new beginning.

First, the new beginning is signaled by the parallels between verses 1 and 25:

> Verse 1. And the man [the *adam*] knew Eve, his woman.
>> Verse 25. And Adam knew his wife again.

The second time, it is not "the" *adam* but simply Adam, as a proper name. Perhaps the idea is that Adam is no longer acting as "the first man" giving birth to his first son, but as one man, part of the line of which he is the beginning. This Adam is, we learn from chapter 5, 130 years old. "The man," the first and fallen Adam, begat Cain. The same Adam, but at a *later* time, begets someone better. There is a first race that came from Adam and then a second race, first Abel and then Abel's replacement.

The word "again" does not mean there had been no sons and daughters between Abel and Seth, but does indicate a new start, and in context a replacement for Abel. Seth is the son begotten first after Abel's death, not Adam's third son absolutely speaking. Evidently a lot of Adam's later sons and daughters, and grandsons and granddaughters, went with Cain, and that is how he could found a city.

Continuing,

> Verse 1. And she bore Cain.
>> verse 25. And she bore a son.
> Verse 1. And she said, "I have acquired a man (*'ish*) with Yahweh."
>> Verse 25. And she called his name Seth, "for God
>> has appointed to me another seed...."

As we saw earlier, Cain means "smith," and there is a pun on "Cain" (*Qayin*) in the word "acquired" (*qanithi*). Similarly, Seth means "foundation," and there is a pun on "Seth" (*Sheth*) in the word "appointed" (*shath*). The parallels indicate a new beginning.

Second, the new beginning is indicated by the use of "God" (*Elohim*), the original creator of man and woman, in verse 25, rather than "Yahweh," as in verse 1. In verse 1, Eve saw the covenant-keeping Yahweh keeping His promise by giving her a son, and though in time that son went bad, she was right to thank Yahweh. Now the emphasis is on God the Creator as the giver of a new creation.

Third, the meaning of Seth as "foundation" indicates a new beginning.

Fourth, Cain was a "man," a male human being (*'ish*). Seth, however, is a "seed," pointing back to the promise made about the woman in Genesis 3. Cain turned out to be "the seed of the serpent." Now we have a new seed, which the woman says was "appointed to me" as a "seed of the woman." We notice that Cain was the son of "Eve," while Seth is the "seed" of Adam's "woman."

("Woman" and "wife" are the same word in Hebrew.) Eve makes clear that the birth of Seth as the woman's seed replaces Abel, who by implication was also her seed. These two sons, the one who died as a human sacrifice and the one who came to life after Abel's death, are the "seed of the woman."

Moreover, the text includes the fact that Cain slew Abel. It is not clear whether this last phrase continues what Eve said (as in most translations) or is a comment by the narrator (as I have it here). Either way, we are invited to consider that the coming of "Foundation" arises precisely from the death of Abel, a foreshadowing of the Church that arises from the death of Jesus Christ.[144] Along these lines we notice that worship of Yahweh in some particular way arises from this new beginning (verse 26). The death of Abel gave rise to the first form of the Church.

THE WORSHIP OF YAHWEH

And to Seth: To him also was born a son.

And he called his name Enosh.

At that time he began to call on the Name: Yahweh (Gen. 4:26).

The word *'enosh* means "man" in the sense of "mankind." It is the most general term for man, lacking the specificity of *'ish*, particular man. It is used the same way as *'adam*, for individuals as considered part of mankind. Unlike *'adam*, which speaks of man as man, as created by God whole, *'enosh* speaks of man as weak, as needing God. "Adam" and "enosh" are like two sides of one coin.

Man's need of God is indicated by the fact that at the time Seth gave this name to his son, he also began to call upon the Name of God: Yahweh. This name, as we shall see, speaks of God as the nurturer and protector of mankind, not as Creator (*'Elohim*) over mankind. The notion that "weak man" (Enosh) is complementary with Yahweh the Protector is reinforced by the parallel phrasing:

He called	his *name*	*Enosh.*
He began to *call*	on the *Name:*	*Yahweh.*

---

144. Notice in Revelation 12 that the woman gives birth to a son (verse 5), who is caught up to heaven, and then the serpent "goes off to make war against the rest of her *seed*." Both Abel and Seth, both Jesus and Church, are the seed of the woman.

The last phrase can be translated "At that time *one* began to call on the Name: Yahweh," and for this reason many translations render it "*they* began." The idea is that the appearance of the name "Enosh" in the text has created a sense of mankind, not of individual man, so that it is not Seth but people in general who begin to worship by the name Yahweh.

I don't think this line of reasoning can be sustained. It may be hinted at, but clearly it is Seth who is calling on the Name.

All the same, since Seth gave this kind of "group name" to his son, it is implied that Seth began to lead his sons and other people—other children and grandchildren of Adam and Eve—in calling upon the Name.

Exodus 6 tells us about the Name "Yahweh." There God says to Moses that He gave the name "Shaddai" to the patriarchs, but not the name "Yahweh." "El Shaddai" means "Almighty God." It is a name associated with promises. Abraham and the other patriarchs did not live to see the promises fulfilled, but they could trust in the Promise-Maker because He is the All-powerful God. His promises are certain to be fulfilled.

"Yahweh" is the name given at the time the promises are fulfilled. Moses and his people can trust God now in a new way, as the One who keeps the promises made to the forefathers. "Yahweh" also has the idea of God as near to His people, as the God who is *their* God, upon whom they can always call when in need.

It is clear from Genesis, indeed from our verse right here, that men knew the name "Yahweh" and used it in worship. Its full meaning was not revealed, not "given," however, until the exodus from Egypt.

Let us now consider the meaning of "Yahweh" in Genesis 4. As we noted several chapters back, the Creator in Genesis 1 is "God" (*'Elohim*). The name used in Genesis 2–3 is "Yahweh God" (*Yahweh 'Elohim*). In Genesis 4 we find "Yahweh" by itself used.

"Yahweh" is displayed in five aspects in Genesis 4, and these five are relevant to why Seth began to use this name in a special way. First, Yahweh helps men and women produce children (4:1). Second, Yahweh is the God that is worshipped (4:3). Third, Yahweh is the God who brings judgment upon the enemies of His people (4:4, 6, 9, 13, 15). Fourth, Cain and his people rejected Yahweh (4:16). Fifth, Yahweh is the God of the weak (4:26).

By calling on the Name "Yahweh," Seth is affirming God's original command to be fruitful and multiply, for Yahweh gives children. By calling on Yahweh, Seth is reaffirming the worship that Abel began. By calling on Yahweh, Seth is asking protection from the Cainites, asking Yahweh to continue to judge them. Finally, by calling on Yahweh, Seth is affirming what Cain rejected. He is siding with Yahweh against Cain.

I think it is primarily the protection and judgment against the Cainites that is in view. This is the main thing we see Yahweh doing in the preceding verses of Genesis 4. Needy man (*'enosh*) needs protection. As we have seen, the Cainites are developing a titanic and oppressive conquering culture. It is Yahweh, the One who judges Cain, who is needed, just as Moses needs Yahweh to judge Egypt and later to judge the Canaanites.

Seth wants his family to affirm the Yahweh that Cain rejected. He wants his sons to bring gifts to Yahweh and worship Him. He wants his sons to be fruitful and multiply. He wants his sons to call upon Yahweh for protection, to restrain and judge their enemies. Hence, he establishes the name "Yahweh" as the special name they are to use for God.

WHAT HAPPENS NEXT

As we draw to an end our studies in Genesis 2–4, it is useful to look at what happens next. We have seen in Genesis 2–4 a series of basic movements through seven events or aspects of things that build on the original movement of the Spirit through the seven days of creation week in Genesis 1. We can see the same progression found in Gen. 5:1–6:8. Gen. 5:1 begins the Book of the Generations (Outflow) of Adam, the things generated by Adam.

We begin in 5:1b–2,

> In the day God created Adam, in the likeness of God He made him.
> Male and female He created them.
> And He blessed them.
> And He called their name "Adam" in the day He created them.

This corresponds to Day 1 and to the creation of Adam as God's human light in 2:4–7.

We have seen that the creation of mankind on the sixth day links chiastically with the creation of the firmament heavens on the Second, for the firmament is the (first) location of man between the highest heavens and the earth. The firmament corresponds to the Garden of 2:8. The firmament people, the godly line of Seth, that are mediators between Yahweh and the rest of mankind, are listed generation by generation in 5:3–32.[145]

Day 3 gives us land and sea, and 2:9–14 gives us the outflow of waters to all the earth, along with the trees of the Garden that were pleasing to *sight* and *good* for food. These good and attractive trees included the temporarily forbidden Tree of the Knowledge of Good and Evil (cf. 3:6). In 6:1–2, mankind gives forth waters consisting of sons and daughters, and we find that the godly (the sons of God) chose wives according to their own desires based on their *seeing* that they were *good*. Since the Spirit strove against these marriages, we can infer that they were evil and selfish marriages, a seizing of forbidden fruit. It is clearly implied that the "daughters of mankind" were largely of the line of Cain, whether physically or spiritually.

Day 4 sees the lights put into the firmament as spiritual rulers, as symbols of Divine rule through godly human beings, and 2:15 sees the first man placed into the garden-firmament to oversee (rule) it. What links with this is 6:3, "And Yahweh said, 'My Spirit will not strive with mankind forever; for he is also flesh [or, in their wandering astray he is flesh]. And his days will be 120 years.'"

"In their wandering astray he is flesh" makes more sense. Why would God cease striving with mankind simply because he is flesh? Leviticus speaks of "wandering astray" (often translated "sin of ignorance," but better rendered "sin of wandering astray")[146] and also focuses attention on impurities of "flesh." That linkage appears to be in view in Genesis 6. God will not overlook this wandering forever. The stars are wandering from their courses, as Adam wandered from his duties in the Garden. The sun and moon and stars governed days and years in Genesis 1. So also here man's time is allotted to be 120 years.

We arrive at Day 5 in 6:4–5, the mighty Nephilim corresponding to the great ruling sea monsters of the fifth Day, and thematically (and chiastically) to the "sons of God" who sinned in 6:1–2, for the evil marriages are mentioned again in 6:4. Following on the mention of the Nephilim, Yahweh evaluates the

---

145. On the astral associations of the numbers in this passage, see my *Chronological and Calendrical Commentary on the Pentateuch*, Studies in Biblical Chronology (October 2001).

146. The best study of the Hebrew word *bishgagah* I am aware of is Van Dam, "The Meaning of *Bishgagah*."

swarms of men (birds and fishes), that their wickedness was *great* (compare the mighty Nephilim) and continual.

As God made man on Day 6, so Yahweh is "sorry that He made man on the earth" in 6:6.

Which bring us at last to sabbath judgment in 6:7–8. The judgment is twofold: Yahweh determines to blot out mankind in verse 7, but finds Noah righteous (faithful) in verse 8.

1. Creation of Adamic Humanity.
2. Establishment of true Adamic Humanity in Firmament.
3. Fall of the Sons of God (true Adamic Humanity); mixed marriages.
4. The time allotted for Adamic Humanity.
5. Mighty men, like Sons of God, great in wickedness; mixed marriages.
6. God regrets His establishment of Adamic humanity.
7. De-creation of Adamic Humanity.

TREES AND THORNS

In Gen. 2:9 the ground brought forth trees good for food, delightful to view, and in two cases, life-giving or rule-bestowing. Adam, made of the ground (2:7), would by implication bring forth new trees, and thus trees and plants are among the symbols for human beings throughout the Bible.

The woman taken from Adam's side was the first such tree. She would have a "seed," language taken from the trees and plants of Gen. 1:11–12. Her womb would yield "fruit" (Gen. 30:2). Like the soil on the original third day, the Adamic soil brought forth a plant seeding seed and trees that had fruit with seed in her.

At the time of Adam's creation, the ground had not yet put forth the "shrub of the field" (2:5). In our study, we saw that this phrase is associated with thorny plants. We can suppose that there would have been a place for such plants in an unfallen world, but 3:18 tells us that because of man's sin, the ground would give forth thorns and thistles "for you" when Adam and his descendants sought to grow good plants.

Fallen Adam, made of soil and seeking good seed, would find as often as not that he had produced thorns and thistles.

Abel was the good tree that sprang from Adamic soil as the fruit of Eve's womb. God found the food he brought good and hence viewed him as delightful.

Cain was the bad thorn that sprang from Adamic soil and also from Eve's womb. God found his food unacceptable and did not delight in him and his tribute.

Sinful men prefer thorns, looking only on the outward appearance. Hence, before the Flood, the sons of God (the line of Seth) saw that the daughters of men (the line of Cain) were "good" and took them, corrupting the witness of God until only Noah was left (6:2, 8–9). This preference for thorns continued after the Flood as well (6:4).

Thorns threaten to choke out good plants. Cain succeeded in choking out Abel, the bad plant murdering the good. The seed of the "daughters of men" overwhelmed and almost completely choked out the good seed.

Crowned with thorns, the Greater Abel was surrounded by evil Cains in His sacrificial death, with His followers standing away from Him, at a distance (Matt. 27:55–56; Mark 15:40–41; Luke 23:49).[147]

Humanity still bears both trees and thorns, but the world has changed. It is now a wheat field, though there are tares in it. It is the wheat who now have the power of the Spirit and who are destined in Christ to triumph over and "choke out" the thorns.

---

147. John 19:25–26 says that initially some had been near the cross, but they did not stay there. "At the cross her station keeping stood the mournful mother weeping, close to Jesus to the last" (by Jacopone da Todi) is not an accurate hymn. Jesus was eventually forsaken by all.

INDEX

A

Aalders, G. Ch., 60
Aaron, 68, 76-77, 83-87, 96, 164, 167
Abel, 2, 4, 190, 216, 224, 239, 294ff.
Abraham, 36, 38, 41, 43, 44, 80, 230 (as 'Abram,' see 40, 74, 108, 109, 110)
Absalom, 44
Achebe, Chinua, 224
'adam, 27, 295-296, 318
Adam, 2-3, 30, 36, 41, 53, 152, 207-208, 348
ambition, 186-188
Ancient East, 40
animals, naming them, 99, 102-103
animals, to teach man, 101-102
Antioch, 45
Ararat, 22, 74
Ark of Noah, 22, 49, 74
Ark of the Covenant, 167, 289
Assyria, 44, 47
author of Genesis, 38

B